1971 TI invents the single-chip microcontroller.

1974 TI secures the High-speed Antiradiation Missile (HARM) development contract.

1975 GSI/TI processes the first 3D seismic surveys.

1978 TI's speech chip enables toys such as its Speak & Spell™ to talk.

1981 TI's corporate quality director is appointed, heralding the start of a Total Quality focus.

TI metallurgy helps save Statue of Liberty from erosion.

1982 TI announces its first single-chip digital signal processor (DSP).

1988 TI produces the first Digital Light Processing™ chip.

1992 TI's defense business wins the Malcolm Baldrige National Quality Award.

1995 TI goes live on the Web at www.ti.com.

1997 A new $25 million DSP University Research Fund is started by TI.

TI announces its Tag-it™ SMART label technology.

1999 TI's eXpressDSP™ Real-time Software technology is released.

TI announces OMAP™ application processors.

2000 Jack Kilby is awarded the Nobel Prize in physics for his role in inventing the integrated circuit.

TI acquires Burr-Brown, strengthening its leadership position in the analog market.

TMS320C64x™ core breaks records as world's fastest DSP.

2002 TI announces its 90-nanometer CMOS process.

2003 TI ships its 25 millionth graphing calculator.

2004 TI incorporates the major functions of a cell phone onto a single chip.

TI announces its 1-GHz DSP, the fastest in the industry.

More than half the cell phones sold worldwide use TI technology.

2005 TI launches digital power integrated circuits.

TI completes a phone call using 65-nanometer silicon technology.

TI introduces DaVinci™ digital video technology.

TI celebrates its 75th anniversary.

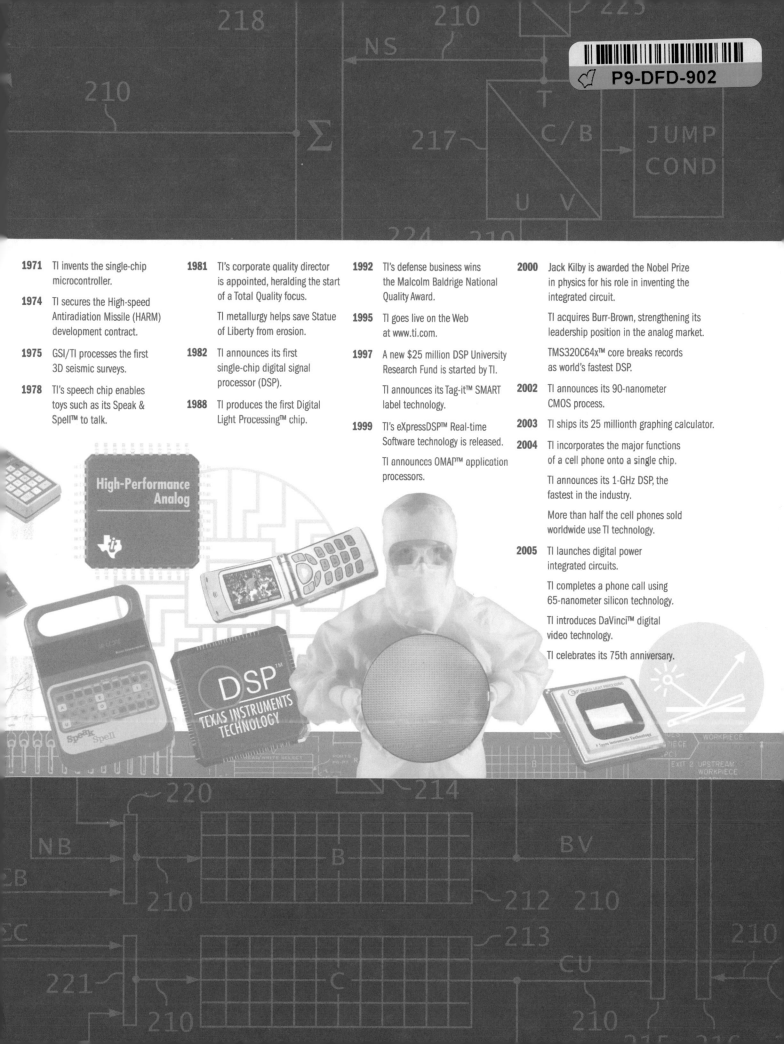

CONTENTS

THE WHITE HOUSE

WASHINGTON

March 7, 2005

Congratulations to the employees of Texas Instruments as you celebrate 75 years of service to your customers and to the communities where you do business. You should take great pride in your accomplishments.

American business is the backbone of our economy, and hard work, innovation, and an entrepreneurial spirit have made our country strong. Since 1930, Texas Instruments has created technologies that have improved industries and lives. From changing energy exploration with reflection seismology; to spurring progress in the defense and space industries through new electronic systems; to ushering in modern technology with Jack Kilby's invention of the integrated circuit, Texas Instruments employees have impacted our lives.

Today, the people of Texas Instruments continue to play an important role in our communities through innovations in technology, outreach, and education. By offering solutions that move us into the future, your company contributes to our country's progress and helps advance America's legacy of exploration and discovery.

Laura and I send our congratulations on 75 years of success and our best wishes.

Letter from President George W. Bush

INTRODUCTION

A common characteristic among the people of Texas Instruments is an impatient eagerness to buck the odds and do something different. TIers just don't seem to know what cannot be done. And so, this company has consistently achieved what others thought was impossible.

This ambitious, risk-taking approach to innovation and business began when a few visionaries left secure jobs early in the Great Depression to establish a new venture using a new technology to search for oil. Seventy-five years later, ambition rooted in ethics, and innovation grounded in integrity continue to drive Texas Instruments to explore and expand the frontiers of technology.

From TI's very earliest days, the objective has been to use the company's unique technical skills to fundamentally change markets and create entirely new ones. When the world dreams, "What if something could be done," TI responds, "Why not?" And after we have brought the dream to life, this restless company has never been afraid to ask itself, "What's next?" Our successful businesses in the past funded developments that became TI's critical operations today, which in turn are now funding efforts to create new growth engines for the future.

On the surface, the connection might seem obscure between our original work exploring for oil and our current core operations that enable the digitization of daily life. But the link between the founding business, Geophysical Service Inc., and Texas Instruments today (the company adopted the TI name in 1951) is fairly simple and precise: For three quarters of a century, this company has used progressively more complex signal-processing technology—with advances ranging from the incremental to the revolutionary—to literally and repeatedly change the world. This book highlights just a few of the amazing things that TIers have accomplished over the decades.

Beyond pioneering technology, TI blazed new business trails by thinking and operating globally, a heritage from our worldwide search for oil. In 1956, TI's facility in the United Kingdom became the first semiconductor manufacturing plant outside of the United States. In 1968, TI became the first foreign semiconductor company to establish manufacturing operations in Japan. We became the first foreign technology company with wholly-owned operations in India in 1985. In 2002, our push into China led to the creation of joint technology development centers in Beijing and Shanghai.

Today, TI has manufacturing, design, or sales operations in more than 25 nations. Even with this enormous global footprint, we have never forgotten our Dallas roots nor have we stopped working to improve the quality of life in North Texas and all the communities in which we operate.

Quite frankly, it's humbling to be tasked with leading a company that has such a rich history and bright future. TI's culture of innovation, ethics, integrity, and inclusion is not something we created as today's leaders of TI. These are attributes we inherited from the company's founders and successive generations of leadership and employees. We are very proud that TIers constantly prove that people with a wide diversity of cultures and human differences can come together and successfully work for a common objective.

Both of us joined TI because, of all the companies where we could have worked, this place offered us a chance to do what we really wanted to do from day one. That's why Jack Kilby and countless other key innovators joined this company instead of any other. Working at TI is not for everyone. The work is demanding, often frustrating, and sometimes even maddening. But for people who want to apply their skills to the very fullest right from the start, for people unafraid of major challenges and who want to do things in electronics that truly matter, there is no other company on earth like Texas Instruments.

TIers can be rightfully proud of this company's past, yet we believe that even bigger and more significant developments are on the horizon. TI's real-time signal processing technology already permeates daily life in many different ways, from digital communications and entertainment to medical services, automotive systems, and wide-ranging applications in between.

As we continue to expand the performance and increase the power efficiency of our technology, we are beginning to enable applications that once were confined to the pages of science fiction. Add in new growth technologies such as Digital Light Processing™ and emerging opportunities such as radio frequency identification, and we can only say that our amazing past is simply the prologue to an even more incredible future.

Tom Engibous
Chairman

Rich Templeton
President & CEO

v

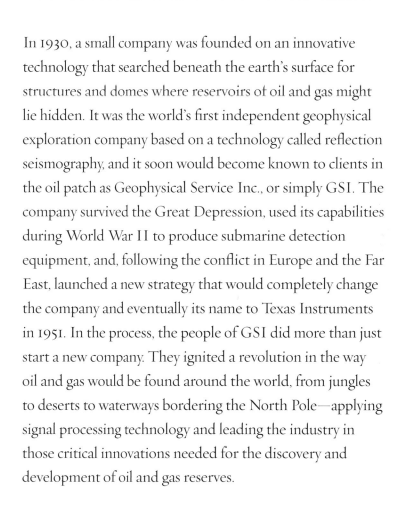

IGNITING A REVOLUTION

In 1930, a small company was founded on an innovative technology that searched beneath the earth's surface for structures and domes where reservoirs of oil and gas might lie hidden. It was the world's first independent geophysical exploration company based on a technology called reflection seismography, and it soon would become known to clients in the oil patch as Geophysical Service Inc., or simply GSI. The company survived the Great Depression, used its capabilities during World War II to produce submarine detection equipment, and, following the conflict in Europe and the Far East, launched a new strategy that would completely change the company and eventually its name to Texas Instruments in 1951. In the process, the people of GSI did more than just start a new company. They ignited a revolution in the way oil and gas would be found around the world, from jungles to deserts to waterways bordering the North Pole—applying signal processing technology and leading the industry in those critical innovations needed for the discovery and development of oil and gas reserves.

Mud and water fly up from multiple shots detonated by this GSI crew in South Louisiana in the early 1930s. They traverse the wetlands in this marsh buggy designed by Ken Burg. The crewman at the bottom right operates the equipment to record the faint seismic signals returning from reflecting horizons far below the earth's surface.

1

THE GENESIS OF GSI

A company is founded on using signal processing in the search for oil.

Even though the odds were stacked against it, a small company faced down the Great Depression and built a visionary geophysical business that brought a new technology to the old-fashioned art of oil exploration. GSI sent shock waves into the earth to map underground structures that might hold accumulations of oil and gas, and its innovative methods sent shock waves through an industry at home and abroad.

Eugene McDermott, a founder of GSI, developed the innovative designs for instruments that improved the business of geophysics.

In early 1930, John Clarence Karcher and Eugene McDermott realized they were making a decision that would no doubt impact the rest of their lives. The threat of a bitter economic depression was beginning to generate anxiety and unrest throughout the nation, but both men were determined to walk away from secure positions with Amerada Petroleum Corporation, a major oil company headquartered in New York City. They would establish a new, revolutionary business—Geophysical Service Inc. (GSI)—founded on their own genius, innovation, and perseverance. The dependability of reflection seismography, which Karcher pioneered, had been proven during the critical five years he and McDermott worked with Geophysical Research Corporation (GRC), a subsidiary of Amerada.

Karcher's concept was based on vibrating the earth's surface by setting off small dynamite explosions called shots, then precisely recording and timing the reflected waves or signals to determine the depth of the substrata.

As early as 1925, Karcher and his innovative oil exploration method had caught the attention of Amerada's president, Everette Lee DeGolyer, one of the preeminent geologists in the industry, who was looking for a competitive advantage in a tough business that had more dry holes than gushers. If oil exploration had a new frontier, DeGolyer wanted to be on the front lines. He firmly believed Karcher's reflection seismograph system would become one of the industry's most invaluable tools in charting the earth's subterranean structures.

DeGolyer met with Karcher that same year and offered him a job. Amerada had agreed to form GRC, and Karcher would be named vice president and given 15 percent of the stock issued for the new company. Karcher immediately began to surround himself with a staff as driven, as inventive, and as ambitious as he.

Karcher persuaded Eugene McDermott to leave his teaching job and research work at Columbia University and join him at GRC. They had worked together earlier at Western Electric, where both men had developed a respect for each other's abilities. McDermott had received two master's degrees, the first in 1919 from Stevens Institute of Technology in Hoboken, New Jersey, the second from Columbia University.

After accepting Karcher's offer at GRC, McDermott recalled, "I didn't know anything about geophysics, but I liked new and exciting things. Anything new interested me."

Karcher thought that McDermott just might be able to make the reflection seismograph method work even better.

Together, they would take Karcher's geophysical exploration

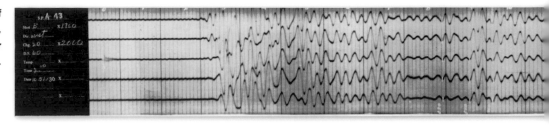

In the early 1930s this type of record, or reflection seismogram, showed structures in greater detail than previously recorded.

concept to a new plateau, building a system that would detect faint impulses from beneath the surface, amplify them hundreds of thousands of times, and record them.

DeGolyer would later liken the technology to "giving eyes to the geologists."

By late 1929, Amerada's owners decided to assign the company's reflection crews exclusively to Amerada projects. No longer would the crews be contracted to other oil companies, even though there was a growing need and demand for geophysical exploration.

Disappointed with the decision, Karcher sold his shares

A charter from the State of New Jersey, signed in 1930 by John Clarence Karcher (at right) and Eugene McDermott, puts GSI in business. The third signature is that of J. Thomas Schneider, believed to be the lawyer who handled the incorporation of GSI.

of GRC stock back to Amerada in September of 1929 and left with McDermott in January of 1930 to start Geophysical Service, a new company devoted to contracting reflection crews to any oil company that was willing to pay for the benefits of their technology. Karcher and McDermott owned 50 percent of the company.

The other 50 percent belonged to a secret partner who had invested $100,000 in the business venture—Everette Lee DeGolyer.

On May 16, 1930, papers were filed in New Jersey to incorporate Geophysical Service, a visionary company that would become recognized throughout the world's scattered oil fields as GSI. With Karcher as president and McDermott as vice president, GSI gambled on an uncertain venture, one that depended on the reliability of signal processing. Its field crews used reflection seismograph equipment to map anticlines, faults, domes, and broken strata beneath the crust of the earth to locate structures that might be favorable for the accumulation of oil and gas.

The formula and geophysical instruments Karcher had originally developed would become legendary and would help turn the art of oil exploration into a science-based methodology, one that would thrive on advancements in signal processing.

During Karcher's years at GRC (1925-1929), he, McDermott, and others like Henry Bates Peacock, a GRC crew chief, worked together to build a strong team. Karcher was the inventor who believed that the ideas of a scientist should be translated into money. McDermott was the designer who had the talent to take an idea or technology and make it work better than anyone imagined. Peacock, who had earned his doctorate in physics in 1925 at the University of Iowa, was content to remain in the field, exploring the geologic mysteries beneath the earth's surface with reflective and refractive seismograph technology. He would become recognized as one of the most able and inventive party chiefs in the field.

Peacock, in fact, had mapped the Viola limestone around Shawnee, Oklahoma, in vain, until his surveys began to detect an underground anomaly not obvious from simple surface geology. All around him were remnants of dry holes, mute testaments to the last stands of wildcatters (independent oil

GSI field crews often moved in convoy-like formations as they deployed to new locations for clients, as shown in this photograph taken around 1939. At times, they would leave town in multiple convoys to throw oil scouts off their trail and keep them from discovering their new seismic survey location.

This seismic recording truck was photographed in 1931, outside of Dallas, during a shakedown test. Henry Happell is checking out the instrumentation and geophones, designed by Karcher and McDermott, and built in Jonsson's laboratory in Newark, New Jersey. The Model S-2 geophones (earth microphones), each weighing 35 pounds, are shown in the foreground. The box on the running board is the photographic developing compartment.

After making their decision to start a new company, Karcher and McDermott rented a room in February of 1930 at the St. Francis Hotel in Newark, New Jersey. It would serve as a temporary drafting room for their first employee, Alfred Morel, who provided the specific schematics to the conceptual ideas they gave him. A month later, they leased 700 square feet of shop space above a Ford Motor Company sales showroom at 185 Clinton Street in Newark, setting up a laboratory—equipped with a drill press and bench lathe—where a new generation of geophysical instruments could be designed and assembled. As soon as a piece of equipment had been completed, it was rushed to crews in distant fields.

On one occasion, when Karcher and McDermott were feverishly working in the New Jersey lab, they badly needed some aluminum castings. They drove down the street to a local office of Alcoa Aluminum Co. to buy the products they needed and rushed into the office of Erik Jonsson, a sales engineer with a degree from Rensselaer Polytechnic Institute. He vividly remembered that the two men were "wearing caps and rumpled suits and looking one cut above the apple sellers in the streets." Jonsson expedited a delivery of the aluminum castings, and, a couple of months later, received a telegram from Karcher offering him a job to manage the GSI machine shop in Newark for $5,000 a year. If GSI had any chance of competing for oil exploration, it needed good management from someone who could guarantee equipment manufactured to exact tolerances.

drillers) and the disappointments of more than a few oil companies. Peacock's survey led to the first oil well to be drilled, in 1928, using the reflection seismograph system.

Twenty-eight-year-old Jonsson was the son of Swedish immigrants who had settled in Brooklyn. He had a solid engineering background, and he seemed to be the right choice.

Jonsson initially had doubts. He realized it would be foolish to leave a secure job at Alcoa. However, he wanted a chance to prove himself in the business world, and GSI just might give him that opportunity. He recalled, "If those two were crazy enough to get into business at a time like that, in my situation I could hardly do worse. I felt there was more of a chance to carve out a career in a short time with a small company rather than a large one."

Jonsson, in July of 1930, decided to risk his talents and future on the vision of GSI. He had the confidence and the ability to develop improvements to GSI's seismic instruments. "I can make them faster, cheaper, smaller, lighter, more usable," he told his new employers.

To be close to the center of activity in the oil industry at the time, they decided to locate their headquarters in Dallas. In June, they leased space on the thirteenth floor of the Republic Bank Building (now the Davis Building) for $100 a month. The cosmopolitan city was regarded as a major financial and distribution center.

———————————

Cecil Green, an amiable Brit who was born in Manchester, England, was working long hours beside Charles Litton in the vacuum tube laboratory of Federal Telegraph Company in California when he received an offer in 1930 of a position at GSI. The salary was $5,000 a year, and he would be required to travel, searching for underground oil structures in some of the

most remote and barren terrain in the Southwest. It would be a "stop here and go there" kind of existence, but business was booming, and GSI was in desperate need of good party chiefs to supervise the reflection survey crews.

It would be a far different kind of life for Cecil Green, who as a child had immigrated with his parents to Canada. He received his bachelor's and master's degrees in electrical engineering from Massachusetts Institute of Technology, and he was ready for a change. Green and his wife, Ida, left California on October 4, 1930, and headed toward Oklahoma. As a survivor of the San Francisco earthquake in 1906, he was no stranger to hard times. The stock market had crashed a year earlier, and many businesses were fighting for survival. Hard times grew bad, then worse.

As Green was driving east to join GSI, an old wildcatter, C.M. "Dad" Joiner, broke and in debt, was completing an oil well in the pine forests of East Texas. With luck, and without the benefit of seismic technology, he had managed to discover the richest oil field in Americans history. Within 18 months, rampant overproduction in East Texas caused the price of oil to plunge to 10 cents a barrel. Companies could no longer afford to drill, much less hire crews to help them locate fields favorable for oil exploration.

GSI had barely launched its business, and already there were doubts about its ability to survive circumstances it could not control. But Karcher, McDermott, Jonsson, Green, and Peacock stood firm. The oil business had made them tough, and tough times wouldn't last forever.

Paul Meeks drilling with a spudder for a South Louisiana field crew in the Jennings area in 1933. The ability to drill holes 20 feet deep for dynamite charges was a major improvement in a crew's productivity. The first holes were dug by hand, using augers.

2

OIL FIELD "WIDOWS"

Wives of doodlebuggers survive the hardships of a nomadic life.

As GSI field crews followed back roads into remote regions to search for oil-bearing structures, their wives traveled with them. They were pioneers, adventuring into new places and experiencing the hardships of a nomadic existence. Always on the move, never staying in any place long enough to have roots or a sense of belonging, these families found it wasn't an easy life. But the GSI wives made the most of it, working hard to ensure that those towns they called home, even for a short time, would appreciate them and their efforts even after they were gone.

Ida Green first learned of Geophysical Service Inc. and the company's pursuit of oil-bearing structures throughout the American outback from the letters she received from an old friend, the wife of GSI Party Chief Roland Beers. To Ida, the constant traveling to new, out-of-the-way places with strange-sounding names seemed an exciting life. She was supportive in 1930 when Beers wrote her husband about the employment potential at GSI.

All Beers could promise Cecil Green was a nomadic existence. As his letter pointed out, *"You will have to give up any idea you may have of having a permanent residence. In this work, we move about frequently, often as much as every two weeks. We are now in Seminole, Oklahoma, and expect to remain here until March at least. We may be here a year, and then again, we might tear up and move in a month or two."* Beers's words were prophetic.

During their first seven months with GSI, Green and his

wife drove the roads that led to field assignments throughout Oklahoma. They wandered down highways they had never known to exist, seldom stayed in any place more than a couple of months, living in shacks and rented rooms, working for an innovative company that offered them every benefit but a home.

The traveling life of those early-day doodlebuggers (the industry's term for seismic field crew members engaged in geophysical exploration) created daunting hardships on their families, who followed them down every makeshift road that led to another makeshift town. One wife wrote: *"Being known as 'transients' is a handicap in the small towns where we have to stay, and it's hard to find decent living quarters. Somehow, having children seems to be considered not quite decent, and the ones with youngsters have the worst time finding accommodations. Apartments (such as are available) are pretty dismal. Usually it's a bedroom, a bath (shared with others) and kitchen (also shared). My food allowance is a dollar a day, but we eat like kings."*

GSI families were always the new faces in town, the people who came to stay awhile, then were gone again, never around long enough to establish either roots or lasting friendships.

Ida and Cecil Green on a Sunday at Turner Falls, Oklahoma —photo taken in 1930 as Cecil began his first assignment as a GSI Party Chief in Maud, Oklahoma. Over the next few years, the couple would traverse the U.S. many times in the search for oil.

Cecil Green once said about his wife, Ida, "She had what it took, and it took a lot." He could just as well have been speaking about any of the wives who, from time to time, found themselves living in shacks that were too hot in summer or too cold in winter, eating their food from plates set on orange crates, brushing the crumbs through the cracks in the floor to feed the chickens scratching in the dirt below. They withstood the miseries of grit and dust storms blowing across the land, summers without any rain, winters without much heat, bare walls, crying babies, busted tires, vegetable gardens withering in the sun, and hard mattresses. Yet the doodlebuggers and their wives were proud of the work they were doing, proud of the company they were building. For families whose lives were dedicated to the open road and the promises of the next oil patch, the wives played a role as vital and important as their husbands'. They kept the families together and learned quickly how to endear themselves to communities they might visit once and only briefly, then never pass through again.

In the 1930s, Cecil Green wrote of one place he and Ida stayed on a long, weary gravel road: *"Didn't sleep much on account of mosquitoes. Heard coyotes howling for the first time. Saw lots of tarantulas."*

Ida was with him all the way, even riding with her husband during those times when he was driving out to a crew, hauling a few hundred pounds of dynamite in the back of his car.

No matter where they were or how long they stayed, a GSI crew formed its own neighborhood, its own sense of respect for the land and those who came to explore beneath it.

One of Ida's letters explains the life faced by GSI wives whose husbands were making geophysical history:

Life moves swiftly since moving about every few weeks seems to be our fate. After dashing around in some small town to find a place to live, we may end up with two shabbily furnished rooms, or in rare cases a nice private home which happens to be for rent. First there, first served is the policy which equalizes living conditions for everyone at some time or other, especially in these Oklahoma boom-times.

"If you end up living in a place where you share the bath with three other families, maybe the next time you'll hit the jackpot and get an attractive home. One soon becomes philosophical. The business is so new that small towns haven't adjusted to oil people and regards them with suspicion and concern. We try to keep a good reputation ...

"First thing the wives do after getting located is to rush around to see what the grocery stores (not more than two) have to offer in foodstuffs. Vegetables are scarce, other than turnips and mustard greens. Fresh killed

yearling beef is sometimes good and then again tough. Chicken for Sunday dinner is found by going down to the local feedstore on Saturday. Sacks of Purina Chow and other feeds fill the place, but out back is a pen or yard filled with fast-stepping chickens. A man snares one with a wire, and I ask him if he would mind cutting the head off. That accomplished, I return home, proceed to remove the feathers and do some major surgery. Come Sunday, golden brown fried chicken with cream gravy graces the festive board.

A DIFFERENT WAY OF LIFE
★ ★ ★

Dorothy Ramsey understood the trials GSI wives confronted in the field. She and her husband, Lewis, a party chief, moved six times during the first three years of their marriage. His career at GSI would take them from Canada, where she traveled 10 miles to town on a horse-drawn sled in temperatures plunging to 72 degrees below zero, to Egypt, which, she remembers, "seemed like the end of the world."

Dorothy recalls, "We always had to keep making adjustments, never really knowing what to expect next. In Canada, it was so cold that the brake fluid in Lewis's car froze, and he had to keep driving into snow banks in order to slow down." She and Lewis lived in a small farmhouse, braced against the bitter temperatures, with a mattress but no box springs. She improvised by spreading the frayed mattress across empty dynamite boxes.

"In Venezuela," she continues, "it was so hot that I felt water splashing against the back of my leg while I was cooking, and I thought the roof was leaking. It wasn't raining. It was only sweat falling off the back of my head.

"Times weren't always easy," she says, "but the wives of a GSI field party had a way of bonding together, and we all helped each other make it through the rough spots. We felt a little like the early-day pioneers who settled the country they had never seen before. Our husbands were always in the field, and we were usually in a foreign country, or a place where we didn't know a soul. We either had each other or no one."

Lewis Ramsey and his wife Dorothy prepare to board a flight at Love Field in Dallas on their way to an assignment in Venezuela in 1952. Lewis is holding their daughter, Susan, and Dorothy holds their young son, Paul.

"Life is settling down, or so it seems. Suddenly, it is whispered around ... rumored that we are going to move. The women begin to lament they have just stocked up on a lot of perishable food or groceries, or someone has been silly enough to have done some extensive housecleaning. Such things always bring on a move. Plans are made to move as quietly and as secretly as possible since the general idea is to outwit the scout and leave him behind.

"Some of the single men are marrying, and the married folks are beginning to have families. Life isn't too monotonous and even has an element of adventure to it. The crew is like family, our joys and sorrows are shared, and we make an effort to get along together.

"The advantages are: time for hobbies, family ties are closer, and appreciation for any kind of entertainment. Children seem precocious and extroverted, meeting people easily. There is less expense in keeping up appearances. Last, but not least, we always see and learn about something new or different, and can put away a nice nest egg for the future. Such is the doodlebugging life."

In 1930, Ida Green didn't know that over the next 12 years, they would live in 53 houses, before finally settling in Dallas.

———

The unexpected challenges facing a doodlebugger's wife were as great in the 1950s as they had been during the '30s. Frances Dunagan would never forget the day her husband, Lillard, walked into their apartment in Houma, Louisiana. They had just arrived in town, and Frances was unpacking her last box. She sighed with relief and looked up as Lillard walked through the door.

"They want us to move again," he said.

"Where?"

"Cairo."

"Cairo where?"

"Egypt."

"When do they need you there?"

"Yesterday."

At a feverish pace, the Dunagans packed again, received their immunizations, and headed to Dallas to say goodbye to their families. Then, as Frances recalls, "We got on a plane for the first leg of the journey to Cairo, and I could not imagine ending that journey in such a faraway place."

The Dunagans landed at two o'clock in the morning, reaching their hotel two hours later. Already the streets were crowded with donkeys, trucks, carts, and vegetable peddlers. "It was a city full of noise, dust, and a strong smell of the desert," Frances says. "We were faced with a new climate, new language, new money, new everything." The Dunagans rented an apartment sight unseen just to get one.

"Through all of the travels for GSI," Frances remembers, "the wives stuck together. We had picnics on the beach where there was a beach and played tennis when there were courts. We had bridge games several times a week and ate potluck lunches together. In Iran, we had afternoon teas in the middle of sandstorms with the temperatures soaring above 120 degrees. We faced a lot of challenges, but complaints were rare."

———

The wives of doodlebuggers left a lasting impression everywhere they stayed. A face might be unfamiliar one day, but it didn't take long before the face belonged to a friend.

These oil field "widows" had time to spare, and they didn't believe in wasting it. While their husbands were in the field, some spent their time volunteering in educational programs and school lunchrooms, as well as in the community and church activities, doing what they could to make life a little better than it had been before they drove into town.

They gave of themselves. And they left behind the spirit of GSI's commitment and the legacy of people helping people wherever the company took them.

3

GOING ABROAD

GSI's international mindset moved the company to the forefront of the geophysical exploration industry.

The Great Depression was taking a severe toll on businesses large and small throughout the nation. When GSI saw its contracts evaporate, the company learned to be flexible and changed its strategy. GSI began looking across oceans toward faraway places where governments and companies were still willing to gamble good money on the discovery of new oil fields. Business overseas would keep GSI profitable even when competitors were failing. No longer simply regarded as a Texas company, GSI would become recognized and respected as a company of global importance. More significantly, GSI developed an international mindset in its early years, which would serve it well as the company grew and entered new markets.

Geophysical Service Inc. stood at a precarious crossroad. By 1931, the Great Depression had tightened its grip on the nation. Oil prices plummeted to all-time lows. And long-term contracts that had seemed certain for GSI were suddenly being terminated or left unsigned. GSI experienced a severe drop in domestic oil exploration, and the company began looking at market potential outside the United States. Many international oil companies and foreign governments still had money to invest in the search for oil.

During 1931, Robert P. Thompson led the first GSI field crew into Mexico. It wouldn't be long before GSI crews under the leadership of Ike Newton, Al Storm, Bill Salvatori, Herb Pernell, and Martin Kelsey would also be shooting surveys across the Mexican terrain. In 1932, crews were heading north and rolling into Canada.

GSI weathered the difficult days of the Depression by risking its business and its future on mapping the undiscovered oil fields of international markets. By the end of 1934, the company had grown to more than 200 employees. GSI ultimately moved reflection survey crews across Venezuela, Ecuador, Colombia, New Guinea, Panama, Sumatra, Java, India, and Saudi Arabia. The decision for GSI to dispatch its crews around the globe was made of necessity. It allowed the company to remain at the forefront of the world's growing geophysical exploration industry and to work with a new, though often unpredictable, base of customers. These included large international oil companies, small independent American oil companies lured abroad by the promise of untapped fields, and foreign governments.

Along the way, GSI developed a strong, inventive international mindset. The far reaches of the world had become its primary market. GSI was working diligently to

This photo shows Ben Melton (center with field boots, unwinding cable) and his crew, who entered Mexico at Laredo on March 11, 1933, and arrived at San Lorenzo (Isthmus of Tehuantepec) on April 2, 1933. Note the poles used to hand-carry equipment through the jungle.

Ellis Schuler's GSI crew in Saudi Arabia in 1939 arouses the interest of a passing caravan. The crew's recording truck is shown on the left. This photo was taken by Cecil Green on his trip around the world to visit GSI crews.

establish and maintain close relationships with its clients, regardless of their customs or the languages they spoke. GSI's managers learned the art of dealing with overseas markets and gained an international perspective on the needs and demands of the petroleum business. Within a few years, GSI crews were as much at home on faraway continents as they were in U.S. oil fields. The flooded jungles of Sumatra didn't stop them. They had survived the swamps of South Louisiana. And they had been prepared for the sands of the Rub al-Khali, known in Saudi Arabia as the "empty quarter," by working the wind-blown, sun-blistered plains of western Texas and Oklahoma.

Cecil Green was named supervisor for all of GSI's field crews in 1934, and he quickly discovered that many of his survey parties were spread across distant locations often too remote to be mentioned on world maps.

In Saudi Arabia, a GSI crew began surveying in 1937 after a grueling three-week trek that involved sailing to Europe, taking the Orient Express to Istanbul, and riding a succession of trains, buses, and boats before stepping ashore on the Persian Gulf coast. Doodlebuggers lived in brush huts and later

in tents, working 24 consecutive days at a time.

Skinnie Holbert, a GSI crew member, recalled, "We built our own trails. We called them roads, but they were trails going out into the desert. We always had a core rig with us, and he (the driller) normally built us a water well for us to have water. All in all, the living wasn't bad."

In 1938, James Gary's GSI crew obtained seismic reflection data that indicated the potential for a vast reservoir of oil below Abu Hadriya. The report was met with skepticism.

Max Steineke, chief geologist for the Arabian subsidiary of Standard Oil Company of California (SOCAL), didn't have much faith in the seismic reflection data, but SOCAL, over his objections, had chosen to drill at Abu Hadriya anyway. During the early days of 1940, the well had reached 8,656 feet, and still there was no hint of oil.

The bit cut its way down past 9,000 feet, and the hole was as dry at the bottom as it had been at the surface of the sand. About this time, Cecil Green arrived for a visit to GSI operations.

He had been invited by George M. Cunningham, exploration manager of SOCAL, to join him on a trip to the Middle East. Green watched the drilling and later recalled, "You might go that deep at home, but certainly you wouldn't go as far away as

WATCH YOUR STEP

★ ★ ★

The jungle terrain of Sumatra was a foreboding curtain of bamboo and mangrove swamps in the shadow of a volcanic mountain range. By 1940, GSI had two crews working along the eastern coastal plain under Al Storm and Sam Stoneham. Members of a third crew lay in a small hospital ward high among the peaks, battling jungle malaria.

Each of the parties had a dozen or more crew members, led from one shooting site to the next by more than 700 local workers who cut trails through the thick forests and hammered together bridges over the flooded flatlands. They hauled everything the crew needed, from supplies and food to explosives.

Cecil Green arrived in Sumatra for a visit

to GSI crews. As he and his party left on the way to visit the field locations, Green took up a position at the front of the train of bearers, alongside their client's geologist, George Cunningham. As Green and Cunningham reached a patch of savannah, the bearers suddenly quickened their pace and ran past, leaving them confused and somewhere near the middle of the pack. "Something's awry," Green thought.

"What's the sudden rush?" he asked Cunningham.

"Well, I hate to tell you," Cunningham told him, "but there are tigers in this jungle, and the tiger finds it easiest to pick off the first man or the last one in the column."

The local workers realized they couldn't afford to lose anyone who might make the difference between oil and poverty in their lives.

Transporting equipment for jungle work in Sumatra, around 1938. Crews in Sumatra would employ hundreds of local workmen to build trails and continuously move the equipment deeper into jungle areas in the search for oil.

Steineke. It said, "Abu Hadriya well just came in for 15,000 barrels per day at 10,115 feet."

GSI's reflection survey and data had been vindicated, and Green remembered the advice Everette Lee DeGolyer had once given him: "Use all the best geology you can and all the best geophysics. But be sure to carry a rabbit's foot in your pocket."

Saudi Arabia and drill 9,000-foot holes looking for oil. It was too expensive."

In mid-February of 1940, Green and Cunningham decided to proceed eastward to visit operations in India and Indonesia. While they were on the Indus River in India, two urgent radiograms arrived.

Cunningham read the first. "Before going on to Indonesia," it said, "you should return to Saudi Arabia to make a post mortem as to why we ever became involved in that $1.5 million dry hole at Abu Hadriya."

Cunningham was crestfallen, and Green wasn't feeling any better. "Why don't you read the other one?" asked Green.

Cunningham shrugged and opened the radiogram from

GSI had a growing number of competitors in the geophysical business, but the company was steadily building its reputation on the strength of its technology in the field. GSI became recognized as one of the world's largest and most successful international contractors. Understanding the protocol for doing business internationally was an asset that would serve the company well in later years as it expanded into other business areas.

4

PURSUING A DREAM

*Cecil Green, Erik Jonsson,
Eugene McDermott, and
Henry Bates Peacock buy GSI to
keep from losing the company.*

*For Green, Jonsson, McDermott, and Peacock,
GSI's internal business structure was becoming too
fragmented and moving in directions none of them had
anticipated. They were concerned that the foundation
upon which GSI had been built was crumbling, and
they refused to let go of a company they had created
with their innovations, technology, and hard work.
Their vision for GSI would persuade them to take the
biggest risk of their lives—
displaying an entrepreneurial
spirit that would guide the
destiny of the company.*

Even though GSI's
international ventures
were going well, their domestic
business was not. The company
had too many crews without jobs.

Since so many of the nation's
oil companies were leaving
the Southwestern oil patch

untouched, GSI decided to launch its own exploration
business in a valiant effort to hold its crews together. Karcher
and McDermott initially chose to operate on a speculative
basis, cataloging valuable data they might later market to oil
companies. GSI, however, began exploiting its own properties,
gaining ownership of a number of producing fields and
acquiring a substantial interest in several others. GSI had
moved beyond the geophysical business and was entrenching
itself in the oil business as well.

Clients throughout the oil field were suddenly concerned
that GSI, long a dependable ally in oil exploration, would
become a competitor. Some were beginning to wonder aloud
about the proprietary aspects of the data GSI had collected
for their companies. It was vital that any information
gained through GSI's reflection surveys be kept secure and
confidential. The faith and trust they had always placed in
GSI were in serious jeopardy.

During 1938, Karcher and McDermott sought to defuse the
situation by separating the producing arm of the company from
the survey side of the business. First, a Delaware subsidiary
of the company, called Geophysical Service Inc. (GSI),
was established on December 23, 1938. In January of 1939,

**Al Morel, the first GSI employee,
hired in 1930, is working at the
front drafting table in this 1938
photo of the GSI office at 2114
N. Harwood, Dallas. Draftsmen
here were kept busy designing and
improving seismic instruments and
equipment for GSI crews.**

the name of the parent company was changed to Coronado Corporation, with Karcher at the helm to pursue oil development. GSI became a subsidiary of Coronado with McDermott in charge of geophysical exploration activities. The GSI team worked long hours to revitalize the company, but, during the first six months of 1940, they were confronted with losses of $31,300 on total revenues of $539,300. Despite the separation of work, some clients were still concerned about a conflict of interest, threatening to cancel their contracts.

Karcher envisioned an easy solution. He decided it would be advantageous if he went his separate way, provided, of course, he could successfully use his expertise, experience, and good name throughout the oil business to align himself with a major petroleum company. In 1941, he negotiated the sale of Coronado to Stanolind Oil & Gas Company, which would become Amoco, for $5 million.

Stanolind Oil & Gas decided that GSI management should be given the right to purchase the reflection survey subsidiary in order to preserve its identity and independence in the marketplace. It was determined that the assets of GSI could be bought for $300,000.

Erik Jonsson, who had remained with GSI as secretary-treasurer, studied the proposal that lay on the desk before him. He, Green, McDermott, and Peacock were being handed a once-in-a-lifetime offer to purchase GSI. As he later recalled, "There's an element of luck involved when an opportunity comes along. You have to recognize it at just the right time. If you recognize it a little bit too soon, a bit too late, maybe it's not an opportunity at all. So you must decide right then what you can do and what you can't."

Jonsson reached for the phone. Green, McDermott, and Peacock were in the field, visiting GSI crews, but he managed to track down McDermott. "Look, Mac," Jonsson said. "There's an option here to buy this company. If we don't buy it, Stanolind will, and I have the feeling that we'll all be job hunting."

McDermott did not hesitate. "Well, you're there," he said. "See what kind of deal you can put together."

Jonsson wasn't sure what he should do. As he later remembered, "We would be buying, in essence, a business that was almost junk, threatened by losses of $10,000 a month. The reason was we had put all our chips on overseas exploration: South America, Canada, Saudi Arabia, New Guinea, Java, and India. We had crews everywhere. But war in Europe was escalating, and oil companies began to pull in their horns and cancel contracts with us. So, in 1940, we had started getting crews out of several countries, and, in only one year, we had gone from 28 crews in the field down to six. Suddenly we found ourselves depending on a very lethargic domestic business which we had almost entirely abandoned to our competitors because we had been going after the larger profits of foreign operations."

The four members of the GSI management team met in Dallas and agreed on a plan to buy the company. Only Green expressed any doubts. He had seriously considered leaving GSI. His own prognosis for the future of the seismograph company appeared bleak, and, during the late summer of 1941, Green wrote a letter announcing he would resign rather than become part of the acquisition team. He was, however, unable to resist Jonsson's well-practiced powers of persuasion. Green reluctantly acquiesced and agreed to become a partner.

The future partners and their spouses were contemplating their impending purchase of GSI at a dinner party in Dallas when Jonsson turned to Ida Green and asked, "What would you most like to do if we all get rich?"

She smiled and said simply, "I'd like to be a philanthropist."

Jonsson was alone in his office when, in late November 1941, the call came from Stanolind Oil confirming the terms of the sale. There was, however, one stipulation that no one had anticipated. If the financing was not completed and in place within ten days by Monday, December 8, 1941, negotiations would be terminated.

McDermott and Peacock managed to come up with $75,000 each to invest in the venture. Jonsson and Green were forced to use their personal property, including stocks and insurance policies, as collateral to get approval by Republic Bank for the loans they needed to pay their share of the purchase price.

Jonsson had been borrowing money for years at Republic Bank to keep GSI in business during difficult economic times. He was aware that Republic bankers understood as much as he did about GSI's growing losses. But Republic Bank had faith in the men.

This Monday, however, was an official bank holiday, so Jonsson worked frantically to complete the financial aspects of the transaction on Saturday.

The next morning, as Jonsson drove toward the golf course for his usual Sunday game, he was thinking that GSI had survived economic crisis before, and GSI would surely do it again. He was feeling more optimistic about the company, which was poised for growth even though the business environment was unstable. He, Green, McDermott, and Peacock owned the business now, and failure was not an option.

Jonsson turned on his car radio that Sunday morning of December 7, 1941, and heard the news that sent a chill through him. Pearl Harbor had been bombed by the Japanese. America would be at war. GSI had crews working abroad and in harm's way. They would have to be brought home as soon as possible.

Overnight, he and his partners had lost their most promising and profitable operations—the GSI crews overseas. Jonsson knew that surviving the hardships of war would be as difficult for a small company as outlasting the difficult days of the Great Depression.

He and Green had gambled every dollar they could borrow to become owners of a company. The feeling of elation had been replaced with one of dread and anxiety. Jonsson realized that GSI must endure even if he and his partners had to reinvent the company and alter its direction in time of war, which is exactly what they would do. They had no other choice.

This GSI machine shop located on Harwood St. in downtown Dallas did precision machining. This gave GSI a competitive advantage which they highlighted in ads in the early 1940s.

5

GEOPHYSICS GOES DIGITAL

GSI pioneers a completely new strategy for oil exploration through digital computation.

For almost two decades, GSI field crews had conducted geophysical operations in deserts, jungles, swamplands, and remote terrain around the globe, establishing the company as a world leader in oil exploration. During the late 1940s, however, GSI understood the threat of competition and realized it could lose its lofty position in the marketplace if the company did not aggressively develop new concepts for seismic exploration. Over the next decade, it pioneered the application of digital field data acquisition and digital signal processing to oil-finding—a development that not only put GSI at the front of the geophysical exploration industry but led to reduced finding-cost per barrel of oil and successive major increases in the world's known petroleum reserves.

As early as 1949, Pat Haggerty and Eugene McDermott had begun working with a team of Geophysical Service Inc. employees including Ken Burg, Bob Olson, and Hal Jones to find innovative analog approaches for the collection and processing of seismic data, and ways to

improve the resolution. In 1952, the Board of Directors heard Burg's request for additional funds and set aside $25,000 as seed money to finance geophysical research.

GSI was not alone in this quest. In 1953, the Massachusetts Institute of Technology (MIT) established a Geophysical Analysis Group to research the application of theories that could lead to seismographic analysis by computer. Despite the fact that MIT had access to some of the brightest academic minds in the country, the university's work proved inconclusive. The research, however, did change the thought processes of Mark Smith, a student involved in the program. [By this time, the company's name had changed to Texas Instruments with GSI remaining as a subsidiary.] After receiving his Ph.D., Smith was recruited by Cecil Green to work in TI's Central Research Laboratories (CRL) for six months before transferring to GSI.

The acquisition of Houston Technical Labs in 1953 greatly expanded the company's ability to move quickly and decisively on the manufacture of a range of instruments used in petroleum exploration, from gravity meters and seismic sensors to truck-mounted and man-portable field recording systems. J. Fred Bucy, who had just completed his master's degree in physics at the University of Texas, joined TI in 1953 and began working with Hal Jones in CRL. They designed a hybrid analog-digital computer called *seis*MAC—the seismic

J. Fred Bucy, who later became president of TI, at controls of *seis*MAC, an analog computer that was a predecessor to systems for digital seismic data processing.

Operator at the controls of the DFS9000, the first generation of GSI's digital field systems, circa 1964.

The DARC measured 6 x 3 x 24 feet, including peripherals, and used two thousand vacuum tubes with a power consumption of approximately 10 kilowatts.

While the hardware was being built in Houston, Mark Smith's group in Dallas was designing software, and the team led by Milo Backus was developing 12 machine diagnostic programs, 30 library programs, and 30 seismic programs. By October of 1959, the DARC was actively processing seismic data for customers.

For researchers and engineers, it was an exciting time as digital technology emerged and transistors became more widely available and reliable. Bucy typified the company's philosophy of doing whatever it took to get the job done on time or ahead of schedule.

Bucy took charge of the mission to develop the TIAC, an all-transistor special-purpose computer for digital seismic processing that used some 15,000 standard alloy-diffused transistors made by TI for computer customers.

The TIAC was faster by an order of magnitude, outperforming commercially available computers for many years in the area of seismic data processing.

The digital seismic strategy continued to move forward as a team effort. While the TIAC was being completed in Houston with Leonard Donohoe as project manager, the GSI research group in Dallas worked on software to exploit its digital capability, focusing on the complex recordings of stratigraphic traps. GSI's research and development team had been studying ways to effectively chart the traps since 1955.

During the fall of 1961, the first TIAC processing center was put into operation by GSI in Dallas. By February of 1962, the first production crew began using the new digital equipment and statistical processing techniques for Texaco, with Walter Thomsen as party chief. Another early digital crew party chief was Dolan McDaniel, who later served as GSI's longest-tenured president.

Thomsen's, McDaniel's, and other GSI crews brought with them the key to success of the digital program—the ability to record seismic data in the field in digital format on magnetic tape. The digital program faced strong opposition in the exploration industry. Among oil companies and seismic contractors alike, conventional wisdom held that it was folly to

automatic computer. It would be the company's first attempt to develop special-purpose computers to advance TI's digital seismic strategy.

With the *magne*Disc, introduced by TI in 1954, the company moved a step closer to developing its first digital field system. Though it was soon supplanted by magnetic tape recorders, the *magne*Disc was used for magnetic recordings in the field and was capable of storing 24 different seismic traces per recording on an 18-inch Mylar disc coated with magnetic material. The *magne*Disc may have been one of the world's first floppy discs.

In the spring of 1957, researchers in CRL started developing the Data Analysis and Reduction Computer (DARC), TI's first digital computer. It was implemented as a vacuum tube computer because engineers did not believe they had time to wait for transistors to become widely available. Technology was moving fast, and TI was moving quickly to establish and maintain its leading edge within the industry.

record digitally in the field.

But, the GSI/TI approach avoided the layer of costs imposed by analog data and made the digital data immediately available for computer processing which was an important benefit. The primary concern was to get better information, and this was done with the increased dynamic range of the Digital Field System (DFS). A GSI Series 9000 System (DFS I), based on vacuum tube electronics, made the first digital field recordings in 1960. It was followed by the TI Series 10000 System (DFS II), which used semiconductor technology and was designed for use in the jungle and similar operations over difficult terrain. DFS III was based on a license from ESSO and was the first binary gain ranging system. Texaco, one of the two oil-company participants in the digital program, developed the instantaneous-floating-point process used in DFS IV.

DFS V, fully designed by TI, was the most successful of all the systems and became the standard of the industry for more than a decade. In total, from eight digital field systems operating in 1962, TI DFS units in operation grew to 583 in 1972 and to more than 1,300 in 1981. TI's leading position in the geophysical instrumentation market ultimately brought it a strong return on its cumulative investment in the digital seismic strategy.

TI developed more powerful seismic computers, such as the TIAC 870, one of the first integrated-circuit computers. It included a cathode ray tube (CRT) for on-line display. The

A NEW DIVISION

★ ★ ★

In April 1959, a new Geosciences & Instrumentation division was announced by TI for the purpose of applying geophysics to underground nuclear test detection and activity. Fred J. Agnich was to head the new division. Agnich began his career with GSI loading dynamite into shot-holes. Seventeen years later, he was president of GSI and helped lead the transition of the company into Texas Instruments and the digital age.

TIAC 870 proved costly, however, and TI was aware that its competitors were rapidly gaining ground in computing performance.

Haggerty had no intention of losing the lead TI had carved for itself in a marketplace that was becoming crowded. The company formed two strategic task forces to study the requirements for the next generation of computers. TI decided to proceed with the development of a special-purpose supercomputer, called the Advanced Scientific Computer (ASC). The task force was convinced that a giant computer and massive software would be necessary if TI was to have any chance of solving the complicated problem of three-dimensional (3D) seismic surveys. TI was ready to take the industry to the next level, and Haggerty believed TI's labs had the research and engineering genius to get there.

Haggerty was right. In 1970, Bill Schneider, who made a number of significant contributions to the company's digital seismic program, became

The TIAC Center, in Calgary, Canada, in 1964, performed digital seismic data processing for clients. The computer printouts in the foreground show the much improved 2D resolution made possible by digital seismic.

This 3D computer generated model represents approximately 32 cubic miles of subsurface, beginning at a depth of two miles and extending downward to about four miles below the surface of the Earth. Horizontal "slices" may be extracted at any depth for closer study by geophysicists. (Photo from TI 1984 Stockholders Report courtesy of Hunt Oil Company.)

the project manager in charge of GSI's visionary 3D seismic technology. As project scientist, he was instrumental in moving 3D imaging out of the research phase and into a production framework where, once again, GSI would revolutionize oil exploration by giving customers greater geological visibility.

A crucial marketing test was mounted by M. E. "Shorty" Trostle. With several important "firsts" to his credit (first fixed-price field operations in West Texas, first digital recording crew in West Texas, first digital recording of surface non-dynamite seismic sources), Trostle now had his chance at yet another. In 1973, he put together the first full-scale commercial 3D survey for GSI, showcasing the concept and allowing six sponsoring oil companies—Chevron, Amoco, Texaco, Mobil, Phillips, and Unocal—to evaluate its success and potential. The 3D survey worked with stunning results.

The technology was startling and effective. But it was expensive, and many oil companies doubted they could justify the cost. Backus said, "GSI never wanted to be the cheapest company, but GSI was determined to be the most cost-effective company by applying advanced technology. That has always been ingrained in the GSI and TI philosophy of doing business. We were seldom the least expensive company, but we made it a point to have the best technology, and that kept us ahead of the rest of the industry for at least a decade."

In 1978, Bob Graebner of GSI and Dr. Cornelius Dahm, who had been chief geophysicist for Hunt Oil Company, presented an important paper titled "Field Development with Three-Dimensional Seismic Methods in the Gulf of Thailand." The data represented 1,400 kilometers of records, and the interpretation made on the 3D data assessed the natural gas deposits of the Gulf at well over two trillion cubic feet. Such studies helped convince customers to evaluate the new technology with a hard, bottom-line look at results rather than costs. A Sandia Laboratories report later reached a conclusion that *"Three dimensional seismic technology will reduce the worldwide cost of finding new oil reserves by an estimated 47%, or $2.20 per barrel."*

During the 1960s and 1970s, explosive charges were replaced by vibrators on land and by air guns at sea, making geophysical exploration much more environmentally friendly. At the same time, major navigation improvements were being made possible by satellites and global positioning equipment.

Graebner once commented, "There have been three major revolutions in the exploration for oil and gas: reflection seismology, digital seismic circuit, and 3D technology, and GSI/TI has led in each one." Though, ultimately, only the drill could find oil, reflection seismology charted subterranean structures favorable to its accumulation. Then digital seismic separated unwanted noise from the desired seismic signal, giving geologists a better reading of underground formations. And 3D seismic technology produced an accurate 3D picture of the earth's subsurface, reducing the number of dry holes. Each revolution changed the nature of the market and was dependent on science to effectively reduce the cost of finding oil.

3D PIONEERS

The first commercial 3D seismic project was carried out in 1973-74 over the Bell Lake Field underlying Lea County, New Mexico, and extending into West Texas. Years later, the *Midland Reporter-Telegram* reported, "Nothing in the past 20 years has turned the oil industry upside down like 3D technology. Providing a sharper, more definitive picture of subsurface geology, it has literally revolutionized the industry.

"When the petroleum history books are written, Milo Backus, M. E. 'Shorty' Trostle, and Bob Graebner (of GSI) may stand in significance alongside Howard Hughes and his rotary bit, the Schlumberger brothers and their logging machine, and Earl Halliburton and his idea for pumping cement behind the casing of oil wells. Because when the final tally is made, the impact of 3D on the oil industry will be in the billions.

"Not only is the [Permian] Basin-born technology an effective exploration tool that has reduced dry-hole odds by 30-40 percent, it is a highly effective exploitation tool that is being used to find and recover millions of barrels of oil from proven reservoirs."

A line of vibration trucks heads to the next site.

The M/V *Sonic*, placed in service in 1953, was GSI's first ocean-going exploration ship. The *Sonic* was retired in 1964.

6

THE GSI NAVY

GSI creates its own fleet to search for oil.

During the 1930s, GSI built a sterling reputation in the unpredictable business of oil exploration by charting unseen structures that lay hidden beneath the earth's terrain, whether blanketed by deserts, swamplands, or jungles. However, many within the geophysical industry were also intrigued by the possibility that oil might be entombed far below the deep-water oceans and shallow bays that covered so much of the earth's surface. Some speculated that crews would not be

able to record seismic reflections offshore. GSI took on the risk to prove that seismic technology would be just as productive at sea as it had been on land. They built a fleet that would become known as a leader in productivity and technology in marine exploration, and would be instrumental in many of the major offshore discoveries in the twentieth century.

Robert Dunlap had been leading Geophysical Service Inc. field parties on seismic expeditions across the country. One day in 1936, he fielded a crew, loaded a boat with instruments, and sailed out into the Gulf of Mexico to test the effectiveness of the reflection seismograph in open water. The weather was calm and the water like glass as he placed shallow-water seismometers in dishpans and floated them out among the gentle waves surrounding the vessel. The crew randomly exploded their shots on the Gulf floor and waited.

Dunlap later recalled, "We didn't know anything about multiples and bubbles at the time. Also, the seismometers kept falling into the water and sinking, which sounds a little comical now. Later, crew members bolted the seismometers to the dishpans and intentionally let them sink to the bottom. We wanted to see if we could get anything. Sure enough, we got some things—probably all bubbles and noise. But we did prove that offshore seismic work could be done."

The vast opportunity for finding potential oil-bearing structures had suddenly expanded for GSI. The shoreline was no longer a barrier in the quest for oil. The company launched its own navy, a deep-water seismic operation that at first depended exclusively on leased ships. GSI would thus begin pioneering its reflection seismology techniques in the difficult environments encountered at sea.

The Motor Vessel (M/V) *Sonic* would become GSI's first self-sufficient, deep-water marine exploration ship, capable of averaging 50-60 miles of profiling a day and requiring the detonation of 200 to 250 explosive charges. The *Sonic*, a converted 425-ton Navy LCS(L), had a crew of eight, as well as 11 party members responsible for operating the seismic instruments. The ship was acquired in 1953 as part of a business venture that gave GSI a 75 percent interest in two marine geophysical corporations: Geomarine Service, Inc., and Geomarine Service International S.A.

By January of 1954, GSI announced total ownership of both companies, the same year that the M/V *Sonic* made its way into Arabian waters. During the next three years, the ship's crew would shoot surveys across more than 14,000 miles of open sea. They had a technological edge in their profiling mission, the benefit of using a neutral buoyancy streamer, which contained seismometers and wiring and was towed by the seismic vessel. GSI's streamer contained a sheath filled with a lightweight oil that made the streamer neutrally buoyant, an innovation that eliminated the need for detector floats or the use of multiple vessels. Traditionally, marine geophysical surveys employed a minimum of two vessels: one for shooting and one for recording.

During the 1960s, the GSI fleet was making a name for itself in such prime oil exploration regions as the North Sea, the Gulf of Mexico, the waters edging Alaska, the western coast of the United States, the Grand Banks off Newfoundland, the Gulf of Suez, the Brazilian coast, and the waters rising toward the shores of Africa and Asia. By 1965, the fleet grew to more than 50 ships, and GSI introduced an experimental gas exploder marine seismic source called Seismic Underwater Explorer and a digital

Cecil Green at the wheel of M/V *Cecil H. Green I* in the waters off Mexico, 1980.

recorder system. Air guns (pneumatic sources) soon became the standard for marine exploration. They got the job done and were regarded as much more friendly to the environment than those early day dynamite charges they replaced.

In order to develop a fleet to service the worldwide demands for offshore oil exploration, GSI often found it necessary to buy or lease ships and convert them to seismic vessels. For example, the M/V *Texin* had been a U.S. Navy escort ship, the M/V *Gunard* a 30-year-old former pilot boat, the M/V *Merino* a wool transport ship, and the M/V *Hans Egede*, a Norwegian fishing trawler. In addition, a World War II vintage landing craft, the LSM371, was retooled to carry fuel, water, and explosives to various GSI ships working in deep water.

The skills acquired in GSI marine operations were extended to areas other than the search for oil and gas. In 1966, TI's Science Services Division, of which GSI was a part, was awarded a three-year ocean survey contract from the U.S. Naval Oceanographic Office. At the time, it was the largest survey contract in dollars ever handed down by the agency to an industrial organization.

As offshore oil exploration continued to gain more prominence in the economic structure of TI, GSI began naming its ships after those visionary men who had played such vital roles in the founding and building of the company. In 1965, the M/V *Cecil H. Green* was christened by Ida Green, wife of Cecil Green. It was the first ship ever designed specifically by GSI for seismic work. The *Green* had been built for operations in the Gulf of Mexico, but its work assignments would ultimately carry the vessel twice around the world in its first few years of operation. After 16 years of service, the *Green* would be replaced by an even more advanced ship, the M/V *Cecil H. Green II*. It was built larger than its predecessor to accommodate changes in seismic technology and improved living conditions aboard.

The M/V *Eugene McDermott*, the second ship in the fleet built to GSI specifications, was lost at sea. Its replacement, the M/V *Eugene McDermott II*, was launched from New South Wales in 1971. The *McDermott II* bravely plowed through the Bass Straits, known and feared for treacherous waters and wind forces bearing the name "Roaring Forties." All around the ship, from time to time, were raging cyclones described by Australians as "Willy-Willies."

A Canadian stern trawler was purchased in 1970 and named for Erik Jonsson. The M/V *J. E. Jonsson* sailed off the coast of eastern Canada a year later, providing nonexclusive seismic coverage from surveys beneath the waters of the Grand Banks, the Newfoundland Shelf, and the northern portion of the Nova Scotia Shelf.

The M/V *Patrick E. Haggerty* was christened on March 28, 1979. A plaque onboard the ship said of Haggerty: *"His technical and managerial abilities played a significant role in such industry firsts as the production of the first commercially available silicon transistors, the invention of the integrated circuit, and the development of digital seismic data collection and processing systems. The results of these revolutionary achievements are pervasive throughout our society and have contributed far-reaching benefits to mankind."*

The GSI marine operations were full of long days, hard work, turbulent waters, and weather that could be miserably hot, thick with ice, or laced with foreboding storms. Seismic explorations were most often conducted in remote oceanic corners of the world, and crews might go for weeks without a glimpse of land. GSI mariners faced, then overcame, each obstacle, no matter how difficult it might seem at the time.

During the 1960s, GSI had as many as eight parties battling the rough waters of the North Sea, profiling a region that would become one of the world's great oil discoveries. More than anything, their primary concern was one of logistics. Data was recorded daily in analog form and dispatched to England, where it was taken by rail to Bromley, near London, for processing at GSI's Seismic Center. Interpretation of each day's findings was an around-the-clock operation. GSI's seismic fleet established records for productivity, and the company's marine exploration was a major factor in accelerating the development of North Sea oil for the United Kingdom and Norway.

In 1972, the company created speculative marine surveys in waters near the Arctic cap. Because of the short recording season, it was vital to have a seismic vessel ready to work as soon as the Arctic ice pack moved out. The M/V *Mariner* was built in Edmonton, Alberta, Canada, and shipped overland in three sections to the Hay River, where the short, barge-type vessel was reassembled, outfitted, launched, and tested on the Great Slave Lake. The *Mariner*, flying the Canadian flag, sailed up the Mackenzie River and waited for the ice to move out before collecting seismic data in the Beaufort Sea. For 19 years, the ship triumphed over the bitter cold, angry winds, and ice-storm challenges it confronted during the short Canadian Arctic recording season. In October each year, the ship was frozen in place, sealed by the harsh winter, hibernating until spring released it from a prison of ice once more. As the *Mariner* slipped gingerly into the Beaufort Sea, fixed-wing and helicopter flights from Inuvik base camp monitored the treacherous movement of ice each day.

In 1974, the M/V *Arctic Explorer*, an icebreaker rigged for seismic operations, accompanied by the M/V *Carino*, made its way hundreds of miles nearer the North Pole than any previous seismic survey ships, cutting through ice that was often four feet thick. The *Arctic Explorer* was built to cruise comfortably at 14 knots, but it would sometimes take hours for the ship to penetrate a single mile of pack ice that kept freezing up behind the vessel as it moved tediously along. The *Arctic Explorer* and *Carino* patiently chopped their way through the previously

unnavigated waters of the Arctic Ocean, breaking all records by coming within 500 nautical miles of the North Pole.

However, GSI's far-reaching marine operation entailed risk, and even though the company applied stringent safety regulations and stringent education and training for its crews, the threat of accidents or disaster rode the winds of every storm at sea. Some ships and men were lost, including the M/V *McDermott*, which struck an uncharted reef off West Africa and sank with no loss of life. The M/V *Arctic Explorer*, which for many years had plowed through Arctic ice, sank off the northeast coast of Newfoundland on July 3, 1981, with a loss of six GSI employees, five ship's crewmen, and two subcontractor personnel. In July of 1977, the M/V *Midnight Sun* burned for 19 hours in the Gulf of Mexico before the flames could be extinguished by the U.S. Coast Guard. The crew, just five days earlier, had practiced fire and abandon-ship drills and were able to abandon ship without any casualties.

On land or on sea, GSI made an impact in the search for oil-bearing structures, often going where neither men nor ships had ever ventured before. Crews baked in the deserts and froze in the Arctic. They suffered in isolation and with loneliness. They battled cyclone winds, high seas, and fortresses of ice. But they did the jobs they were asked to do, and

In this 1963 North Sea photo, Party Manager Bill Blakeley directs operations of the shooting boat *Fokke de Jong* from the bridge of the M/V *Kyle Anne*. The water plume aft the *Fokke de Jong* resulted from detonation of explosives, the seismic energy source used prior to airguns.

M/V _Arctic Explorer_ made history in 1974 as first ship ever to have entered Kellet and Fitzwilliam Straits in the Canadian High Arctic.

few ever did them better. When revenues from both land and marine operations were combined, GSI, for many years, was recognized as the number one geophysical exploration company in the industry.

In 1988, TI sold a 60-percent interest in GSI to the Halliburton Company. In 1991, the remaining interest in GSI was sold to Halliburton, whose objective was to expand the technology-driven capabilities of its oil field services business. Later, portions of Halliburton's seismic operations were purchased by Western Geophysical.

For a few years, the honored name of GSI virtually faded from sight. But its name lives on again.

Davey Einarsson served as an executive with GSI for many years, and his responsibility included marine operations. He acquired the rights to the GSI name, and, in 1992, formed a new company—hiring a new generation to provide land and sea oil exploration services to the world's petroleum industry.

GSI is now an independent company with offices in Houston, Texas; Calgary, Alberta, Canada; and Milan, Italy. GSI also has associates and agents in other countries, including China, Turkey, England, and Argentina.

A ship uses streamers to gather 3D data deep below the ocean floor.

THE LEGACY OF GSI
★ ★ ★

In reflecting on the company's history, Harvey Cragon, a retired TI scientist, pointed out: "It's a good thing that TI's founders came out of the oil patch. They knew what it was like to hit a dry hole. They weren't afraid to take risks."

Such an entrepreneurial spirit formed the backbone of the GSI legacy. The company, its founders, its employees, and its parent company all possessed a can-do attitude and the belief that a person's responsibility always exceeded his or her authority. The mission was always to do the job right.

With its vision and innovation in the oil exploration business on land and sea, GSI established a solid foundation for TI. Even when the name changed, the company's values, its integrity, and its ethics remained as they were during the vibrant years when Karcher, McDermott, Green, Jonsson, Peacock, and all the GSIers were struggling through the Great Depression.

IN PURSUIT OF DEFENSE

To counter the sudden decline in oil exploration during World War II, GSI decided to pursue business within the U.S. defense industry. The hiring of Pat Haggerty in 1945 became a key step in the company's strategy. Haggerty had been in the equipment purchasing section of the Navy's Bureau of Aeronautics, and he knew what was needed to write winning government proposals. Early defense projects focused on manufacturing the designs of other companies using its precision machine shop. By the mid-1950s, TI received its first contracts for internally designed systems, a side-looking radar for the Air Force and an infrared linescanner for the Army. In 1961, TI was selected for the Shrike Missile project because of its position as a leading supplier of solid-state technology transistors. By 1997, the company became one of the nation's top missile contractors, created a multi-billion dollar military infrared market, and was a principal supplier of tactical radar systems to military markets worldwide. TI would help change the balance of power by revolutionizing tactical warfare.

The Navy's Neptune anti-submarine aircraft had TI's magnetic anomaly detection equipment located in the elongated tail.

7

MAD: A TICKET FOR SURVIVAL

The hunt for submarines forever changes the direction of GSI.

The attack on Pearl Harbor was just the beginning. On December 6, 1941, less than 24 hours after Eugene McDermott, Erik Jonsson, Cecil Green, and Bates Peacock took ownership of GSI, America found itself at war, and GSI's business prospects darkened. GSI took advantage of an opportunity to manufacture a system designed to detect enemy submarines, called Magnetic Anomaly Detection (MAD). The risk paid off for GSI and the U.S. Navy. Although the value of the defense contracts received during the war would only total about $1 million, it would be enough for GSI to pay off its bank loans and survive a difficult period. The company would go on to make its own innovations and, years later, become one of the highest quality defense electronics manufacturers in the world.

The day after Pearl Harbor, Jonsson later recalled, "A million worries crossed my mind, not the least of which was that I probably had lost a lot of money I really didn't have. So maybe I was broke again. I didn't know." McDermott had been named president of the company, with Jonsson serving as vice president and treasurer. Green and Peacock were assigned the task of building and supervising GSI's geophysical work at home and abroad, even though oil exploration was as troubled as the times. Field crews went from 26 to six. It would have been easy for the partners to wonder if they had foolishly purchased a doomed company. But they never wavered, though GSI had very little borrowing power and its reserve capital was rapidly eroding. All prospects for expanding the company's lucrative overseas operations had come to an end as GSI survey crews had to return home due to the war.

Erik Jonsson wrote: *"To a casual observer, it might well have seemed that a foundation had been built, not for a growth company, but for an industrial fatality ... To those of us who knew the facts, the outlook seemed rough, but we had good people, the job was worth doing, and we were in Texas, where the expression, 'You can't get there from here' has still not been heard. We rolled up our sleeves and went to work."*

Jonsson realized GSI's situation was "serious, but not hopeless." The war, he believed, was destined to be long and demanding, making it imperative for GSI to continue its geophysical exploration for oil. The supply of oil could make the difference between victory and defeat.

The partners began working to find a new business that might supplant the company's decline in geophysical exploration. They had a few engineers and technicians, a first-class machine shop, some electronics design knowledge, and assembly capability. The answer could well be defense contracts connected to

This Magnetic Anomaly Detection (MAD) equipment was built by GSI in 1942 and was the genesis of TI's military equipment business.

electronics—work that would utilize their skills in precision machining. But, they wondered, "How could a small company without prior experience compete successfully within the large established defense contractors?"

Jonsson began spending much of his time in Washington, D.C., learning his way around the Defense Department, walking long hallways, and knocking on as many doors as he could find, seeking military contracts that might boost GSI's revenues. Initially, he came home with some small engineering and development tasks for the U.S. Army Signal Corps. These marked the beginning of a new era and a new direction for GSI.

Jim Wilhite arrives at the remote MAD test site to calibrate equipment near today's D/FW Airport.

I n Washington, D. C., the National Defense Research Committee (NDRC), headed by Vannevar Bush, was uniting the brightest minds from university and industrial environments, assigning them projects that the military deemed important to its war strategies. It was at that time Eugene McDermott received a fortuitous phone call from Dr. Dana Mitchell of Columbia University. Years earlier, the men had taught together at the university. Mitchell was a member of Bush's wartime countermeasures group in Cambridge, Massachusetts. On his way to meet with a group of scientists at Los Alamos, New Mexico, Mitchell stopped in Dallas, toured the GSI facilities, and talked with McDermott.

Soon after the visit, Mitchell was on the phone, asking McDermott if GSI would manufacture some devices the Navy needed for a test. "I know you can build them," he said.

"What are the devices for?" McDermott wanted to know.

"I can't divulge that information," Dr. Mitchell answered.

McDermott agreed to help the NDRC, though he had no idea what GSI was supposed to build, the cost, or price the company could put on the highly classified devices. But GSI had years of experience keeping customer data confidential. The fewer questions asked, the better.

Jonsson immediately left for Washington, and, when he returned home, he had a small contract to manufacture six MAD systems. Because of security, the NDRC refused to release an assembly drawing. That didn't matter. It didn't take long for Al Morel, chief of drafting and mechanical design, to make subassembly sketches by carefully matching the piece part drawings. GSI realized for the first time exactly what kind of devices its team would be building: magnetic anomaly detection systems, designed to help the Navy track down enemy submarines by detecting slight changes in the earth's magnetic field caused by the steel hull of the submerged sub.

When the first circuit diagram was hand-carried to Dallas from NDRC headquarters, the circuit, as drawn, wouldn't work. Darwin Renner, in charge of GSI's electronics development, redesigned the circuit, and it functioned exactly the way it was supposed to. Renner, who was GSI's only electrical engineer at the beginning of the war years, and Jim Toomey, superintendent of the geophysical lab, loaded up the first GSI-produced MAD units and flew with them to Quonset Point, Rhode Island. One of the units was set up for a test in a shack beside the landing field. As Toomey recalled, "Immediately it began to detect aircraft on the nearby runway... Our MAD was a success."

GSI was a relatively small company among the industrial

RESCUING SKINNIE AND L.C.

★ ★ ★

Al Storm's GSI crew was working in the Sumatra jungle, unaware that Japanese troops were moving swiftly from one island to another. As Skinnie Holbert recalled, "They wanted the oil that Sumatra had."

News of the 1941 hostilities finally reached Storm, and he dispatched a runner to the field with an optimistic note that said: *"The Japanese have attacked Pearl Harbor and destroyed a lot of ships. War has been declared, and it looks pretty bad. But keep shooting (the geophysical shots). It should all be over in about three weeks."*

Ten days later, Storm frantically sent out a runner with a second note that told his crew, *"Stack it up. We're going home."*

While Japanese invaders were marching across Sumatra, the GSI doodlebuggers sought to secure passage to freedom before enemy troops stormed into the port of Sunbaja. They could already hear bombs exploding on the outskirts of town. Two GSI crew members, Holbert and L.C. Craig, climbed aboard a small, coal-burning Dutch rubber transport, and were only a few hours out of port when a Japanese torpedo ripped the ship apart. Holbert and Craig jumped in a crowded lifeboat and floated out to sea. All their possessions were left behind, and Holbert had lost his shoes. He remembered, "We had one water bottle and passed it around. Everybody only took one swallow. We had no idea how long we would be adrift at sea."

Holbert and Craig, along with the crew of the ship, were rescued several hours later from the sea and were returned to the port they had recently departed. In the midst of chaos, they found passage aboard a freighter headed for New York. But after a few days of sailing, the ship was diverted and they disembarked at Ceylon, then made their way by rail across India and joined GSI crews at work in Saudi Arabia. Eventually, Holbert and Craig were able to journey to Dallas, ready for their next assignment.

giants who became suppliers to the Navy's Bureau of Aeronautics, but, by the time Toomey and Renner returned to Dallas, Jonsson had received an order for 50 more MADs. Priority for production in the GSI shops promptly shifted from oil exploration to the MAD work. The MAD systems were critical to the Navy's task of tracking down German submarines operating along the Atlantic coast, menacing the shipping lanes. At first, the detector systems were placed on blimps; later they were attached to Navy patrol aircraft flying low over the ocean. The plane would tow the MAD sensor at the end of a 200-foot cable, detecting minute changes in the strength of the earth's magnetic field to pinpoint submerged enemy submarines.

Within a few years, GSI would be recognized as the nation's largest producer of the submarine-hunting equipment. The company's survival had been dependent on its ability to apply its skills to a new field.

As a teenager, Tommy Chaddick joined GSI in the machine shop on Harwood Street in Dallas. He epitomized the machinists' skills critical to the company's early defense contracts.

8

THE BEST AND THE BRIGHTEST

A "good, little company" sets its sights on becoming a "good, big company."

After WWII ended, GSI was determined to take advantage of the crucial contacts Erik Jonsson and Eugene McDermott had made inside the military complex—they would keep building equipment the U.S. needed to keep the peace. Jonsson decided it was time for GSI and its 550 postwar employees to begin diversifying the company's business structure, and he knew just the person to make that happen—Pat Haggerty. This decision would have a major impact on GSI and eventually on the electronics industry—setting a new and exciting direction.

Exposure to techniques and technology in military manufacturing helped chart the future course of GSI. While doing business with the Navy's Bureau of Aeronautics, Jonsson was in close contact with men who excited his interest in the potential of electronics. One of them was Lieutenant Patrick E. Haggerty, the Navy's procurement officer on the Magnetic Anomaly Detector project. At the war's end, Haggerty was embroiled with canceling contracts and rescheduling the department's postwar priorities. He was ready for a change and a new challenge. He admired GSI's work and knew Jonsson's vision for the company's future. Haggerty was not surprised when Jonsson said, "Why don't you come on and join us?"

Haggerty thought for a moment, then replied, "We've talked a little about this manufacturing stuff and where we think deficiencies are. I think I see an area for opportunity; and if

Pat Haggerty joined GSI in 1945 and soon became manager of the Laboratory and Manufacturing Division, consisting of 85 people.

you will set up and cut out this part of the company where we can start an activity to do this engineering and manufacturing job in electronics—not just for the geophysical—then I'm damned interested."

Haggerty had built one of the first ham radios in his home state of North Dakota and won a scholarship to Marquette University's School of Electrical Engineering. He graduated in 1936 with the highest grades ever awarded by the engineering school.

Jonsson would later say, "Haggerty was a hard worker and a man of integrity. I made my mind up long before the war was over that the day it ended I'd be after Pat for our company. I realized that would be a competitive mistake if you enjoy power, because in many respects he was smarter than I, but it was the way to go. One of the first principles of good management is that you have your successor ready."

During the spring of 1946, the Laboratory and Manufacturing (L&M) division of GSI was established in a corner of the company's automotive shop. Haggerty was named general manager in charge of the 85 employees who had been assigned to work with him. As the *GSI Grapevine* pointed out: *"For a business venture without products or markets, a new plant emerged from the drawing board."*

Jonsson recalled, "It signaled a period of rapid and substantial growth. For five years, the story was work, build, expand, hire, train, borrow, earn, and get ready to grow again."

Haggerty did not hesitate to staff the new division with key personnel who had worked with him at the Bureau.

31

Even before he left Washington, D.C., Haggerty had hired Robert W. Olson, a senior engineer with the Bureau who became chief engineer at GSI. Olson had worked his way through the University of Minnesota, earning a degree in electrical engineering, while repairing radios and taking odd jobs.

Under Olson, GSI established experimental labs to create and develop seismic, electronic, mechanical, and electrical products.

Carl J. "Tommy" Thomsen, who had roots in the Bureau, was hired as controller of the L&M division in 1946. Thomsen, with a degree in industrial engineering from Rensselaer Polytechnic Institute, had served as a time-and-motion analyst at Westinghouse and taught industrial engineering at Johns Hopkins before the war.

The foundation of Haggerty's team was set, and others with Bureau expertise would soon follow.

Haggerty initiated the three-pronged rollout of GSI's strategy: first, he wanted the company to become a long-term provider of military electronics, starting as a "second source" supplier and eventually becoming a major producer. Second, he supported Jonsson's belief that GSI should set its course toward becoming a manufacturer of nonmilitary electronics. And third, he understood the importance of GSI's continuing to manufacture geophysical equipment.

GSI's emergence as a manufacturing company would take longer than anyone had anticipated. In 1948, the company's sales neared $5 million, but manufacturing had accounted for less than $1 million in sales. During the year, McDermott decided to step down from the presidency to devote his time to guiding an expanding GSI research program. Henry Bates Peacock was named president of GSI.

Haggerty expressed the company's vision best. He said, "We are a good, little company. Now we must become a good, big company."

"What do you consider big?" someone asked.

"Around $200 million in sales," he answered.

Jonsson remained vice president, secretary, and treasurer of GSI. Green was vice president for GSI's field operations and international business. Under his leadership, GSI was able to return to the oil exploration sites of Saudi Arabia, as well as to secure long-term contracts from government-owned oil companies in Mexico and Brazil.

During 1948, GSI strengthened the nucleus of its management team when Haggerty hired 25-year-old Mark Shepherd, Jr., a graduate of Southern Methodist University's School of Engineering. His father, a veteran Dallas policeman, had been immobilized by a stroke, and the young Shepherd helped support his mother by cutting lawns and working in grocery stores—finishing high school at the age of 14. As a college student at SMU, Shepherd had sought summer employment at GSI but had been turned down.

Years later, Shepherd was working for the Farnsworth

Company in Fort Wayne, Indiana, when a company executive asked him, "What about this GSI in Dallas?"

Shepherd outlined his working knowledge of GSI, then inquired, "Why are you so interested in the company?"

"Well, GSI just took one of our more lucrative government contracts, the APA-5," came the answer.

Shepherd later recalled, "I wanted to get in touch with an outfit that could do that. And I wanted to go back home anyway. So I dropped them a line, and the next time I got to Dallas, I went to see them."

His visit paid off for Shepherd and for GSI. He was assigned to work on the Navy's USQ-1 Radiac detector, then served as project engineer on the ASQ-8, a redesign of MAD. Shepherd rapidly advanced to the position of assistant chief engineer under Olson. As Shepherd later said, "There was never any question as to what I would do. From the time I read my first quasi-technical magazine, it would be electronics." Eventually, Shepherd became Chairman of the Board and was instrumental in TI's international semiconductor manufacturing.

Haggerty looked to men with Navy experience for his next two critical hires.

S. T. "Buddy" Harris had taken a job with a plastics company in Virginia after the war, but on a sales trip to Dallas, he dropped by GSI for a visit with Olson. Harris had drive. He had the kind of unabashed enthusiasm Haggerty wanted in a man who wouldn't be afraid to reach for $200 million in sales. Harris, with an electrical engineering degree from the University of Tennessee, and radar experience with the Navy's Air Development Center, was offered a job before he left Dallas.

Haggerty had been trying to recruit W.F. "Wally" Joyce for a long time. Joyce had worked as a mule skinner in a Montana copper mine and prospected for gold in Nevada before returning to Marquette University and studying chemistry, physics, and math. Haggerty tried to persuade Joyce to join him when both men left the Bureau, but Joyce declined, moving instead to New York. Haggerty never gave up, finally convincing Joyce in 1949 to head up GSI's manufacturing division.

Defense spending was increasing, and Haggerty got GSI on the bid list for government contracts. GSI was establishing an enviable record of submitting lower bids, then working faster

JONSSON'S DREAM CASTLE
★ ★ ★

In 1946, Haggerty began making preparations to build a stronger foundation for the company's manufacturing business. GSI needed space, and he proposed the construction of a new plant to accommodate the expected expansion.

Jonsson persuaded the Travelers Insurance Company to loan GSI $150,000 to build a new plant on Lemmon Avenue at the north edge of the city, near the airport (Love Field). Some questioned building so far away from downtown Dallas in a new and empty industrial district surrounded by oat fields, tall grass, and sunflowers.

GSI sought top-rated architect Harwood K. Smith to design a modern 38,000-square-foot facility, called Jonsson's "dream castle" by employees. *Architectural Forum* described the plant as having *"striking industrial facades."* By the time the plant was completed, the cost had risen to $350,000—a major statement of confidence by GSI in its future.

The machine shops moved in several weeks before work was completed on the building. In rapid succession came automotive, engineering, manufacturing, administration, and purchasing. The main office, computing department, and personnel didn't move from their downtown offices until June 1947. By that time, three shifts were already engaged in manufacturing.

It was the first and last time the company would be housed under one roof.

and more efficiently to complete the projects. The military took notice. GSI was still a "good, little company," but its business was on the upswing. By 1950, GSI's sales topped $7.6 million, about equally divided between the geophysical business and the manufacturing division.

With his team in place, Haggerty's goal was to reach $200 million in sales by 1960. It was a lofty goal, perhaps, but Haggerty believed it was attainable. Defense electronics would have to play an even larger role—taking the company in new directions.

9

INNOVATION IN
TACTICAL RADAR

*TI helps the military fly
under the enemy's radar.*

*TI bootstrapped its way from a small producer of other
companies' radar designs to a position of prominence
as one of the major radar suppliers. With its innovative
radar systems, TI provided solutions for many of the
tactical surveillance and airborne attack problems
facing the nation's military.*

**Dallas is mapped by TI's revolutionary radar, producing
near-photographic information with certain advantages over
conventional aerial photos. The APQ-55 radar, developed in
1957 for the Air Force, mapped thousands of square miles of
terrain per hour, night or day, in any weather in which man can
fly. Unlike an aerial photograph, perspective of distance is
adjusted electronically so areas on the edge of the photo
are of the same scale as those at the center.**

Even as many electronics companies were moving in
other directions after WWII, GSI in 1947 decided to
remain solidly entrenched within the fading military market
because of its success during the war with submarine detection
equipment. Many throughout the industry questioned the
company's wisdom, but the monumental decision proved
prophetic. Because of GSI's vast knowledge and experience in

using precision electronics for recording seismograph data, the
company was able to secure its first sizeable military contract
in 1947. The APA-5A electronic bomb sight sparked a genuine
interest in pursuing work on radar for military applications. In
1949, even though GSI had never built a radar system, it outbid
Philco, one of the nation's largest electronics firms, and stunned
the industry by winning a Navy contract to manufacture the

APS-31, an airborne ocean surveillance radar for locating sea targets. The project represented the largest single contract in the company's history, and TI committed to build the first radar at a fixed price in nine months. However, it wasn't until Jonsson assured the Navy of a guarantee of financial support from Republic Bank, that GSI received production orders for several hundred of the radar systems.

W. F. "Wally" Joyce, head of the company's defense business in the 1950s, characterized the early management team as "a group of individualists and independent thinkers with a keen appreciation of the efforts of each other and the team as a whole." They sought out new challenges and took risks together. They faced problems together. They found solutions together. As Jonsson pointed out, TI's management and production teams "were hardworking, ambitious and ready to go—ready for expansion on a major scale."

The Korean War triggered a boom of defense equipment business, and, from 1949 to 1953, the company's revenue rose from $5.8 million to $27 million. Winning new business was all about being the lowest bidder, and profit margins had to be drastically reduced. The end of the war had devastating effects on the defense business. Most open contracts were canceled, and, during one period, TI lost 28 bids before finally winning its twenty-ninth proposal. This was one of the most difficult procurement periods, but the military learned that it could depend on TI to provide high quality equipment without unnecessary delays, even though TI's defense business, at times, had to rely on selling spare parts to keep the business viable.

Historically, TI had always been content to seek military business with the Navy, a traditional customer of the Bureau where Haggerty and many of his management team had worked during the war. Desperately searching for new business, the company chose to bid on a radar project for the Air Force. And even though TI offered the lowest bid, the Air Force was unfamiliar with the company and apprehensive about doing business with a new, unproven supplier.

Ron Keener, an engineer who would later manage the company's defense business, packaged up bits and pieces of key components required by the radar project and, in 1955, presented them to the Air Force with a persuasive argument

that TI could indeed do the job. By accepting a fixed price of $1.4 million and agreeing to a 1957 delivery date, the company assumed a tremendous financial risk while committing to produce the radars in record time.

That radar, the AN/APQ-55 side-looking radar, became the first radar totally designed by TI. Before delivering engineering models of the radar system to Wright Air Development Center, TI engineers worked out bugs in the program by logging 6,000 air miles at the company's own expense in a modified B-25 airplane. Flight testing its radar equipment in the skies above North Texas became standard procedure on future radar projects, and the extra effort paid off. The radar system was delivered on schedule, and, while the project did not reach volume production, TI had managed to enhance its credentials as a prime developer of new projects, as well as significantly broaden its customer base.

With the side-looking radar, the stage had been set in early 1957 for the design and development of a revolutionary concept that was destined to have a dramatic impact on TI's defense electronics business for decades to come.

The Soviet Union had introduced the surface-to-air antiaircraft missile, and there was a greater need than ever to protect aircraft flying over hostile environments. The military was faced with two options: planes would be forced to fly extremely high, which negated their effectiveness, or they had to fly extremely low to the ground during reconnaissance, damage assessment, and close air attack missions. But skimming close to the mountainous earth at high speeds was often more dangerous than taking a chance on enemy missiles at higher altitudes.

TI hired Bart Bechtel, a former Navy engineer, who had designed a radar "scan template" control technique that permitted safe aircraft descent in adverse weather. The concept was the basis of winning a $750,000 U.S. Army contract to develop a radar system to automatically guide a drone aircraft. The Army did not pursue the project to production, but the Air Force became interested and was willing to gamble that Bechtel's innovation just might be able to protect the low-flying planes. TI was awarded a contract to develop APN-149, the first terrain-following radar for use on manned aircraft.

Prototype flight-testing always played a key role in the military equipment business. Norman Chandler (left) checks out APQ-55 equipment as John Chandler (center) and Ray McCord (right) look on.

Jim Sherill, Dwain Manning, Audie Herriott, and Lloyd Tuttle (left to right) check radar antennas in the test tower.

The pressure was on. A pilot's life was at stake and Bechtel's idea and TI's engineering innovation had answered the call.

In 1962, the Air Force experience with the APN-149 was the basis for the company to be awarded the APQ-99 radar development for the McDonnell RF-4 aircraft. TI, however, had ambitiously underbid the APQ-99 project, and problems began to appear immediately. McDonnell tested the radar and bluntly explained that the radar didn't work the way it was supposed to. TI's Russ Logan, a radar engineer and later a TI Principal Fellow, was a novice pilot and volunteered to fly in McDonnell's simulator to prove the effectiveness of the radar. He said, "I was accustomed to flying tri-pacers, and now I found myself stuck into an F-4 simulator. It was like jumping off into the Grand Canyon with an umbrella for a parachute. I drove the simulator through the second mountain I came to."

Logan admitted that a legitimate technical problem did exist. He pointed out, "The company had a secret resource, Bob Davis, a former Marine pilot, and TI was depending on him to fly in an RF-4 to prove that the radar really worked." He did. The radar didn't.

The whole project was in jeopardy. TI's Sam K. Smith explained, "In reality, McDonnell Douglas was flying around an RF-4 with a piece of lead ballast in its nose. The radar just didn't work." Smith went to Ray McCord and said, "We don't have any choice. We have to start the whole project over, and it'll cost us a million dollars."

McCord replied, "Do it. It's worth millions of dollars."

As Logan pointed out, "TI gave McDonnell Douglas a commitment it hadn't counted on receiving. We said we would fix the problem, and we did. TI had strong individuals who weren't afraid to step up when necessary and accept responsibility if a job happened to be going bad, and that made all of the difference. When a company proves that it is ready to stand behind its work, then its work begins to mean something. McDonnell Douglas wasn't easy on us, but the company didn't cancel the contract. McDonnell Douglas stayed with us, and the terrain-following radar became one of the systems that kept

A tail-mounted camera captures an F-111 aircraft in terrain-following flight.

TI and the free world out front."

In reality, this technology made it possible for America's aircraft to fly under the enemy's radar as low as 200 feet, effectively creating the nation's first "stealth" penetration fleet of fighters and bombers. They arrived at high speeds, completed their mission, and were gone without ever showing up on an enemy's radar screen. During the life of TI's defense business, the company produced more than 6,000 terrain-following radar systems for the F-111, A-7, F-16, the European Multi-Role Combat Aircraft, the B-1, C-130, and HH-53 Pave Low helicopter.

Texas Instruments never lost its vision for seeking out the next best idea, and, as Russ Logan pointed out, "Ideas always make the difference as long as a company has people capable of making those ideas a reality."

TI did.

TI's expertise in semiconductor technology, which began in 1952, had always played a central role in the growth of the radar business. In 1964, the company was awarded a development contract for MERA—Molecular Electronics for Radar Applications—which called for an intriguing new design. MERA, a joint effort between TI's defense and semiconductor businesses, was an all-solid-state radar system with no moving parts. An important part of the system was the 1.5-cubic-inch electronic module, small enough to fit in the palm of the hand. Less than two years earlier, it would have measured a cubic foot, weighed 25 pounds, and cost $5,000 instead of the $50 to $100 TI projected for volume-production units of the new integrated-circuit version.

CONTROLLING THE SKIES

★ ★ ★

In the fall of 1957, the company received a Federal Aviation Agency solicitation for the ASR-4, Airport Surveillance Radar, whose purpose was to ease the increasingly complex problems of aircraft control around major metropolitan airports. TI had little interest in pursuing the project and lay the request aside. However, Warren Lowery in TI's Washington, D.C., office persuaded the company to bid, even though time had grown too short for TI to prepare a thorough cost proposal. All emphasis was on the technical side of the ASR-4, and Glenn Bandy, TI's first systems engineer, remembered the TI team worked day and night to complete the proposal as the company went head-to-head with such major corporations as General Electric, RCA, and Bendix. To almost everyone's surprise, TI received a $4.7 million contract to build and install 16 ASR-4 systems. Over the next 40 years, TI would deliver more than 250 of these systems to customers around the world.

MERA replaced not only the microwave electronics rack of conventional radars, but also made conformal antennas possible. In addition, MERA's operating reliability was significantly greater than any previous airborne radar system, and its distinctive weight and performance advantages gave the company a future that appeared to have no limits. Perhaps just as important, the project spawned development of a monolithic microwave integrated circuit capability that would be critical to future successes in radar and missile projects.

TI had gained a leadership position early with electronic surveillance equipment, and it was a position that the company never lost. The ideas and concepts involved with radar development moved TI into another domain. Radar work changed TI's professional landscape from a build-it-to-print company to a design-and-make-it-happen solutions company. TI's way of doing business was changed forever.

TI equipment including optics and data storage on the *Voyager I* interplanetary spacecraft helped make this image of Jupiter. (Photo by Jet Propulsion Laboratory.)

10

THE RACE TO SPACE

TI was one of the first companies chosen to work with NASA in America's exploration of the planets.

The development of the silicon transistor in the early 1950s provided TI with the competitive edge it needed for designing and building lighter electronic packages placed aboard tactical military systems. TI's ingenuity for developing an array of unique materials, detectors, and innovative designs allowed the company to play a critical role in America's exploration of those unsolved mysteries in deep space. The National Aeronautics and Space Administration (NASA) recognized that TI had the capability to produce lightweight electronics systems for launch missiles and satellites. Between 1957 and 1977, the missions to the planets carried more than 450 TI systems and hundreds of thousands of the company's semiconductor components and electrical control products, making a major contribution to America's leadership in space.

On October 4, 1957, the Soviet Union shocked the world by launching *Sputnik*, a satellite weighing 183 pounds and orbiting the earth every 98 minutes. The battle for space had begun in earnest, and America was lagging far behind. The country's valiant struggle to catch up with a foreign power that had gained a definite advantage in the Cold War would have far-reaching political, military, technological, and scientific ramifications.

The U.S. responded quickly on two fronts. Always fearful of an impending attack by the Soviet Union, the military began work on the Titan Intercontinental Ballistic Missile, and TI supplied the digital programmers and the signal-conditioning package. In January of 1958, America launched its answer to the Soviet Union's *Sputnik* with *Explorer I*, equipped with TI's transistors. Subsequent payloads using TI transistors would help discover the magnetic radiation belts around the earth.

Space had suddenly become a bold new frontier, and TI was helping make it possible for a nation to go where no one had dared venture before, far beyond the elliptical orbit of *Sputnik*. The company's flight programmers on Thor-Delta rockets helped put *Telstar*, the first communication satellite, *TIROS* weather satellites, and the *Explorer II* satellite into orbit.

As the emphasis on space exploration grew, so did TI. In the early 1960s, the company established a Space Systems Branch and began designing an advanced series of power transistors, high-voltage rectifiers, and ultra-fast silicon rectifiers which permitted reductions in size and weight of power supplies in space vehicles.

TI built telemetry packages for the rockets that launched the Mercury manned-space capsules, as well as the *Mariner 2* Venus

semiconductors, precision switches, and thermostats on board. The company had been part of a scientific and technological team that helped astronaut Neil Armstrong make a "giant leap for mankind."

Mariner 4's 1966 mission for a closer encounter with Mars utilized TI components and guidance programmers on the launch vehicle. The payload carried TI recorder electronics, Data Encoder, Gyro Electronics, and Helium Magnetometer. TI would ride with Mariner explorations for years to come.

During the 1960s, TI developed and successfully flew IRIS, an Infrared Interferometer Spectrometer, on the Nimbus D spacecraft series for NASA Goddard Space Flight Center. When the decision was made for Voyager's ambitious mission to unlock some of the puzzles surrounding Mars, Jupiter, Saturn, Neptune, and Uranus, TI was awarded a sole source contract for an advanced IRIS system to implement into the program.

As Don Vanous, TI's program manager, wrote, *"IRIS was used in space exploration for the measurement of both atmospheric constituents of the targeted planets, as well as a measurement of the temperature profile from space to the surface of the planets. This information was used at NASA Goddard to then simulate and understand the atmospheric physics of the planets. These measurements could only be achieved with the degree of accuracy required with the IRIS operating at 200 degrees Kelvin or less in the space environment."*

Weight was at a premium on the *Voyager* spacecraft, so

probe. By tucking astronauts into the cramped confines of the Mercury craft, America had surged ahead in the frantic race to space, and a nation began to breathe a little easier.

In 1964, TI built the command detector and decoder for the *Ranger 7* photo mission to the moon. TI's Walt Riley was an integral member of the mission control team for the project, and, he recalled, NASA was feeling an extreme burden of pressure to achieve a successful mission. Six Rangers had been shot toward the moon before, and their missions had all ended in failure. *Ranger 7* arrived and sent back the photographs that NASA needed to expedite man's historic journey to the lunar craters around Tranquility Base five years later.

The Apollo vehicles all headed toward the moon carrying TI

A composite image shows the *Ranger 7*, which used TI equipment to photograph potential moon landing sites in 1964.

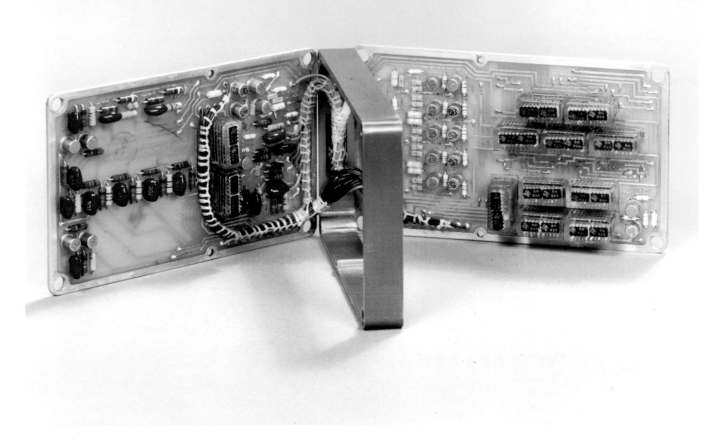

This Digital Data Signal Conditioner was built by TI for Dr. James Van Allen at the University of Iowa in 1962. It was the first use of integrated circuits in space.

designs had to be made from exotic materials that TI had never used before. For example, the front optics on the IRIS was a 20-inch diameter-beryllium mirror that needed to be rugged enough to withstand the vibration environment of the spacecraft launch and yet maintain its optical quality while operating in the temperature of space. The spectrometer took 30 months to develop, and when IRIS was placed on board *Voyager* for its long journey to study Jupiter, Saturn, and Neptune in the early 1970s, it weighed a mere 3.25 pounds.

———————

On *Voyager*, the data storage subsystem, a tape recorder operated by TI electronics, was periodically transmitting data to Earth for computer analysis and visual display. As Verie Lima, who was responsible for the project, pointed out, "These programs are examples of designing quality into a product. We knew there would be no opportunity to repair on such a mission." After passing Neptune, Jupiter, and Saturn, the *Voyager* probes began traveling into darker space beyond the known planets. The TI products were still performing in 1989 after 12 years in deep space, and as of January 2005, they have passed 10,000 days since launch.

A similar IRIS system designed by TI was used on *Mariner 9* in the early 1970s, the first mission to orbit Mars for the purpose of observing and mapping at least 70 percent of the Red Planet. Ted Pounder, acting manager of the project, said later, "The scientific productivity of *Mariner 9* surpassed everyone's dreams. In just the area of surface mapping, *Mariner 9* has mapped the entire planet... When all the data obtained has been analyzed, we will have learned more of the planet Mars than man knew in his entire history up to November 1971."

TI's participation in space continues to this day. TI integrated circuits are aboard every space shuttle and many of the payloads. TI imaging chips are an integral part of the Hubble Space Telescope. In 1995, TI researcher, Mary Ellen Weber was accepted into the NASA astronaut program and flew Mission STS-70 aboard the Space Shuttle *Discovery*.

When the great abyss of space beckoned and America realized the political and scientific importance of traveling there, TI, with its silicon transistors, integrated circuits, and innovative solutions, helped pave the way to the planets and beyond.

11

OWNING THE NIGHT

TI's innovation in infrared technologies helped the military expand its operations to include effective night fighting.

Infrared technology offered a lot of potential in tactical military equipment, and it was a natural for the company. Crystalline infared materials could be grown like silicon and silicon itself could be used for infared lenses. TI's vision, dedicated work in basic materials and systems engineering would result in it's leadership in military infared systems and change tactical warfare.

I n 1956, Haggerty organized an interdisciplinary team to determine if infared technology could have a future in TI's defense business. Willis Adcock immediately took a special interest in the feasibility of using indium antimonide as a detector material. In 1956, TI acquired the rights to indium antimonide technology from Chicago Midway Labs, and, before the year ended, purchased the William I. Mann Company, a California electro-optics expert whose inventory was stocked with such silicon-based products as absorption cells, missile guidance heads, fire-control sights, and light source devices. The Mann Company would form the core of the TI Optics Division with founder Bill Mann serving as general manager.

TI had a definite vision for the potential of infared technology, and, from 1956 through 1962, Adcock and George Pruett in the Semiconductor Research and Development Labs received contract funding from a host of government agencies. TI achieved one major breakthrough when it was able to integrate a detector and preamplifier on the same chip, and the company was also on the leading edge of pioneering work that involved longer wavelength, mercury-doped germanium detectors. The longer wavelength (8-14 micron) was critical for creating and manufacturing usable infared systems. With these basic technologies firmly in place, TI won an Army contract in 1957 to develop a wide-angle infrared mapper, the UAS-5, that used a single-axis scanner to image the earth directly below an airplane.

Although the UAS-5 was never produced in large quantities, it marked the genesis of an infrared systems business for the company, leading in 1961 to the production of the AAS-18 linescanner. Installed on the RF-4C aircraft, the linescanner earned its reputation by mapping the entangled jungle terrain of Vietnam.

An aerial photograph of TI's Semiconductor building on the Central Exressway in Dallas (left) compared with the UAS-5 infared image of the same view (right). The UAS-5 was the first infared line scanner built by TI.

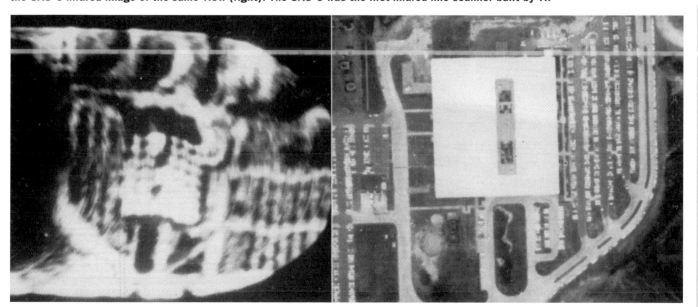

41

well as possible.

The official report was negative. Haggerty was seated on the prestigious Defense Science Board when it received the disheartening news. TI was maligned. Haggerty was appalled, and the briefing greatly eroded his support for TI's continued research in Forward Looking infared (FLIR) development.

But some people in the Department of Defense also realized an important lesson from the test. During night missions, gunships could greatly benefit from having a sensor on board to locate and define targets in the dark terrain while the aircraft circled at a constant altitude and fired large-caliber guns. In 1967, the Air Force ignored its own criticism of the lab model and awarded TI a million-dollar contract to further develop the idea for FLIR. FLIR would bring the advantages of real-time viewing to infrared systems.

Manager Ray McCord, believed strongly in the technology and was willing to battle for critical resources necessary to finance the research of infared detectors, even though management's skepticism had reduced the amount of research money allocated for the project. Many in TI were willing to eliminate or at least lessen the emphasis on the infared program. McCord was determined to keep it a priority.

Key customers stood firm in their support of TI's research endeavors, but they wanted results. When one appealed directly to McCord to provide improved performance, he gave his commitment to solve all problems associated with the project without any additional costs being passed on to the customer. TI backed McCord's pledge, and the company began successfully producing a series of gunship FLIR systems that were capable of detecting radiated heat from an unseen, unknown target and providing operators a displayed image of the heat source.

I n 1963, TI's Kirby Taylor began visualizing a real-time, two-dimensional infared viewer, and was given $30,000 in company funds to investigate the possibility of adding another scan mirror to the single-axis linescanner optics. The study determined the feasibility of the concept, and TI wasted little time in preparing and delivering an unsolicited proposal to the Advanced Research Projects Agency, long recognized as the venture capital, visionary arm of the Department of Defense.

The response came back quickly. The company's concept was "interesting," the agency said, but no military requirement existed for such a sensor. TI was disappointed but not willing to give up on the program. The company turned next to the Air Force Avionics Laboratory, which had been involved with TI on its infared detector development, as well as the linescanner source selection. The Air Force decided that the infared sensor was certainly worth studying further but insisted that the project be bid competitively. TI's original idea was no longer proprietary, and eight companies were battling for one of two contracts, each valued at $250,000. Within months, all competitors but TI had dropped out, and by the end of 1965, TI delivered a crude lab model. It was a simple prototype, nothing more, and certainly not yet ready to be tested in a critical airborne environment. The imagery was marginal at best.

The Air Force in Washington, D.C. was excited about the technology and wanted to see what it could do in practice. Ignoring TI's protests, the model sensor was placed onboard a DC-3 aircraft named *Puff the Magic Dragon*, and an operational test flight was scheduled over the battle zones of Southeast Asia. For TI, it was a bad engineering situation, and Kirby Taylor flew the test missions to assure the system worked as

B y the late 1960s, as the U.S. broadened its war involvement in Southeast Asia, TI's AAD-4, 6, and 7 FLIR became the eyes of Air Force gunships, flying missions throughout the night. From that point forward, night vision would be required for virtually every air, ground, and tactical

The economies of scale offered by TI's common-module FLIR concept enabled nighttime capability for man-portable anti-tank weapon systems.

1 S 6 6 - 4 4   TEXAS INSTRUMENTS

warfare system. Strategic military actions would never be the same again. FLIR made the difference.

With FLIR, the U. S. military owned the night.

After the end of the war, planners saw the power of FLIR but recoiled at its relatively high cost. In March 1972, TI received a letter from the director of Advanced Research Projects Agency, Dr. George Heilmeier (later TI's Chief Technical Officer), explaining that the Department of Defense could no longer afford the FLIR system. And he also asked for reasons why each unit cost several hundred thousand dollars.

TI answered by underscoring the enormous development costs required to make FLIR an integral and effective part of each gunship mission. The company had invested a lot of time and money in the project, and the costs simply added up.

The Department of Defense promptly rejected the explanation.

TI recognized that FLIR had become a major financial success for the company, and it did not want to lose a system it had invented to a growing number of competitors. Something had to be done and done quickly.

After a thorough analysis conducted by Dennis Lacy and Dr. George Hopper, TI concluded that each FLIR application had its own unique set of requirements. Since 1964, 385 FLIR systems had been produced with 55 different configurations, and the production rates of each configuration were too low to achieve any economies of scale.

TI set about developing a common-module FLIR concept, based on the premise that certain functions of an infared sensor were not sensitive to the mission application and could be made universal from system to system without affecting the mission performance of the sensor. Such a commonality not only made custom design and development unnecessary, it also decreased the time committed from inception to availability, made volume production possible, and greatly reduced the cost. But the challenge was daunting because such a concept had to be endorsed by all three military services for it to be effective.

Even though the common-module FLIR demanded significant changes to TI's designs, the company adopted the concept as the central theme of its infared strategy. TI's John Chandler assumed the responsibility for making the methodology work. Resistance within the engineering department was sometimes suffocating because of the success of the unique gunship designs and management was worried that a common-module approach to FLIR would commoditize the business and possibly even minimize its value to the company.

From the initial definition of the common-module concept in April 1972 through December 1972, TIers were

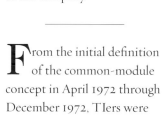

This forward-looking infrared image of a TI parking lot was taken one night in the late 1970s.

GO RENT SOME ELEPHANTS

★ ★ ★

During the peak of the gunship FLIR development program in 1968, the complexity of the system had grown to such an extent that the customer was concerned that both the sensitivity and the resolution of the system would be adversely affected.

TI scheduled a night demonstration for its key customers on the North Building roof, located on the Central Expressway site. The project manager was nervous about the customers' opinion of the image quality he would be able to achieve. He needed something big to make the point.

He had read in the newspaper that a circus was in town, so he dispatched a project engineer to rent elephants for the demo.

By the time the customers arrived, the elephants were stationed in the parking lot and could clearly be seen with the FLIR, which, on that night, was indeed the "greatest show on earth" for TI.

constantly on the road trying to convince the government of the economic viability of the common-module concept. Competitors and some customers thought it was just another marketing ploy, but TI pressed on and in November 1972 began to build prototype common modules.

In early 1973, all three military service chiefs declared support for the common-module concept (it wouldn't become an official standard until 1976), and TI began to win development programs using common-module designs. But the competitive technologies would not go away easily, and TI was involved in competitive developments for a number of programs, most notably the tow launched, optically tracked, wire guided Dragon sight. The pressure also grew to develop second-sources for the modules even though TI had developed much of the common-module technology on its own (a second-source award would be made in 1980.)

In the early 1980s, manager Pat Weber was an ever-present figure in Washington, D.C., working to broaden support for the common-module concept. Weber would later become president of the company's defense electronics business and an executive vice president.

But TI's determination to stick to a strategy based more on economics than technical wizardry paid great dividends. The company regained the businesses it had originally lost. It won production of the sight, the M-60A3 Tank Thermal Sight, the Bradley Fighting Vehicle sight, the M-1A2 gunner and driver sights, and many others. The F-117 stealth fighter fire-control system was built around a TI common-module FLIR. All of these systems were used in Desert Storm and the subsequent Gulf War. The Federal Republic of Germany, Taiwan, South Korea, and Denmark also adopted TI common-module FLIR systems for use on their armored vehicles.

The company's business strategy, rather than military requirements, drove TI's unique common-module concept. Historically, because of the high cost, TI had only received orders for tens of FLIR systems each year. After introducing the common-module FLIR, however, TI was able to market thousands of systems a year. As the price sharply decreased, the orders dramatically increased, and by 1998, TI had produced more than 30,000 FLIR systems.

Many are convinced that the company's commitment to infared technology, even when the odds were less than favorable, ultimately furnished the U.S. Armed Forces with a distinct military advantage. FLIR allowed them to see through the darkness and own the night.

12

IN HARM'S WAY

*TI combined its system skills,
including signal processing,
to become a force in
tactical guided missiles.*

*TI began to look at the potential of the missile
business during the 1950s in response to Pat
Haggerty's mandate to use the company's transistor
technology in its equipment designs. The company
had worked hard to build a solid foundation with the
Defense Department, and when they found they could
help develop anti-radar missiles that rendered enemy
radar useless, the relationship was solidified. TI's
serious venture into the missile business made sense.
It was a decision that would change tactical warfare
in the twentieth century.*

In 1954, the company had supplied a guidance system for Bell
Aircraft Corporation's Rascal surface-to-air missile, using
recycled APS 31 vacuum tube components. But Jim Wisseman,
chief engineer for the defense business, was already envisioning
a time when TI could exploit transistorized electronics to
become a major player in the future of America's missile
strategy. He hired Gene Helms as the company's first missile
systems engineer from Hughes Aircraft and Tom Weaver from
the U.S. Army Missile Command.

In 1955, TI won a proof-of-concept contract from the
Applied Physics Lab at Johns Hopkins University to build a
30-MHz silicon transistor amplifier for the Talos surface-
to-air missile. A year later, TI received new contracts to
develop stripline mixers for the Sparrow Missile, transistorized
telemetry systems that could be used in the Boeing Bomarc

**TI developed the seeker for the Shrike
anti-radar missile in 1961. Shrike was the
company's first significant missile contract and
was a forerunner of the HARM.**

In an early test, HARM homes in on a ship's target.

Missile, and a transistorized inertial reference unit for Temco's Regulus missile. TI's involvement with the Navy's Corvus program launched its thrust in anti-radar missile technology. It also introduced the company to Grant Dove, who would later join TI and become one of its top officers.

The Corvus program was ultimately canceled, but TI's interest in anti-radar technology had been aroused. TI then funded a core technical team to study and develop anti-radar missile technology, and from 1958 to 1960, Helms and Weaver devoted their full attention to studying the emerging requirements for anti-radar missiles with various defense agencies and laboratories. Their team wrote a series of white papers on missile design issues and began distributing them throughout the government customer community.

The Navy Bureau of Weapons decided to build the Shrike anti-radar missile using the Naval Ordnance Test Station at China Lake as technical directorate. TI won the guidance and control system contract over a number of traditional and established defense suppliers. When the $1.7 million contract was awarded in 1961, the project was too large for TI's Lemmon Avenue plant in Dallas, and the company rented space at the old Manor Bakery on Maple Avenue. The project manager predicted that the Shrike program would last five years. Instead, it brought TI consistent revenues for the next 19 years. More than 20,000 missiles were built in the decade

between 1965 and 1975, and Shrike was the country's principal counter-radar weapon throughout the Vietnam War.

During the late 1960s, enemy missile radar systems were becoming more sophisticated and posed a lethal threat to American aircraft. More advanced technology was required to counter the threat, so the Navy began making plans to develop a new, high-speed antiradiation missile (HARM).

Several years earlier, Glenn Penisten had established an engineering facility near the Naval Weapons Center (China Lake) at Ridgecrest, California. Long before any information about the missile was announced, TI-Ridgecrest was working with the Navy to define requirements for the HARM targeting system, the on-board electronics that would sort enemy missile radar signals and provide initial targeting coordinates to HARM before its launch. The knowledge Penisten's group gathered provided TI with valuable information about the Navy's ideas and technology, as well as those enemy signals and tactics pilots face during air warfare. The TI-Ridgecrest staff spent an enormous amount of time on analyses and design of critical missile functions, and in 1972, built and flight-tested a full guidance unit. The weapons center was impressed.

A TI-built anechoic chamber was used in testing the HARM missile. HARM is a key element in the defense-suppression mission for the U.S. and its allies.

An F-18 aircraft armed with a HARM. (Photo courtesy of Department of Defense.)

When the Navy solicited proposals to build HARM in 1973, TI was ready to compete with such defense industry giants as General Dynamics, Lockheed Martin, and Hughes Aircraft. Now, TI had its chance to be a prime contractor responsible for all aspects involved with designing, developing, and manufacturing the missile. The program had an annual budget of several hundred million dollars and was a line item in the national defense budget.

As Russ Boughnou pointed out, "The other companies were bidding on a missile specification. We had put together a small team dedicated to solving a customer's problem, and the Navy realized we had the technology and the expertise to make it happen. TI was willing to take some risks and try things that hadn't been tried before. If it took putting together a demo model, we were ready to do it."

TI built a mockup of the missile, and Boughnou and Dean Clubb, a project engineer who later would become president of the

defense business, brought it into a Washington, D.C., hotel room. They invited the Navy to view TI's vision for HARM.

As Clubb remembered, "We showed them what we had in mind, and the Navy told us what it had in mind for the missile. It gave us an opportunity to broaden our thinking on the project and improve our offering to the Navy. Our competitors may have known so much more than we did. But they didn't listen as well as we did."

Late in the afternoon of May 24, 1974, a phone call from Washington, D.C., made four years of hard work worthwhile for TI. The company had been named the prime contractor for HARM, making TI a force to be reckoned with in the competitive wars of defense contracting.

For TI, however, the battle had just begun.

The company faced an onslaught from competitors with political clout who fought long and hard to make sure TI's program failed. Other companies wanted the government to choose a second source to share in the revenue. China Lake was angry because it had wanted to be in charge of the operation, and, Clubb recalled, "China Lake had its own ideas about design configuration and was finding fault with everything we did." China Lake was as worthy and as technologically proficient as any competitor TI had on HARM.

Defense contractors and their lobbyists kept parading up to

Capitol Hill, trying to persuade congressmen to remove the prime contract from TI and pass the wealth around. TI's every move was being scrutinized by Congress and the Department of Defense, and virtually every day, the contract was under threat of being canceled.

But TI's William B. "Bill" Mitchell, HARM program manager and later Vice Chairman of TI, faced the critics, week after week, delivering the company's unwavering commitment to performance and excellence. Just when it appeared the battle might be lost, an unflappable Bill Mitchell would win another round and keep the contract alive another day. He and TI would be under the gun for the next two years, facing, as Hank Hayes, HARM deputy program manager, said, "a constant barrage of live or die situations that covered everything from engineering to production." Mitchell, with strong support from the company's Washington office, effectively worked the political system, the press, the users, testers, developers, and

purchasers in two military services (Navy and Air Force) to keep the project sole source for TI.

Immediately, the technical specs began to change dramatically, and they kept changing month after month, always driving the costs up despite the fact that TI had been forced to submit a fixed-price bid. Fred Bucy, TI president at the time, knew the company was at financial risk, but he didn't budge. TI stood behind its original bid. Bucy even invested $150 million for a factory in Lewisville, just north of Dallas.

The performance requirements for HARM, however, were daunting. The missile seeker had to cover a broad range of frequencies, and whenever a target profile changed, the design had to change. HARM was designed to suppress enemy air defense radar, which direct surface-to-air missiles and anti-aircraft gunfire at tactical aircraft. It was supersonic, which demanded innovative requirements on control, airframe structure, radome, and software processing that had never been tried before. And it had to be compatible with a variety of Navy and Air Force fighter planes. Never in its history had TI's defense unit been confronted with such a formidable task.

The first HARM flight test and the first guided missile firing were successfully conducted in 1979 on board an A-7E aircraft. Eighty production missiles were delivered two years later, and, in April 1986, they were used in action during the raids on the terrorist camps of Libya. By 1988, the four thousandth HARM had been delivered, and production rates were topping 200 a month.

During Operation Desert Storm, more than 2,000 HARMs shut down 95 percent of the enemy's radar defense, opening air space and allowing the F-117 stealth and other allied attack aircraft to safely penetrate enemy territory.

More than 20,000 HARMs have been built. HARM remains the principal weapon for suppression of enemy air defenses by U.S. and allied military forces. Equally important, the experience as prime contractor led to other missile prime contractor wins for TI on programs such as Javelin and the Joint Standoff Weapon system.

TI had succeeded in leveraging its initial advantage in transistorized electronics, building along the way an array of missile systems skills to become one of the world's major producers of tactical guided missiles.

13

PAVING THE WAY IN AIR WARFARE

TI harnesses the laser for improved precision weapon guidance.

TI's success in the missile guidance business kept the company on the cutting edge of defense work as the military sought more precise and effective ways to target bombing missions. Through teamwork and a focus on systems solutions, TI designed a weapons system that gave the military the ability to precisely guide missiles thereby improving aim and dramatically reducing civilian casualties.

In 1964, at the urging of Tom Weaver, a missile engineer, TI submitted a proposal and received $100,000 from the U.S. Army Missile Command to study the feasibility of adapting an earlier guidance system for a laser-guided artillery shell. TI was convinced laser guidance was viable, but the Army program bogged down, and the company's engineers, directed by Weldon Word, began searching for someone in defense who might be interested in developing new technology. TI had the knowledge and expertise, but the company needed a new project, or, Word feared, the Missile Guidance and Tracking team might be dissolved.

During the 1960s, the Air Force owned the skies above Vietnam, but, more often than not, its superior air power was going to waste. Bombs were raining over Southeast Asian

jungles, but critical targets were still intact when calm returned to the battlefield. In 1964, Colonel Joe Davis from the Air Force Armament Test Center met with Word and showed him tactical photos of a bridge surrounded by more than 800 pockmarks in the ground—ragged holes left by exploding bombs. The bridge, critical to the flow of Viet Cong supplies heading north, was unscathed. Colonel Davis said, "We have a bombing problem, and there may be some money available if you think you can fix it."

Word immediately thought the military might be willing to spend at least $70,000 on a laser-guided missile study, a project that would allow him to keep his team together. His solution for reducing the Air Force's large margin of error was using a new technology to guide a bomb to a target with a laser beam. His goal was "one bomb for one target."

Glenn Penisten, head of TI's missile and ordnance business, scheduled a Friday afternoon appointment with the customer to discuss the potential of laser-guided bombs. After 15 minutes, the customer stood up, closed his windows, and walked out the door without another word. He went home and left Penisten staring at an empty room. His official duty for the day had ended.

Penisten angrily called Colonel Joe Davis. He didn't appreciate being treated that way, especially not when TI was working on the colonel's own bombing concerns.

Davis told him, "If you have me a proposal by Monday morning, and you can build a dozen laser-guided bombs in less than six months, and the cost to the Air Force is less than $100,000, then I'll find the money."

Penisten was aggressive in marketing, and, as Word remembered, "Glenn never backed away from any challenge. For him, it was always full speed ahead. He never saw an opportunity he didn't believe he could make real. He knew how to keep customers happy and the train on the track. He figured it was up to the engineers to put the train on the track."

Before 7 a.m. on Monday, Word placed an 18-page, handwritten proposal for $99,000 on the colonel's desk.

Word recalled, "Unfortunately, a marketer and an electrical engineer doing aerodynamics work over the weekend delivered

A naval technician works on a Paveway laser-guided bomb, the principal weapon used by F-117 stealth fighters.

BUSTING BUNKERS

★ ★ ★

On February 1, 1991, Air Force officials revealed they had a problem during Operation Desert Storm. They needed a laser-guided bunker buster bomb capable of destroying an Iraq air defense sector command and control bunker located in an isolated section north of Baghdad.

The bunker lay buried deeper than 12 feet. High-powered bombs may have shaken it but had not been able to destroy it.

On February 14, the Air Force submitted a request for the GBU-28 bunker buster bomb. Time was running out. A team of Army technicians at the Army's arsenal in New York was already working around the clock to reshape eight-inch artillery barrels rescued from the scrap heap.

Cameron Forging Company in Houston reforged hardened steel nose sections to fit the superbomb.

And TI, with a handshake, but not a written contract, worked with the Air Force Development Test Center to adapt existing guidance sections into the GBU-28 configuration. TI technicians were responsible for reprogramming computer chips used in Paveway III laser-guided software to accommodate the larger weapon.

By February 23, TI had completed its reprogramming assignment and flown upgraded nose guidance sections on a corporate Learjet to Nellis Air Force Base. Tests proved that the 4,000 pound bunker buster was powerful enough to penetrate more than 20 feet of reinforced concrete.

Still warm with molten high explosive, two GBU-28s were flown on February 26 to Saudi Arabia. Five hours later, the bombs were dropped, and the Iraq air defense sector command and control bunker ceased to exist.

From start to finish, the TI team, in collaboration with the Air Force team, had developed, tested, and dropped the GBU-28 bunker busters in just 12 days.

a prescription for disaster. We knew what we wanted. We had no idea how to realistically do it."

Jack Sickle, a TIer and retired Navy test pilot, told his associates at TI to keep the design of the laser-guided system simple, user-friendly, and completely disconnected from the aircraft. He explained, "It's important for the Air Force to be able to slap one of the missiles on any plane that has a bomb rack."

Dick Johnson, regarded as one of the country's premier aeronautical engineers, returned from an international soaring competition in Yugoslavia and began retooling the proposal Word and Penisten had developed. While evaluating various ideas on an analog computer, he began defining ways for TI to place a guidance system on a missile with fins. Johnson, along with engineer Ron Hirsch, devised a unique floating head, a so-called "birdie head," to house the seeker. Their approach enabled the bomb to stay fixed on the laser-designated spot without the use of stabilization gyros or input from the launchcraft. The birdie head directed the bomb precisely toward its target.

The seeker was simple. It was low cost. And it gave TI the potential of providing the Air Force with test hardware in a mere 60 days after receiving the $99,000 study contract.

Because of the tight, 60-day deadline, however, Johnson did not have time to conduct full up-wind tunnel modeling, so he improvised, using his own lathe to machine a one-sixteenth-inch scale model of the precision-guided bombs. He then dropped them in a swimming pool to establish critical centers of pressure.

At the same time, Bob Wagner, a missile engineer, was working on a laser guidance system that, he figured, would require a material capable of generating a pulse legnth of ten nanoseconds at the most. In the lab, germanium proved to be acceptable at room temperatures, but it was of no value when placed aboard an aircraft cruising twenty-five thousand feet above the ground at a temperature of minus forty degrees.

A transistor device of ultra-pure silacon was the answer. Again, TI's leadership in silicon materials and semiconductors would make the difference, but not without a battle against military tradition.

As Word remembered, "The Air Force was still operating with a WWII mentality. The effectiveness of a bombing run was measured in how many tons of bombs were dropped."

The F-117 stealth fighters, armed with Paveway III laser-guided bombs, led raids in Operation Desert Storm. (Photo courtesy of Department of Defense.)

Colonel Davis, however, fully understood that technological changes needed to be made in the way air warfare was conducted, and he managed to provide TI with some 750-pound bomb bodies, arranging for the company to test its guidance system on the Eglin range. The Air Force laughed when it first saw TI's birdie head. They thought it looked like a toy. The tests, however, were as successful as TI engineers believed they would be, and they pressed management to pursue the laser guidance business.

Unfortunately, for TI, the Air Force was already committed to the 3,000-pound TV-guided bomb being developed by a competitor, North American Aviation. TI's idea was good, and it might even work. But the Air Force was moving forward with a bomb that could be directed remotely to the target by human eyes and hands.

_____

Because of this commitment to alternate technology, management wanted to kill TI's laser-guided program. While TI did offer the best technical solution for a laser-guided projectile, the company did not have the resources to support a project the customer did not support, especially when TI was already stretched so thin.

Penisten was in no mood to walk away, not without a fight anyway. He persuaded management to give him $50,000 to continue a low-level study of the laser-guided project.

In 1966, again with an assist from Colonel Davis, TI successfully tested its innovative guidance system on a 3,000-pound bomb. TI's system made it feasible for an aircraft to fly

over a target zone at 20,000 feet, roll in at a steep, 45 degree angle dive, and release its laser-guided bombs at 12,000 feet. Throughout the mission, the aircraft remained safely above enemy ground fire and once released, the laser-guided bomb headed for the target, making its own guidance corrections without any help from the pilot. Additionally, the Air Force could purchase TI's laser-guided bombs for only $2,000 to $3,000 each. The Air Force's solemn commitment to the $100,000 TV-guided bomb began to waver, then unravel altogether.

By 1969, the first guidance kits, designated as Paveway 1, were delivered to the Air Force and fitted to the MK-117 bombs. A year later, the Air Force significantly increased production rates for laser-guided bombs, and the Navy began purchasing the weapons as well. In 1977, TI created Paveway II for the Air Force by adding laser countermeasures to the bombs, and from 1967 to 1977, TI delivered 110,000 of the weapons, which generated hundreds of millions of dollars.

_____

Allied countries began ordering Paveway bombs, and the weapon became a factor in Great Britain's 1982 war in the Falkland Islands. A year later, the Air Force contracted with TI to develop Paveway III, laser-guided bombs that could be launched from attack aircraft flying as low as 200 feet above the ground. Paveway III, regarded as the most sophisticated bomb the world had ever known, was used in combat for the first time during the 1986 raid into Libya.

In the 1991 Gulf War, F-117 stealth fighters led the raids of Operation Desert Storm, dropping Paveway III laser-guided bombs. The U.S. military reported a 90 percent accuracy rate for the weapons used during Desert Storm, which destroyed a full spectrum of targets, including aircraft shelters, bridges, buildings, command bunkers, SCUD missile launchers, tanks, and underground bunkers.

TI's laser guidance systems ushered in a new era for air warfare. By 2004, more than 250,000 Paveway systems had been delivered by TI (and after 1997, Raytheon); their precision was regularly seen around the world on televised news programs reporting from the war zones of Afghanistan and Iraq.

TI, for four decades, had given pilots the technological advantage they needed. Wars could now be fought and won because of it. Former Air Force historian Dr. Richard Hallion has said of precision-guided weapons, "It was as revolutionary a development in military air power as, say, the jet engine."

14

NATIONAL RECOGNITION FOR QUALITY

TI becomes the nation's first defense contractor to win the prestigious Malcolm Baldrige National Quality Award.

Since its earliest days, the company has been conscientious about preserving its international reputation for designing and engineering quality products and services. During the late 1980s, TI integrated a policy of total quality management throughout the company, giving its defense business, the impetus to pursue the nationally acclaimed Malcolm Baldrige Award. This decision would have a long-lasting impact not only on TI's defense business, but on the company as a whole—propelling it to focus on total quality leadership.

In 1990, TI's defense business progressed to the second stage of the Baldrige review process, and, a year later TI's improvement initiatives were rewarded with a site visit by the selection committee. But TI didn't win the award in 1991. For defense business president Hank Hayes, there was no doubt about "staying the Baldrige course," which, he believed, provided a sound framework for managing the company.

"The criteria are demanding," he said. "They stretch us, and sometimes it's painful, but the gains are worth it. Our competition gets tougher each year. If we drop out of the race, for whatever reason, we risk losing touch with increasingly stringent criteria. We risk losing the momentum that all of us have worked so hard to build over the last several years." In typical TI fashion, there was no turning back.

In 1992, after receiving feedback from its 1990 and 1991 applications, TI's defense business began concentrating on five areas of improvement: customer satisfaction, stretch goals such as six sigma (no more than 3.4 defects out of every million opportunities for that defect to happen), leadership benchmarking against all manufacturing industries, employee and teams empowerment, and an integrated quality strategy.

As Hayes pointed out, "It was important for every TIer to understand the company's quality strategy and the critical role that he or she must play."

It was easy for TI to measure the improvements engineered by total quality management:

- Revenues per TIer were up 50 percent during the past four years, from $80,000 in 1987 to $125,000 in 1991.
- Product development time had been reduced 25 percent during each year.
- In 1983, only four TI quality teams were in operation. By 1992, the defense business had implemented more than 1,900 teams.
- Aggressive environmental protection goals were set to reach international standards much earlier than imposed deadlines.
- Eighty percent of the processes in the printed wiring board factory had reached world-class six sigma levels.

TI, a designer and manufacturer of precision-guided weapons, as well as other advanced defense technology, believed that dedication to quality made the company a stronger competitor in the battle for market share in a shrinking defense industry.

The reliability of TI's systems was exceeding specifications of Department of Defense customers by as much as five times.

President George H.W. Bush presents the Malcolm Baldrige National Quality Award to TI CEO Jerry Junkins as Commerce Secretary Barbara H. Franklin looks on.

TI's defense business was the 1992 winner of the Malcolm Baldrige National Quality Award.

Effective strategic planning, wide use of concurrent engineering methods, and strong relationships with key suppliers had helped TI penetrate new defense markets, while increasing its share in five of the company's six existing markets.

TI's performance had been well documented by customers. For example, a Navy evaluation of 17 missiles found TI's HARM and Shrike were the Navy's most reliable missiles. A Navy study evaluating the manufacturing operations of 35 defense contractors pointed out that 106 processes and techniques used by TI's defense business had been designated as having the "best manufacturing practices"—more than any other company. And an independently conducted survey of 2,000 company customers revealed that DSEG topped its primary competitors in all 11 customer satisfaction categories—including cost-effective pricing, deployment of technology, and product support.

In 1992, the concern for quality paid off. TI's defense business became the first business devoted solely to national defense to win the Malcolm Baldrige National Quality Award.

As Hayes said, "I can't tell you how proud I was to receive the call from the Secretary of Commerce. It could only mean one thing—we had won the Baldrige award. When I say, 'we,' I really mean we. This was a team effort all the way."

THE LEGACY OF DEFENSE

★ ★ ★

TI's years of meritorious work for the Defense Department, beginning with its pursuit of enemy submarines during World War II, were perhaps best exemplified during Operation Desert Storm in the early 1990s.

TI Chairman, President, and CEO Jerry Junkins said, "TI's Paveway precision-guided weapons, HARM defense suppression missiles, forward-looking infrared systems, airborne radars, and other TI systems made major contributions to the success of that operation. We've heard it from field commanders, from the front-line troops, and from the highest levels of our government—and the TIers who designed and built those systems deserve our thanks for a job well done."

Pilots appreciated HARM because of its performance and reliability. In a letter to TI, Lt. J.D. Klas of Attack Squadron 46 said, "The air superiority we enjoy is a direct result of the success we've had employing HARM against Iraqi radars. All 18 pilots have shot HARM. I know I speak for all of us when I say I would be extremely proud to have a HARM patch for my flight jacket."

But the legacy of TI's defense operation goes beyond what it meant to the U.S. military and its allies. Defense operations helped give TI a focus on systems solutions that remains today, and many of the defense initiatives in project management, quality, and teamwork made a lasting impact on the company.

In the 1990s, the company faced a shrinking defense budget and the realization that it would either have to acquire other defense companies and become much larger, or divest its defense business. On January 6, 1997, TI announced the decision to sell its defense operations to Raytheon for $2.95 billion, ending one chapter, but starting a new one as the people of TI's defense business joined one of the nation's largest defense contractors.

CREATING A NEW INDUSTRY

Texas Instruments was no longer just a little company with big ideas. The company had a new name, it was armed with the revolutionary new technology of semiconductors, and it was determined to build a worldwide business. With the production of the world's first commercial silicon transistor, TI ruled the semiconductor world, and when Jack Kilby invented the integrated circuit, he helped trigger the world's second industrial revolution. Reaching a leadership position in the market, however, involved more than designing new circuits. TI had to learn to grow its own silicon crystals, develop its own manufacturing and test equipment, and establish a worldwide marketing force. TI produced the first pocket transistor radio to demonstrate the potential of transistors and later underscored the value of integrated circuits by building the first digital integrated circuit system. With hard work and strong capital investment, TI became one of the electronic giants of the world.

Famous close-up photo of a red-hot crucible of molten germanium and a partially grown crystal—used on the cover of TI's *1953 Annual Report*.

15

NAME THAT COMPANY

Wanted: A new name to reflect the changing culture and direction of GSI.

Erik Jonsson explained it best: "By 1951," he said, "history repeated itself. Manufacturing and exploration activities had increased so much that it was necessary to set them up in separate corporate structures." Jonsson and Pat Haggerty thought GSI needed a new name, one that would project the image of an aggressive company in the national and international marketplace. They were determined to change its focus, its culture, and its direction.

Geophysical Service Inc. was chartered to build its foundation on the success of the reflection seismograph. Even though oil exploration remained an integral part of the company, Jonsson and Haggerty were ready to bet the future of GSI on the growing strength of its manufacturing division. They wanted to increase the company's research and development efforts while GSI sought to enter a widening range of industrial business opportunities.

Jonsson had been elected president of GSI on June 25, 1950, a day when the local and national news centered on the outbreak of hostilities in Korea. Under his leadership, the company had seen the potential of defense contracts during World War II. The Korean War was destined to create even

larger military markets. Within the next two years, the U.S. military's demand for GSI's airborne radar system and other defense equipment would increase the manufacturing division's production output and be responsible for 80 percent of all the division's electronic sales.

As defense orders kept rolling in, GSI searched for a new manufacturing business. It became evident to Jonsson that it would be difficult for GSI to transform itself into a diversified technology-based electronics company when its name at home and around the world was so closely aligned with geophysics. The company's original charter had become obsolete.

Throughout the company, people were talking about a new name for the manufacturing division, but an increase in business delayed them from taking action. Weeks passed, then months. Priorities kept changing, the workload kept growing, and after a while, the search for a new name had been shelved.

During late 1950, a frustrated Haggerty decided he couldn't wait any longer. He called a group of managers together, closed the door, and said, "No one leaves this room until we have a new name."

When the door reopened, Haggerty emerged with the name General Instruments Inc. The new name was formally announced on January 1, 1951.

There was only one problem.

A defense contractor based on the East Coast was already using the name of General Instruments and had been for many years. People within the Department of Defense, especially the Navy, began complaining about the confusion.

Early morning strategy meeting with Pat Haggerty. Seated left to right, around Pat's gray Steelcase™ desk, are C.J. (Tommy) Thomsen, Mark Shepherd, Jr., S.T. (Buddy) Harris, and Haggerty.

They kept receiving bids from two different companies using the same name. Orders were getting mixed up. Something had to be done.

In October 1951, Jonsson appointed a committee, with Haggerty as chairman, to choose another name. His instructions were brief and explicit: "Just be sure to have Texas in the name."

The meeting didn't last long. The new name, Haggerty told Jonsson, would be Texas Instruments Incorporated, or TI for short.

It was a fortuitous selection. The name gave instant recognition to the company, particularly in international markets, where anything Texas had flair and mystique. The new name helped open doors, and customers had no trouble remembering Texas Instruments. Soon, those customers simply referred to the company as "the guys from Texas," or just "Texas." In time, the name Texas Instruments would become synonymous with a distinctive culture that had carved a special niche for itself around the world.

On January 1, 1952, it became official. Texas Instruments became the parent company in the corporate structure, with Eugene McDermott named as its first chairman and Jonsson serving as its first president. GSI was organized as a wholly owned subsidiary of TI, with Cecil Green as GSI president. Under Green's leadership, new crews were hired, trained, and sent to Latin America, as well as to Spain and Saudi Arabia. New and more accurate field equipment was designed and put in operation. Methods of data analysis grew more sophisticated, which led to interpretation improvements of seismic data for clients.

In less than six years, Haggerty and his team had reshaped TI, creating a manufacturing culture that would take deep roots within an expanding marketplace. TI had new policies, a new direction, and Jonsson was preparing TI to become a publicly owned company. At the same time, Haggerty was interested in developing a transistor program, which, he believed, could become pivotal for TI's manufacturing business.

He launched a campaign to convince the owners of the company that they could be successful in the transistor business, pointing out, "If we are to be a giant and compete with the giants, where are we better fitted to take on a giant than in a field where the giant is also just starting?" Jonsson

was enthusiastic. Cecil Green, who worried that defense orders would decline if there were a lasting peace with the Soviet Union, supported the transistor effort. Dr. Henry Bates Peacock wasn't convinced it was a good idea. He believed the company should focus its efforts on the geophysical market.

It would be a tough road in the national marketplace for a small Texas company, but Haggerty had confidence in the talent of his engineers, most of whom had been recruited to support military contracts. Transistors would become their new challenge, and change forever the way the world perceived the name of Texas Instruments.

DESIGNING THE TI LOGO
★ ★ ★

When the name Texas Instruments was finalized, Erik Jonsson began thinking about an official company logo. He engaged Torger (Torg) Thompson, an artist with the advertising agency that had handled GSI's business, to design the TI logo.

"How much will you charge?" Jonsson asked.

"Five hundred dollars," Thompson replied. Both men agreed. It was a fair price.

After several revisions, the artist presented Jonsson an acceptable logo design, essentially the same that TI has used ever since, although the lines of a ragged Texas coastline would be smoothed out in later revisions of the design. It would affectionately be called "the TI bug" by employees.

Jonsson, always frugal with the company's cash, offered Thompson 500 shares of the new company's unlisted stock instead of the $500.

"It may be worth a lot more someday," Jonsson said. Thompson replied, "I'll take the cash."

16

TAKING ON THE GIANTS

TI boldly enters the semiconductor market.

The announcement of the invention of the transistor by researchers at Bell Labs in 1948 received little notice in the world press at the time. But for a small company in Dallas, it would become the ticket to its future. The transistor would turn out to be one of the most significant inventions of the twentieth century. Scientists and engineers at TI would create their own innovations in semiconductors that ultimately would help build a $200 billion industry—changing the way the world lives, learns, works, and plays.

Pat Haggerty, by 1951, had a strong conviction that his company's future growth would be tied to the transistor. But the key to that future lay in the offices of Western Electric, which held the patents for the transistor. Haggerty and his team began to formalize a strategy that called for the creation of a new operating division and a research lab devoted to attaining a better understanding of solid-state physics, while placing bold emphasis on development of semiconductor materials and devices.

Haggerty and Erik Jonsson had been fascinated by the business potential of transistors since the Bell Labs' announcement on June 30, 1948. Bob Olson, TI's chief engineer, received a copy of the press release outlining the intriguing new discovery. It stated: *"An amazingly simple device, capable of performing efficiently nearly all the functions of an ordinary vacuum tube, was demonstrated for the first time yesterday at Bell Telephone Laboratories, where it was invented.*

"Known as the transistor, the device works on an entirely new physical principle discovered by the Laboratories in the course of fundamental research into the electrical properties of solids. Although the device is still in the laboratory stage, Bell scientists and engineers expect it may have far-reaching significance in electronics and electrical communication ...

"Its essential simplicity, however, indicates the possibility of widespread use, with resultant mass-production economies. When fully developed, the transistor is also expected to find new applications in electronics where vacuum tubes have not proved suitable."

The transistor, Haggerty and Jonsson decided, could well signal the company's entry into a new, perhaps even revolutionary, manufacturing business. The problem confronting them, however, seemed to be insurmountable. Western Electric had a firm grasp on the patents and was not aware that TI even existed.

Bell Labs had the scientific expertise of Dr. Walter Brattain, Dr. John Bardeen, and Dr. William Shockley at the company's disposal. Their invention of the transistor

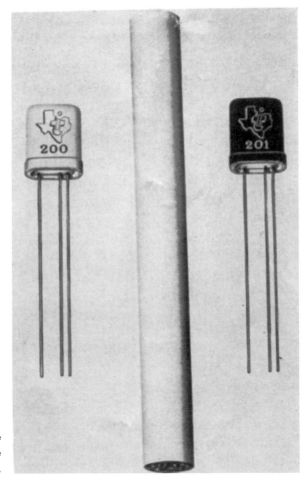

Early examples of TI germanium transistors shown beside a cigarette for size comparison. The transistors were encased in hermetically-sealed metal cans.

Germanium crystal puller—designed and built by TI in 1952. The first puller was nicknamed "Old Betsy" and was eventually sent to TI's plant in Bedford, England.

would later earn them the Nobel Prize. TI was simply a geophysical exploration company in the process of building its defense manufacturing capability. The talent and brainpower working within TI was, as yet, unrecognized by the scientific community. Haggerty and Jonsson, however, were determined to enter the semiconductor business. Together with Olson, they launched a barrage of phone calls, letters, pleadings, and trips to negotiate with attorneys, who considered TI a marginal company at best. After one stormy session, an attorney for Western Electric turned to Jonsson and said, "This business is not for you."

Olson remembered, "I got the impression they were amazed and amused that our little company would have the effrontery to even think we could make transistors."

As Western Electric would learn, if anyone told Jonsson and Haggerty they were incapable of doing something, then, rest assured, it would somehow get done. They weren't afraid of risks or giants.

In the fall of 1951, Western Electric finally relented. It began offering licenses to any company willing to pay an advance of $25,000 on royalties. TI had its check in the mail the next day, after a hasty phone call by Jonsson to Fred Florence, president of Republic National Bank, to obtain a loan to cover the check.

Around the TI offices, a feeling of elation was gradually

replaced by frustration and anxiety as people eagerly waited for the technical details that would allow them to move forward with their strategy of transistor manufacturing.

During the spring of 1952, Bell Labs held an eight-day symposium in Murray Hill, New Jersey, to teach transistor technology to the 39 companies that had paid fees for a license. When Haggerty, Olson, Mark Shepherd Jr., and Boyd Cornelison walked into the Murray Hill auditorium as representatives of TI, they glanced around the room and saw engineers and scientists from GE, RCA, Westinghouse, Sylvania, IBM, NCR, Raytheon, Minneapolis Honeywell, Motorola, and Sprague Electric—the well-known, well-respected giants of the electronics industry. Most of the companies had one thing in common. They either manufactured vacuum tubes or used them in huge quantities in electronic products such as radios, stereos, and television sets.

Sitting virtually unnoticed in the auditorium was an engineer named Jack Kilby, a representative of the Centralab Division of Globe-Union in Milwaukee. He, like so many others at the symposium, was mentally working on applications for the new technology, wondering if transistors could be built in volume and at costs low enough to be profitable. Years later, he would find the answers to those questions after moving to Dallas

to work for TI. Kilby would invent the integrated circuit, a technology that would change the world.

The TI representatives took detailed notes and asked a lot of questions, especially when visiting the transistor manufacturing plant in Allentown, PA. TI may have been one of the smallest companies attending the symposium, but no one had bigger ideas. The giants within the industry had the manpower and the financial strength, but TI had some distinct advantages of its own. The company possessed an entrepreneurial spirit, and, because of its size, knew how to work fast and efficiently. It had a history of being innovative and, unlike others in the electrical industry, was not burdened by having a vacuum tube business to protect.

Back in Dallas, Shepherd was named project manager and immediately established a small group of 15 engineers whose sole purpose was to fabricate transistors. He was told by management, "We want to make semiconductors. It's your problem."

As Haggerty later admitted, TI, at the time, did not have a semiconductor research lab, and not one single hour of effort had been invested in research and development of semiconductor devices. Nevertheless, Haggerty began building an organization that, within 18 months, would become the semiconductor-components business of TI. Within two years, he would be forced to move the business to a vacant bowling alley two doors down from the Lemmon Avenue plant, just to accommodate the operation's growth.

As an assistant vice president at the age of 30, Shepherd found himself faced with the unending challenge of prevailing upon TI's physicists, chemists, and electrical and mechanical engineers to all apply their various disciplines in concert.

First, TI had to build a crystal puller to produce the vital material needed to make transistors since there were no commercial pullers available. The assignment was handed to Cornelison, whose rough pencil sketch was promptly converted into workable machine shop drawings. In the shop, Tommy Chaddick carefully machined the large screw that would slowly turn to pull the seed upward from the melt. Production began on a crystal puller that could accurately control temperatures near 1,000 degrees Celsius. The completed control unit, engineers would say, resembled a regular totem pole of electronic and mechanical devices, all stacked on top of each other.

Cornelison's crystal puller, dubbed "Old Betsy" for good luck, and two small seed crystals shipped from Bell Labs became the critical tools utilized by Shepherd's team as they arduously began the task of growing a successful germanium crystal. In late June 1952, researchers were well into their second seed, aware that their narrow window of opportunity was rapidly closing, when they managed to create their first good crystal. After a series of tests, the small crystal was sliced into wafers, placed on ceramic blocks, and cut into tiny squares. By August, commercial production of TI's first point-contact transistors was underway. The company soon learned how to produce 500 units from one small crystal.

On December 30, 1952, TI received its first semiconductor order from the Gruen Watch Company. John Dutton made the first sale—10 transistors at $10 each for a total value of $100.

TI had made the most of those few critical months after the Bell Labs symposium. Even though only one sale was made during 1952, management could envision a huge potential market simply because transistors let the industry escape the size and power requirements of vacuum tubes. It was not surprising that Shepherd projected a $250,000 budget for 1953, earmarking $75,000 for additional equipment. It would be quite an investment for a product that had brought in only $100 in revenue for the company. But TI was in a race to determine who had the talent and tenacity to gain an early lead in the transistor market. Every day and every dollar counted.

TI may have been regarded as a small company at the time, but it boldly entered a marketplace dominated by the giants of the electronics industry and walked away a winner. In June 1957, *Fortune* magazine, in a major story on the emerging semiconductor market, commented, *"Texas Instruments, a little-known company, is placed first by a comfortable margin."* In a few short years, TI had made significant innovations in semiconductor technology and emerged as the world leader of an exciting new market.

Helen Bryant peers through a binocular microscope inside a "dry box" in 1953. The job required dexterity and patience to assemble transistors, which at the time had to be done manually under microscopes.

The crowd at the New York Stock Exchange, including Erik Jonsson, looks on and cheers as the first trade of the morning is executed on October 1, 1953.

17

TXN LISTING

How TI bought a rubber plantation and got its stock listed on the New York Stock Exchange.

In 1953, Texas Instruments took extraordinary steps to become a public company. Capital access was needed for rapid expansion in semiconductors, and this meant the company needed to be listed on the New York Stock Exchange (NYSE), and quickly. Erik Jonsson and the TI Board of Directors looked at many alternatives. None was as attractive as merging with a company with cash, rubber plantations, and a listing on the NYSE. Negotiations took more than a year, but in the end the goal was achieved. Over the years, many shareholders have joined the initial group of TI shareholders, and the market has seen the company successfully transform itself more than once. But through it all, the company has focused on growth, and long-term shareholders have shared in TI's success.

As early as 1951, Jonsson began preparations for TI to become a public company. One of his first actions that spring was to hire a young lawyer, Bryan F. Smith, as TI's first general counsel. Smith, who had been recommended to TI by the Massachusetts Institute of Technology (MIT), was hired after meeting with Jonsson in New York City. A five-page annual report was issued in 1952 as part of the preparations to become a publicly traded company, but TI needed to retire $1 million in debt and increase its working capital.

TI did not qualify for listing on the NYSE, because it had only 28 shareholders in 1952. Even after Dr. Peacock sold his shares to other TIers, the number rose to only 47 shareholders—all insiders.

Intercontinental Rubber Company (IRC) was brought to TI's attention by the New York firm of Hamond & Braxton. IRC was attractive to TI because, if the companies were to merge, IRC had a broad stock ownership and was listed on the NYSE. The company had another benefit—cash ($1.3 million in cash and government securities plus fixed assets conservatively valued at about $300,000). Hamond & Braxton also introduced Jonsson to the Equitable Life Assurance Society of the United States, and a long relationship began, with an initial loan to TI of $2.5 million in May 1953.

Merger negotiations began in 1952 in New York City with Jonsson, Haggerty, and Smith representing TI and a team from IRC on the other side, led by Anton Bestebreurtje, IRC's chairman—reputed to be a tough negotiator. IRC produced rubber from the guayule shrub in Mexico and natural rubber from trees in Sumatra. However, its operations were at a standstill due to price declines in rubber. The IRC Board was looking for a way to invest its assets in a growth opportunity, but not everyone on the Board was convinced TI was the right answer. After more than a year of on-and-off discussions, it finally came down to Bestebreurtje and Jonsson alone in one room in New York to strike the deal.

Under the terms of the merger, TI would be the surviving company and would split its existing shares, bringing its total outstanding to 4 million shares. IRC would exchange its outstanding stock for 595,832 shares of TI stock (or 14.9 percent of the total TI shares).

After all the negotiations, there were last-minute difficulties in getting the NYSE to approve what was called a "backdoor" listing. After more discussions, Jonsson persuaded the NYSE to move ahead on the approval process. On the morning of October 1, 1953, Jonsson stood on the floor of the NYSE, and at the sound of the bell at 10 a.m., he purchased the first shares of TI stock, which were traded under the symbol TXN. He bought 100 shares for 5 ¼, and a cheer went up as trading in TXN was launched—fulfilling the dreams of TI's founders that TI would become a publicly owned company.

With the first trade at 5 ¼, TI's market capitalization (the number of shares outstanding times the share price) was $21 million. As TI grew through the years, the shares have split eight times, so that 100 shares in 1953 would equal 24,000 shares in 2004. At year-end 2004, TI's market capitalization stood at more than $42 billion.

The stock exchange listing made it possible for the company to raise capital. In May 1955, TI issued preferred stock to raise about $4 million, which was used to repay bank loans and for additions to working capital and equipment for plant expansion, primarily in semiconductors.

Three IRC directors, E.G. Ackerman, A.D. Bestebreurtje, and Ewen C. MacVeagh, joined the TI Board, bringing their wisdom, experience, and an introduction to the New York investment firm Morgan Stanley & Co. This was invaluable knowledge in helping TI learn the ways of Wall Street. Jonsson spent much of his time the next year visiting financial firms in New York. He shared TI's vision to assure there would be capital to finance TI's dreams.

On December 13, 1956, Jonsson was invited to speak at the New York Society of Security Analysts. In his remarks, he recapped some of the company's history, including several of its early mergers and acquisitions, and described three areas of focus: geophysics, military electronics, and electronic components. Jonsson told the audience, "Many people seem to think that most of TI's growth has stemmed from mergers and acquisitions. This is not so. Our increased earnings power may be attributed almost entirely to internal development and will probably continue to be so."

Jonsson's words were prophetic. TI has been viewed as a growth company since its inception. The most recent transformation of the company into primarily a semiconductor company has changed the way Wall Street values TI. Investors increasingly perceive the company's core technologies of digital signal processors (DSPs) and analog chips as critical technologies that underlie electronics products that represent some of the best growth opportunities in the coming years,

The original stock certificate issued to John E. Jonsson for 100 shares of Texas Instruments Common Stock in 1953. Jonsson kept the certificate during his lifetime. After his death in 1995, the Jonsson family made the original certificate available to TI.

H.A. Rob, manager of TI's Sumatra rubber plantation, checks a tapped tree while a local worker looks on. The 12,000 acre plantation and processing plant was acquired in 1953 as part of the merger with Intercontinental Rubber Company. The plantation produced almost 1 million pounds of rubber in 1954.

As a publicly held company on the NYSE, TI has delivered more than $2.7 billion in dividends to its shareholders, uninterrupted since it began making dividend payments in 1962. As the company's profitability increased over time with improved cash flow, TI has been able to increase the repurchase of company stock, thereby increasing the value returned to shareholders.

TI is today one of the premier technology companies listed on the NYSE, and on the 50th anniversary (October 2003) of its listing, of the nearly 2,800 listed companies, only 230 (or about 8 percent) preceded TI's listing. Commenting on TI's growth through the years, TI Chairman Tom Engibous said, "That growth, fueled by decades of technological advancements that have changed the world, is a legacy that few companies can match and TI is proud to own."

including new generations of wireless cell phones, portable digital consumer electronics, digital TV, and Digital Light Processing technology (DLP™). TI is also viewed as having higher levels of profitability than in the past, reflecting its more differentiated product mix.

But TI operates in a cyclical industry, and as semiconductor stocks move through upturns and downturns, TI at times also becomes attractive to value-oriented investors who recognize the long-term opportunities being offered by the company. "We try to communicate broadly to both growth and value-oriented investors as we move through cycles. TI stock appeals to value investors, who are also important to TI," stated Ron Slaymaker, current Vice President, Investor Relations. In commenting on the changes in TI's shareholder base, Slaymaker pointed out that "increasingly, for many of our largest shareholders, TI represents a core holding, meaning they will remain invested in TI over time, though the size of their holdings may increase or decrease as TI moves through its business cycles." Since its listing in 1953, TI's stock has become widely held, and at year-end 2004, there were some 700,000 shareholders. About 70 percent of TXN shares are held by institutional investors, with the remainder held by individual investors or employees.

WHAT HAPPENED TO THE RUBBER PLANTATIONS?

★ ★ ★

The rubber plantations which TI acquired in the IRC merger were eventually sold or disposed of because they did not fit the company's electronics vision. The Sumatra plantation was donated to a charity in 1958, but not before its manager rescued an 18-foot python from locals who were about to do it in, named it "Pat," and shipped it to Dallas to the attention of Pat Haggerty. TI promptly donated the snake to the Dallas Zoo around August 1955, where it resided as the star in the zoo's herpetarium for many years. The Dallas Zoo claimed that "Pat" was bigger than Fort Worth's famous snake "Pete," a claim roundly disputed by the Fort Worth Zoo. This led to a series of good-natured press stories about the rivalry and high-tech suggestions on how to measure the length of the snakes.

18

STUNNING THE WORLD

TI produces silicon transistors years ahead of the industry.

As early as 1951, Pat Haggerty had learned that silicon was far superior to germanium for transistors, and set Texas Instruments on the path to prove it. He discounted the difficulties of growing silicon crystals with the junction required for the transistors, but he knew TI had to have one scientist and his knowledge to succeed—Dr. Gordon Teal. The goal was worth the risk—the silicon transistor could move the electronics world to a higher and immensely broader level.

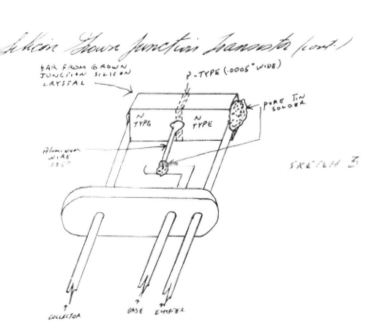

This drawing from the engineering notebook of Mort Jones shows his sketch of the original design for TI's grown junction silicon transistor. The page is dated 5/6/54. Note the arrow pointing to the small bar cut from a grown junction silicon crystal.

Near the end of 1951, Gordon Teal answered a blind ad in *The New York Times* for a semiconductor research and development director. Haggerty had placed the ad in a newspaper near Bell Labs, where most of the innovative semiconductor work was taking place. Teal was a soft-spoken physical chemist considered to be the resident single-crystal and materials expert at Bell Labs in New Jersey. He met with Haggerty and Bob Olson but was not convinced that moving to a small, unknown company in Texas would be the right choice. Teal had been working at Bell Labs for the past two decades, and it would be difficult for him to leave the world-renowned research facilities. Even though Texas was his home state and TI had big ideas, Teal declined the offer.

During the interview Haggerty pressed Teal for his ideas on the future of semiconductors. "Is germanium the best material for transistors?" "No," said Teal, "silicon is better."

Haggerty knew he had the world's best-educated guess on the direction transistor technology was heading. But the key piece of the puzzle for TI was to get Teal to head up the silicon transistor project. Teal had investigated semiconductor materials at Bell Labs, and along with John Little, developed a crystal puller to generate single-crystal germanium from a crucible of molten material. In the spring of 1951, Teal then discovered how to make the theoretical grown-junction transistor a reality by selectively "doping," or adding impurities to the melt as the crystal was growing.

In 1952, Haggerty again contacted Teal, urging him to relocate in Dallas to head up TI's semiconductor research and development. Those who worked with Haggerty could vouch for his powers of persuasion, and near the end of the

When TI announced commercial availability of the silicon transistor in 1954, this photograph of a silicon transistor superimposed on a three-cent U.S. postage stamp was used to show its relative size.

year, Teal could no longer resist the open-ended opportunity to head up his own laboratory at TI.

Haggerty told him to build a team of scientists and engineers that could keep TI at the leading edge of the semiconductor industry. Teal's name was respected throughout the scientific community. Mark Shepherd, heading up the semiconductor business, remembered, "We could never have attracted the stable of people we did without him. And we got some really outstanding scientists..."

Teal's first step was to contact his doctorate alma mater, Brown University, about outstanding graduates. The first name the school gave him was Dr. Willis Adcock, a physical chemist working at Stanolind Oil in Tulsa, Oklahoma. Adcock joined TI in April 1953, followed by Mort Jones, a chemist from Cal Tech. The team was augmented with Jay Thornhill, a physicist, and Ed Jackson, a polymath who had been with GSI/TI since 1948. The small research group immediately began to tackle the problems of first growing silicon crystals, then making silicon transistors.

They faced a daunting challenge. Many scientists predicted it would be years before a production-worthy silicon transistor process could be developed, and others theorized such a transistor could never be built in quantity. But Haggerty's plan was now in place, and TI had the team to meet the challenge head on.

Teal immediately began to work with Boyd Cornelison, designer of TI's now highly successful germanium crystal puller. Cornelison had designed the puller after little more than a long glance at the Teal-Little puller he was shown during his visit at the Bell Labs symposium. Teal gave Cornelison the task of upgrading the red-hot germanium puller into a 1,400-degree Celsius white-hot silicon puller. Adcock was assigned to work with Cornelison on the project, and was given his own unenviable task of growing the silicon crystals. The other team members, Jackson, Jones, and Thornhill, had the job of sawing the transistor bars (or dies) from the silicon crystals, making electrical contacts to the ends of a bar, and somehow melting a microscopic wire into the bar itself at the razor-thin junction.

By the summer of 1953, the team was working literally night and day on the dual tasks of producing the silicon crystals with electrically satisfactory junctions, and developing methods of fabricating silicon transistors. The seemingly never-ending problems were addressed, and overcome or side-stepped, and progress inched forward. The new silicon crystal puller required major changes in its temperature control and timing systems—far beyond industrial norms—to grow the crystals. But Adcock finally began to grow silicon single crystals, each better than the last. And the doping of the melt to form the elusive junction was beginning to respond to science rather than art. He could see a glimmer of light at the end of the long, dark, and exhausting tunnel.

Adcock sent a memo to Teal on March 12, 1954, saying that the grown-junction silicon transistor was getting close.

A month later, it all came together. Using high-purity silicon material purchased from DuPont, Teal and his team grew a silicon crystal with a negative-positive-negative structure (NPN) having an emitter region doped to enhance current gain and a p-type base layer about a thousandth of an inch thick. They cut a quarter-inch bar from the crystal and attached the electrical contacts to it on the morning of April 14.

Teal called Haggerty and asked if he would like to witness the test. A few minutes later, Haggerty recalled, "I was observing transistor action in that first grown-junction transistor." TI knew how to make the silicon transistor.

The team had succeeded, Adcock always said, because none of the members knew how difficult it would be. It was a defining moment for TI. The company had suddenly

The silicon transistor development team from a photograph in the company's internal publication, *texins*, in June 1954. Pictured, left to right, are Willis Adcock, Mort Jones, Ed Jackson, and Jay Thornhill. Pat Haggerty honored the team at the company's strategic planning conference in 1980.

become a world leader in the semiconductor business, though the world didn't know it yet.

For Teal, the timing of the breakthrough couldn't have been better. He was scheduled to speak on May 10, 1954 at the Institute of Radio Engineers National Convention in Dayton, Ohio. His speech already had a title: "Some Recent Developments in Silicon and Germanium Materials and Devices." Four days before the convention, Teal approached Haggerty with the proposal that TI announce not only the invention of the silicon transistor, but that TI was in production. He pointed out that the team now had several crystal pullers running and a pilot line set up and assembling units. They had already built about 150 very good transistors, and had characterized and written specifications for them as TI types 903, 904, and 905. Haggerty agreed, and Teal now had a technical one-two punch far beyond anyone's expectations for the conference.

All Teal needed to do before heading to Dayton was rewrite a few sentences and build a couple of props. At the conference, Teal remembered, "During the morning sessions, the speakers had unwittingly set the stage for us. One after the other [speakers] remarked about how hopeless it was to expect the development of a silicon transistor in less than several years. They advised the industry to be satisfied with germanium transistors for the present. We of TI listened with great respect and mounting exultation, because I had a handful of excellent silicon transistors in my pocket."

As Teal began his presentation, he read through 24 of the 31 pages without mentioning his team's achievement at TI. The crowd was less than attentive after listening to a day of technical papers. Then Teal dropped his bombshell. "Contrary to what my colleagues have told you ....," he began. His message stunned everyone who heard it: Silicon transistors were a fact. TI was producing them.

After a moment of silence, someone in the audience yelled, "Did you say you have the silicon transistor in production?"

"Yes," Teal answered, "we have three types of silicon transistors in production. I happen to have a few in my pocket." Now came the props.

Teal turned and switched on an RCA 45-rpm turntable,

playing the swinging sounds of Artie Shaw's "Summit Ridge Drive." The germanium transistors in the amplifier of the record player were dunked in a beaker of hot oil, and the sound died away as the devices failed from the high temperature. Then Teal switched over to an identical amplifier with silicon transistors, placed it in the hot oil, and the music played on. One conference attendee was heard shouting into a pay phone in the lobby, "They've got the silicon transistor down in Texas." The silicon age had arrived in Teal's coat pocket.

TI began production of the grown-junction silicon transistor several years ahead of the industry's best estimates and surged to the forefront. TI was no longer a small company with a big idea; TI had become the industry leader.

KEEPING CONTROL

Early in the project, the formidable task of growing silicon crystals ran into a serious snag. The temperature of molten silicon in the puller was not being controlled accurately enough to achieve the required uniformity. The store-bought temperature controller could hit within two degrees of the 1,400-degree Celsius target, but Adcock needed to hold it within two-tenths of a degree.

Mark Shepherd called the manufacturer, probing to determine if the company would build a temperature controller for TI that was at least ten times more precise.

The engineer bluntly told him, "Quit wasting my time," and hung up without another word.

An angry Shepherd turned around and snapped, "Well, we'll just build our own."

Art Evans, an electrical engineer, was brought in and built a controller that solved the temperature control problem with room to spare, and the silicon transistor project again moved ahead.

19

THE SILICON AGE

TI had the silicon transistor, but had only one source of the high-purity silicon material needed for mass production.

Texas Instruments stunned the world in 1954 by making the first commercially available silicon transistors, but the next step was to move forward to capture the emerging market. At the time, DuPont was the only domestic supplier capable of providing the high-purity raw silicon material needed to produce the crystals. It looked as if TI's future lay in the hands of a chemical giant that might or might not be willing to increase its output of silicon and lower the price as the volume grew. So, TI set out to make its own material, and succeeded beyond its dreams—producing enough silicon to become a major supplier to the industry, thereby accelerating the market.

Texas Instruments had stormed into the marketplace with silicon transistors three years ahead of its competitors and was recognized as the world leader in the technology. The germanium transistor's reign as king of semiconductors would come to an end because of silicon. Germanium transistors failed at even moderate temperatures, limiting their use to room-temperature applications for the most part, but silicon transistors could operate at boiling temperatures and beyond. TI wanted to build enough of them to bring the price down, and the market would grow accordingly.

Gordon Teal, the inventor of the grown-junction single crystal technique during his days at Bell Labs,

had convinced Pat Haggerty that TI should focus on silicon for the future. He and Haggerty had early on considered the idea of TI manufacturing its own high-purity silicon. In 1953, they set up a Transistor Materials team in Teal's Central Research Labs, with Willis Adcock as the leader, to investigate a process of extracting high-purity silicon from commercially available chemicals.

Dr. Ray Sangster joined TI in the fall of 1954 and took over the technical leadership of the materials team, reporting to Adcock. By 1954, silicon transistor manufacturing was operational, and the goal of producing in-house silicon material was a priority. To add technical horsepower to the group, Adcock went to see Jim Fischer, who was in Boston completing his master's degree in chemical engineering at MIT. Adcock had worked with Fischer at Stanolind Oil Company in Tulsa, Oklahoma, and knew him to be a top-notch chemical engineer. Fischer became one of TI's first chemical engineers. He started at TI in December 1955, reporting to Sangster, on the silicon materials project. Fisher rose rapidly in TI, eventually becoming head of TI's worldwide semiconductor business in 1978, and later, a TI executive vice president.

After reaching a dead end in an attempt to adapt the current commercial process of reducing the chemical silicon tetrachloride with hydrogen, Sangster and Fischer made a leap of technology with a shift to reduction of the chemical trichlorosilane (TCS) instead. In an interview years later, Fischer understated the accomplishment, "We had a good deal of difficulty in the development of the process." But this

Dr. Gordon Teal and Dr. Willis Adcock examine crystals grown by the company's crystal pullers in 1954.

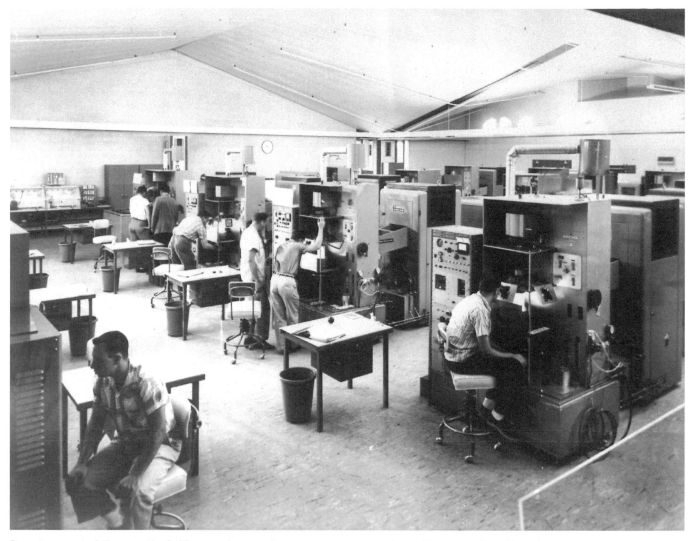

Operators control the growth of silicon and germanium crystals, purer and larger than gems found in nature. TI operated the electronics industry's largest battery of the intricate machines in its new Semiconductor Components plant around 1958.

crucial change proved to be the right one, and a pilot plant was built in the rear of the TI Lemmon Avenue facility. The silicon materials team transferred from research to semiconductor manufacturing under Cecil Dotson and Steve Karnavas.

The start-up production facility consisted of four small silicon reactors in a specially designed room. Each reactor was brought on line in turn, with the production of silicon increasing at each step. When the fourth reactor was brought up to temperature, the room overheated, set off the sprinkler system, and automatically dialed the Dallas Fire Department. Fischer recalled, "They all immediately rushed over to find out what was going on with their axes and fire hoses." But by 1956, Sangster and Fischer had reached Haggerty's and Teal's goal of an independent supply of ultrapure silicon for the ever-growing needs of TI's silicon transistor.

In 1960, TI took the bold step of constructing a Materials Building on the Central Expressway site for a much larger silicon production operation, headed by Ralph Stroup. It

eventually contained more than 100 reactors for producing high-purity silicon material from TCS, a room full of crystal pullers for converting the material into single-crystal ingots, and diamond saws to slice the ingots into the thin wafers required for transistor production. Later, TI built a fluid-bed reactor to produce its own TCS. It took miles of pipelines to complete the task and tie it into the reactor room in the adjacent Materials Building. From the outside, the TCS tower looked like an offshore drilling platform. TI now had a complete in-house facility to produce silicon material with impurities controlled to 1 or 2 parts per billion.

TI stopped purchasing silicon from DuPont and had extra capacity of a hot commodity. A marketing organization was created under the leadership of Bill Haynes, and TI began to solicit trade customers. For several years, TI supplied silicon materials to semiconductor companies around the globe. DuPont ultimately dropped out of the silicon business entirely, but Monsanto, Dow Corning, Wacker Chemical of

TI's silicon reactors supplied the ultra-pure material for the crystal pullers. Silicon crystals were then sliced into thin wafers for use in transistor manufacturing.

Germany, and Shin-Etsu Chemical of Japan began to invest heavily in new plants and eventually produced semiconductor-grade silicon for the booming worldwide market.

A t its peak, TI produced 3.2 million wafers a year in a variety of sizes: 100-mm, 125-mm, and 150-mm diameters. However, when the semiconductor industry moved to 200-mm wafers, TI decided it would be more efficient to purchase ready-to-use wafers than to invest in the equipment to upgrade production to the larger diameter wafers. In 1995, TI entered into a strategic alliance with an established supplier of wafers, MEMC Electronic Materials, which took over operation of TI's wafer production facility in Sherman, Texas. This move allowed TI to concentrate on the design and manufacture of integrated circuits. In time, TI sold its interest in MEMC but has remained one of the industry's largest and growing users of high-purity silicon wafers. TI's innovations in the chemistry of high-purity silicon material had served its purpose—accelerating the world's movement into the Silicon Age.

SILICON ACREAGE

The metric used to report the industry's annual silicon wafer production is millions of square inches of silicon, or MSI. For the last 30 years, the MSI of silicon wafers has increased at an average compound rate of approximately 10 percent. The MSI of silicon wafers doubles about every 7.4 years. In 1997, wafer production was 4,000 MSI, almost exactly equal to 1 square mile. The October 2004 SEMI forecast was that 6,313 MSI would be produced in 2004—about 1.6 square miles of optically flat surface.

There have been many changes in silicon production since TI's first process in 1956. The earliest silicon crystals pulled were only 0.65 inches in diameter, less than 6 inches long, weighing just over 0.5 pounds. In 2004, the 300 mm silicon ingots in production are typically 45 inches long and weigh over 450 pounds.

20

A MAJOR BREAKTHROUGH

TI showcases transistors by designing the world's first transistor radio.

By the summer of 1953, Pat Haggerty believed that the future of Texas Instruments was tied to semiconductors. TI was producing germanium transistors, but the market had been slow to respond. The industry was comfortable with vacuum tubes and had taken a wait-and-see attitude. Transistor sales had been just a trickle with a few applications, but Haggerty's goal was to produce them by the hundreds of thousands. A daring plan would herald the world's acceptance of transistors and help launch TI into a new industry.

Haggerty turned his attention to the computer giant, IBM, which he believed one day would buy a lot of transistors. IBM, however, was barely aware of TI and had shown little interest in transistors. Haggerty decided that IBM and the electronics industry in general needed a transistor wake-up call and that a small radio would provide it.

Haggerty urged Mark Shepherd's semiconductor business to develop less expensive ways to build transistors. Shepherd directed Boyd Cornelison and Elmer Wolff to create a method for mass-producing germanium transistors. The existing fabrication consisted of skilled operators working through microscopes, assembling tiny bars into individual transistors. It was a slow and tedious task and would never reach the production levels Haggerty envisioned.

Cornelison and Wolff came up with the indium dot ladder process, a radical approach that allowed for batches of transistors to be built at the same time in a furnace. Mort Jones of the Research Group described it as "a pan of cookies." It was a creative method that eliminated the old one-at-a-time procedures.

In the spring of 1954, Haggerty decided TI would develop the transistor radio business, even though, at the time, transistors were poorly suited for the job and much too expensive. Haggerty and S.T. "Buddy" Harris began asking large radio manufacturing companies if they might be interested in teaming up with TI to build a transistor portable radio. Most companies said they would wait and see what happened. Vacuum tubes were cheap and dependable.

Celebrating the introduction of the world's first transistor pocket radio, Pat Haggerty (left) shakes hands with Ed Tudor, president of the Regency division of IDEA, Inc.

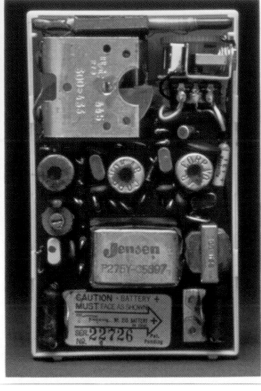

The first transistor radio—
the Regency TR-1. Early
models of the first radios
are in the Smithsonian
Museum and can be viewed
on the museum's website.

As Haggerty pondered his next move, a Chicago investment firm inquired about the possibility of TI's merging with a small, innovative Indianapolis electronics manufacturer—Industrial Development Engineering Associates (IDEA), Inc. The firm was producing television accessories such as signal boosters and UHF channel converters, all sold under IDEA's trade name, Regency. Haggerty was interested. The acquisition of IDEA might provide TI with an expeditious, low-cost route to move transistor radios to the consumer market. He and Harris met with IDEA President Ed Tudor to discuss the matter at a consumer electronics show in Chicago in May 1954.

A merger was ruled out, but during discussions with Regency, Haggerty called TIer Paul Davis to his office late on a Friday afternoon and asked him to design and build the "breadboard" model of a transistor radio—one that would receive all the AM

stations in Dallas. He could select anybody he wanted to work with on the project.

Davis, an electrical engineer who had previously served as chief engineer at Watterson Radio of Dallas, nodded. He would begin work immediately.

"Fine," Haggerty said, "I won't need it until next Wednesday." On Wednesday, Haggerty would be meeting with IDEA, and he knew that having a working transistor radio playing on his desk would give TI leverage during discussions of a business deal.

Davis later recalled, "As TI engineers, we were accustomed to meeting tight schedules on development projects, like a goal of six months for a product where most companies would have a goal of at least a year. TI engineers seemed to thrive on such projects."

His assignment bordered on the impossible. In four days, Davis and his team had to develop and build the working model of a transistorized radio at a time "when the basic circuits had never been conceived, much less designed," Davis recalled. "We not only did not know the solutions, we still did not even comprehend what all the problems were that lay ahead. It wasn't exactly your typical Friday afternoon."

Roger Webster, an electrical engineer and top-notch transistor circuit designer, agreed to tackle the toughest assignment—developing the Intermediate Frequency amplifiers. According to Davis, Webster had to build "a circuit that would amplify high-frequency electrical signals by a factor of many thousands." He, along with Ed Jackson, fresh from the successful silicon transistor team, and Mark Campbell, another experienced electrical engineer, plunged into the uncharted world of designing and building a transistor radio. They had no suitable coils or transformers and were using transistors that performed poorly at radio frequencies. They were joined by Jim Nygaard, a fresh Texas A&M graduate. Nygaard recalled, "I was really quite awed by the fact that I was only out of college for two months and was involved in what was going to be the first transistor radio in the world. Very few people ever get an opportunity like that."

His opportunity was a chance to work night and day and over the weekend, on a project that was an extraordinary technical challenge. But it was also the rare opportunity to work with some of the best engineers at TI on a Haggerty project that could alter the course of the company.

———————————

Tuesday afternoon, a day early, the weary and jubilant team carried a working radio to Haggerty's office and turned it on. As Davis later reported, "It clearly received all local AM stations, and the tone quality of the audio was quite good." Haggerty was pleased. The team had accomplished their four-day miracle.

When Haggerty welcomed the representatives from IDEA into his office on Wednesday, he had a transistor radio to show them. Any doubts they might have had were quickly erased, and negotiations began in earnest. TI and IDEA would begin immediately to design the production model jointly, and IDEA would then assemble and market 100,000 of the Regency-brand radios.

The revolutionary new transistor radio would be introduced in New York and Los Angeles by mid-October 1954 to take advantage of Christmas sales.

Haggerty, Shepherd, and Harris argued about the retail price while waiting on a plane at Love Field in Dallas. Shepherd recalled that the three men finally agreed on $50. He said, "We went out and caught our airplanes, and that was it." Haggerty said later that they thought if it was any higher it wouldn't sell,

and if it was any lower TI would lose money.

TI was still facing an improbable deadline if IDEA hoped to have a miniature transistor radio in production by October. It was time to design a radio. The TI team of Webster and Nygaard moved into their new home-away-from-home—a radio-shielded screen room. Along with the IDEA team of Ray Morris and Dick Koch in Indianapolis, they began the radio design in earnest. At the same time, Cornelison, Frank Horak, and Wolff began their night and day project to stretch the performance of the newly developed indium dot transistors far enough to make a practical radio.

———————————

Webster's engineering notebook page dated June 30 had a wiring diagram of a six-transistor radio with the optimistic note *"To Ray Morris—final design."* But at the combined design team meeting a few days later, Haggerty insisted that six transistors were too many. It could have no more than five. Koch and Webster consulted briefly, left the meeting, and headed for the screen room. Back within an hour, they reported that they had replaced the detector transistor with a diode, and it "worked just about as good." Five transistors it was.

But this, too, Haggerty rejected. It must be four. Haggerty knew how to reach his original goal of four transistors—one transistor at a time. And Koch of IDEA pulled off the miracle a few weeks later by inventing a method of combining the two transistor functions of oscillator and mixer into one "converter" transistor. And on August 30, Webster's notebook, once again, showed a "final design." Only this time it had four transistors.

IDEA now had six weeks to mass-produce the transistor radio. One of many obstacles was that tooling to stamp out the steel chassis would take a minimum of six weeks to produce. TI's Tool Shop took on the challenge and supplied the tool in nine days. Not to be outdone, TI set up production for the tiny audio transformer to drive the loudspeaker.

On October 18, 1954, the Regency TR-1 radio was officially announced to the world: "The radio receiver measures 5 x 3 x 1 ¼ inches—the smallest set commercially available—with the semiconductor devices themselves occupying less than 1/10 of a cubic inch. The 'pocket size' is a significant achievement since it includes a high-fidelity, high-volume speaker, and single-battery supply, as well as all associated receiver circuit components. The introduction of this first mass-production item to use the tiny transistor to replace the fragile vacuum tube leads the way for the long-predicted transistorization and miniaturization of many other mass-production consumer devices."

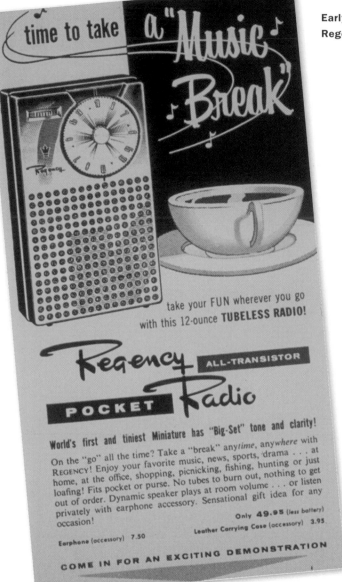

The transistor radio was never a profitable venture for TI. The strategic plan was to use the pocket radio to introduce transistors to the world market, as well as to the consumer, and, within two years, TI led the radio market, supplying almost 2 million transistors to such customers as Admiral, GE, Magnavox, Motorola, Westinghouse, and Zenith.

Haggerty had wanted to attract IBM's attention, and he did. Tom Watson, IBM's president, bought 100 or so of the miniature radios and passed them out to his skeptical executives and key managers. He reportedly told them, "If that little outfit down in Texas can make these radios work for this kind of money, they can make transistors that will make our computers work, too."

As Haggerty later said, "We signed an agreement with IBM and began supplying large quantities of transistors for many, many years."

The Regency TR-1 radio had given TI instant recognition as a serious semiconductor manufacturer and opened doors for business opportunities the company had never imagined. And it reinforced a growing belief within TI that the company had the ability to pull together a small, talented team and succeed at virtually any market it chose to tackle.

A national sales campaign formally introduced the arrival of the transistor age with ads touting a *Revolutionary NEW Tubeless Radio.* More than 100,000 pocket radios were eventually sold. IDEA's Ed Tudor said, "The industry was caught napping. TI had the only mass-production transistor facility in the world."

H aggerty later admitted he had made a serious strategic mistake. The TR-1 should have been priced at $60-65. The $49.95 retail price was simply "the minimum for us to break even."

IMPACT OF THE TRANSISTOR RADIO

★ ★ ★

The transistor's contribution to the world may have been best described by Walter Brattain, one of the inventors of the transistor at Bell Labs, as reported by Robert J. Simcoe in his brief history of the Regency Radio: *"Even the loneliest nomad on the steppes of Asia can have the news of the world by twisting a dial. He doesn't have to read. Once the common man has a chance to learn what is going on, he has a chance to control his destiny."*

Minutes after the doors opened, and almost constantly thereafter, Booth 776 was jammed to capacity at the Institute of Radio Engineers tradeshow in 1954.

In October 1953, TI received its first big production order—7,500 transistors for Sonotone hearing aids. Success with the Regency Radio in 1954 stimulated interest in transistors; inquiries were handled by mail and telephone. Before the semiconductor business set up its own sales force, S.T. "Buddy" Harris, who headed all of TI's marketing, had assigned Jim Willis to work with government customers, and W. E. "Bill" Love to semiconductor customers. In 1955, TI opened its first regional sales offices in New York City, Chicago, and Los Angeles. Jay Rodney Reese, the first Eastern Regional Manager, operated out of the trunk of his car until an office was set up in New York. Reese soon moved to Dallas to head Semiconductor Field Sales.

Rapid growth soon generated the need for a semiconductor sales force. Richard "Dick" Hanchen joined TI in 1956 and continued the campaign to hire a semiconductor sales staff. Semiconductor added a distribution channel (the first authorized distributor was its own TI Supply Company). The company's game plan called for the sales team to qualify products in a customer's engineering department, then work to secure purchase orders from procurement. Mike Corboy, an FSE in Chicago and later vice president of sales and marketing, remembers that the FSEs in his office would meet the incoming Dallas flights at Midway Airport at 5 a.m., deliver the products to the customer promptly at 6:30 a.m., and make sure they reached the production lines by 7 a.m. Customers appreciated the personal attention, which was important for driving growth in new markets and forging strong business relationships.

21

CREATING A WORLDWIDE SALES & MARKETING FORCE

TI sales engineers experience life in the fast lane as role changes.

Texas Instruments entered the semiconductor market in late 1952 with its first customer order, but the company had no Field Sales Engineers (FSE) dedicated to the products. As demand grew, TI developed a worldwide marketing organization. Over the years, the role of FSEs has changed dramatically. Initially, they sold a wide variety of products; their focus was on price and delivery. As semiconductor products became more complex, FSEs needed to understand customers' technical design needs and software; they also had to be able to help the customer with the logistics of product delivery and inventory control. Today, FSEs face many challenges around the world, spending most of their time at the customers' system design locations battling competitors and building long-term customer relationships for TI.

According to Corboy, FSEs during those early days were trained for three weeks at the new training facility on Lemmon Avenue in Dallas. If, however, a salesman was immediately needed in the field, he received his training under fire and on the job. Bachelor of Science in Electrical Engineering degrees were required. Sales meetings were held in Dallas to provide sales updates and motivation for an expanding sales force. Factory product managers made routine visits to the field to receive customer reviews, often described as a "socket-by-socket" analysis of a customer's requirements,

and to investigate strategies necessary to give TI a competitive advantage. Expansion of the sales organization stepped up in the U.S., and by the early 1960s the sales force had grown to 154.

In 1959, TI received its first commercial integrated circuit order from American Bosch of Long Island, New York—for $17,500. As the demand for integrated circuits increased, TI added integrated circuits specialists to the marketing team to insure customers had the knowledge to apply the technology in their products.

During the early 1960s, TI formed the nucleus of a sales force for European operations in Bedford, England, and Paris, France. Pat Haggerty and Buddy Harris made many trips to the U.K. to study prospects for business, and Don Burrus, TI's marketing research manager, gathered data on the European semiconductor market. Because of business contacts made by Bob Cohen, a French national selected to manage TI's liaison office in Paris, TI was able to begin selling directly to customers instead of importers, thereby establishing a close factory-to-customer relationship.

Although customer contacts from management, purchasing, and manufacturing departments continued to be important, the SC sales focus shifted into design engineering. Field Sales Product Specialists were given extensive training in areas such as optoelectronics, analog, and distribution support.

An important change occurred in the sales force in the 1970s. The Category 1 (CAT 1) program was established to focus on smaller customers and to identify significant new opportunities. The sales force was also segmented into Computer, Consumer, Military, and Distribution segments. The sales force was reorganized, and factory and field meetings were scheduled to review objectives and customer strategies. During these CAT 1 account reviews, product departments

and FSEs analyzed sales strategies and tactics with senior management, helping managers understand the changing needs of TI's customers, giving them a better idea of what TI needed to maintain its status as a major supplier. According to Charles "Charley" Clough and Kevin McGarity, both former vice presidents of semiconductor sales and marketing, "This was the most significant change to covering customers since the sales force inception."

Advanced customer system development drove the creation of the Regional Technology Center concept in the mid-1970s, which positioned hardware and software specialists (with advanced degrees in Electrical Engineering and Computer Science) at field locations where they were most needed. The first of six domestic technology centers opened in Detroit and focused on automotive customers.

Semiconductor hired its first female FSE, Dorothy Kubicek, in the Minneapolis sales office in 1974. A growing number of women graduating with electrical engineering degrees have been recruited for TI's sales and marketing operations.

As the 1980s approached, TI continued its emphasis on technical and system training. The sales training

Jay Rodney Reese, left, field sales manager for the semiconductor marketing department, greets Barbara and Tom Connors of New York when they arrived in Dallas on May 30, 1957, for an annual sales conference. To become better acquainted with TI, wives of regional salesmen were invited to attend the first four days of the meetings.

program, evolved into a yearlong effort, with trainees integrated into the product marketing organization. There was crossover between sales and marketing. Several TI senior managers have come through the sales training program including Rich Templeton, TI's current president and CEO.

In the 1990s, another significant change in sales focus took place as semiconductor sales began to measure and track customer "design wins." This effort began in Europe and became a worldwide method for identifying and tracking achievements for the "design-in" process for customers around the world. As customers expanded their design and manufacturing globally, worldwide "flex teams" were formed by semiconductor marketing personnel within the regions to provide global support for both design wins and production. For example, the flex team for Apple Computer consisted of 120 people working together around the world, which resulted in improved service to the customer and increased sales for TI.

TI's marketing presence in Asia has continued to grow. In 1964, TI-Asia was incorporated in Delaware to serve customers in Japan and elsewhere in Asia. The TI-Asia's Japan branch was established May 1964, with Joe Emery as the first manager. Eiji Kamisaku was the first Japanese sales engineer hired. By May 1967, TI-Asia had opened a branch in Hong Kong. In August 1970, Don Hall moved to Taipei to head up sales in Southeast Asia, and TI's semiconductor business in Asia continued to grow. Later additions included offices in Korea and China. Asia has emerged as one of the largest segments of the world semiconductor market.

During the first years of the 21st century, TI's semiconductor sales force grew and deployed around the world, working in all aspects of sales account management, field applications, inside sales support, centralized technical support, and distribution channel management. In addition, TI established several business development product specialists and a worldwide strategic marketing team.

According to Jeff McCreary, vice president of worldwide semiconductor sales and marketing, "The greatest challenges of semiconductor customers going forward are the demands for more complete product solutions and support." For FSEs, this means a better systems understanding ranging from cell-phone chipsets and digital cameras to high-performance analog, catalog DSP, standard logic, and large custom Application Specific Integrated Circuits. It means a commitment to spend more time with customers at every level of sales, marketing, and management.

The King Customer program began in January 1959 to strengthen customer awareness throughout TI.

KING CUSTOMER

★ ★ ★

In January 1959, a new program, "King Customer," was announced to TIers. Stories about customers were featured monthly in the internal employee news publications and in department meetings to encourage TIers to understand customer requirements and their own role in supplying that need.

Over the years TI has teamed with major customers such as Sun Microsystems for microprocessors, General Motors for single-chip microcomputers, ITT Europe for electronic braking systems, CMM for electronic numeric controls, General Dynamics for military programs, and IBM for many technology and system requirements.

Semiconductor marketing has evolved from its early days as a parts supplier to a systems solution provider focusing on a breadth of topics to better serve customers' needs including supply chain management, ship-to-stock programs, Electronic Data Interchange, and global tracking programs. Coming full circle, the "King Customer" concept initiated in 1959 is just as relevant today.

22

STAYING A STEP AHEAD

TI builds its own production and test equipment.

Rows of CAT machines testing transistors in the Semiconductor Building in 1960.

Mark Shepherd believed the company could cut costs, as well as maintain a business advantage, by designing and building its own equipment to make semiconductors. So TI set up teams of engineers to do just that. The TI-made equipment helped the company set the standard for productivity and paved the way for a whole new industry of specialty semiconductor equipment suppliers.

While the production of transistors was in its infancy, TI formed separate mechanization and test equipment

During the mid-1950s, rows of operators tested TI's transistors, one at a time; each transistor required ten to twenty different tests. It was a slow and methodical process that called for more manpower as the number of transistors grew.

In 1956, six engineers in the test equipment group generated an idea and submitted a proposal to build a tester, The Centralized Automatic Tester (CAT). Its design was not funded, because it was deemed too complicated.

Two years later, Jim Nygaard needed more help supplying new equipment for the rapidly growing semiconductor business. He contacted TI's plant in Houston, and Ed Millis got the task of putting together a support group. One of their first projects was the prototype of the CAT. Millis recalls, "It resembled a pile of electronic and mechanical junk, but we thought it was the most beautiful thing in the world." Fortunately, so did Shepherd, who persuaded semiconductor product areas to purchase CATs from Houston.

By the end of 1958, CATs were capable of testing 2,000 transistors an hour. When the improved version, the Super CAT, was developed, *Dun's Review*, in 1967, reported: *"The machine performs more than 40 sequential tests, at high temperatures, for each semiconductor unit. And it does so at the incredible production rate of 6,000 devices per hour."*

groups, which triggered a never-ending battle between mechanical and electrical engineers to determine who could build the best equipment in the shortest time. A section leader in the test equipment group bragged that, since his team didn't have access to a draftsman, they could build a tool wrong twice then right the third time, more rapidly than the mechanization group could create proper drawings and build the tool wrong the first time.

The first installation of the ABACUS II, integrated circuit wire bonders, in TI's Sherman, Texas, plant around 1973.

TI's in-house teams were limited only by their imaginations. If an engineer wasn't sure how a piece of equipment was supposed to perform, he walked to the production lines, tried it, and found out. And if he wanted to see whether his idea for a new invention was practical, he would temporarily install a prototype on a line and conduct the necessary tests with skilled production personnel at the controls.

The groups were under pressure to produce equipment that gave TI a quicker response for new products, superior performance or technology, and lower costs to justify the expense involved. Expenses were growing all the time. From the inventive minds of Boyd Cornelison and Gordon Teal came the crystal pullers that gave TI its head start in silicon transistors. Centralized Automatic Tester (CAT) machines offered unprecedented quality and provided TI with a major cost reduction in the testing of transistors. Front End Processor (FEP), the industry's first computer-controlled manufacturing system, enhanced the company's manufacturing uniformity, which paid off in higher yields, lower costs, and greater reliability. The ABACUS II (an acronym for Alloy, Bond, Assembly Concept, Universal System) integrated circuit wire bonder drastically cut assembly labor costs and allowed TI to capture the plastic Dual In-line Package market.

ENTER ABACUS

★ ★ ★

One of the final steps in manufacturing an integrated circuit is connecting microscopic electrical pads—placed around the edges of the tiny silicon chip—to the electrical connection pins of the package.

TI had tried several times to automate this delicate process without success. A major missing piece of the puzzle was a controller, and in the 1960s, computers were too expensive.

Then along came the HAL-9 computer, the result of a 1969 TI bootleg project. It was designed to run machinery, and it cost only $5,000, although a 4,000-word core memory added $7,000 to HAL-9.

TI's third attempt at creating an automatic wire bonder produced the ABACUS.

As soon as TI introduced its new TI-960A computer, ABACUS B was upgraded, but the price for each unit exceeded $65,000. TI went back to work designing a modular bonder that would cost less, and be more adaptable. ABACUS II cost $15,000; it could perform at the rate of 375 (16-pin) devices per hour, assuring its success. During the next decade, almost 1,000 systems were built and put in production around the world.

Thirty years later, the ABACUS III SA models were bonding units at the equivalent rate of 2,000 devices an hour.

CREATING THE FEP

★ ★ ★

In the 1960s, silicon wafers were processed one at a time. Others were collected in plastic cassettes or quartz carriers, then dipped, dunked, and subjected to the irregularities of batch processing.

Ed Jackson came up with an idea to remove the wafer from the batch tank. He proposed to automate each of the dozens of process steps for every wafer—one wafer at a time—as they progressed down an assembly line of machines. He proposed to run the concept with computers.

Jim Nygaard took the revolutionary idea to Pat Haggerty, who funded the FEP project, which, more than likely, was the first large manufacturing system ever run solely by computers. When the FEP began production in April 1970, led by Herby Locke, it consisted of five lines of equipment, each with 10–15 processing stations, as well as a room of diffusion furnaces. Don Benefiel and Bob Falt supplied the process engineering support that made it hum. The FEP remained operational for 10 years, and, at one time, was processing more than 100,000 2-inch wafers per month.

The final FEP system was a grand and difficult mixture of engineering, chemistry, physics, and innovative software developed by Claude Head and team. TI's patent for computer-controlled manufacturing is still considered one of the company's most valuable intellectual properties.

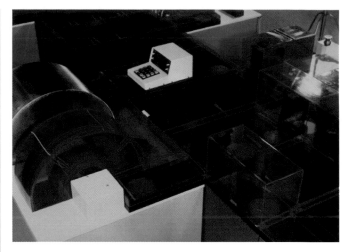

Several processing stations of the Advanced Front End Processor manufacturing system in 1979. The orange shields protect the light-sensitive silicon wafers.

Texas Instruments realized it was time to reshape its strategy. It no longer made sense to design and build its own equipment. It was more logical and cost-efficient to buy production equipment from specialized companies around the world. However, TI dutifully evaluated those suppliers on technology, environmental responsibility, responsiveness, assurance of supply, cost, and quality. TI needed the best equipment available to succeed.

By the late 1980s, an optical printer or an ion implanter could cost as much as $1 million, and chips were becoming as complex as the tools to manufacture them. The task of designing new equipment seemed to have no end. As soon as a wafer fab was running smoothly and profitably, the size of the available silicon wafers would increase an inch or two. Bigger is better, was the common thought. Early wafers were an inch in diameter; the worldwide standard would grow to about a foot in diameter. The equipment that cost millions of dollars to process 200-mm wafers wouldn't work with 300-mm wafers, and TI was faced with buying larger and more expensive equipment.

Today, TI buys equipment and materials from hundreds of companies worldwide, with the largest equipment suppliers generating billions of dollars of their own revenue each year. TI established Supplier Excellence Awards in 1983 to honor businesses that provide exemplary service. These awards communicate the standards TI expects of its suppliers.

23

THE CHIP THAT CHANGED THE WORLD

Jack Kilby's invention of the integrated circuit triggered a new age of electronics.

At 6 feet, 6 inches tall, Jack St. Clair Kilby stood out in a crowd. Among contemporary engineers and inventors, his stature became extraordinary. Kilby's invention of the integrated circuit at Texas Instruments in 1958 launched what the National Academy of Sciences would later call "the second Industrial Revolution."

After completing his electrical engineering degree at the University of Illinois in 1947, Kilby devoted the next 11 years to building components for the cost-driven consumer electronics market at the Centralab Division of Globe Union. He faced the challenge of reducing costs in production and assembly at a time when many believed miniaturization held the greatest cost-cutting promise.

While he was working at Centralab and pursuing a graduate degree from the University of Wisconsin, Kilby attended a lecture by John Bardeen, a coinventor of the transistor at Bell Labs in 1947. As soon as Western Electric Company announced it would issue licenses for producing these transistors, Centralab began making plans for Kilby to learn about the technology. The company acquired a license, and Kilby began working to develop and improve point-contact transistors, resistor-capacitor networks, and ceramic-based silk-screened circuits.

By early 1958, Kilby was convinced that Centralab did not share his interest in miniaturization and began sending out a few résumés to companies that might. TI was one of them. Willis Adcock, manager of the Development Department for TI's Semiconductor Components division, offered Kilby a position that would allow him to work full-time on miniaturization. Kilby immediately accepted the offer and joined TI in May.

At the time, TI was working with the U.S. Army Signal Corps to determine whether the micro module approach might serve as an acceptable miniaturization method for circuits. TI proposed making all the electrical components the same shape and size, then inserting them into a pre-wired matrix to eliminate discrete wiring.

Kilby wanted to see if repackaging the circuits might be a better alternative to the micro module approach. Initially, he designed an intermediate frequency amplifier, using components in a tubular format, and put a prototype together. After completing his cost analysis, Kilby realized the

Jack Kilby and his famous notebook showing the sketch of his integrated circuit invention, which sparked the multibillion dollar electronics industry and led to the information age of wireless cell phones, personal computers, and other high-tech products.

Jack Kilby's first working integrated circuit, tested on September 12, 1958, consisted of a transistor and other components on a sliver of germanium, 7/16 x 1/16 inches, which revolutionized the electronics industry. Kilby often remarked that if he'd known he'd be showing the first working integrated circuit for the next 40-plus years, he would have "prettied it up a little."

manufacturing costs would be too great for the concept to be practical or profitable. As he recalled, "I felt it likely that I would be assigned to work on a proposal for the micro module program unless I came up with a good idea very quickly."

During the summer of 1958, TI shut down for the annual two-week, company-wide mass vacation. As a new employee, Kilby had not yet accrued vacation time, so he stayed on the job and began looking for a viable alternative to the micro module program. While studying the problem, he decided the only product a semiconductor house could make cost-effectively was a semiconductor. Perhaps other circuit components could be made from the same material as the semiconductors.

Kilby drew up a few sketches and showed them to Adcock as soon as the vacation period had ended. Adcock was optimistic, but cautious, about the new idea. He suggested that Kilby try building a working circuit, utilizing components made from silicon. With Adcock's orders in hand, Kilby carried his sketches to the lab and asked the technicians to fabricate some silicon resistors and capacitors. He wired these parts into a transistor flip-flop circuit and demonstrated the working device to Adcock on August 28. Kilby was given the go-ahead to continue his

project, and when he designed the next circuit, he integrated all the individual components onto a single bar of semiconductor material. He sketched in his notebook the complete circuit of a phase-shift oscillator on a bar of germanium.

Within two weeks, the first three oscillators were completed and ready to test. What TI managers saw on that historic day of September 12, 1958, was a tiny bar of germanium, measuring 7/16-x 1/16 inches, with protruding wires, glued to a glass slide. It was a rough device by anyone's standards. But when Kilby applied the voltage, an unending sine wave undulated across the oscilloscope screen.

It worked just as Kilby thought it would. He had solved one of the most perplexing problems associated with miniaturization. Once his invention was accepted, it would revolutionize the electronics industry. As Kilby said, "What we didn't realize then was that the integrated circuit would reduce the cost of electronic functions by a factor of a million to one. Nothing had ever done that for anything before."

TI officially announced the technological breakthrough in New York on March 6, 1959. Mark Shepherd, vice president of TI's semiconductor business, said, "I consider this to be the most significant development by Texas Instruments since we divulged the commercial availability of the silicon transistor."

Pat Haggerty predicted the first applications of the circuits would be further miniaturization of computers, missiles, and space vehicles. Consumer applications were several years away.

Although Kilby's invention was a major technological breakthrough, the electronics industry reacted with doubt and skepticism. Kilby later commented that the integrated circuit and its relative merits "provided much of the entertainment at major technical meetings over the next few years."

TI immediately began searching for applications that would demonstrate the promise of integrated circuits in systems. The U. S. Air Force wanted to reduce the size and cost of airborne computers. A TI team was able to develop a small digital computer with 587 circuits in 1961. This success helped TI win the design of the Minuteman II missile computer, completed with more than 2,000 integrated circuits in 1964.

Because of Kilby's integrated circuit invention and the contribution of many other pioneers in the industry, the global market for electronics equipment mushroomed. In 1960, the world market for electronic end equipment was $24 billion. By 2004, it had increased more than 48 times to $1,175 billion, becoming one of the world's largest industries. The integrated circuit had become the backbone of electronic systems. Even Jack Kilby never expected its impact to be so great.

Winning the Nobel Prize in Physics, the National Medal of Science, or the National Medal of Technology is any inventor's dream.

Kilby won all three.

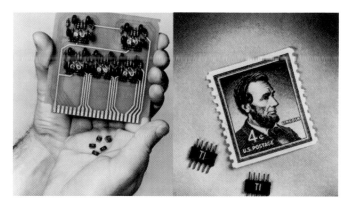

TI's Series 51 Solid Circuit product line consists of six microelectronic digital circuits, each containing the equivalent of two dozen conventional components. The five networks alongside the conventional etched card at left are the functional equivalent of the entire assembly shown. Two integrated circuits networks at right are compared to a postage stamp for size.

MIND OF THE INVENTOR

★ ★ ★

According to Jack Kilby, an inventor has to define a need or problem, have the proper knowledge of those technologies or the techniques available for reaching a positive solution, then develop a specific product or structure that allows him to select the right technologies necessary to achieve the desired result. For Kilby, that meant writing everything down. He kept copious notebooks to document his inventive endeavors. He saw value in his efforts, even the ones that didn't work out. He often learned what was possible by discovering what wasn't.

Kilby said an idea, particularly a new one, was a fragile thing. He began each process by thinking about the problem, taking notes, and drawing sketches—sometimes for several months. He used colored pencils to illustrate various layers, progressions, or sequences, which showed the order of putting things together. He knew he was near the end of the process when he had the inspiration to build something.

Proud of his achievements, Kilby preferred to be known as an engineer, not a scientist. "There's a pretty key difference," Kilby explained. "A scientist is motivated by knowledge. He basically wants to explain something. An engineer's drive is to solve problems and make something work. Engineering, or at least good engineering, is a creative process."

A problem solver by nature and by training, Kilby always understood his inventions must be practical and cost-effective. Yet within those constraints, creative ingenuity was still the driving force for Kilby. TI gave his creativity a home, and that made a difference to him, to TI, to the electronics industry, and to the world.

The *Wall Street Journal* named Jack Kilby as one of the five members of its High-Tech Dream Team in November 1994, and his picture hangs in the National Inventors Hall of Fame™ between the portraits of Henry Ford and Ernest Lawrence, who created the atom smasher. The Smithsonian Institution displays Kilby's first integrated circuit. Kilby's influence spans the globe. In 1993, he received Japan's Kyoto Prize in Advanced Technology, honoring those who have contributed significantly to the scientific, cultural, and spiritual development of mankind.

Kilby's body of work, including more than 60 patents, underscores the critical role he played in the advancement of electronics. However, Kilby himself always looked on his achievements with a touch of good humor and great humility.

During the mid-1990s, he was asked his thoughts on the general public's lack of awareness about his accomplishment that had changed the world in which they lived. Kilby shrugged and said, "Well, there aren't many history books that work [touch] on technology and its development. I suspect that I'll get a footnote in some of those that deal with electronics."

"How does it feel merely being a footnote?" he was asked.

"I guess it's probably better than not being a footnote," Kilby replied. "The history of technology is not a subject that many people pay attention to. They don't know who invented the ballpoint pen and don't much care. You can use it without the need to know what makes it work."

At an event honoring Kilby at Texas A&M University in 2001, TI chairman Tom Engibous commented that Kilby's invention was the single most important innovation of the Information Age—virtually creating the computer industry and setting the foundation for digital communications and modern electronics. He added, "Such is the power of one man, and one idea, to change the world."

24

THE MINUTEMAN CHALLENGE

Minuteman missile helps boost TI into the integrated circuit market.

In the early 1960s, America was nervous about the Soviet threat. The Minuteman missile had been designed to give the U.S. a primary capability of striking back in case war invaded its boundaries. However, the missile was in need of improved accuracy, increased flexibility, and reduced weight. Texas Instruments was sure that Jack Kilby's invention of the integrated circuit, which shrunk many electronic functions onto a single chip, was the answer. But there were several competing programs within the military for microminiaturizing electronics. It took the courageous support of a U.S. Air Force contracting officer and hard work by many TIers to get integrated circuits designed into the Minuteman and to move them into mass production, giving TI the boost it needed to transform the market.

After Jack Kilby invented the integrated circuit, Pat Haggerty immediately began searching for customers who might have a product or system in need of the microminiaturized devices. In 1959, the integrated circuit was little more than a laboratory creation. Without contracts, TI would not have the funding needed to develop and expand the program, even though integrated circuits potentially could reduce the space and power used in electronic equipment and improve reliability.

Kilby and Charles Phipps, a key manager in TI's strategic planning and marketing of integrated circuits, developed a good working relationship with Richard D. Alberts, chief of the transistor section at the Air Force Electronic Components Laboratory in Dayton, Ohio. Phipps described Alberts as "somewhat of a maverick," but someone who "did have the

technical foresight and imagination to see where he was going, and who relished twisting the tails of the other services and some of the people above him in the Air Force." Alberts was intrigued by Kilby's concept of silicon integrated circuits, and he defied established Air Force priorities by funding a small TI research program.

Previously, Kilby had faced the task of making each integrated circuit by hand. But Alberts circumvented Air Force

The U.S. Air Force Minuteman II missile was the first to fly with a fully integrated microelectronics system, proving in action the high-reliability semiconductor integrated circuit. Each missile contained over 2,000 TI circuits of the types shown.

policies a second time, providing additional funding for TI to research manufacturing processes. Willis Adcock, whose research and development lab produced the first integrated circuits, pointed out, "I think we would have dropped the program had it not been for the Air Force's support." Alberts made it possible for TI to develop a pilot manufacturing line, which made a handful of devices that were ultimately sold for $450 apiece.

Texas Instruments had not been able to convince skeptics that integrated circuits were reliable. They thought that if you multiplied the yield of each component in an integrated circuits together, the overall yield would be so low you could never expect to build a good unit. Also, some feared the amount of heat dissipated within a densely packed group of circuits would keep them from functioning properly. Alberts and

Phipps decided TI needed to build a model to demonstrate the viability and reliability of the technology. Alberts backed the project by funding $600,000—enough to let TI build a small digital computer using integrated circuits. It was a "bootleg" project that Alberts decided to keep secret. The Air Force could not interfere with a project it didn't know existed.

Harvey Cragon, an engineer in TI's defense business, was assigned the task of building a tiny 10-bit computer capable of assorted mathematical functions. Cragon later said, "Along about that time, I hired Joe Watson. The two of us sort of designed the thing, and Jack built the circuits."

To refute critics of integrated circuits who said they would never be practical because of yield and power dissipation, the demo computer was built as small and dense as possible. A stacking concept was used to interconnect five or six integrated circuits into each module. This packaging scheme was years ahead of its time—a decade later memory stacks were used in the industry to save space in electronic equipment. And, the little computer was the first to employ solid state memory.

When completed, the computer used 587 integrated circuits and weighed a mere 10 ounces. To focus attention on its size, TI built a second unit offering the same proficiency, but assembled it with discrete solid-state devices. This machine was 150 times larger than the integrated circuit computer and almost 50 times heavier. And it used 8,500 discrete components, 14 times more than the unit built with integrated circuits.

The demo and tour of the tiny computer helped tip the scales in TI's favor and made it possible to start applying integrated circuits to defense equipment in 1961 and to Minuteman and other programs in 1962.

Autonetics, a division of North American Aviation in California, held a major subcontract from Boeing on the Minuteman. TI had never been able to secure any business from the company. It took TI two years of determined efforts, including visits by Kilby and Phipps, and Air Force support to convince Autonetics that integrated circuits held the key to success for the Minuteman before TI finally won its first contract at Autonetics for slightly more than $9 million.

The Minuteman II, with its extended range, was valued as an essential part of America's strategic arsenal. Its new guidance computer, armed with more than 2,000 TI integrated circuits, was 50 percent lighter than its forerunners had been. It earmarked the integrated circuit as one of TI's major breakthroughs. Just as it had been with the introduction of the transistor, the electronics business was on the verge of undergoing another rapid growth period.

At TI, the work had only begun. Haggerty, no longer concerned with marketing integrated circuits, was suddenly faced with the fact that TI could not make enough integrated circuits to fulfill the Autonetics orders. TI had seriously miscalculated the problem of designing so many custom circuits in such a short time. Complications arose in trying to handle some 19 different integrated circuit types, both analog and digital, for the Minuteman computer—an unprecedented task in integrated circuit development. Phipps recalls that from the spring 1963 until almost year-end, TI struggled with the manufacturing process.

As Kilby remembered, "When we began to try to put all those different circuit types into production, and then to build up the production rates on all of them simultaneously,

things began to fall apart." Phipps commented, "Instead of delivering 1,000 per month, we were ripping off 50, 100, or 200 per month." Autonetics had schedules to keep, and TI was falling behind in its deliveries. In shifting engineers to solve Minuteman production problems, TI lost control of its Series 51 manufacturing process for integrated circuits used by other military customers—a major setback for TI.

Haggerty himself took charge of the production crisis, assuring Autonetics, "The next month or two will be critical, but I am more confident than ever that we will support your program adequately." He realized that TI was paying the price of pioneering a new technology. Nelle Johnson, his administrative assistant, would say, "I don't suppose that I saw him more than 10 minutes a day for two and half or three months because he was meeting with those guys [in production] from 8 in the morning until 7 at night until they hammered out whatever the problem was."

In September 1964, the Minuteman II was launched in a successful test flight from Cape Kennedy. TI received substantial follow-on contracts, and a 1965 Air Force decision to retrofit 800 earlier Minuteman missiles with integrated circuitry provided another $11 million in revenues for the company. The Minuteman III system, with improved warhead deployment and increased range, entered the silos in early 1970; the missiles contained large quantities of TI's integrated circuits.

Haggerty later could proudly point out the Minuteman II guidance computer was half the weight, used less than half as many devices, and consumed about half as much power as its predecessor. The new guidance computer was a little more than 36 pounds, but its heart and soul, the integrated circuit, weighed only two and a half grams. That was only the beginning. Within a short time, TI was selling devices similar to those designed for the Minuteman missile in the commercial marketplace, helping to spawn a new industry. As Phipps commented, "The Minuteman program allowed us to get integrated circuit complexity under our belt." Gene McFarland, a key marketing manager in the early integrated circuit years, added, "It also taught us about the learning curve and how to get our costs down."

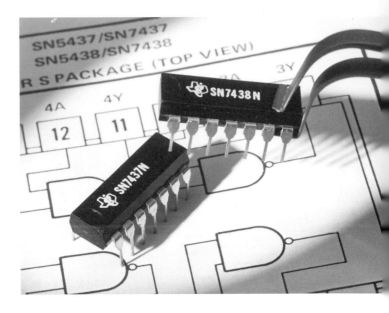

25

TTL TAKES THE MARKET

TI creates a revolution in circuit design and captures market leadership.

The decade of the 1950s was filled with technological fantasies of the vast potential of electronics. During the 1960s, those far-fetched dreams slowly began to take shape. Computers were no longer as large as the rooms that held them. Affordable semiconductor circuitry had made it possible for computers to be reduced to a reasonable size with sufficient capability for use in an office or factory. As integrated circuits came into the marketplace, manufacturers were under pressure to lower the cost to consumers by increasing the number of circuit elements on a chip. The industry tried many approaches to solve the problem. Through a series of innovative developments, Texas Instruments triggered a revolution in design, creating the standard for digital integrated circuits that would transform the electronics industry.

Early computers used vacuum tubes to perform logic functions, but they were seriously limited by the power and space required by the tubes and their poor reliability. Substituting transistors for vacuum tubes provided a solution to the power consumption issue. In 1958, however, Jack Kilby's integrated circuit offered the total solution that had been evading the industry. Kilby's technology made it feasible to convert older diode-tube solutions, and subsequently the diode-transistor logic models, to an integrated circuit implementation known as DTL, which integrated the diodes, transistors, and resistors on the chip. Other circuit configurations began to appear as companies battled for a competitive edge, but, as time went on, most of those

configurations faded from the marketplace.

One remained, however, and held the promise of simplifying circuit design. Developed outside TI, it was called Transistor-Transistor-Logic (TTL); its prime feature was smaller usage of silicon area, which could lead to lower costs. TI weighed the advantages and realized that TTL designs offered the potential for providing better speed-power performance than could be achieved with the older DTL designs.

When TI began working on a TTL product line in 1962, the company was focused primarily on military customers. TI had more than 100 military contracts and by 1963 was struggling with what seemed to be an unending sequence of manufacturing problems. The semiconductor division was hard at work to ensure that all possible corrective actions were taken, fully aware that schedules for military customers demanded top priority. TTL product development slowed dramatically as TI diverted its resources to resolve the problems threatening military integrated circuit production.

Fairchild, one of TI's chief competitors, was not engaged in a broad spectrum of military programs, and had invested its future on the familiar DTL circuit designs. An eager commercial market realized that DTL was the only immediate solution available for its needs. TTL might be better. It might be faster. But TTL was not yet ready for the market. Fairchild had the commercial market to itself, with a few other competitors rushing to produce their own brand of DTL.

TI's patience with TTL paid off. The company's step-by-step analysis of its production problems and its one-by-one application of solutions allowed the military's demanding schedules to be met, and TI began directing its focus on TTL. The task was to design a product and a process that would give TI an advantage over anything else in the marketplace.

The TI effort culminated in 1964, when Howard Moss unveiled an advanced series of high-speed integrated circuits at the National Electronics Conference in Chicago. TI's Series 54/74 featured eight distinct digital semiconductor networks that offered an unprecedented combination of advantages, including high-speed performance and lower power usage. As the company's press release pointed out, TI's multi-function concept employed in the Series 54/74 allowed up to four or more complete circuit functions to be fabricated within a single monolithic bar of silicon in a package measuring less than a thousandth of a cubic inch. With as many as 56 circuit elements—such as gates or inverters—available in each package, the cost per circuit function could be reduced by as much as 70 percent. In 1964, those were impressive numbers.

TI's TTL devices tripled the speed of DTL parts and, in a short time, became the preferred choice by customers. TTL was clearly superior, and DTL would soon fade from the marketplace.

Charles Phipps was put in charge of TI's marketing effort for integrated circuits. His team, led by specialist Bill Martin, worked closely with the principal design engineers, Billy and Bob Martin, who were brothers but not related to the marketer. Their strategy boiled down to two key points: field engineers must know and understand the product and be able to recite the advantages of the product as easily as they could remember their own names. And the design team would work shoulder-to-shoulder with field and internal marketers to define which circuit functions should be invented next. The designers had many ideas, and the TTL strategy was sound. The famous TTL Data Book emerged, changing the way a new generation of engineers would design electronic equipment.

The real breakthrough was the reduction of cost. Integrated circuits had typically been packaged in ceramic or metal packages with the chip connected to the external leads inside the hollow package. The package was held together with a glass sealing process. Plastic encapsulation would

MOON SHOT

The 54L low-power family had the distinction of being selected as NASA's choice to go to the moon and back. Tim Smith recalled, "After the return of the successful moon shot using 54L in its instrumentation, NASA personnel brought a printed circuit board that had been to the moon to the manufacturing line. The production workers were allowed to handle the product that made history. There were many tears of joy on that production line."

TI began publication of its TTL Data Books in the early 1970s; these became the standard reference for design engineers across the industry.

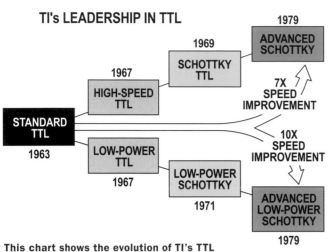

TI's LEADERSHIP IN TTL

STANDARD TTL — 1963

HIGH-SPEED TTL — 1967

SCHOTTKY TTL — 1969

ADVANCED SCHOTTKY — 1979

LOW-POWER TTL — 1967

LOW-POWER SCHOTTKY — 1971

ADVANCED LOW-POWER SCHOTTKY — 1979

7X SPEED IMPROVEMENT

10X SPEED IMPROVEMENT

This chart shows the evolution of TI's TTL products. By 1979, TI reported a 7x speed improvement and 10x power improvement over its 1963 technology.

HOW LOW-POWER SCHOTTKY (LS) WAS BORN

★ ★ ★

The idea for an LS family of chips was presented, but not approved by TI. Ed O'Neill, head of the Special Circuits department, squirreled away money within his budget and gave Tim Smith the go-ahead to "unofficially" work on the project. Years later, when Mark Shepherd presented the Patrick E. Haggerty Innovation Award to the key players on the LS design team—the Martin brothers, Smith, and Steve Baird—he said, "This is for having invented the single most profitable product line in the history of Texas Instruments." O'Neill himself also received the award for his vision.

have a significant cost advantage, but moisture might penetrate the plastic-to-metal lead interface, and it was well known that moisture and integrated circuit chips were incompatible. Also, the electrical connection from the bond pads on the chip to the external metal leads required extremely fine gold wire, which might be broken when plastic molding compound was forced into a cavity defining the shape of the finished product.

In 1961, TIers developed an innovative molding process that met the rigorous reliability and quality criteria of industry standards. A pilot production line was organized, and TI now had another substantial competitive advantage—manufacturing plastic packages, which cost about half as much as the ceramic packages. TI now had the competitive edge it had been seeking. Its TTL designs offered faster circuits, lower power usage, less noise, more complex circuit functions, and lower cost.

Those associated with America's space program were immediately attracted by the emerging TTL technology. Its ability to provide low power consumption was critical. The very low-power 54/74L family was introduced, followed by very high-speed 54/74H versions. Ultimately, the addition of a Schottky process provided the winning market acceptance of the 54/74LS low-power Schottky product.

With its TTL technology, TI gained a major share of the market. As Tim Smith recalls, "The bipolar designers at TI in the 1960s knew how to design products right the first time and on short schedules. We outpaced competition by advancing complexity faster, driving power per gate down, and by driving the TI volume cost learning curve."

Since TTL was in the midst of explosive growth, TI initially made the decision to produce integrated circuits in its Houston operation. Capacity was needed in Dallas fabs for a host of other product lines. Ultimately, however, TTL production was centered in the Sherman plant. Over the years, volume declined as TTL technology yielded to newer technologies, such as Complementary Metal Oxide Semiconductor (CMOS) and BiCMOS. Many applications remain, however, and TI produced more than a quarter of a billion TTL chips in 2003.

26

EARLY MOS DAYS: OPPORTUNITIES AND CHALLENGES

TI catches up in a promising new semiconductor technology.

The semiconductor business has evolved through many process technologies, each with inherent advantages and disadvantages, depending on the application. As with GSI's experience in the oil patch, there were "gushers and dry holes" in semiconductor process technology. Bipolar was a gusher in the early days of the semiconductor industry, and Texas Instruments resources were focused on bipolar for military and industrial applications. When consumer applications needed lower power, Metal Oxide Semiconductor (MOS) was the technology of choice. When customers needed more complex integrated circuits, Complementary MOS (CMOS) was the answer. Although TI was late to the market with MOS products, it mounted a determined effort in the early 1970s that made the company a process leader in MOS and later in CMOS, both from a revenue and a patent perspective.

Beginning in the mid-1960s the need for a class of large-scale integrated (LSI) circuits (greater than 100 gates per circuit) became evident. Two alternatives were considered: MOS (an approach being developed by competitors) and a bipolar discretionary wiring approach that showed promise, which was under development at TI.

The decision would affect the company for years to come. After much discussion, management decided to go with MOS and to offer discretionary wiring as an alternative.

In 1967, a fledgling MOS project was underway in Dallas but soon got into trouble on several military contracts due to process variables and cycle time. Charles Phipps was placed in charge of a small group of engineers who were working to develop the MOS process, with L.J. Sevin as the lead engineer. By the end of the year, the team succeeded in getting the process stabilized, and the first P-Channel MOS (PMOS) logic products were offered to the market. A 256-bit static MOS memory was introduced in 1968, and the team began to plan for complexities of 100 to 300 gates or more per chip. The MOS area was the first to take advantage of TI's new integrated circuit computer-aided design automation tools.

In 1968, TI established MOS manufacturing in its Houston plant, and some production people were moved from Dallas. Then, in the spring of 1969, the decision was made to move MOS design and administration people to Houston. Some engineers left the company rather than move to Houston. Several joined Mostek Corporation, which had

In 1978, TI's position was strengthened in MOS—the largest segment of the solid-state memory market—by the introduction of the single-voltage 64K-bit dynamic RAM. This product established a new benchmark for performance, as measured by power consumption, speed, and bar size.

64K-BIT DYNAMIC RAM

1/4 in.

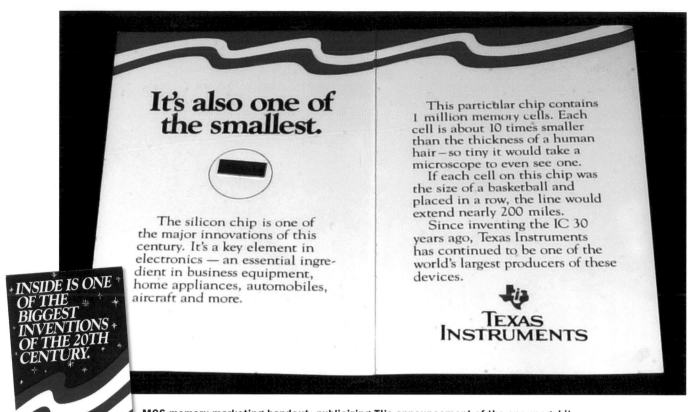

It's also one of the smallest.

The silicon chip is one of the major innovations of this century. It's a key element in electronics — an essential ingredient in business equipment, home appliances, automobiles, aircraft and more.

This particular chip contains 1 million memory cells. Each cell is about 10 times smaller than the thickness of a human hair—so tiny it would take a microscope to even see one.

If each cell on this chip was the size of a basketball and placed in a row, the line would extend nearly 200 miles.

Since inventing the IC 30 years ago, Texas Instruments has continued to be one of the world's largest producers of these devices.

TEXAS INSTRUMENTS

INSIDE IS ONE OF THE BIGGEST INVENTIONS OF THE 20TH CENTURY.

MOS memory marketing handout, publicizing TI's announcement of the one-megabit CMOS dynamic random access memory (DRAM).

been founded by Sevin and other former TIers, in nearby Carrollton, Texas. Notwithstanding that blow, by March 1970, the MOS manufacturing process in Houston was producing standard products and some custom products. However, a semiconductor industry slowdown the next year blunted TI's MOS efforts.

———

By 1972, the industry's MOS activity began a period of rapid growth. TI MOS logic then developed a series of multi-chip calculator sets for several customers. This new endeavor, using TIers with both technology and software backgrounds, led to early development work that successfully generated a single-chip calculator chip, implemented in PMOS.

PMOS product calculator demand, both internal and external (all custom), would soon swamp the design resources for MOS logic. By 1972, TI had split the MOS business into memory and logic. The company attempted to share in the growing microprocessor market by offering a product similar to Intel's 8080, but with limited success. The memory side of the division was grappling with the 1K Dynamic Random Access Memory (DRAM), and development was underway on the Electrically Programmed Read-Only Memory (EPROM).

In the early 1970s, a customer approached TI to develop a

1-K MOS memory, but the company elected not to pursue the contract because of insufficient design resources, so the customer went to Intel. Memory activities began in earnest when TI second-sourced Intel's 1-K DRAM. Later, TI began a conversion from metal gate to silicon gate designs, led by memory designer Clinton Kuo. In 1972, a decision had to be made to predict the next generation of DRAM, either 2K or 4K. TI started a 4K program which turned out to be the right choice. The 4-K DRAM became a significant product in the industry.

By 1974, TI had 4-K DRAMs (both an 18- and a 22-pin version) available and was set to become the market leader. However, Mostek introduced a 4-K DRAM (a 16-pin version) with a multiplexing system, which afforded improved speed, smaller size, and simplicity of installation. By 1977, TI decided to second-source the Mostek device.

———

In 1975, TI started development of the 16-K DRAM, but was late to market due to another semiconductor market recession. Major Japanese competitors began to enter the memory market at the 16-K level. The Japanese also had the 64-K in development. TI began development of the 64K in 1976. Dean Toombs remembers heated meetings where some thought it was too early to leap ahead to the 64K, and he did all he could to persuade the company to start early and do it right. He prevailed. TI's early position in the 64-K DRAM market and its innovative approach allowed development of strong memory patents which would prove to be a great asset. The company also entered the EPROM business—initially with a 12-volt device and later a 5-volt version, as well as the Static RAM market with a 1-K and 4-K product.

In 1981, market pressure for lower power revitalized TI's CMOS process development efforts. Combining efforts in research and design automation, the business groups under Tim Smith developed working CMOS products in record time. These processes formed the baseline for CMOS LSI products in memory, EPROMs, and many other activities, including analog-compatible processes. Bob England, who later ran the MOS memory business, recalled TI switched from NMOS to

TI pioneered the concept of small outline packages, making possible automated assembly which reduced the total system cost for customers.

CMOS at the one-megabit level in DRAMs. He commented that "Memory was the first semiconductor business in TI that had worldwide responsibility. At first, we had a U.S. manager, a Europe manager, a Japan manager, but we found we were competing against ourselves as our customers were going global. We had no choice but to switch to global pricing."

In 1986, 8 percent of TI semiconductor revenue was from CMOS products, compared to about 27 percent for the industry as a whole. Six years later, TI had closed the gap, reporting that its CMOS revenues were expected to be on par with the industry at about 70 percent of semiconductor division's total revenues. Significant breakthroughs were achieved in processes and designs, at increasingly high levels of quality, which became a way of life at TI. The MOS people responded with passion in getting the job done. Silicon-gate transistor cells, single-chip calculator chips, single-chip microcontrollers, cell interconnects, testing and packaging all positioned the semiconductor business for successful areas such as Digital Signal Processors and Charge-Coupled Devices.

LET'S MAKE A DEAL

★ ★ ★

On a business trip to Japan in the mid-1970s, Mark Shepherd bought an assortment of sleek, new Japanese calculators in the famous Tokyo shopping district. Back in the U.S., he dumped the calculators on the desk of Ron Ritchie, who headed TI's consumer operations, and grumbled, "Why can't you make them like this?" Ritchie called K. Bala into his office and said, "You have 24 hours to figure out how they do it." Bala, who was head of circuit design for the consumer business, together with his team dissected the calculators through the night. Well before the deadline, Bala announced, "They have CMOS." Ritchie told Bala to figure out a way to get CMOS. TI's semiconductor business had been focused on bipolar and had no interest in CMOS. Bala scratched his head, wondering how to catch up.

Jerry Moffitt, design manager working in TI Japan, just happened to be in Houston on a business trip, when he ran into Bala in the hallway. Bala explained his CMOS problem. Moffitt also had a problem; he had agreed to design circuits for TI consumer products in Japan, but was short of resources. Moffitt said, "Let's make a deal. I'll do the CMOS process if you'll do the chip designs." Bala said, "It's a deal." Moffitt agreed, with the provision that he would be able to sell the CMOS chips in Japan to outside customers.

By 1977, TI Japan had a metal-gate CMOS process, and Bala's team performed their end of the deal. As a result, TI's consumer business was first to have access to CMOS technology within TI.

27

THE EXPRESSWAY SITE

TI "bets the farm" on 300 acres of farmland.

TI has never been afraid to take risks. By 1955, the company had ambitious plans for growth on the drawing board and was ready to defy conventional wisdom by purchasing farmland about 11 miles north of downtown Dallas to be the site for a new semiconductor plant. The business and real estate community wondered about Texas Instruments' decision to build a plant so far out of town. Disregarding criticism, TI moved ahead. The site would become the crown jewel and headquarters for TI's growing network of worldwide facilities. The state of Texas later erected a historical marker on the site, recognizing the Semiconductor Building as the location of Jack Kilby's invention in 1958 of the integrated circuit—the chip that changed the world.

Erik Jonsson, always keeping an eye on the future, recognized the need to secure land for the company's long-range expansion. TI had already been forced to temporarily move its fledgling semiconductor operation to a vacant bowling alley down the street from its Lemmon Avenue plant. To relieve the crowding, TI began construction on a 33,000-square-foot addition to the Lemmon Avenue facility. Jonsson and Pat Haggerty realized that if TI's semiconductor plans materialized, the company would need even more room to grow.

Several sites were surveyed, but one patch of ground adjacent to U.S. 75, a major highway running north and south through Dallas, captured the imagination of the TI managers. The triangular-shaped site was bounded on the east by Floyd Road and on the south by Valley View Lane, stretching almost to Spring Valley to the north. The gentle slope of the landscape was drained by creeks, shaded by patches of trees, and dotted with a few farmhouses and an old sanitarium.

It would have been easier had the acreage all belonged to a single farm. But the tract consisted of more than 20 parcels of land, ranging in size from 1 ½ acres to 60 acres. This required negotiations with 23 different owners or their representatives for almost two months before the purchase was completed. More acreage was later acquired across Floyd Road, but by 1956, TI owned the 300 acres it needed to begin expansion.

During the mid-1950s, TI was a relatively small company for such a sizable real estate investment, and it was a gamble that employees could be persuaded to drive so far out of town to work. Ultimately, TI's move north helped spark a remarkable wave of growth and development in the communities surrounding Richardson, the town just north of TI's site.

Portions of the 300-acre tract had, in earlier times, belonged to John B. Floyd, who had served two terms in the Kentucky legislature before he and his wife and six sons journeyed to the fertile prairies of Texas in a covered wagon—driving their livestock as they went. They arrived on Christmas Day in 1855 at the village of Breckenridge, near the 900-acre farm Floyd had bought earlier for $4 an acre.

A year later, the pioneering Floyd family built the first two-story house in Dallas County on their farm, using lumber hauled from Jefferson, Texas, more than 100 miles away. For 17 years, the home served as an inn for travelers on the stage line between Houston, Dallas, and Denison. It was rumored that the famous and infamous alike stayed at the Floyd Inn, including such legendary outlaws as Belle Starr, Sam Bass, and Cole Younger. With the coming of the railroad, which ran across the Floyd property and through the small town of Richardson, the inn closed for good in 1873. Floyd's sons farmed, as well as operated a grocery store and lumberyards, after the death of their father. So many Floyd family members remained in the area that the Interurban Railway had its own "Floyd Stop" when the electric Interurban made its way north from Dallas to Denison.

In 1954, improvements were made to U.S. 75, and it became Central Expressway. Richardson became a thriving.

As TI looks to the future, it also pays tribute to the landscape's heritage. The early settlers who came to Texas brought with them vision and determination to establish a better community. They pioneered the land. TI is pioneering new technologies. Both made indelible legacies on the face of Texas.

progressive city—businesses and homes now dot the landscape where cotton and wheat once grew. In time, the sector from TI's property north would become known as "Telecom Corridor" because of the numerous technology companies serving the telecommunications field located there.

When TI began to develop the Expressway site, some doubted the company would ever need all the acreage. However, within 10 years, several major buildings were completed on the site, including the Semiconductor Building, Central Research Labs, Materials Building, North Building (for defense business), and the multi-purpose South Building. In time, three large semiconductor wafer fabs would also be built on the site, including Dallas Metal Oxide Semiconductor Six (DMOS 6), a 1 million square-foot wafer fab. DMOS 6 and the Kilby Research Center are recognized as technical marvels, involved in some of the most innovative, high-tech developments in the industry.

In the late 1960s, with continuing growth, TI took steps to secure a 135-acre site north of Forest Lane and east of the railroad track, which ran along Floyd Road. A 1.2 million square-foot facility was built for defense electronics on the Forest Lane site, and in 1997, the company's executive offices moved from the Expressway site (now called the North Campus) to the Forest Lane (South Campus) site.

In 1999, TI worked with the Dallas and Richardson city councils to change the name of a section of Floyd Road to TI Boulevard. The company worked with the Floyd family to preserve and protect the early heritage of North Dallas County by commissioning an oral history from the Dallas Public Library and building the Floyd Family Memorial alongside TI Boulevard.

WHAT HAPPENED TO THOSE FARMHOUSES?

★ ★ ★

When TI acquired the Expressway site, three weathered farmhouses and the old Elm Rest Sanitarium were still standing during construction of the Semiconductor Building. The first group to occupy the site was TI's defense business. In November 1957, an infrared optics testing group set up operations in the old sanitarium. TI engineers believed they would have to build a special tunnel for infrared testing, but discovered the 140-foot hallway in the center of the rock hospital building could be easily adapted as a testing tunnel. The optics team moved in and began conducting tests even before the building could be renovated.

Some of the farmhouses were used as offices for a few years before they were removed to make way for further development of the site. The farmhouses stood in stark contrast to the marble facade of the modern Semiconductor Building, the last link of two economies that shaped Texas—agriculture and technology.

28

INNOVATIONS IN ARCHITECTURE

Art and functionality combine to express TI's high-tech image.

Soon after acquisition of the 300-acre Central Expressway site, Texas Instruments began to plan a facility for its rapidly growing semiconductor business. It would be a building like no other. The overall specifications were given to three competing architectural firms; they were given one month to present their designs. The building had to be "exceedingly expansive." Each of the business entities in the building must have its labs, offices, and manufacturing space in close proximity. The building needed to express the institution and its overall character. Some might have walked away from the challenge, but one of the architectural firms had the vision to create a landmark of Texas architecture— the Semiconductor Building.

The winning team was O'Neil Ford of San Antonio and Richard Colley of Corpus Christi. Ford provided the creativity; Colley worked out the details and made the drawings, based on long hours of discussions with Erik Jonsson, Pat Haggerty, and the semiconductor managers. Sam Zisman, well known as a master planner, joined the team to handle site planning, and Felix Candela was recruited for his expertise in concrete shell construction. Candela provided the innovative hyperbolic paraboloid roof shell design to provide wide spans in two directions with minimum structural truss interference and a minimum of construction materials. A.B. Swank, a Dallas architect, joined the team as resident consultant. The Ford & Colley design would come to be known as the space-frame building concept.

The genius of the design was the space-frame floor—a 9-foot-high space sandwiched between an upper manufacturing floor and a lower floor for administrative and engineering space. A young architect working for Colley, Wally Wilkerson, is credited with designing the precast concrete tetrapods that made the space frame viable. He made a model of cardboard and toothpicks, which was brought to Dallas to explain the concept to Haggerty. The model passed its test and TI gave the go-ahead to the final design. The space frame supported the manufacturing floor with a large unobstructed space between columns (60.5 ft. x 60.5 ft.) and a loading of 200 pounds per square foot. The space frame was used to deliver utilities and gases up to the manufacturing floor and down to the office/lab level. Jonsson pointed out later that some 38 varieties of pipes could be found in the space frame. By having room for technicians to walk through the space frame, utilities and gases could be added or deleted anywhere in the building without interrupting business. This provided the ultimate in flexibility since processes changed frequently and new manufacturing lines were added overnight.

Space frame under construction at the site of TI's Semiconductor Building—1956–58. (Photograph by N. Bleeker Green.)

TI's Semiconductor Building after completion in 1958. (Photograph by N. Bleeker Green.)

As important as the structural details of the building and its flexibility were its decorative aspects, its charm and beauty, which could be seen in the durable Georgian marble on the exterior of the building and the beautiful artwork throughout the building. The interior garden courts, or patios, were designed to give employees visual relief from work requiring their close attention.

In a presentation in 1965, Haggerty said of the Semiconductor Building, "In the first two years of occupancy, there were about 250 new installations and approximately 650 moves requiring work on services...but no floor or wall openings, no structural or major building changes had to be made to accomplish these moves and installations." His dream of "exceedingly expansive" had been realized.

The first phase of the Semiconductor Building, containing some 300,000 square feet, was completed in 1958 by the construction firm of Robert E. McKee. Within a year, Phase II was added to the building. By 1965, there had been two more additions; the building ultimately reached 725,000 square feet—one of the world's largest semiconductor manufacturing buildings at the time.

The space-frame design concept, with modifications, would be used for many other TI manufacturing plants, including those in Attleboro, Massachusetts; Sherman and Houston, Texas; and international locations in England, Germany, France, and Italy. In time, TI's needs would change, and the architects would respond with innovative designs to keep TI competitive.

In the mid-1970s as TI's facility needs continued to grow,

TI's Dale Cunningham and Bill Lawson worked with Richard Colley's team in Corpus Christi to develop a new building concept. It addressed the growing cost of the space-frame building, with its heavy concrete structure requiring special forms, and the need for better space utilization for both manufacturing and special-purpose needs such as warehousing, cleanrooms, and taller equipment. TI wanted to make large buildings seem more human and to add small increments of space quickly, cost-effectively, with no disruption to adjacent operations. The Lubbock building was the first example of this new generation of TI buildings, which became known as the modular concept.

A long central spine tied to a central utilities plant near the center served as the backbone for the modular facility. Separate modules of 35,000 square feet each were "plugged into" the backbone as needed. There were special-purpose modules of different shapes and sizes to meet the needs for warehousing, wafer fabrication, cafeterias, lobby space, and hiring centers, as well as general purpose, office, and light manufacturing modules.

In the mid-1970s, as the line widths of semiconductor products continued to shrink and the processing became more complex and sensitive to air and chemical purity, it became necessary to build facilities and infrastructure that did not easily fit in conventional buildings or the TI space-frame buildings. The key issues were the volume of air that needed to be circulated and filtered, the height of the manufacturing equipment, and the amount, size, and complexity of infrastructure equipment that needed to be close to the manufacturing equipment. The resulting building design became the special-purpose Wafer Fab Building concept.

The first special-purpose design was constructed for Hiji, Japan. A concept initially used in the Dallas South Building was enlarged, and a two-level, flow-through building design was created. The entire metal grid floor was perforated with large fans on the lower level, which then pressurized a large plenum overhead that fed special air filters in the ceiling of the cleanroom. Utilities and special infrastructure such as vacuum pumps, electrical transformers, chemical and gas delivery systems, drains, treated exhausts, and process cooling systems were housed in the clean air return space on the lower floor.

The design evolved from a two-level building with variable

DEDICATION OF THE SEMICONDUCTOR BUILDING

★ ★ ★

On June 23, 1958, TI's new Semiconductor Building was officially dedicated. The ceremonies included a dramatic ribbon cutting by a high-voltage arc activated by a beep from the U.S. satellite *Vanguard*. The honor of pushing the button to activate the beeps, which had been prerecorded on a TI *magne*DISC recorder, went to Mark Shepherd, then Vice President of the Semiconductor Division, and Walter H. Brattain, co-inventor of the transistor at Bell Labs, who attended the ceremonies.

After speeches by Jonsson, Haggerty, and other dignitaries, an army of 60 white-coated TIers conducted tours through the new building. The day before, they had escorted some 9,000 TIers and their families on tours. The celebration continued the following day, with a seminar on transistor technology, which included discussions from military representatives and prominent scientists.

pitch vane axial fans and large infrastructure spaces to a three-level design with fan-filter units for air distribution. The latest version is a two-level fab for 300-mm production. These wafer fab buildings cost thousands of dollars per square foot of cleanroom and must allow change-out of equipment and processes without disruption to the manufacturing processes. The systems must be reliable so that production on over $2 billion worth of equipment is never interrupted.

Lewis McMahan, current manager of TI's worldwide facilities commented, "As we enter the 21st century, the facility design challenges revolve around reliability and cost. Most of TI's facilities assets are related to semiconductor wafer manufacturing and assembly. Both operate around the clock almost 365 days per year. As the value of the products in production continues to rise, the avoidance of unplanned interruptions from facilities infrastructure systems becomes critical. We also have the challenge of lowering our operating cost to be competitive with Asian foundries. A key is the lowering of initial capital investment as well as efficient systems with many energy conservation features such as high-efficiency equipment, heat recovery exhaust systems, and recycling systems, for deionized water processes."

Pat Haggerty watches while Mark Shepherd, left, and Walter H. Brattain, co-inventor of the transistor at Bell Labs, push the button to cut the ribbon at the opening of TI's Semiconductor-Components Building.

In commenting on plans for TI's newest fab, McMahan said, "The results of this approach are being incorporated in the new fab to house 300-mm manufacturing and development in Richardson, Texas." The design was developed with architect Alfonso Mercurio of Rome, who is renowned for his high-tech designs around the world. The Richardson Fab will cost approximately 30 percent less per square foot than the DMOS 6 design and be more reliable.

Mercurio's first wafer fab project for TI was in Avezzano, Italy, in 1990. Because of his grasp of the complexities involved in air handling, gas and chemical distribution, and the support systems, Mercurio's designs have evolved with the business. He has been involved in every major TI semiconductor facility since that time, including the Kilby Research Center and DMOS6 in Dallas.

TI continues to see its image and values expressed in its architecture.

EXPANSION TO EUROPE

TI becomes a leading force in the European semiconductor market.

In the mid-1950s, Texas Instruments recognized the importance of European semiconductor markets and realized they could not be effectively handled by sales efforts or exports from the company's U.S. operations. The European markets warranted special treatment, and TI decided to develop wholly owned manufacturing facilities in major European countries. Such a move would help establish a stronger liaison with European customers, satisfying their desire for indigenous suppliers. Bold, early steps in Europe positioned TI to meet overseas competitors head on, and lead the market in the shift from local plants for local markets to worldwide strategic management affecting all phases of product development, manufacturing, and marketing.

Texas Instruments' first semiconductor operation in Europe became a reality in 1957 when TI began production in Bedford, England, using a small, leased facility on the appropriately named "Dallas Road," until a permanent plant, designed by TI architect Richard Colley, could be completed in 1960. A year earlier, Cecil Dotson had moved to England as Chairman of the Board of Texas Instruments Limited.

The operation was quickly up and running, producing the crystals needed to make transistors. There were no local suppliers of the material. Texas Instruments Limited soon was manufacturing transistors, including what would be a very successful line of power transistors.

After successfully launching operations in Bedford, Dotson was chosen to head TI's International Operations. In 1959, he and Mark Campbell traveled across the continent to assess market potential in other European countries. They selected France as the next expansion site primarily because of a growing computer market there being efficiently developed by IBM, one of TI's most important customers.

Buddy Harris convinced TI's management that the availability of labor in Nice, along the French Riviera, and its beautiful location would attract professionals with technical expertise. According to Dotson, "TI wanted a super, permanent location on the French Cote d'Azur, and the company found one on a hill overlooking Villeneuve-Loubet, a town at the outskirts of Nice. It was situated

TI's European sales force in early 1959 studies maps of countries within this marketing area. Standing (left to right) are Monroe Maller and Cecil Dotson, head of European operations, and seated, Bob Cohen and Mark Campbell.

The TI-Nice facility, built in 1963, sits atop a mountain overlooking the Mediterranean Sea. This facility served as headquarters for TI-Europe.

on land rich with history, even topped by a ninth-century castle owned by a noble family—Marquis Panese Pacis. The family sold part of their land to TI, provided that a row of trees be planted to hide the building."

Under the management of Mark Campbell, the facility opened in 1964 as an assembly and test site located in a temporary factory building. Many transistors were assembled there and in the beautiful new permanent plant that succeeded it.

The consumer products market drove TI's choice of Freising in Bavaria as its next manufacturing location in Europe. Near the cosmopolitan center of Munich, the plant had access to a good labor supply, and the facility went on line in 1966 with 20 women producing diodes. In February 1966, a TI-designed plant became operational, and a large order from Siemens—requiring a German manufacturer—launched TI's integrated circuit production a year later.

In 1970, an assembly plant opened in Rieti, Italy, to serve the European market. Rome and its airport were nearby, and there was a good labor supply. The operation paved the way for a large memory wafer fab to be established in neighboring Avezzano in 1990.

Jim Hubbard, who later ran European operations, recalls that, "In the early 1980s, the political impetus toward the European Common Market gained momentum, and it was obvious that the long-discussed union would finally happen. In order to lead the inevitable Common Market transition, the managers for TI's sales, products, and support functions now reported to TI's Europe manager instead of the historical 'by-country' setup. This was a ground-breaking step in the European culture. For example, the responsibilities of a French sales manager or a German product manager spanned all European countries. It was a definite early challenge, but one in which TI excelled ahead of most competitors and customers."

A significant organization change came in the late 1980s when TI-Europe moved toward TI globalization. A matrix structure was established wherein the European product and sales organizations were tied directly to the TI worldwide organization, as well as to the European managers. The resultant improvements in TI synergy in interfacing with customers were significant.

These changes accompanied some shifting of resources. As the world increasingly turned toward integrated circuits, Bedford manufacturing was committed to mature technologies, including the successful power transistor to support European customers who required discrete semiconductor devices. Bedford's manufacturing facilities were divested from TI in the 1990s as part of the company's decision to focus its semiconductor business on Digital Signal Processing and Analog. Operations in Rieti and Avezzano were also divested because of changes in TI's business plans. TI marketing began serving U.K. and Nordic countries from offices in Northhampton, whose design center specialized in combining analog and digital design techniques.

The Nice plant eventually became recognized as TI's Wireless Center of Competence. TI's wireless business originated in Europe, thanks to the expertise and the regional presence of such major Original Equipment Manufacturers as Nokia and Ericsson.

The wafer fab at Freising ultimately grew with the success of TI's analog semiconductors; the competencies at Freising were defined by its high performance analog, low-power microcontrollers, Application Specific Integrated Circuits, automotive, broadband communications, and radio frequency identification activities.

TI's product thrusts were further enhanced during the late 1990s with selective acquisitions to support the present and future product roadmaps. ATL Research in Denmark, Condat in Germany, and Butterfly in Israel are now part of TI's worldwide wireless activities. Libit, also in Israel, is part of the company's DSP Systems group. From these locations came the vital design effort for TI wireless products. Currently, TI has 25 sites in Europe in 14 different countries.

The company's partnership with Nokia flourished with shipment of the first Nokia phones containing TI's DSP chip in 1996, and, in 2004, TI and Nokia celebrated the shipment of 1 billion DSPs. Ericsson's work with mobile platforms and

TI's plant in Freising, Germany, was officially opened in June 1970 and specializes today in the manufacture of mixed-signal integrated circuits.

Third Generation (3G) gave TI the edge over semiconductor competitors around the world. Alcatel and Siemens continue to partner with TI on expanding opportunities for the company's wireless capabilities.

As the years passed, TI's European customer list was headlined by companies with a diverse range of products. Bosch and Continental Teves primarily served automotive markets. Philips used TI DSPs, as well as components for several other consumer electronic products. Thomson introduced televisions using TI's Digital Light Processors, and SAGEM was instrumental in taking TI technology to military, consumer, and office markets.

In order to maintain a highly competitive posture and a major market presence in Europe, TI progressed through three critical organizational transitions. During its first four decades in European markets, TI encountered and successfully resolved numerous obstacles. But dealing with the many challenges meant growth, and growth was tantamount to success in countries whose culture and language were very diverse. TI's aggressive early moves into Europe, coupled with a highly developed and flexible marketing organization, provided TI with a firm foundation for the critical penetration of an ever-expanding global market.

As Jean-Francois Fau, current President of TI-Europe, said, "As a result of our efforts to be close to our customers, developing unique technological competencies in Europe and adopting a solutions-based approach, we have been able to seize outstanding growth opportunities at major market players

in sectors such as communication, automotive, and industrial. In a region as diverse as Europe, being close to customers, speaking to them in their own terms, and sharing their work culture has been instrumental to our success."

BUSINESS EXCELLENCE

★ ★ ★

In 1993, TI-Europe adopted the European Foundation for Quality Management business excellence model, providing a common methodology across the company to bring TI's diverse businesses into harmony. A year later, TI-Europe was named a finalist for the European Quality Award, and, in 1995, the company was recipient of the award.

TI-Europe won Dataquest's European Semiconductor of the Year Award four times in a row, with the last one in 1998, which was the last year the honor was bestowed. Based on an extensive survey of 200 leading purchasers of semiconductors throughout Europe, the award rated companies on delivery, quality, responsiveness, technical support, price, supplier flexibility, and overall performance.

[30] ENTERING THE JAPANESE MARKET

It took six years for TI to gain its own facility in Japan.

Texas Instruments' struggle to enter Japan was long and arduous, but rewarding. No one dreamed it would take six years for TI to establish its own facility on Japanese soil. Negotiating rules were different. Final terms were extraordinary. It would have been easier for TI to leave the bargaining table and search for opportunities elsewhere, but TI had long regarded the Japanese market as a prime target, and ultimately TI-Japan became a major contributor to TI's growth.

Mark Shepherd (TI President), Alexis Johnson (U.S. Ambassador), Masaru Ibuka (Sony President), Bryan Smith (TI Senior Vice President), Akio Morita (Sony Vice President) at a TI reception in Japan for the patent licensees in 1968.

In the early 1960s, Japanese customers such as Mitsubishi, Sony, Canon, IBM Japan, and Furukawa, the parent company of Fujitsu, had expressed interest in having TI provide supply and support from one or more locations in Japan. Accordingly, TI mapped out a plan for placing sales, engineering, and manufacturing facilities in Japan to serve its customers. TI would use virtually the same blueprint for expansion it had implemented elsewhere. At the time, TI was relying on Japanese trading companies, such as Marubun and Sumitomo, to supply TI products to Japanese customers.

TI invested time and resources in an effort to bring business operations to Japan. In 1963, Joe Emery was sent to Hong Kong to conduct TI business, as well as to assess potential factory locations. Earlier, Ben Schranil had been sent to Japan as TI's first sales representative. He located in Nagoya in 1962 to support Mitsubishi, a customer for TI's electrical control products. Mitsubishi Heavy Industries had licensed a compressor from Tecumseh, a major North American electrical control customer, and was manufacturing the compressors, which used motor protectors and starters made by TI's M&C operation.

In early January 1964, working with representatives of Japan's Ministry of International Trade and Industry (MITI), TI submitted a formal application to establish a wholly-owned subsidiary in Japan. Discussions continued sporadically, but

it took more than two years before Japan officially replied to TI's request. Informally, MITI explained that it would be necessary for TI to form a joint venture with a Japanese partner, which would then market and sell the company's products.

In November 1964, MITI agreed to continue its evaluation of TI's application, if the company would license its integrated circuits to Japanese companies, but TI would not agree to license until all of the major issues in its application had been worked out. By licensing its patents, TI would lose its only leverage in the negotiations. For two years, neither side showed any signs of budging.

To service the market while the negotiations continued, TI formed a TI-Asia sales subsidiary, which began with three employees: Mitsi Yako, the first employee, who handled administrative work; Eiji Kamisaku, as salesman (based in Tokyo); and Joe Emery, as manager. TI-Asia moved into its office—one small room in the Osaka Grand Hotel. Emery later recalled, "I could hold my arms straight out ...and touch both sides of the room. We took out that single bed and put in two desks for the three of us. One had to stand up. The files and brochures were all dumped in the bathtub." They soon hired Norio Yamada as a sales representative for semiconductor products, convincing him during his hotel room interview

Located on a hilltop in Hiji, Oita Prefecture, on Kyushu Island, the plant was TI-Japan's second manufacturing facility. The first phase was completed in 1973.

NEGOTIATING A SITE

★ ★ ★

When Bill Sick moved to Tokyo as president of TI-Japan in 1971, he found a small operation with a single assembly plant in Hatogaya, with Bill Dees as plant manager. The Hatogaya plant became a worldwide leader in productivity and yields. As demand increased, TI decided to build a second Japanese plant at Hiji. A beautiful site was chosen, perched on a hilltop overlooking the sea, but a lengthy negotiation was required to acquire the site.

Akira Ishikawa, who had been hired earlier by Sick and sent to the U.S. for training, returned to Japan to supervise construction of the Hiji plant and to manage upon its completion. Working with Ando Construction, Ishikawa developed a detailed project plan consisting of eight-hour increments for completion of the construction in about seven months, half the normal time for a plant of this size. Ishikawa told Sick, "You don't need to worry about this project, just set the date for the opening ceremony from my project plan and show up."

From time to time Ishikawa would report on how many hours he was ahead or behind the schedule. When Sick arrived for the opening ceremony on the projected date, the plant was nearly perfect. Even the landscaping was in place, although steam was still rising off the hot asphalt, which had been completed the night before. The employees presented the first day's production to Sick, who later said, "I cannot remember that the Hiji plant ever missed a production schedule. Productivity, yields, and quality were outstanding and attendance was nearly perfect."

The plant also became a leader in quality. Ishikawa engaged the leaders in the Japan Quality movement, called TQC, which was several years ahead of quality efforts in other countries of the world. TI-Hiji would later win the Deming Prize, the first time  this prestigious award was given to a foreign-owned company. This experience in Japan became a primary foundation for the TI Total Quality Program, at first in the semiconductor business and later throughout TI.

The first phase of the Miho site was completed in 1980.

that TI was indeed a "big corporation." A small beginning, but the team had big plans.

To speed up MITI approval, TI notified the U.S. government that Japan had not yet replied to its application for foreign investment in the country. During the Japanese-U.S. cabinet meetings held in Kyoto during July 1966, Secretary of Commerce John T. Connor brought up Japan's lack of response to TI's investment request, now two and a half years old.

Two months later, MITI sent a written response to TI's original proposal, giving specific conditions for approval of the company's petition: the new company must be a 50-50 joint venture with a Japanese company, production would be limited for the first three years, and TI was obligated to license its patents to Japanese industry.

TI did not believe a joint-venture structure would work in the fast-paced, competitive electronics marketplace. TI was also determined to withhold the licensing of its patents until all issues had been resolved. Neither TI nor MITI would back down. The contentious negotiations placed MITI in an awkward position. Many Japanese companies wanted to export their products to Europe and the U.S., but they needed TI's patents, particularly the Kilby integrated circuit patent.

While discussions continued with MITI, TI began negotiating with the Sony Corporation as a potential joint-venture party. TI had a good relationship with Sony, and Pat Haggerty had great respect for Dr. Ibuka and Dr. Morita of Sony. In 1968, TI and Sony defined and agreed on a partnership capitalized at 100 million yen. TI would retain management control of the company, and, after three years, TI would have the option of buying Sony's share for 50 million yen, thus becoming the sole owner. In return, TI agreed to license its patents to Japanese industry. TI-Japan was incorporated under Japanese law on May 24, 1968. The next step was to find a manufacturing facility.

Eiji Kamisaku had been scouting possible locations as he drove his Nissan around the country on TI-Asia business. In three months, he had checked out more than 70 sites. The best of these was a 40,000-square-foot building about an hour's drive north of Tokyo in Hatogaya. The facility was previously owned by Simplicity Patterns, then rented by Colgate to manufacture toothpaste. It would soon become a semiconductor assembly plant.

In December 1971, MITI approved TI's acquisition of Sony's interest in the joint venture, and TI-Japan became a wholly-owned TI subsidiary.

Two years later, TI-Japan added a Metal Oxide Semiconductor (MOS) fab to its Hatogaya factory and built a new semiconductor factory in Hiji on Kyushu Island, Oita Prefecture. Oyama, almost in the shadow of Mt. Fuji, was chosen as the site for an electrical controls plant in 1979, and in 1980, TI-Japan opened a major MOS facility in Miho, near the Narita airport. TI's first research and development center outside of the U.S. was built near Miho in the 1980s.

TI-Japan's wafer fabs were to remain competitive with other fabs around the world. Miho played a major role in TI's global success when the techniques pioneered there were replicated at other TI fabs around the world. The plant also gained recognition as the worldwide center for TI's mixed-signal process development (with digital and analog functions on one chip).

As the electronic age moved into the 21st century, K. Bala, then chairman of TI-Japan, said, "The first thing I noticed when I came to Japan in 2002 was that the Japanese are always striving for perfection in anything they do. For instance, trains that arrive every three minutes are not late even a few seconds. This is part of the Japanese culture, and our Japanese customers demand perfection from TI more than any other customer anywhere. We, at TI-Japan, always expect that product specs and delivery requirements are met as contracted, or, if possible, we do even better than that."

TI-Taiwan plant was completed in 1970 in Chung Ho. The plant has since been expanded and is a key supplier of integrated circuits to TI customers throughout the world.

31

WORLDWIDE SEMICONDUCTOR ASSEMBLY

TI builds a world-class semiconductor assembly operation benefiting from diverse cultures around the globe.

Texas Instruments faced competitive pressure when the company belatedly began to develop semiconductor assembly and test sites around the world. There were logistical problems and language barriers and unfamiliar customs, but with determination and creativity, TI developed a world-class assembly and test operation, strengthened by the diversity of many cultures.

As demand for semiconductors grew rapidly in the early 1960s, TI needed more assembly capacity. Wafer fab operations were highly capital intensive but not labor intensive. The assembly operation was labor intensive although it employed machines to help operators connect and test millions of semiconductor units. The demand for integrated circuit assembly was so critical that TI initiated free bus service to transport production operators from all over the Dallas area to the South Building in the late 1960s.

Major semiconductor competitors such as Fairchild and Motorola did not have an organization like TI's internal equipment operation—the Process Automation Center (PAC). Instead, those competitors solved their assembly needs by moving to locations in the Far East. At the time, TI thought the cost challenge could be offset with greater productivity from machines built by PAC. However, explosive growth within the industry enticed many small equipment makers to improve the manual workstations Fairchild and Motorola used in overseas operations. TI could no longer rely solely on the benefits of PAC and automation to maintain a competitive balance.

Other challenges appeared, as some countries erected import barriers, giving preferential treatment based on the location of a company's factories. For example, Canadian products—but not U.S. products—could be imported into England duty free.

TI responded by opening a small transistor assembly operation, led by Ron Ritchie, in the M&C electrical controls plant in Richmond, Canada.

Pat Haggerty strongly preferred to keep the assembly business at home by relying on automation. But as costs rose and unit demand steadily increased, Haggerty searched for other options and soon realized he had none.

When the decision was made to set up overseas operations, TI moved quickly. Curacao, under the direction of Ritchie, became TI's first major assembly operation outside the U.S., opening in April 1968. The transistor assembly operation was moved from Canada to speed the startup. Since Curacao was an autonomous state within the Dutch kingdom, products produced on Curacao were given tax-free entry into the European Common Market, making it possible to serve a broader base of customers in Europe. As transistor orders later slowed, the Curacao plant became surplus capacity, and its doors were closed after five years.

Assembly operations began in Malaysia in 1972 in a leased facility and later moved to this new TI facility in Kuala Lumpur, Malaysia.

During a trip to Asia in 1967, Haggerty met with industrialists from Taiwan and Singapore who encouraged him to consider placing assembly operations in their countries. They appealed to Haggerty's economic sensibilities, explaining that TI's foreign investments would benefit their countries. Haggerty returned home, and TI, without hesitation, decided to open its next major assembly and test facility in Taiwan.

In August 1967, TI began planning for a plant in Taipei, asking for guarantees from the Taiwan government that TI's patents would be respected. The negotiations and TI's application for investment dragged on for months. It took two years to start production. Because of the delays, plans for increasing capacity were at a standstill, and TI had to consider other alternatives.

In 1968, when Mark Shepherd met with the Economic Development Board in Singapore while searching for other potential assembly plant sites, he looked around the city and concluded "this could be the place." He asked Cecil Dotson to lead a fact-finding mission throughout Asia to choose a prime location with stable, cooperative governments, and skilled people, including graduate engineers.

In Dallas, Chuck Anders and his team, preparing for the Taiwan start-up venture, were told to exchange their airline tickets. They were to head to Singapore instead. The Singapore negotiations had been quick and decisive; it took only 50 days for TI's Board of Directors to approve the move, relocate personnel, refurbish exsiting facilities, install equipment, hire and train workers, and begin the assembly phase. The press would refer to the start up enterprise as "the 50 day wonder." At the official opening of the Singapore plant in 1969, Shepherd said, "We have achieved the fastest operation start-up in the history of TI."

In 1968, TI established an International Semiconductor Trade Organization to address the challenges of a large multinational assembly operation, with John Brougher serving as its first manager. TI's assembly operations were designated as Fabrication Customer Centers (FCC), and as service centers, they were evaluated by cost, quality, and on-time delivery. A communications and computer system was developed to share production specifications and information around the world. Scheduling, shipping, and other logistical functions were transferred electronically in a seamless, automated fashion. It was critical that a product manufactured in one plant be able to meet the quality and performance standards of the same products made in other company facilities.

With growing demand, the FCC structure made it possible for TI to establish a major assembly facility in Kuala Lumpur. The Malaysian government was cooperative during the negotiations and the country could provide sufficient assembly personnel. Malaysia offered incentives, and a pool of technical expertise was available in nearby Singapore. In November 1972, only 83 days after TI officially opened its discussions with Malaysia, plant manager Mike O'Brien flipped the switch inside a temporary building to trigger the assembly of integrated circuits. In another part of Kuala Lumpur, the Malaysian government was already preparing a new building TI would lease as a permanent factory.

TI's worldwide assembly network enabled the company to remain competitive with semiconductor producers in Japan and the Far East. As Haggerty commented in 1972, "Our plants in Taiwan and Singapore have allowed us to manufacture products at costs which, when combined with our own superior U.S. technology, both product and process, enable us to feel confident in our ability to compete on an equal basis with any Japanese producer."

During the mid-1970s, integrated circuits evolved to higher pin counts and more complex packages. The new designs required different assembly approaches, and TI's facilities in Asia had run out of space. The company began looking elsewhere.

TI decided to build a new plant in the Philippines in Baguio, tucked on the crest of a mountain about 100 miles north of Manila. The view was breathtaking, but all materials had to be trucked in from Manila. Labor was plentiful, but TI found it difficult, but not impossible, to persuade Manila's young professionals to move to such a remote region. Problems were immense, but not insurmountable, and in April 1980, under the leadership of Mike O'Brien, a dedicated start-up team began production. Today, Baguio has become a popular mountain resort city, and TI continues to expand facilities on its 62-acre high-country site.

Investment considerations and incentives were important factors when TI prepared to develop assembly plants in South America. Profits from the company's M&C operation in Campinas, Brazil, were coupled with export incentives to establish a facility in the city. By the end of 1973, TI employed 1,400 workers to assemble semiconductor products there.

TI helped El Salvador expand its economy beyond farming, adding technology with an assembly operation there in 1974. Bernie Yurin headed the team that trained farmers and textile workers to become assemblers of integrated circuits. Though the plant was a boon to the economy in El Salvador, TI had to close the facility in 1985 because of a downturn in the world semiconductor market.

When Mexico wanted to increase exports in 1984 (TI's M&C business had been long established there since the 1950s), it was logical for TI to bring its semiconductor manufacturing to the region. Cliff Gibbs, after almost two years of negotiations, obtained approvals and started up the Aguascalientes site. The plants would work side by side— the semiconductor operations located in Aguascalientes, and Sensors & Controls, formerly M&C, in nearby Ciudad Morelos.

TI's worldwide assembly operations were successful because each of the plants was part of a system that included leadership, equipment, and motivated TIers in addition to excellence in information technology and quality. The plants gave TI the flexibility to move product from one site to another, or have multiple products sourced from multiple international locations. The cultures may have been diverse and the languages different, but the productivity and quality TIers achieved in the assembly plants were major factors in TI's position as a leader in the world semiconductor market.

The TI-Philippines plant completed in 1980 is on a hilltop in Baguio, Philippines.

Charles Liu in front of an office supply store in Beijing, China—the first retailer of TI calculators in China. (Photo courtesy of Charles Liu.)

32

PROGRESS IN CHINA

TI emerges as a major supplier to a country once isolated by culture and political ideology.

Few countries captivated the imagination of the semiconductor industry quite like China. It was the unknown country, veiled from the rest of the world by culture, distance, and political ideology. Deng Xiaoping, who emerged to lead China after the death of Chairman Mao in 1976, recognized the opportunity for opening up China's markets to competition and established special economic zones where foreign trade and investment could flourish. According to the World Bank, since 1978, these reforms have brought 250 million people out of poverty, creating an ever-expanding base of new consumers. In 1975, with no direct business in the country, Texas Instruments began a far-reaching strategy of building a long-term relationship with China. During the next three decades, TI emerged as a major supplier of a broad range of products to customers throughout China.

In 1972, President Richard M. Nixon startled the world by traveling to Communist China in a bold attempt to break down the barriers of the Cold War. His journey signaled a new era of political relations and trade opportunities. In Dallas, this presidential visit gave hope to a young Chinese engineer, Charles Liu, working in TI's defense business. He was separated from his parents when he was sent to Taiwan

In December 2004, TI's Sensors & Controls (S&C) business announced the opening of a new factory in Changzhou, Jiangsu Province of China, and the establishment of Texas Instruments (Changzhou) Co. Ltd. The 200,000-square-foot factory is scheduled to begin production of thermoelectric motor protectors for customers in China in early 2005. Operations will expand to include production of pressure switches and pressure sensing devices for the heating, ventilation, and air conditioning markets, as well as export sales. The new factory adds to S&C's capacity for manufacturing sensors and control products in China, serving the growing Chinese market and markets around the world.

to attend school. Then he went to college in Plainview, Texas, and finally received his BSEE and MSEE degrees from the University of Illinois. He joined TI in 1966 and longed for the day he could return to visit his parents. It would be a long wait.

Liu began reading everything he could find about China's technological needs, comparing those to TI's product lines. He decided to focus on energy, transportation, and communications—talking to everyone in TI he could about the vast opportunities awaiting TI in China. Associates quietly warned Liu, "You better be careful. Don't stick your neck out. It might get chopped off."

But Liu was undaunted. He decided GSI might be the best way to build a bridge between TI and his native country, so he enrolled in two Dallas universities to improve his knowledge of geophysics. He later moved into TI's Corporate Marketing and studied ways to develop a China strategy for TI. His big break came in 1977 when the company dispatched him to China to solve a customer's problem, and he finally had a chance to visit his family. Liu traveled to China a year later and was successful in establishing contacts with the China National Petroleum Company.

In 1979, Liu was selected as the one TIer to accompany TI President Fred Bucy as part of a trade delegation to China appointed by President Jimmy Carter. It was TI's first high-level contact with China, marking the beginning of the company's effort to penetrate China's burgeoning markets.

Within three years, GSI, under the leadership of Dolan McDaniel, was awarded more than $65 million for a three-year contract for land seismic exploration in the remote Tarim Basin within the Gobi Desert. It was the single largest contract in GSI's history, and was followed by a $35 million seismic data collection equipment contract. Liu continued to work on business opportunities for other groups within TI, including consumer products. In 1977, he was able to convince a store in Beijing to be the first to sell the TI-59 scientific calculator in China.

When he was in charge of the Ministry of Electronics, Chinese President Jiang Zeming led a delegation to Dallas in 1984 which led to TI establishing its first representative office in Beijing a year later with only two TI staff members. The number of employees in China grew exponentially during the following years. Today, TI has sales and marketing offices in Beijing, Shanghai, Shenzhen, Suzhou and Hong Kong providing full application engineering support for semiconductor customers.

TI's semiconductor effort has evolved from customers choosing individual devices from TI's portfolio of products (a catalog approach) to a total system solution focus that emphasizes both hardware and software. Today, TI works to create a system design support model, which is engineered to help customers compete globally on the leading edge of product development. By working with top Chinese equipment manufacturers, TI influences a broad range of other companies that are considering TI solutions for their individual designs.

Boosted by growth in China's electrical appliance market, TI's Materials & Controls business formed a joint venture in China, opening a plant in the Baoying Economic Development Zone in Baoying, Jiangsu, China, in 1996. Within two years, TI acquired 100 percent equity in the joint venture, which supplied motor protectors and other control products.

Tom Engibous, TI's CEO at the time, met with President

Baoying is the site for the first manufacturing facility of Sensors & Controls in China.

Jiang Zeming in 2000, strengthening TI's relationship with China. TI became involved with communities where its employees worked and supported engineering programs at Chinese universities. In addition, manufacturing relationships were established with key Chinese foundries (companies providing wafer manufacturing services), including Semiconductor Manufacturing International Corporation (SMIC).

TI is involved in several joint ventures in China including DigiPro, DigiVision, and Commit which are involved in standards development. These joint ventures focus on the digital consumer, broadband, and wireless markets. TI's DLP™ business is committed to being an active player in China because the country is the world's number one producer of television sets, as well as the world's number two market for television sales..

China has emerged as the world's sixth-largest economy, with a gross domestic product of $1.4 trillion in U.S. dollars. China is recognized as the third-most-active trading nation, ranking behind the U.S. and Germany. In 2003, China's

1.3 billion people purchased 23 percent of the world's television sets and 20 percent of the world's cell phones—both critical markets for TI in China.

By 2004, China was moving aggressively into the semiconductor foundry business. After working with SMIC, TI realized the Chinese were capable of performing additional process steps on wafers started in TI's 130-namometer (nm) copper-interconnect process, thus freeing up capacity in one of TI's wafer fabs in Dallas. (A nanometer is a billionth of a meter.) SMIC qualified its 130-nm process for TI in mid-2003 and promptly began working to develop its own 90-nm process.

China could become the world's second-largest economy, and TI plans to be part of China's continuing growth. This critical partnership has been forged, in part, from the early work of many TIers, a long-term commitment by TI, and the dedication of one young man—Charles Liu—who yearned for a chance to go home again.

33

THE QUALITY CHALLENGE

TI launches a company-wide emphasis on quality and reliability to counter increased Japanese competition.

TI's semiconductor business had always emphasized the quality and reliability of its products. During the early 1980s, however, the bar was raised. The company became increasingly aware of Japan's emergence as a market leader, particularly in color televisions, automobiles, and even in semiconductor. Texas Instruments could either defend the quality of its products or find new ways to improve them. TI made a commitment to Total Quality throughout the company and achieved international recognition for its quality and reliability.

For almost a decade, TI had been grudgingly aware that Japan was making steady but significant advances in improving the quality of its products. As early as 1973, TI's analyses of competitors' semiconductor products suggested that the Japanese might indeed be producing superior products, considering their reduced defect rates and longer-term reliability. Neither TI nor most other U.S. companies gave the information as much credence as they should have. TI's global reputation for quality and reliability had been built on the production of a broad range of products and systems for the nation's missile and space programs.

During the 1950s, two of America's most influential thinkers and foremost quality and statistical experts, Dr. Joseph Juran and W. Edwards Deming, were dispatched by the U.S. to help Japanese industry improve the quality of its products. They urged companies to apply statistical quality control throughout the manufacturing processes instead of merely inspecting products after they had been produced. It was a revolutionary way of thinking for Japanese executives, who embraced the concept with a religious fervor—immediately introducing it throughout their plants and factories.

Sachi Nagae, (left), Hiji plant manager, and Akira Ishikawa, president of TI-Japan, visit with W. Edwards Deming in 1985 when TI-Japan's Hiji facility won Japan's top quality award, the Deming Prize.

Texas Instruments responded to the Japanese challenge by initiating its own commitment to the Total Quality concept. Morris Chang was named TI Corporate Quality Director in 1981, responsible for a company-wide effort to guide business managers in making quality and reliability improvements. He understood that TI and Japanese competitors had many of the same strategic approaches to improving business. He explained, "Our emphasis on strategic planning, our emphasis on automation, our emphasis on people effectiveness, and our extensive use of team improvement programs are all examples of such similarities."

TI organized a corporate quality council made up of the quality managers in each business. Top operating managers were immediately trained on quality improvement, and a *Quality Bluebook* was used to measure the quality performance of each business.

By 1984, TI commented we intend to make TI the quality leader worldwide for all our products and services as measured against our best competitors." A year later, Bill Sick, head of TI's semiconductor business, announced, "We have earned a preferred position on quality and service with our customers. In a survey that we conducted in the fourth quarter [1984], 67 percent of our customers ranked us number one on quality and service. Last year, we received 29 quality excellence awards. And 33 of our major customers are receiving TI semiconductor products directly into stock without incoming inspection. This results in a built-in preference for TI products and a natural tendency to purchase TI products for their next requirements."

It was a strong beginning, but as Sick pointed out, TI "must continue to improve our quality and service toward our goal of 100 percent on-time delivery of defect-free products in order to stay ahead of the competition."

TI was using the same Total Quality idea Juran and Deming had taken to Japan three decades earlier. George Graham, who later served as TI's corporate quality director, explained that, prior to the 1980s, TI had not understood the total quality concept. He said, "We always have believed in quality, but concentrated primarily on product quality. Hence we made quality a manufacturing responsibility. We also did not appreciate the value of total quality as it applies to all aspects of the corporation." Graham later referred to the 1980s as the decade when "we learned what Total Quality was all about."

In mid-1986, TI assembled a team from its wafer fabs in the U.S. and Japan to improve costs and yields of MOS memory products—with the focus on quality. The team achieved results that were competitive with the best in the market.

With the advent of Total Quality, TI's emphasis shifted to improving all aspects of the business, including staff/support organizations, business processes, leadership, people involvement, strategic quality planning, customer satisfaction, and supplier development.

Later, Pat Weber, head of TI's semiconductor business, challenged everyone at TI to get onboard because "the quality train was leaving the station." Weber utilized TI's Total Quality thrust to achieve increased performance within all areas of business.

The results spoke for themselves.

During 1987 to 1995, customer returns in the semiconductor business were reduced by more than 70 percent. Product defect levels were reduced by 65 percent. Manufacturing cycle times were reduced by more than 60 percent, decreasing work in progress by millions of dollars. Not-on-time deliveries were reduced by 83 percent, and, according to customer satisfaction surveys, TI's semiconductor business was regarded as the

Akira Ishikawa, in 1982, then Japan Semiconductor Operations Manager, along with Shin Ohkura, Hiji plant manager, and all TI-Japan employees, decided to accept the challenge to win the Deming Prize, one of the most prestigious quality awards in the world. It took years of dedicated effort by the Hiji plant management team and all its employees. Every employee was trained in every aspect of quality—how each of their jobs related to producing quality products and services and how this related to the objectives and success of the plant. In the final examination for the Deming Prize, the gardener was among the many people interviewed. He was asked how his job related to quality. He answered, "A beautiful and well-kept garden provides the first impression of quality for customers as they enter the plant and a spirit of quality for all employees as they come to work."

After the Deming examiners had interviewed many of the employees and reviewed numerous files of data and procedures to support answers to their questions, they made the decision to award the Deming Prize to TI's Hiji plant in 1985. In a formal ceremony similar to that of the Nobel Prize, the Deming Prize was presented to Sachi Nagae, Hiji plant manager at the time. TI-Japan's Hiji plant was the first wholly-owned foreign plant to win the Deming Prize, an honor for all the TI-Japan people.

industry benchmark for on-time delivery. Increased productivity in wafer fabrication resulted in additional output from existing capacity that was equal to two free wafer fabrication facilities, and TI received more than 400 quality awards.

The Total Quality effort spanned all areas of the company. TI's efforts received national recognition, including Japan's top quality award, the Deming Prize, won in 1985 by TI's plant in Hiji, Japan. In the U.S., TI's defense business in 1992 won the Malcolm Baldrige Award. In 1995, TI-Europe won the European Foundation for Quality Management Award, which is similar to the Baldrige, except that it is awarded by a consortium of top companies from all European countries, instead of a government.

Today, quality continues to be a critical measure for customer satisfaction, and TI has put increased emphasis on protecting its customers. Catching errors early, long before the product enters the market, is critical. The process is much more proactive than reactive today. Just as TI measures safety in its manufacturing, TI recognizes the factories with the least customer disruptions to spread awareness and accountability for quality.

"Design for Reliability" became a quality mantra in the late 1990s in a drive to create business rules that became part of the design process, taking into account the natural distribution expected from manufacturing. Soft Error Rates, for example, are random errors in integrated circuits caused by charged particles that are constantly hitting the earth and can cause a bit of data to switch its value. Soft Error Rates, although they rarely impact operation, are an increasing concern and need to be accounted for early in the development process because they cannot be fixed later.

Instituting uniform quality measurement across the company has become increasingly important since TI products are manufactured, assembled, and tested around the globe. A product shipped from multiple factories must not only have the same quality, but must be labeled and packed uniformly. Many semiconductor products are now systems-on-chip, so the quality and reliability of embedded software at the component level are now even more critical in the Total Quality performance of the end equipment. Managing the quality process is becoming as complex as the systems TI supports.

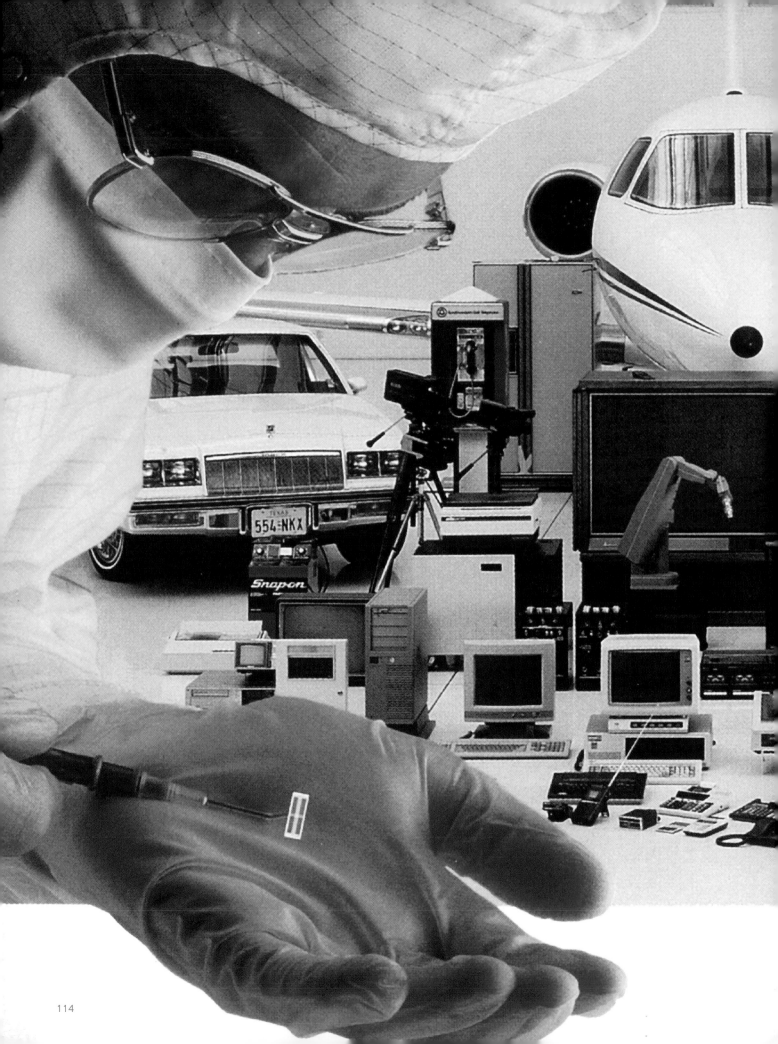

NEW HORIZONS

`01101010110101`
`01011010101101`
`10100001010000`
`11011011101101`

TI's powerful microchips ushered in a new era of vertical integration, with new opportunities in a wide variety of end-equipment markets. The invention of the calculator-on-a-chip made handheld calculators affordable—creating a whole new market and changing the way math is taught in schools. The revolutionary ability to synthesize speech on a single chip led to a series of learning aids, the first major application of digital signal processing technology in consumer electronics. Development of ever more powerful microprocessors and memory chips led to new computer products and applications. Vertical integration propelled the company into new ventures, bringing some disappointments and some new and unexpected businesses. It was the beginning of the digital age, and it would be an exciting and bumpy ride.

Programmable single-chip microcontrollers and microprocessors, coupled with software and innovative designs, ushered in a wide range of applications in the Digital Era.

34

THE DECISION TO DIVERSIFY

TI's first planning conference resulted in a roadmap for diversification to add stability in a global marketplace.

Armed with Texas Instruments' first germanium transistors produced during the summer of 1952, Pat Haggerty was convinced that semiconductor manufacturing would usher in a new era for the company. But with the war in Korea winding down, opportunities for future defense contracts were dwindling, and Haggerty decided the company needed a new plan for growth. Out of a three-day conference came a strategy that would have a major impact on TI's direction: a plan featuring growth and diversification that would help shape the future of TI and the world's electronics industry.

Texas Instruments held its first formal planning conference at the Broadmoor Hotel in Colorado Springs, Colorado, in October 1952. Haggerty described the meeting as "a tough, three-day session." Managers arrived enthusiastic about the company's progress since 1946, boosted by revenue projections that would top $20 million—divided almost equally between geophysical exploration and manufacturing, their

primarily defense electronics. Their enthusiasm, however, was tempered. No one could predict the potential revenue from future defense contracts after the final battle in Korea had ended; they only knew it would be drastically cut.

Haggerty wanted diversification, and he wanted it soon. Options were discussed, including the possibility of mergers and acquisitions. TI decided to step up its seismic instrument manufacturing for external customers; there was talk of the possibility that TI would become a public corporation.

Dr. Bates Peacock, one of the four GSI managers who had purchased the company in 1941, believed the company should focus on geophysical exploration. Realizing TI was becoming more interested in pursuing the semiconductor business, Peacock, on November 6, 1952, sold his shares back to the company, resigned from the Board, and left to involve himself in the global search for oil. He is credited with many contributions to the industry.

The company's first annual report, published in 1952, stated, *"It is believed that several desirable companies can be acquired during 1953, adding further to our diversity and stability, as well as total profits. The rate at which our family growth continues will, however, be in part dependent on our success in obtaining satisfactory long-term financing. It is hoped that this can be accomplished during the first half of 1953."*

TI immediately set out to acquire or merge with those companies whose products would help diversify its business. One of the first actions was a merger with Engineering Supply Company (ESCO) in February 1953. ESCO, which traced its history to Wink Supply, had been founded in 1937 to help supply GSI crews. ESCO would later be known as TI Supply

Joe Rodgers, left, manager of Components Division, and Ray Kidder, in charge of components production shops, watch Billie Smith (seated) electrically sort resistor slugs by an improved method that increased production on this operation by about 300 percent.

Company, or TISCO. It became a worldwide distributor of TI products and those of other manufacturers.

Al Cranford, left, and Pete Damrel testing gravity meters at Houston Technical Laboratories (HTL) before shipment to faraway places.

I n early 1953, TI began advertising its first non-military, non-seismic product—a magnetic clutch meter/positioner developed as part of the readout for the ASQ-8 submarine detection equipment. In 1954, the recorder in which it was used was painted a non-military color and sold for rugged applications such as the General Motors proving grounds.

In November 1953, TI acquired Houston Technical Laboratories (HTL), a manufacturer of scientific instruments, including the famed Worden Gravity Meter—used in the exploration for oil and minerals throughout the world. The lab was founded in 1946 by Sam Worden and Boyd Cornelison, and with its acquisition, TI could rapidly expand industrial electronics manufacturing.

As the TI newsletter later reported, *"In the high-tech world of rapid technology turnover and instant obsolescence, it is startling to find a successful product that is basically unchanged after more than three decades. Such a product is TI's Worden gravimeter ... used for broad reconnaissance of gravitational anomalies that reveal geological structures such as faults, anticlines, basins, and salt domes. Such broad detection is then followed up by seismic surveys."* The Worden meter could tolerate the heavy vibration of fieldwork.

I n December 1953, TI reorganized into a divisional structure and placed its new organization on a fast track. Four product businesses were established: apparatus (defense), semiconductor products, components (passive devices, such as resistors and capacitors), and petroleum instrumentation.

By 1954, all GSI seismic manufacturing had been moved to Houston. Bob Olson, who had been instrumental in TI's entry into transistors, was named president of HTL which had the responsibility for designing and manufacturing equipment for GSI crews and the geophysical industry.

In 1956, based on its earlier military experience, TI introduced a rectilinear strip-chart recorder called the recti/riter. Project engineer Ralph Dosher, sales engineer Orm

Henning, and the development team moved with the recorder to Houston to launch a commercial business. The recti/riter could be used wherever there was a need to record electrical phenomena—in studies of radar networks, in nuclear energy projects, in aircraft and missile research, in public utility

PRODUCT CUSTOMER CENTERS
★ ★ ★

Pat Haggerty believed TI must be "product-customer centered," a concept the company had been using since 1946. Each Product-Customer Center (PCC) manager had responsibility for the "Create, Make, and Market" functions for a product area. By 1964, TI had 43 product-customer centers in five divisions. In some cases, an entire division might be considered one PCC, while in other cases, some divisions might be comprised of a dozen or more PCCs.

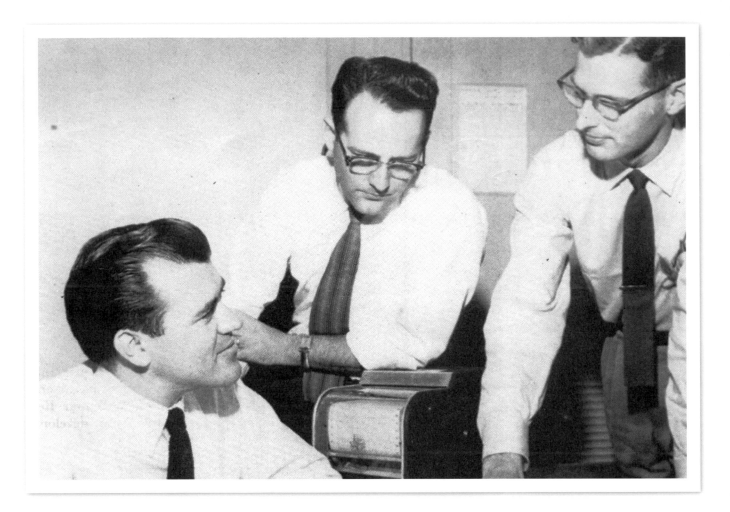

Ralph Dosher, left, discusses a point of interest about the new recti/riter recorder with Jim Thurmond, center, and Gilbert Clift, right. These three were primarily responsible for the engineering of the new recorder introduced in 1955.

operations, and in analog computer work. The recorder was a lower-priced product expanding TI's recorder market opportunities, which began with the converted military recorder several years earlier.

To diversify its components business, TI acquired the carbon resistor product line from the Radell Corporation in 1955 and moved the operation to Dallas. Later, TI entered the capacitor business, using technology licensed for tantalum capacitors. The portable and panel-indicating instruments line of Burlington Instrument Company of Burlington, Iowa, was acquired in 1956, and moved to Dallas. TI had ambitious plans to build a passive components business to complement semiconductors.

TI added to its defense capabilities in 1956 by acquiring the William I. Mann Company, a manufacturer of optical components based in Monrovia, California. It would later be moved to Dallas to support TI's growing interest in infrared technology.

TI was thinking big in an era of big conglomerates. The company briefly considered contacting Haloid Corporation (which later became Xerox) about a possible merger, but ultimately decided not to pursue the idea.

The company's rapid expansion in an ever-widening market caught the attention of the financial community, as well as that of the business press. In 1961, the company was featured in two major stories in *Fortune*, which called TI *"one of the most sensational growth companies in the U.S."*

As far as Haggerty was concerned, the seeds had been sown in his drive to instill innovation across the company. His goals weren't merely about growth or size. They were about setting in motion an organization that could set goals and systematically focus its technical skills on fundamentally changing a market or, even better, creating entirely new markets.

As the semiconductor business evolved, TI recognized the opportunity to leverage the technology into selected electronic end-equipment markets. TI predicted that new consumer and computer products would ultimately create a huge market.

35

THE M&C EXPERIENCE

TI takes advantage of an unexpected merger to diversify into electrical controls and metallurgical materials.

As Texas Instruments searched for ways to diversify, the company became involved in an unlikely merger in 1959 with a New England firm that, at first look, seemed to have little in common with a Texas-based high-tech outfit. Metals & Controls (M&C) Corporation was a successful Massachusetts company known for its innovative metal technologies, thermostats, and motor control products. TI viewed the merger as an opportunity to apply electronics technology to new markets. For M&C, the merger would provide stability and an opportunity for growth. For both companies, the merger came along when each firm needed the other, although few within the industry were far-sighted enough to realize it at the time.

The Klixon™ Type ST Control was designed principally for use as a limit control—to restrict boiler temperatures for safety, economy, and room temperature control.

M&C began with the founding in 1916 of General Plate, a company that specialized in bonding gold to a base metal for the Rhode Island jewelry industry. Founder Rathbun Willard, a jewelry salesman, referred to the technique as "gold filled." Expertise in handling thin-gauge rolling and metal cladding ultimately launched an international thermostat, controls, and materials business. By 1925, the company had outgrown its space, and Willard purchased more than 200 acres of land in the Cat-O-Nine-Tail swamp in Attleboro, Massachusetts.

Unbeknownst to General Plate, a research and experimental laboratory in Cambridge, Massachusetts, had spent several years working to develop the thermostat. The Spencer Thermostat Company, primarily a research company, had been incorporated by John Albee Spencer, Lawrence Marshall, and an MIT professor named Vannevar Bush. Spencer was a machinist and inventor who discovered that a piece of thermostatic bimetal, formed into a dished disk, would snap back and forth at pre-determined temperatures. The disk movement could then be connected to electrical switches to shut off overheating motors. Marshall later served as president of Raytheon, and Bush became World War II chief of research and development for the federal government.

Willard had decided that thermostat metal might be a good way to fill in the seasonal gaps in the jewelry business. Spencer was looking for a supplier of the high-temperature bimetal needed for an electric flat-iron temperature controller for Westinghouse. Willard provided the sample material, Spencer successfully created a demonstration device, and Westinghouse bought the exclusive rights for electrical applications using the snap-acting disk. Spencer used revenue from the sale to develop a line of gas controls, including a safety shutoff burner for the Electrolux gas refrigerator.

Willard wasted no time hiring Westinghouse's engineer on the project, Victor Vaughn, to initiate and manage controls activity for General Plate. By 1931, Willard had successfully completed a merger agreement with Spencer Thermostat, which established M&C.

After the merger, General Plate, one subsidiary, expanded its work in industrial-clad metals, and Spencer Thermostat, the other subsidiary, became the company's most important customer for bimetals. General Plate was able to obtain Spencer's patents, fortifying its position in the thermostat metal field. Spencer Thermostat started a manufacturing program devoted to a line of Klixon™ controls it had developed.

The basic function of the 4TM Thermal Protector is to protect the motor in a refrigeration compressor from overheating. The 4TM provides this protection by sensing the current and temperature of the motor.

After Vaughn moved to M&C, his first bimetal disk application was designed for electric motor thermal protection. Although the idea was widely acclaimed, the market grew slowly because of the Great Depression. However, Vaughn managed to secure contracts with Westinghouse that led to the application of Klixon actuators as thermostats for water heaters, appliances, and fan motors. Vaughn regained the rights from Westinghouse to pursue applications for other customers, and Klixon controls kept the company in business as the Depression wore on. In 1936, General Plate was dissolved to become a division of M&C.

One of the first products the newly formed corporation developed was the B3100 gas shutoff valve, which was used on all Servel gas refrigerators produced for the next three decades. A major break for M&C came when the company worked with Emerson, an electric motor manufacturer, and Tecumseh, a manufacturer of refrigerator compressors, to develop motor protection devices. Tecumseh captured the majority of the refrigeration market, and M&C prospered as Tecumseh expanded around the world.

During World War II, M&C halted its peacetime production and introduced 78 new control devices to support the defense effort. During the war years, Klixon electrical protective devices were used on all military land vehicles and practically all aircraft. As a result of effective service in manufacturing, M&C was awarded the coveted Army-Navy E Award in 1943.

During the 1940s and 1950s, Americans came to understand the term nuclear power. M&C learned that the Knolls Atomic Power Laboratory was having trouble rolling enriched uranium into strips practical for making nuclear fuel plates. After experimenting with the process, they succeeded in producing longer strips without the danger of the uranium cracking. In 1952, M&C became the first privately owned facility to obtain a license from the Atomic Energy Commission for the handling of enriched uranium. The company initially manufactured nuclear materials for test reactors and later for the Naval Reactor Program. Within six years, M&C was the world's largest nuclear fuel fabrication plant—supplying fuel for the original nuclear-powered aircraft carriers and submarines.

During the mid-1950s, M&C needed to build a second-source controls facility away from the risk of the hurricanes and winter storms that pounded New England. A manufacturing plant was established in 1954 in Versailles, Kentucky, which had the added benefit of being closer to motor and compressor customers in the Midwest.

International expansion began in 1955, and during the next three years, facilities were opened in Almelo, Holland; Aversa, Italy; Buenos Aires, Argentina; and Adelaide, Australia.

Although M&C had entered a period of great expansion, there were differences among M&C's Board in the vision for growth. Part of the Board supported Carroll L. Wilson, president of the company since 1956 and a former general manager of the Atomic Energy Commission. Another faction stood behind Jerome Ottmar, who had become president of M&C Nuclear in 1958. Rathbun Willard, who had started the original company in 1916, supported Ottmar.

Neither side was willing to compromise. As a last resort, the M&C Board sought the counsel of a consulting firm, Booz, Allen, & Hamilton, which, in the final analysis, recommended that both Wilson and Ottmar resign; that George L. Williams, the treasurer of M&C, serve as acting president; and that the company seek a merger with a larger company. The Board, to the consternation of some, chose to follow all three recommendations.

M&C hired a brokerage firm to look for companies that might be interested in a merger. Several were suggested, TI among them. A scoring method was devised to evaluate and rate the firms. TI—the smallest of the companies, the one with little in common with M&C or its product line—was judged to be the best choice because of its growth potential.

Vannevar Bush, who had reached legendary status because of his role in the development of the atomic bomb, was still a director of M&C. Bush had long known and respected TI's Cecil Green, and he concluded that "TI must be a good company."

After meetings in Dallas, M&C and TI agreed in principle to the merger in December 1958. Carl J. Thomsen, vice president and director of TI, was assigned to serve temporarily as president of M&C, and Ed Vetter, assistant vice president of TI, as executive vice president of M&C. After the merger was completed in April 1959, M&C began operating as a division of TI with Vetter as the division's manager.

During the 1960s, the supply of silver was decreasing, but the demand for coins was on the rise. The U.S. Mint began considering ways to eliminate or reduce the amount of silver in coinage without wreaking havoc in the vending machine industry. When it was learned that Battelle Memorial Labs had been assigned to investigate materials that could be substituted for silver, M&C began supplying a variety of lead metal combinations of both precision and base metals.

Unto Savolainen, an M&C engineer, was assigned to convince the Mint of the merits of cupronickel-clad copper. It would produce a bright coin, not the color of copper. It was already being used for the nickel coin. M&C would be able to

save and recycle 100 percent of the scrap. Copper was the least expensive metal with low resistivity; and Savolainen demonstrated that the material would work without difficulty in vending machines.

In 1965, M&C received a $30 million contract to deliver 60 million pounds of clad metal, and it eventually provided 5 million pounds per month. Because of the quick ramp-up, there was no building available for production. The first coinage material was rolled under tents with heaters, until a new building could be built. Although the contract only lasted until early 1968, the ability to bond 24-inch-wide material became a key factor in TI's becoming a market leader in the production of stainless steel clad aluminum automotive trim during the 1970s and 1980s.

TI helped develop the clad metal material for the U.S. Mint used in replacement of scarce metals in coinage, such as the twenty-five cent piece.

A key technology of M&C was the ability to metallurgically bond dissimilar metals in large bonding mills.

In the late 1960s, an M&C operation was started in Dallas. The purpose was to capitalize on the semiconductor technology in Dallas and develop new electronic products. The design of Polaroid camera controls and the Kelsey-Hayes automobile skid controls were moved from Semiconductor into M&C for design completion and production. In addition, the Dallas operation developed a microwave oven control and a line of electronic industrial controls. A new plant was built in Johnson City, Tennessee, to manufacture these and other M&C products.

It is estimated that a typical U.S. household, by 2004, contained about 30 of TI's sensors and control products.

Today, M&C, whose name was changed to Sensors & Controls when the Materials portion was divested in 2000, generates revenue of more than $1 billion annually, and has three major global business units—sensors, controls, and radio frequency identification (RFID)—operating in nine locations throughout the Americas, Europe, and Asia.

Over the years, the innovative solutions of this business have made automobiles, airplanes, and home appliances safer and more efficient around the world. More recently, Sensors & Controls systems have dramatically changed the face of security, logistics, and retail with a new line of RFID electronics-based products.

JOHN ALBEE SPENCER'S INNOVATION
★ ★ ★

When he was a boy of 15, working on the night shift in a little lumber mill in northern Maine, John Spencer's principal job was tending the fire in a wood-burning steam boiler. Young Spencer observed that when his fires were burning briskly, the old cleanout door would snap out into a convex position with a loud report, and then when the fires burned down, it would snap back into a concave position.

"This gave Spencer what proved to be a big idea. He placed a log against the door and waited for the results. When the fire died down, the faithful door snapped back into its cold position, thereby signaling the fire's need for more fuel by letting the log fall and awakening the drowsy young fireman.

"Spencer carried the idea of the old cleanout door in his mind for 18 years, turning over the principle involved and searching for a practical use to make of the phenomenon. During those years, Spencer acquired a thorough knowledge of mechanical engineering and, after a decade of experiment, tinkering, and study, he gave the world that little piece of thermostatic bimetal known as the Spencer disc (Klixon.)

"This innovation was utilized by M&C to bring added convenience and safety to many millions of homes, factories, automobiles, and airplanes." (Taken from the *M&C Corporation Employee Manual*.)

36

INNOVATION IN THE DIGITAL AGE

Haggerty sets TI on a course for continued growth by creating a plan to instill innovation.

In 1960, Texas Instruments revenues topped $232 million, exceeding Pat Haggerty's announced goal of $200 million. TI, in his words, had finally become a "good, big company." Haggerty, never satisfied with the status quo, proclaimed a new goal of $1 billion dollars in revenue. Within a year, however, TI faced a business recession and saw its stock price drop sharply. The booming growth of the 1950s slowed to a crawl. Haggerty realized it was time to begin aggressively pursuing opportunities in the new and waiting world of digital electronics. TI would help shape the emerging consumer, computing, and factory automation electronics markets.

The digital age was already altering TI's market and product mix. IBM was TI's largest customer. The integrated circuit was gaining momentum, and the digital seismic program was in full swing. Haggerty concentrated on developing a system to instill innovation and spur TI's growth. He gave that job to Buddy Harris at the 1962 Planning Conference, after a year of no growth. Harris assembled a team to work on the process for which there were no textbooks, no models, and no easy answers.

Haggerty looked at TI's successes in the past, searching for common characteristics in the development and marketing of the Regency Radio, the silicon transistor, and high-purity silicon. He found that each successful venture had a clear objective, a strategic concept, the tactics necessary to achieve that objective, along with a manager who could pull it together. Haggerty formulated the Objectives, Stratigies, and Tactics (OST) approach.

Guided closely by Haggerty, the team put together an initial document that provided guidelines to TI's businesses. After a year, it was obvious that the company needed a more extensive system. In 1965, Harris gave the task to Ralph Dosher, who had just completed a long-range plan for the Industrial Instrumentation Division in Houston. Dosher developed a set of standard procedures and coordinated a new Long-Range Planning Conference.

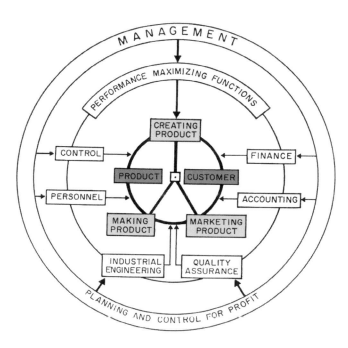

This chart was used to explain TI's Product-Customer Center (PCC) concept, shown at the center of the rings, surrounded by performance enhancing functions, such as finance, quality assurance, and industrial engineering. The outer ring, labeled "Management," had the task of moving all of these decentralized efforts toward TI's short- and long-term profit goals.

Even though the goal structure of the OST system was simple in concept, it was complex in its implementation. Each OST manager had operating, and strategic, responsibilities, some of which were in conflict, and managers worked hard to resolve the inevitable problems.

Haggerty had promoted the plan, but Mark Shepherd implemented the management and control systems that would maximize productivity and minimize risk. Shepherd emphasized the fact that TI's ability to earn a profit was based on creating, manufacturing, and marketing products and services. Innovation, he said, was important in all three areas.

A broad range of strategies surfaced, but Haggerty was always searching for a "breakthrough" strategy, one that would have a major impact on TI's growth and prosperity. He thought that all research and development should lead to new or improved strategies or tactics in fulfilling a clearly expressed company objective. At the time, TI was focusing on three critical strategies: the integrated circuit, digital seismic, and the Shrike missile design. Strongly supported by the OST approach, each of the programs eventually provided significant revenues and profits to the company.

In the late 1960s and early 1970s, the OST system became institutionalized across TI. When the company began leveraging its semiconductor technology into such selected equipment markets as consumer electronics and computing, the OST system was modified to encourage cooperation between TI business units, which was a key factor in using vertical integration to enter new markets.

On the left is a 15-ounce pulse code modulation encoder (using 285 TI integrated circuits) for the U.S. Air Force. It was 50 times lighter and 100 times smaller than the transistorized encoder in the background. Developed in the early 1960s, the small encoder was a harbinger of the changes to come in consumer and commercial markets as soon as integrated circuits could be made in volume and at lower costs.

Morris Chang, who led TI's semiconductor and consumer businesses, commented in a London conference in 1974 that "the most important motivation for vertical integration by semiconductor manufacturers is the opportunity for higher growth resulting from increased value added for products where the principal function is already performed by semiconductors." He cited calculators, where the semiconductor dollar value was 30 to 35 percent of the product's end value. He also cited minicomputers, data terminals, point-of-sale systems, and electronic watches as areas of opportunity for vertical integration by semiconductor makers.

By 1973, one of Haggerty's goals had been realized. TI revenues soared above $1 billion, and the company set a new goal of $3 billion. TI was regarded in the market as an electronics giant that led the world in fast-moving, high-tech markets such as semiconductors, calculators, and digital watches.

Business Week, in a cover story on TI in September of 1976, said, *"The company's rapidly building momentum, orchestrated by one of the world's most finely tuned management systems, is causing some observers to point to TI as the prototype of what a U.S. company must be to compete in the surging worldwide electronics markets of the 1980s."*

As TI refocused its business over the years, the number of strategies gradually declined. In planning, there was less interest in form and more emphasis on content. By the 1990s, digital signal processing (DSP) and analog products were the core businesses of TI. Planning methods at TI were described by such terms as strategic product mix, strategic focus, business segments, and research investment.

As *Business Week* saw it, the 1980s would loom *"as a bloody battlefield for U.S. industry. But no U.S. company is working harder than Texas Instruments Inc. to foster innovation and to focus an entire corporation on boosting productivity—a crucial factor in an era of seemingly endemic inflation."* The magazine noted that TI had been able to accomplish in the 1970s what no other American company had been able to achieve—to build a world-leading consumer electronics business from scratch. *Business Week* cited TI's complex system designed to stimulate and manage innovation as a key factor in attaining that success.

As a measure of that success, in May 1981, TI moved into the *Fortune* Top 100 list for the first time, ranking number 92 in terms of annual revenues.

37

SINGLE-CHIP MICROCOMPUTERS AND MICROPROCESSORS

Putting it all together on a chip creates new opportunities.

Invention of single-chip microcomputers and micro-processors triggered a major expansion cycle for the electronics industry. These chips made possible a new generation of portable electronics and more powerful, lower-cost computers that would usher in the era of personal computing and factory automation.

As early as 1970, Texas Instruments worked with Computer Terminal Corporation to develop a central processor unit (CPU) on a chip for the Datapoint 2200 terminal. In March 1971, TI produced and delivered the industry's first 4-bit microprocessor, the TMS1795. Gary Boone received the patent in September 1973 for the first microprocessor, strengthening TI's intellectual property position.

The customer decided, however, to use TI's popular Transistor-Transistor Logic (TTL) integrated circuits for its terminal instead of a microprocessor. TI shelved its 4-bit design because of other priorities, but Intel continued its work and brought its 4-bit microprocessor to the market.

The bit-parallel architecture that evolved from TI's early microprocessor work became the basis for invention of the single-chip microcomputer by Michael Cochran and Gary Boone at TI in 1971. The microcomputer chip was the first integrated circuit with all the elements of a complete calculator on a single chip of silicon. In contrast, a microprocessor used other chips, such as memory, to complete a design. In announcing the single-chip microcomputer, TI commented, "This single chip may make full electronic calculators available to everyone at prices that can put a calculator into every kitchen or businessman's pocket. The chip incorporates all

the logic and memory circuits to perform complete 8-digit 3-register calculator functions, including full precision add, subtract, multiply, and divide operations." The chip soon became the most widely used integrated circuit for handheld calculators. This invention allowed TI to realize its ambition of a consumer business—first with the introduction of the Datamath calculator in 1972, and later on in a family of educational products.

Michael Cochran holds the single-chip integrated circuit, or "calculator-on-a-chip," announced in September 1971. This chip made it possible for TI to enter the calculator market in 1972.

In 1974, TI introduced the TMS1000, a general-purpose 4-bit single-chip microcomputer supported with peripheral circuits, design tools, software aids, and training for customers. The TMS1000 was a major success, giving TI the lead in the market for 4-bit consumer, automotive, and industrial applications. When TI announced the award of the patent for the single-chip microcomputer in 1978, Mark Shepherd said: "The semiconductor industry now has entered an era where the entire system function of an end product can be accomplished by a single chip or by a few semiconductor chips, with enough versatility to permit adaptation to many different applications through programming. This change carries enormous implications for the system designer: (1) the lead time for system implementation is shortened because no special chip development is required; (2) the development cost will be low because it will be limited to software, which may be executed in hardware; and (3) the required degree of electronics sophistication on the part of the user is much less." Single-chip microcomputers, or microcontrollers as they were later called, would become an important leadership area for TI's semiconductor business.

Company plans reflected the growing contribution of digital products, as the company worked quietly on a completely new strategy. By 1975, TI was ready to

disclose its 9900/990 software-compatible family of 16-bit microprocessors and minicomputers—the heart of its strategy for vertical integration. This strategy was the outgrowth of a task force put together to look at next-generation computers.

The TMS9900 was the industry's first 16-bit microprocessor. The 9900/990 family was designed with an innovative memory-to-memory architecture. However, in the embryonic microprocessor market, designers were just learning how to use 8-bit microprocessors with a register file architecture. The most popular microprocessors were those with the most complete range of development tools. The 8-bit microprocessors, especially Intel's 8080 and evolutionary designs such as Zilog's Z80 and Motorola's 8085, enjoyed the widest range of development tools, leading to a development community that preferred register file architectures to solve their system designs. TI developed its own 8080, although it had limited success in the market.

By 1978, to strengthen its program, TI assembled a team of some of its brightest engineers to focus on the development

TI highlighted the TMS1000, the first microcomputer on a chip (logic, control, and memory on a single chip), in its 1975 *First Quarter and Stockholders Meeting Report.*

MOS MICROCOMPUTER

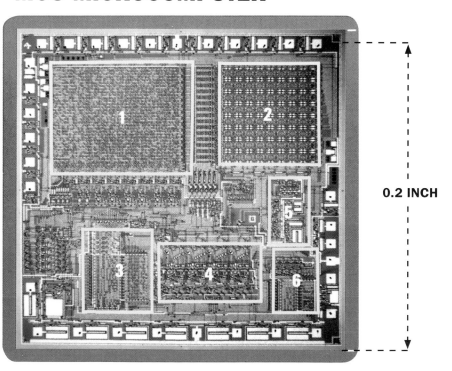

1 READ ONLY MEMORY

2 RANDOM ACCESS MEMORY

3 CONTROL DECODE

4 ARITHMETIC LOGIC UNIT

5 CLOCK

6 INPUT/OUTPUT DECODE

0.2 INCH

of programmable products. Evolution of the 9900 family continued with the 9995 and 99000 microprocessors but came to an end in 1982 when IBM chose the Intel 8088 for its first personal computer. It was clear that TI's future microprocessor success would require differentiation from what Intel and others were doing. The newly formed team embraced a concept called function-to-function architecture that emphasized microprocessors tailored for particular system functions. Digital signal processing, local area networks, floating-point arithmetic, and graphics were selected as areas of focus. Joint development with market-leading system companies such as IBM, Compaq, Hewlett-Packard, and Sun Microsystems was a key element in the strategy. The talented engineers produced a string of innovations, including the TMS320 DSP family, token-ring Local Area Network chipsets for IBM to network computers, and later Scalable Processor Architecture (SPARC®) microprocessors developed jointly with Sun Microsystems. SuperSPARC® was announced in 1992, and many developments since have powered Sun's advanced workstations and servers.

Delivering complete systems on a single-chip continues to be an advantage for TI, including the first single-chip cell phone solution. At the heart of many of these systems-on-chip devices are powerful DSP cores that evolved from the original TMS320; they are prized for their programmable nature, making them adaptable to a wide range of applications. Integrated with analog components, the DSP families power many of the highest-volume applications such as cell phones, broadband gateways for the home and office, and a wide range of consumer electronics, such as digital cameras.

In 1975, TI introduced the industry's first microprocessor that used software language compatible with a minicomputer family. The 16-bit 9900 pictured here is next to a U.S. quarter for size comparison.

38

CALCULATED INNOVATIONS

TI launched a new strategy by entering the consumer and educational markets with handheld calculators.

The first handheld calculator was invented at TI in 1967. The project was code-named "Cal Tech." This model shows the application of TI's thermal printhead to the calculator.

Texas Instruments' decision to enter the consumer market with a handheld calculator was a departure from the company's traditional method of doing business. The handheld calculator offered the company a new opportunity. From the outset, TI realized it had the technology but needed to develop marketing savvy to break into the consumer business by identifying the right markets, alliances, and product mix to build a successful worldwide venture. TI's calculators would make a major impact on business, education, and everyday life around the world. By 2004, TI's Educational & Productivity Solutions Group, the name of the calculator business, had grown to more than half a billion dollars in annual revenue.

During the early 1960s, Pat Haggerty discussed the possibility of a handheld calculator with Jack Kilby on a business trip. There were other priorities, but in 1964, Dean Toombs, head of semiconductor research and development, formed a team consisting of Kilby, Jim Van Tassel, and Jerry Merryman to develop a calculator small enough to fit in the palm of a hand, yet powerful enough to perform basic math functions.

By December 1966, the group had a working model, and, within a year, Kilby, Van Tassel, and Merryman filed a patent application, which would be issued eight years later. The functional heart of the first miniature calculator was a set of integrated circuits able to perform addition, subtraction, multiplication, and division. It had a small keyboard with 18 keys and a visual output that displayed up to 12 decimal digits.

An integrated circuit development program was established in 1969 to supply chipsets to the calculator market, which were produced for both Bowmar and Canon. In April 1970, Canon introduced the world's first commercial handheld calculator, developed with TI semiconductors and carrying a retail price tag of $400. It wasn't long before Bowmar introduced the competitive Bowmar Brain, which used a TI-made keyboard and integrated circuits and retailed for $250.

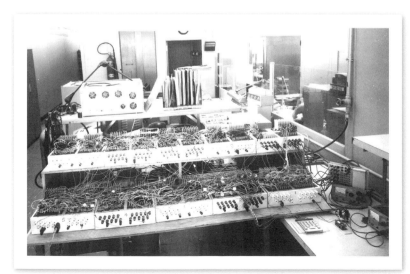

Without today's computer-aided design tools, engineering was messy in the 1960s. This is the laboratory where the handheld calculator was invented, using breadboards to build and test all the functions in conventional logic, before reducing the circuitry to fit in a box that could be held in one hand.

Early versions of business calculators might employ up to 90 integrated circuits and sell for $1,000. TI thought a calculator-on-a-chip could significantly reduce the cost of a calculator for the consumer and business markets. TI engineer Mike Cochran, under the direction of Gary Boone, began work in 1970 on a single-chip design to process a variety of mathematical functions. A year later, two prototype single-chip calculators had been developed, and work was underway on a production design.

In April 1972, the company revealed its TI-2500 Datamath single-chip calculator to a market that was as excited about its $149.95 retail price as it was about its revolutionary technology. The Datamath, which marked TI's formal entry into the market, was introduced in September along with the TI-3000 and TI-3500 high-tech desk calculators.

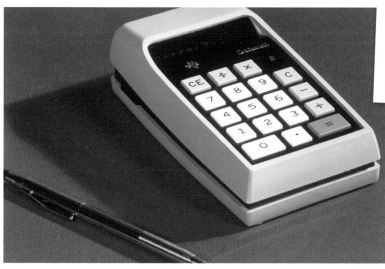

TI entered the calculator market in 1972
with the Datamath single-chip calculator.

In the press release announcing TI's entry into the calculator market, Jay Rodney Reese, who was given the job of building the business, said, *"Our company is dedicated to the belief that electronics will pervade all segments of our society. As electronics continues to open up new markets, Texas Instruments will analyze these high growth opportunities to determine if our company can make a real contribution to society. We believe that an exceptionally good match between the needs of the market and our technological and manufacturing capabilities exists in the electronic calculator field."*

The SR-10 scientific calculator soon followed, and high volumes were being shipped before the end of 1973. Selling for under $150, the SR-10 was positioned as

The SR-50, a full-function scientific calculator, was introduced in early 1974. It was based on algebraic notation and was popular with engineers and the technical community.

a portable slide rule calculator with scientific notation. It performed reciprocals, squares, and square roots quickly and more accurately than traditional slide rules. In early 1974, TI introduced a full-function scientific calculator, the SR-50, based on algebraic notation. It competed against Hewlett-Packard's notation calculator. Initially, the SR-50 was sold only by mail order, and it was soon in short supply.

Reese led the rapid expansion of the calculator business to an annual rate of more than $100 million in revenues, but a worldwide recession in 1974 provoked a price war that staggered the market. To cut costs, TI reduced the number of models it was producing, and a design-to-cost program was implemented to shrink part count—a move that led to the closure of some manufacturing sites in the U.S. and Europe. Design headquarters was transferred to the Lubbock, Texas, manufacturing facility. The price collapse had occurred so quickly that TI's inventories became overvalued, resulting in major write-offs for the company.

Despite the economic downturn, TI continued product

development, and, in 1975, brought out the SR-52, a programmable calculator with nonvolatile magnetic card storage. It featured more programming and memory power than comparable models offered at twice the price. The SR-52 was based on TI's algebraic operating system. It came with 22 program cards and a retail price of $395. And it signaled a new era in calculator functionality, hastening the end of the engineer's love affair with the slide rule.

Texas Instruments began to venture into a new business strategy that focused on opportunities in education. In 1986, the company fulfilled a request from Connecticut for 10,000 simple "four-function" calculators. A year later, Professors Frank Demana and Bert Waits of Ohio State University contacted TI, and other companies, to discuss their idea of using graphing calculators in precalculus classes.

TI's first graphing calculator, the TI-81, was brought to the market in 1990. It has been replaced by an expanding line of more powerful graphing calculators, such as the TI-84 and TI-89.

Most students did not have access to computers, the professors explained, and graphing calculators might be an ideal solution for them if, of course, there was a way to make the product easier to use.

Professors Demana and Waits were impressed because TI, more than any other company, was willing to take a chance on their idea, even though TI did not yet have a graphing calculator on the market. TI immediately began working with the professors, as well as with other math educators, to design and develop a unit that would be simple to use, yet incorporate all of the features required by math students.

Within four years, TI offered a graphing calculator, the TI-81, which proved to be popular because it helped students visualize abstract concepts. Educators appreciated the fact that TI had listened to them and implemented their ideas to create such a valuable educational tool. Word began to spread throughout the educational community that TI had reached out to teachers like no company in the market had ever done before.

The "Teachers Teaching with Technology" (T³) idea germinated in annual workshops conducted by Ohio State University. Math teachers came together to discuss the latest technologies available in the educational marketplace, as well as to share their successes. TI saw that the company could hold workshops on a more frequent basis, thus forming a tighter bond with math educators and helping them to effectively use technology in the classroom. TI would be able to incorporate ideas from the workshops into future versions of graphing calculators, as well as other educational technology. TI was able to reach a greater number of educational decision-makers, which ultimately led to the company's achieving a greater share of the graphing calculator market. The T³ program enabled TI to develop a network of users that provided the company with invaluable insight for future uses of technology developed primarily for education.

By 2004, more than 100,000 educators worldwide had been involved in T³ regional conferences, summer institutes, do-it-yourself workshops for individual schools and districts, college short courses, professional development packages, online coursework, and the annual international conference. They left with the resources, networks, and technologies necessary to teach more effectively and inspire their students to strive for greater achievement in math.

Throughout the 1990s, TI's graphing calculator evolved to help students better understand higher levels of math concepts and theories. Calculator-active questions moved from the research and workshop arenas into a number of leading standardized tests, including the College Board Scholastic Aptitude Test (SAT). As a result, more teachers began recommending TI graphing calculators and adopting the technology into their lesson plans and teaching methods.

During the early years of the 21st century, many teachers, scholars, and textbook publishers are developing curriculum that integrates the use of the TI graphing calculator into everyday lessons. Some mathematics textbooks are incorporating keystrokes and screen details into teachers' manuals and recommending methods for integrating the technology into their classrooms. TI collaborates with all the major mathematical textbook publishers, providing them technical information for each new edition.

39

ELECTRONIC LEARNING AIDS

TI creates a family of innovative learning aids for children.

It began with an "IDEA." It captivated a nation and helped teach millions of children how to spell. The little talking box from Texas Instruments made it all the way to Hollywood, to the cover of Business Week, and finally to the Smithsonian Institution. It was featured on national television with comedian Bill Cosby, and it created a new business for TI, opening the eyes of the electronics industry to a new technology.

One of the most visible and successful manifestations of TI's early efforts in consumer electronics was Speak & Spell™, a portable learning aid designed to help children learn how to spell. It began in 1976 as a three-month feasibility study and a $25,000 budget. Four TIers worked on the project in its early stages: Paul Breedlove, Richard Wiggins, Larry Brantingham, and Gene Frantz.

The concept for Speak & Spell grew out of Breedlove's brainstorming for products that might demonstrate the capabilities of bubble memory (a TI research project). He concluded that speech data took a lot of memory and would be a good application. He came up with the idea for the "Spelling Bee," an electronic device to teach spelling to kids. Frantz was

assigned to design the system, Brantingham to be the integrated circuit chip architect, and Wiggins to specify the speech synthesis algorithm.

The team took the concept to TI's research labs to see if it was possible to create a speech synthesizer to handle the speech data. Most of the research team didn't think it was possible, except Wiggins, who had only been on the project two weeks. Now, the team needed funding. Years earlier, TI had set up a program called IDEA to fund and test creative ideas before they went through the formal process for new research and development projects. IDEA managers were named in each division, with the authority to approve an idea on the spot. Ralph Dosher, the IDEA manager for Consumer Products, approved $25,000 to test the concept. Frantz was named project leader. His team started in the fourth quarter of 1976, and by the end of the year, demonstrated that the concept was viable.

But there was still a tough road ahead to turn the concept

The team that invented TI's Speak & Spell—(left to right) Gene Frantz, Richard Wiggins, Paul Breedlove, and Larry Brantingham. The Speak & Spell was introduced in June 1978 at the Consumer Electronics Show in Chicago.

into a product. The speech synthesis function required that 200,000 additions and 200,000 multiplications be performed in one second. Everyone thought this would mean a custom designed integrated circuit, which could take a year-and-a-half to develop and cost $1–2 million. After three months of computer simulation, the circuit was designed and made to fit on a single chip. The final design for Speak & Spell included a 4-bit microcontroller to run the system, two 128k-bit read-only memories to store the words used, and the speech synthesis chip that made it all possible. Speak & Spell was the first commercial application of digital signal processing technology in a consumer product.

The Speak & Spell was soon joined in the market with other TI talking learning aids—the Speak & Read™ and the Speak & Math™.

Frantz worked with consumer focus groups to develop the right voice for Speak & Spell and to research word lists to use in the product. In some of his focus groups, parents and educators were skeptical, but kids liked the product. He settled on a target market of preschool through third grade and hired a leading educator to sort out the conflicting results of the focus groups. The consultant was generally negative about the concept and reported that children no longer learned spelling by rote. The team met to consider their next (or last) move. They decided to continue the project, with a planned 1978 introduction; they were able to sell their managers on the potential of Speak & Spell and got official funding.

George Doddington, an expert in speech technology in TI's speech lab who had come to the company from Bell Labs,

supported Frantz. Speech synthesis was understood in the industry and could be performed on large computers at the time, but no one had reduced it to a handheld instrument. Frantz and the team applied TI's design-to-cost techniques to develop a product that could be sold at retail for under $50. After analysis, the team realized it could not use bubble memory and would need to use two semiconductor read-only memory chips to store the vocabulary, as Breedlove had recommended earlier. The team also decided to provide plastic plug-in modules containing read-only memories to add more words to the vocabulary.

Brantingham remembers it took nine iterations of his designs through the Houston MOS fab, with the help of K. Bala, before the final speech synthesis chip was ready. The read-only memory chip was also a challenge, because at the time it was difficult to squeeze that much memory onto one chip—it hadn't been done before. Brantingham had good support from TI's consumer operations in Lubbock and its Central Research Laboratories in adapting the TMS1000 as the microcontroller chip for Speak & Spell. Work on the chips began in February 1977, and by May 1978, the team had a product ready for the Consumer Electronics Show. The team was elated when it realized that not only did the product work, but it would also meet the cost goals.

An educational merchandising team was assembled under Don Scharringhausen, and Ralph Oliva was assigned the responsibility for learning factors engineering and deciding on the final word list to be stored in Speak & Spell.

With design and production problems solved, Speak & Spell, the first commercial device to use synthesized human speech, was introduced June 11, 1978, at the Consumer Electronics Show in Chicago. It was a big hit and was featured on the cover of *Business Week* in 1978 in a major story about TI. The magazine proclaimed, *"The $50 Speak & Spell is the first of what is expected to be a flood of products over the next several years using the revolutionary chip."*

The success extended TI's thrust in educational products to Speak & Math, Speak & Read, Speak & Music™, and a whole collection of speaking children's toys. Speak & Spell went around the world—in several languages. In 1982, TI introduced Vocaid, which helped people unable to speak to communicate using touch-sensitive panels to activate spoken messages in a solid-state speech module. In 1983, TI shipped its newest learning aid, the Magic Wand speaking reader for preschool children. It featured an optical "wand" children would wave over specially printed bar codes in a book that prompted the machine to read and speak.

Four years after the introduction of Speak & Spell, a loveable alien rigged the device with an antenna to "phone home" in Steven Spielberg's blockbuster movie, *E.T. the Extra-Terrestrial*, giving TI international exposure and a permanent place in movie lore.

Although it was introduced more than 25 years ago, the basic learning principles and design concepts behind Speak & Spell remain the standard for educational toys. Speech synthesis and voice recognition applications are pervasive today—ranging from telephone applications for checking airline schedules, to voice-assisted navigation systems in automobiles, computers for the blind, and security applications.

The Speak & Spell product line was sold as part of a restructuring of the consumer business, but TI remains active in the education field with calculators and digital solutions that continue to expand the education market.

Family portrait of TI's learning aids, showing the evolution into the preschool market with the Magic Wand, in the center, surrounded by other learning aids, such as the Touch & Tell (upper center). Notice the Little Professor™, TI's first learning aid, just to the right of the Speak & Spell Compact™.

THE LITTLE PROFESSOR
★ ★ ★

Although Speak & Spell was the star of the show, it was not TI's first learning aid. TI had introduced a nontalking learning aid, the Little Professor, in 1976. It functioned as a handheld drill-and-practice aid for basic math, and was designed to resemble a wise and friendly owl. Kirk Pond headed the business responsible for Little Professor and Jim Moore was the engineering manager. The Little Professor suggested problems to students and rewarded them with a message on its display when they gave the correct answer. The Little Professor was priced to sell at retail for under $20 and was an instant hit. Although production ramped up, TI couldn't make enough units to fill the orders for the Christmas season in 1976. Demand in 1977 was more than 1 million units.

40

TI DEVELOPS A SUPERCOMPUTER

By creating a massive computer, TI makes important advances for digital signal processing.

In the mid-1960s, the world needed large-scale computers. Government-sponsored research laboratories were running into computational limitations as they tried to increase the accuracy of their results by using more data. To help with this dilemma, significant government funding was allocated to laboratories and universities to develop bigger and faster computers. GSI also needed a very large-scale computer for 3D seismic analysis. TI decided to join the race—launching a six-year project to build its own supercomputer. In the process, several innovations were made that would advance the state of the art in both the design and manufacture of electronic systems and in the application of digital signal processing (DSP).

The Advanced Scientific Computer (ASC) project was started in 1965 by the Dallas team who had previously designed Texas Instruments' seismic computer, the TIAC 870. While the initial emphasis was for seismic processing, the scope was broadened to scientific applications, which made it possible to utilize government research and development funding. Harvey Cragon and Joe Watson were the principal designers. The team realized that the way to do faster computation was to design a machine that would have several parallel pipelined computing streams, which was common thinking in the industry. But the great advance made by the team was invention of the hardware and software techniques required to process data much more efficiently with these multiple parallel arithmetic vector processors, or pipes. The TI design let application programmers write software in the familiar FORTRAN language and have the support software do the heavy lifting required to use the hardware efficiently. The fundamental techniques developed during the ASC project are still in use today in DSP products.

The ASC team would grow to about 200 people and include design, software, and manufacturing engineers. Their first hardware decision focused on the memory system. The high-speed memory of choice in 1965 was magnetic thin-film memory. A number of research projects on this technology were underway in the U.S., including at TI. It seemed to be the most promising solution for the ASC's memory requirements.

The design was set for a four-way interleave of 32K word modules, for a total memory of 128K words. The memory words were 256 bits (eight 32-bit words) to meet the bandwidth requirement of the processor. But a few years into the design process, TI abandoned thin-films in favor of bipolar memory. After several trial designs, the final design was based on a 256 x 1 bipolar chip. As the design proceeded, memory technology improved, and the design was changed to eight-way interleaving of 128K word modules, resulting in a total memory of 1 million (128-bit) words. Emitter Coupled Logic integrated circuits were vital to the project—they were fast, but generated a significant amount of heat. A 17-layer printed circuit board was used to hold the 308 integrated circuits and/or terminating resistor packages (154 mounted on each side of a board). Power requirements for the total system varied between 250,000 and 350,000 watts. It took 80 tons of chilling capacity to cool the water that flowed in cold plates between the circuit board racks and the air that blew through the cooling coils and between the boards. Maintaining a uniform temperature in the system was critical to keep the circuits operating properly.

In 1970, the ASC project was moved from the South Building in Dallas to the Austin Research Building near the University of Texas-Austin campus. This TI site was the target of several student demonstrations, one of which included fire bombs, because of TI's high profile as a military contractor. Soon after these demonstrations, the ASC project was moved again—this time to TI's new Research Boulevard facility north of Austin.

When the ASC was completed, it was a marvel—capable of doing 80 million floating-point computations per second using a 50-nanosecond clock. This pipelined vector processor demonstrated the viability of the design and set the standards for subsequent vector processors. Other supercomputers available in the industry around the same general time frame were the IBM 360/95 and the Control Data Corporation (CDC) 7600. Although close to the same speed as the ASC, the 7600 was not operational for another two years.

The first ASC was for GSI production use in the Austin facility. The second machine was delivered to the GSI office in Holland in 1971 to process data for Royal Dutch Shell. This house-sized, 3,000-square-foot machine was disassembled in Austin, trucked to Houston, and shipped by air to Holland. The number 3 ASC was sold to the U.S. Army Ballistic Missile Agency for research on anti-ballistic missiles and installed in Huntsville, Alabama. The number 4 machine (the first four-pipe machine) was sold to the U.S. Weather Bureau and installed in Washington, D.C. ASC numbers 5 and 6 were installed in Austin to support seismic processing, and number 7 was used by the Naval Research Laboratories in Washington D.C. Machines from number 4 on were all four-pipe machines.

Even with eye-catching performance, the ASC was among the leaders for only a few years. CDC had a lock on markets such as the Atomic Energy Commission at Los Alamos, the Lawrence Livermore Lab, and the National Security Agency. Valiant marketing efforts were directed at these three major agencies without success. Simultaneous with the ASC development, CDC was developing a faster machine, compatible with the CDC 6600, which could be assembled into lower-performance models. The competition could not be dislodged, and the ASC project was shut down. In total, eight large computers were built, far short of the number the company hoped to see, and TI turned its resources to other fields.

The real benefit to TI from the ASC program was not the computer itself, but the experience and technology developed, and the lessons learned. First, the engineers who were trained during the ASC program were a resource to other TI businesses, including the defense business as it went digital, and took advantage of experience in designing systems with a complex parallel vector architecture used in DSP applications. Second, the complexity of the ASC required the development of computer-aided design techniques useful

in other TI applications. Third, the importance of software design systems used by both TI and its customers to design systems and integrated circuits was recognized, which led to the development of tools to support future TI programs.

The greatest legacy of the ASC was the impact made by 200 engineers directly assigned to the project and several hundreds more in support organizations who spread these technologies

A fish-eye camera view, *left*, of TI's supercomputer— the Advanced Scientific Computer (ASC). It was used primarily for high-speed processing of 3D seismic data and other scientific calculations, including weather forecasting and defense applications.

across TI as the electronics environment of the world became more dependent on digital electronics, and DSP technology in particular.

41

HOME COMPUTER

TI attempts to create a new consumer market and pays a big price.

In the early 1970s, Pat Haggerty and his management team had many strategic discussions about the potential for low-cost semiconductor functions to make possible a computer for the home with implications for commercial, educational, and recreational uses. These discussions led to a home computer project. After the commercial success of Texas Instruments calculators, the home computer seemed the logical next step. The home computer became TI's biggest bet in the quest for vertical integration, but the venture proved to be a dry hole. The huge negative impact on TI's financial health might have sunk the company, except for its strong balance sheet, diversified position, and determination to learn from the experience.

Visitors to the Consumer Electronics Show in Chicago in June 1979 were able to see TI's 99/4 home computer for themselves, confirming rumors that had circulated for months. Its central processor was TI's 16-bit TMS9900 microprocessor, designed to give it a leg up on 8-bit home computers in the market. Equipped with a 13-inch video color monitor, it was designed to use plastic plug-in modules of read-only memory, which contained programs such as games, personal finance, and educational software. The reaction was generally favorable, although some were surprised at the high price tag of $1,150.

Feedback from the market indicated the need for more software titles, a better keyboard, more peripherals, and a lower price. A redesigned home computer, the 99/4A, was introduced in June 1981, priced at $525. One of the most popular options was the speech module, which could be used to read a document out loud.

A major marketing program was created to build sales. The primary channel of distribution was shifted from computer stores to high-volume retail outlets. A team of more than 2,000 school teachers was recruited and trained to demonstrate the product in the stores. A creative TV ad campaign was developed using Bill Cosby as spokesman. The International 99/4A Users Group became an important source of additions to the rapidly growing library of software. As TI gained market share and volume, the 99/4A price at retail dropped to $299 to meet increasing pressures from competitors.

In April 1982, TI reported it had a major position in the emerging home market, with more than 5,000 retail outlets carrying or committed to carry the 99/4A. Although the market had been slow to develop, it began to expand rapidly in 1982, and production was increased.

By August 1982, 99/4A sales were growing rapidly, but the success of the home computer was causing stiff price competition. TI decided to offer a $100 rebate. In a TV ad, Bill Cosby joked about how easy it was to sell a computer if you paid people $100 to buy one.

By early 1983, TI had shipped the one millionth 99/4A home computer. The distribution network had expanded to 20,000 retail outlets worldwide. More than 2,000 software packages, developed largely by third-party authors, were now available for the computer and agreements were in place with several educational and game publishers.

Then, it was discovered that under certain circumstances, a person might receive an electrical shock from the computer's power supply, although no user had yet experienced such a problem. TI armed itself with the facts, reported them to the safety regulatory authorities, and made the decision to temporarily shut down the 99/4A program while new power supplies were manufactured and shipped to TI. All 99/4A retail inventories and customer returns were reworked and returned. TI accrued $50 million as the estimated cost to solve the problem. Even more damaging was TI's two-month absence from the retail marketplace. Competitors made the most of the situation by raising questions in the marketplace about the safety and quality of the 99/4A.

A rescue team of seasoned TI managers was formed and sent to Lubbock, Texas, headquarters and manufacturing site for the home computer. This team along with the Lubbock home computer team mounted an intensive effort to recover from

TI introduced the TI 99/4A Home Computer in 1981, as a redesign to the 99/4 computer. It is pictured here with peripherals, plastic plug-in software modules (lower right), and color TV monitor. In 1981, this was state-of-the-art graphics in home computer displays, made possible by TI's 16-bit 9900 microprocessor.

the transformer problem, restore the sales momentum at retail, adjust production and inventories, and reduce costs. They faced a tough situation.

On October 28, 1983, TI announced it was withdrawing from the home computer market. When the smoke cleared and results were in for the year, TI reported that the total segment losses from the home computer were approximately $680 million, including operating losses, write-downs, write-offs, and other accruals associated with the shutdown.

The withdrawal from the market hurt TI's finances, but the damage to its psyche and reputation was just as painful. Many worried that TI's profitable and successful calculator and learning aid business would be adversely affected. What TI did next, however, was a testament to the character of the company: TI decided to continue support for 99/4A users

during the withdrawal, to honor warranties, and to help dealers with their inventories. It was a big price to pay, but TI thought it was the right thing to do. TI's calculator and learning aids business thrived.

Although TI's shutdown of the 99/4A Home Computer was the one most widely reported, over the next year or so, most of the major home computer manufacturers quietly left the market after experiencing their own disappointments. Many years later, an array of quite different digital products emerged tailored to serve specific subsegments of the home market, including games, education, communication, and small business/home office applications. TI continues to provide semiconductor solutions to customers in many of these applications—with a valuable perspective earned from the painful lessons of the home computer market experience.

42

OTHER CREATIVE CONSUMER PRODUCTS

TI leverages technology to create innovative consumer electronics products.

With its successful entry into the calculator market in 1972, Texas Instruments was ready to turn up the heat on its consumer strategy. At the stockholders meeting in 1976, having announced a $10 billion revenue goal just two years earlier, TI was ready to make it official—consumer electronics products would be one of its three major growth thrusts in addition to semiconductors and distributed computing. The company launched a succession of new consumer products, including digital watches. Innovations helped create new markets, changed the way consumers perceived the usefulness of electronics, and made TI a household name around the world.

Texas Instruments' introduction of electronic digital watches was a business landmark at the 1975 Consumer Electronics Show in Chicago. TI brought out three high-fashion Liquid Crystal Display (LCD) watches; three Personalized Watches with Light-Emitting Diode (LED) displays for men and women; and a compact, seven-function LCD digital Travel Alarm. TI had earlier developed custom integrated circuits and LEDs for the watch market and had an established distribution channel for calculators. It was a small step to make low-cost cases for the watches and purchase the bands and batteries for a complete watch.

TI chose to enter the watch market at under the $40 price point and targeted mass distribution, such as department stores, discount stores, and large catalog companies. At the time, there were few digital watches available to consumers for

under $100. The chip design began in December 1974 for TI's first watches, which were shipped in September 1975. The LED display was illuminated by pressing a button on the side of the watch.

TI's first LED digital watch featured a black plastic case and a red light-emitting diode digital display. Eventually, watches of this type were cost-reduced to sell at suggested retail prices of $9.95.

In July 1978, TI introduced the "Starburst" watch, the first totally electronic quartz LCD analog display watch.

By 1976, TI announced it was the leading supplier in the emerging digital watch market, which was projected to grow to 18 million units that year, up from 3.5 million in 1975. The largest part of the market was the under $20 segment, and in March 1976, TI delivered the first solid-state watches to retail for under $20. TI's product development in watches proceeded in two directions—the low-end (under $10) and the high-tech end of the market, exemplified by the "Starburst" watch. TI's analog electronic watch, the "Starburst," introduced in July 1978, was the first totally electronic quartz LCD analog watch; it was manufactured until 1981.

Not to be outdone, several semiconductor manufacturers, including National Semiconductor and Intel, offered digital watches. In 1978, Hewlett-Packard introduced a digital watch with a built-in calculator. Eventually, all these would disappear from the market, as conventional watch manufacturers reclaimed the market, which ultimately proved to be more of a fashion market than an engineering timepiece market.

TI's introduction of its $9.95 digital watch, which featured a red LED display and a plastic watchband, was the beginning of the end for TI's foray in the watch market. Although the inexpensive watches were popular in the market, TI was roundly criticized for the low price, which generated higher revenues, but not profits. In 1981, TI exited the business and focused on other opportunities.

TI opened a few retail outlets in high visibility locations to display consumer products and create consumer interest, such as in this retail store in Slough, England. TI also had stores located in many of its plants so employees could purchase consumer products at a discount.

As part of its consumer strategy, TI opened a few retail outlets in high-visibility areas to create consumer interest in its calculators, digital watches, and future consumer products. On July 3, 1975, a consumer retail outlet, or "TI Store," was opened at NorthPark shopping mall in Dallas. Noted retail merchant Stanley Marcus attended the opening. Locations for other TI stores included Milan, Italy; Berlin, West Germany; and the United Kingdom.

In 1977, the company announced it was entering the marine navigation and communications market with a microprocessor-controlled Loran-C navigator receiver and a VHF/FM radiotelephone transceiver. These new products, targeted at

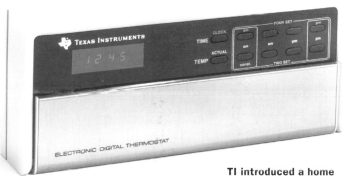

TI introduced a home digital thermostat in 1978 for use in energy conservation.

the high end of the commercial marine market, came out of TI's expertise in defense electronics.

In 1979, a talking language translator was introduced—the first to provide synthesized speech. Using a plug-in read-only memory module, the translator converted about 500 English, German, or French words to spoken Spanish. The device could link these words to speak more than 3,000 phrases and sentences. Modules were available for other language translations. TI also introduced First Watch, which taught five-to seven-year-olds to read any digital or analog timepiece.

Other consumer products introduced by TI during this period included digital thermometers, a home thermostat, a video game, and a Citizens Band (CB) radio (announced, but not put into production because of low prices in the market). In 1980, TI announced an online computer service for consumers—about 20 years ahead of the Internet. It was based on a TI-designed subsystem called TIFAX, which decoded information such as weather data broadcast to consumers' TV sets in the United Kingdom. VIEWDATA was an extension of this concept, which used the telephone system to transmit information selected from a central database containing up to 2 million pages.

Under Willis Adcock, advances in TI's semiconductor technology, such as Charge-Coupled Device imagers, led to use in medical instruments and exploratory research into the market for digital cameras and home video cameras. TI continued to develop Charge-Couple Device technology in its TI-Japan operation and became a major producer of these special chips, which are used today in a wide variety of digital cameras and camcorders.

43

PIONEERING DISTRIBUTED COMPUTING

With vision and breakthrough technology, TI launches a distributed computing thrust.

Computer technology was not new to Texas Instruments. By the early 1970s, the company already had more than a decade of experience in producing special-purpose seismic computers and small military computers, as well as growing expertise in the use of computers for factory automation and communications networks. Mark Shepherd envisioned a dramatic new trend sweeping across America and believed the time was right to shift from centralized computing to a strategy he called "distributed computing." This shift had major implications for TI and the computer industry as a whole.

TI's Silent700™ data terminals moved into volume production as the company raced to meet demand in its Houston and Temple, Texas, plants.

The first steps in TI's commercial computer strategy turned out to be in printers and terminals. In 1965, researchers in Jack Kilby's lab developed an exciting new use for silicon. Stephen Emmons, who had joined TI three months earlier, was investigating the feasibility of using monolithic silicon integrated circuit technology to build a printhead. Under Jack Kilby's direction, he and his associates solved a variety of technical challenges while they developed the first semiconductor thermal printhead—a device that allowed them to print on heat-sensitive paper. Jerry Merryman and his team later took advantage of the breakthrough technology to adapt a design for adding a printed tape output to TI's handheld calculator.

Working in TI's Digital Systems business in Houston, Texas, Herman Pope and Don Boren developed an innovative product based on the thermal printhead—the Silent700™ data terminal. It accessed computers and could be used to replace noisy mechanical printers in the workplace. In 1969, the Silent700 weighed 38 pounds and had a retail price of $3,300. Three years later, Shepherd challenged the team to create a breakthrough product that would weigh 10 pounds and could be sold for $1,000.

Tom Stringfellow's team began work on the project with the code name of Mark-10, referring to Mark Shepherd's 10-pound terminal challenge. As Stringfellow recalls, "The team met its goals and delivered a product that could be sold for $1,000. But since there were no competitive products on the market anywhere near this price, the decision was made to introduce it at $1,995." Almost a half-million of the high-profit-margin printers were sold.

For TI, the commercial computer market was tempting. As early as 1968, a team had been formed to study the potential of the minicomputer business. A huge market was developing on the horizon, but TI was confronted with a serious issue: IBM ruled the computer business, and TI didn't want to compete head-to-head with the company's largest and most valued semiconductor customer.

It was common knowledge that IBM had begun expanding its in-house semiconductor capability. In 1970, TI cautiously entered the market with its first minicomputer, the TI 960, a special-purpose machine used in factory automation. Close behind was the TI 980, a general-purpose minicomputer.

TI's Professional Computer (shown on the desktop in the background and portable unit in the foreground) as featured in a 1983 company brochure.

These were successful, but Shepherd's vision was much greater. He was one of the first to see that semiconductor technology would in time make it possible to distribute logic and memory to its final point of use—the desktop in the office, the factory floor, and the home.

Shepherd formed a task force led by Gene Helms to provide technical guidance to those businesses involved with Distributed Computing. By 1975, TI introduced the 9900/990 software-compatible family of microprocessors and minicomputers. These products were at the heart of an innovative strategy TI hoped would create an entirely new business. In 1976, the company made it official—distributed computing would be one of TI's three major thrusts.

In 1976, the TI 990 became the first in a growing family of minicomputers based on software compatibility with TI's 16-bit microprocessor. By the end of the year, there had been 10,000 shipments of the Model 900 series. TI produced a series of multi-user business minicomputer products based on TI's proprietary DX-10 software operating system marketed through an extensive network of value-added resellers.

TI had access to another valuable and familiar resource, the calculator, which gave the company insight into the applications a customer might need. The SR-52 calculator, which reached the market in 1975, had many features usually associated with a personal computer. TI formed a committee to define the specifications for a general-purpose personal computer that could bridge the gap between a programmable calculator and minicomputer.

Behind closed doors, the debate was lively and often stormy as TI tried to decide on the software format for the computer. Some thought TI would be better off using its own proprietary design. Others argued in favor of the existing IBM design.

When the discussions ended, TI bet on its own format, convinced that in time the company would profit from both the hardware and its own software. The first computer was called the "Office of the Future," or OOF among TIers.

The OOF products were installed throughout TI's offices, and the feedback was largely positive. However, by the late 1970s, several other manufacturers had also entered the market, but they adopted the IBM format. TI's software was still not compatible with the IBM format, and the IBM software was useless on TI computers. TI had positioned itself on one side of the market, while most others were fighting for a place on the other side, which offered more software, a wider range of applications, and a larger customer base. The "Office of the Future" concept never captured a significant share of the market. The OOF was terminated just as the market for general-purpose personal computers was exploding. By 1981, IBM had its own PC ready for the market.

Rod Canion, Jim Harris, and Bill Murto left TI in February 1982 and later established their own company, Compaq Computer Corporation. They developed a personal computer that could operate with all the software being developed for the IBM PC. At first, TI viewed Compaq as a rival. In time, however, the two companies resolved their differences over intellectual property, and Compaq became a valued customer for TI's semiconductor products.

The TI Professional Computer (TIPC) was not available until 1983. Technically, it was solid, but it was still not compatible with IBM's format. The TIPC achieved modest success, but the IBM format continued to dominate the market. The TIPC never gained a competitive edge and was eventually phased out in favor of laptops.

When TI moved into laptops, the company partnered with Sharp Corporation to bring out the smallest, thinnest, lightest product in the marketplace. It was fitted with an Intel microprocessor and designed to be compatible with the IBM format. Around 1992, TI introduced a series of competitive, award-winning notebook computers under the TravelMate™ logo, which ultimately became fourth in the market.

By the early 1990s, TI began focusing on its core businesses of digital signal processing and analog semiconductors. In 1991, the industrial automation business was sold to Siemens; in 1992, the multi-user computer systems and services business was sold to Hewlett-Packard, and the notebook computer business was sold five years later to Acer Computer Company.

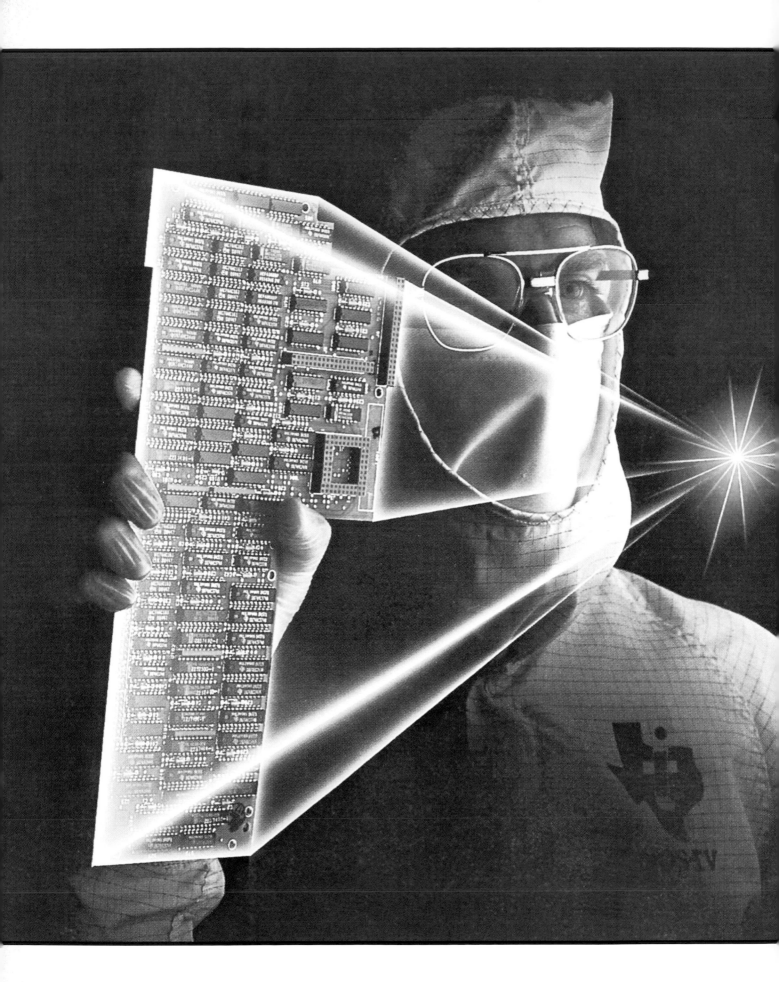

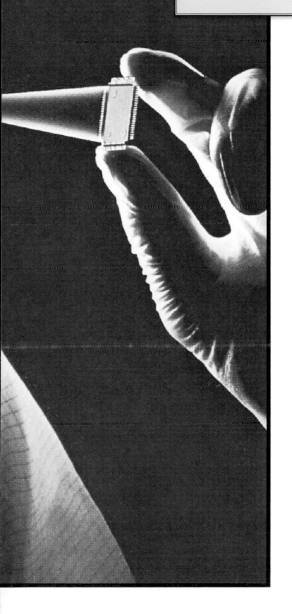

REINVENTING TI

In 1989, Jerry Junkins, TI's CEO at that time, led a process designed to better understand the changing world and TI's position in it. By 1993, a Strategy Leadership Team was formed with a mandate to develop a new course for TI. In a series of divestitures and acquisitions, TI was reshaped and refocused to take advantage of the projected growth markets for the next decade. There were some painful changes, such as the decision to leave the commodity memory market and apply TI's leadership manufacturing capability to the more profitable, differentiated portions of the semiconductor market. TI targeted system solutions for customers in large, global vertical markets, such as wireless, broadband access, and emerging consumer electronics. TI also focused on new opportunities in sensors, radio frequency identification, and digital light processing. The result of the multi-year process was a leaner, more focused company—one that would become the number one analog producer in the world and an even stronger leader in digital signal processors. By the start of the new millenium under the leadership of Tom Engibous, TI had reinvented itself, as it had many times before.

As TI moved to reinvent itself, the company worked closely with customers to shrink complete systems into powerful single-chip solutions.

44

VISION 2000

Under Jerry Junkins' leadership, TI developed a visionary strategy that would reshape the company's focus and direction in the 21st century.

The crumbling of the Berlin Wall signified the thawing of the Cold War. It also heralded the shrinking of defense budgets, and TI realized its traditional electronics business for the military could soon decline. The company was competing on many fronts, and the semiconductor industry was in the midst of dramatic changes. Out of the challenges, a leaner TI would emerge—focused on competing in the global market.

In 1989, CEO Jerry Junkins established TI's Vision 2000 "to signify the type of company we wanted to be as we moved into the new century." The change in TI's way of doing business needed to "match the dynamic change in our world markets," he pointed out. He challenged the company with three primary questions: Where is the world going? What will be TI's position? How will we get there?

As Tom Engibous remembered, "We saw an emerging world of digital communications, and we realized that this new world would require real-time signal processing, which relied on digital signal processing and analog semiconductors. Both were well-established capabilities inside TI. Our strategy was to grow by expanding signal processing's reach into new markets and further penetrate existing ones."

Vision 2000 identified semiconductors as TI's principal market and began strategic planning for world leadership

The TI Strategy Leadership Team was formed in 1993 as the focal point for key decisions in the company. Seated, left to right, are Bill Mitchell, Jerry Junkins, and Hank Hayes. Standing, left to right, are Bill Aylesworth, Dick Agnich, Pat Weber, Dave Martin, Tom Engibous, and Dean Clubb.

in selected markets. Throughout the world, the semiconductor business was in the midst of a transition in products, process technology, and global deployment. TI's goal was to maintain the strength of its standard products while shifting more of the company's business into proprietary products such as application specific integrated circuits, advanced linear devices, microcontrollers, and special-purpose processors. All of these had the potential for becoming an important part of the market but required TI to have a greater understanding of its customers' businesses and their product needs. TI's strategic plan for semiconductors, based on the premise that the company would become more involved with its customers, would one day become the hallmark of TI's business decision to focus on proprietary products, high-growth markets, and eventually, digital signal processing solutions.

TI made severe cost reductions in the defense electronics side of the company, consolidating to match the defense market's tighter constraints on spending. Vision 2000 created a new information systems business unit that focused on the advanced productivity of software tools. TI believed the high-growth business could potentially expand beyond areas of internal expertise. In addition, Materials & Controls used semiconductor technology to open new opportunities in electronic sensors for automotive applications and electronic identification and registration systems.

TI recognized that its strength would depend on its success in developing strong leaders who could manage, as well as capitalize on change, which was the only constant in the company's business. The 1990 company newsletter reported, *"Our vision is to select, develop, reward, and plan the succession of key leaders who possess the leadership skills TI must have to accomplish global business objectives in the year 2000."* TI looked for leaders who were visionary, decisive, focused, results-oriented, risk-taking, flexible, customer-oriented, empowering, and multidimensional. In addition, they needed to be role models, excellent communicators, and developers of high-quality subordinates.

Junkins believed in the power of teams, and, in December 1993, he created a Strategy Leadership Team (SLT), comprised of the company's top operations and staff officers. They were charged with defining and nurturing a direction for TI. As Junkins said, "We have the chance to build a unified, long-term strategy for our company."

Junkins intended for the team to become the focal point for top management decisions across the company. He said, "If we do it right, then all the other functions of the company

Yukio Sakamoto (center) of TI-Japan was among the TIers who met in early 1995 to help refine drafts of a new TI strategy and vision. More than 200 TIers participated in a yearlong series of workshops.

will interlink with that team, and we can effectively manage the company that way. This structure will give us more time to spend with customers. It will allow us to make faster and better decisions and to take full advantage of growth opportunities."

For the next two years, the SLT established the goals and roadmaps that would take the company into the next century. In its final report, the SLT set forth its strategy *"to focus on developing the products and services that make it easy for people to be interconnected via digital technology."* The report went on to explain, *"We believe the most significant added value in electronic equipment is the ability for people to form networks that enable them to share information more effectively.*

"We see the development of a networked-society pattern of digital connections that is global, unprecedented, vital, and exciting in the way it propels the opportunities for entirely new markets.

"Much of TI's strategic emphasis in semiconductors is focused on

digital signal processing which is at the heart of many of the multimedia technologies, such as communications and full-motion video that are critical to the digital revolution.

"Over the next few years, TI expects to make a major contribution to the critical technologies driving the digital revolution across a broad base of capabilities in sensing, processing, transmission, and display.

"The most exciting part of TI's story is still ahead. The networked society offers boundless opportunities for our technology and our creativity. TI's core competencies and technologies play right at the heart of the digital revolution."

———

During 1995, TI identified the longer-term market environment and core competencies required to meet the needs of its customers. They believed that the company had only begun to tap its potential and was determined to achieve world leadership in digital solutions for a networked society.

TI knew it had a strong position in high-growth markets, including DSP, wireless communications, digital imaging, and networking. The common denominator for those successes had been a high market share with above average return. The company would build its future business strategies on that model, and management was committed "to invest to win."

Implementing this new vision wouldn't be easy and might even be disruptive. But this was the map management believed TI was destined to follow. As Junkins said, "If I could change one thing, it would be the cultural resistance to the kinds of change we're going through. We are products of our past. We have to focus our anxious energy toward a positive change. We'll be more competitive if we do that."

Junkins had the vision and understood the need to keep pace with a changing marketplace. The quiet revolution had been his idea. But tragically, Jerry Junkins was not there to see it realized. He died on an overseas business trip in 1996.

Reflecting on this period in early 2005, Rich Templeton, now president and CEO, said, "Jerry taught us how to find our heart again as a company. It wasn't just the mind that TI needed, but the heart and mind working together. Then Tom Engibous stepped up and showed us how to win; the importance of getting our customers at the center of the way we thought and the way we operated."

———

Engibous, who had been working closely with Junkins, was handed the reins as TI's President and CEO, and a reorganized management team accelerated the execution of the vision as the final decade of the 20th century drew to a close.

Engibous remembered, "That process was the initial beginning of TI's management saying that the path we've been on for the last few decades—the one that has brought us so much success—will not be the path that allows us to

The icon adopted by the semiconductor business as a result of the Vision 2000 process featured the customer at its core, and emphasized teamwork, policy deployment, excellence, and management-by-fact as key elements.

be successful during the next few decades. It was the first realization that TI needed to make another major reinvention of itself to become a long-lived, successful, high-tech company.

"We examined the whole company. Nothing was off-limits. We tried to figure out where the world was going because that determined where TI would be steered next. And digital signal processing and analog began to emerge as the answer.

"The world had shifted from the mainframe era—dominated and accelerated by TTL logic—to the minicomputer and personal computer, where microprocessors and memory served as the semiconductor growth engine.

"And we believed the next era would belong to the telecommunications and Internet markets. It would be fundamentally different. All applications would be real-time. Our vision was to put TI's financial, energy, technological, and intellectual focus on those areas where we were the industry leaders. No longer would we be distracted by other businesses where TI might not be as competitive as other companies at the time. No longer would we be simply designing integrated circuits. We would be designing entire systems."

This quest for a new vision and strategy improved TI's competitive position in the semiconductor industry. During the Strategy Leadership Team's work in 1994, Jerry Junkins said, "I assure you that if you look back in a few years, you'll find we've created a company unlike anything that exists today, and we will have developed a much more competitive position in the marketplace."

45

MAKING MEMORY

TI gambled that large amounts of memory would be vital to the future of computers and computing.

The years TI spent pursuing the high-growth but volatile memory market enabled the company to learn how to optimize die size, improve yields, ramp to volume quickly, reduce test time, and work closely with joint-venture partners. And, perhaps as importantly, the memory business gave TI an opportunity to understand the lessons of quality and reliability within the company's culture and its semiconductor operations.

During the 1960s, Pat Haggerty and Mark Shepherd devised ways in which semiconductor applications could literally change the world. They felt memory had the potential for a high-growth, high-volume, low-cost market that could become one of the keys to unlock chip pervasiveness and, in the process, enhance TI's manufacturing skills.

Originally, computers had been viewed as the obvious test bed for the company's early breakthroughs in transistors and integrated circuits. Dean Toombs, who headed semiconductor research, recalled, "Haggerty would philosophize that one of the key things to the future of computers and data processing would be large amounts of very low-cost memory storage." Harvey Cragon and Joe Watson built the first semiconductor digital memory, using TI integrated circuits in a small Air Force computer.

Research on memory technologies at TI had varying degrees of success for more than a decade. Metal Oxide Semiconductor (MOS) memories achieved great success, but eventually Complementary Metal Oxide semiconductor (CMOS) memories became the company's dominant memory technology.

For TI, semiconductor memory was a way to achieve a high-volume product in leading-edge process technology quickly. High-speed bipolar memories found applications in high-performance central processors, buffer memories, and high-speed peripherals. MOS, on the other hand, was being used in add-on memory systems and in the main memory storage of most computers. During a six-month period in 1972, the company announced a milestone: it shipped more semiconductor memory bits than any other semiconductor manufacturer, propelling TI to a leadership position in the technology.

Manufacturing innovations continued to enable greater chip density. For memory products, the one-transistor cell design increased the capacity of MOS random access memories (RAM). By the end of 1975, semiconductor memory, supported by further cost reduction, continued to displace

A gowned worker in the DMOS4 wafer fab cleanroom in Dallas tracking wafers as part of the memory chip production process.

magnetic cores. As the year ended, TI led the industry in the shipment of 4K RAMs, which just happened to be the fastest-growing memory component.

Despite its success, however, the memory business was not for the weak of heart. TI managers had to deal with the impossible task of forecasting accurately, building manufacturing capacity ahead of demand, driving costs down in the midst of declining prices, and seeking innovative ways to develop more highly integrated products for each new generation. It was a tight wire few could master. The costs gradually escalated because the wafer fabrication facilities, or fabs, had become very capital intensive. During the 1980s, a new high-volume fab could cost as much as $100 million, and generally more, at a time when the 64K DRAM was selling for $4 each.

The downturn of 1975 was severe, but the recession that swept over the semiconductor industry a decade later was the worst the world had seen up to that time. The emergence of large, well-financed competitors on the international landscape changed TI's long-standing memory strategy. The company had established itself as a strong leader in the 64K market and announced production of a 256K DRAM, projected to be the largest-selling component in semiconductor industry history. Within four years, it was predicted that 3 billion units would be shipped worldwide. But in May 1985, the Japanese unexpectedly introduced their version of the 256K

Photo of 16-Mbit DRAM chip on multi-colored wafer—taken around 1990. As TI moved to next-generation technology, costs escalated for wafer fab equipment.

DRAM, and competition grew intense.

TI's company newsletter reported, *"Japanese competitors were ahead of us, and further exacerbating the situation was a semiconductor downturn. In May 1985, the industry was predicting a 15 percent decline. In spite of the downturn, we are not delaying implementation of our key capital investments and new product development, and TI will be in a good position when the upturn comes."*

The Japanese, and later Korean manufacturers, understood the value of memory and its process development as a way to leverage designs into a high-volume market. TI witnessed its position in the marketplace rapidly erode with the onslaught of highly competitive and well financed Japanese producers.

To minimize its capital expenditures and keep the company's investments at a reasonable level, TI sought joint-venture partners interested in participating in the memory business. On the research side, TI and Hitachi began sharing technology related to the development of the 16-Mbit DRAM, making it possible for both companies to produce new products faster and at a lower cost. TI entered into agreements with Acer Corporation in Taiwan (1989) and Kobe Steel in western Japan (1990). TECH, a joint venture, was formed as a partnership among TI, the government of Singapore, Canon, and Hewlett-Packard in Singapore (1991).

Because of its joint ventures, as well as its cooperative research and development programs, TI was able to remain active in the memory business. TI expanded its operations to include such differentiated products as video RAMs for graphic applications and the industry's first x4 DRAM. In 1996, TI and Hitachi established the first joint venture in the U.S. Known as TwinStar, the operation began just as the price of DRAMs declined. Within two years, TI purchased Hitachi's share, leaving TwinStar as a wholly owned subsidiary of TI.

During the 1980s, TI launched its digital signal processing business and, by the start of the 1990s, began gaining traction in a growing line of proprietary products. Among the businesses that would emerge from this focus was wireless. A wave of change swept over TI, and memory technology started to fade as a primary revenue and margin generator for the company.

By the late 90s, TI no longer believed it could maintain a global edge in memory chips, and, in 1998, TI sold its memory business to Micron Technology Inc. Included in the transaction were TI's wafer fabrication facilities in Italy, the TwinStar facility in Richardson, Texas, and an assembly/test facility in Singapore. Micron also received TI's internet in two joint ventures: TECH Semiconductor Singapore and KTI Semiconductor in Japan. Micron expanded its leadership in the memory market, and TI, retaining its ownership of memory patents, focused on digital signal processing and analog semiconductors.

Tom Engibous announced, "Several years ago, TI set a course to become a company focused on its leadership position in digital signal processing. With this latest transaction [the sale of the memory business], TI truly becomes a DSP Solutions company." For TI, memory was a highly volatile commodity that cost a fortune to sustain. Yet memory helped TI learn a lot about signal processing, hone its manufacturing skills and taught the company about high-volume production of leading-edge technologies while focusing on finding ways to reduce production costs.

CUTTING COSTS
★ ★ ★

One of the ongoing legacies of memory was a focus on cost containment. Everyone got involved. To reduce costs, paper was recycled so the blank back side could be used, every other light bulb was removed from some buildings, and office supplies were closely monitored. No cost savings were too small to ignore. During periods of DRAM oversupply, add-in memory board manufacturers on the West Coast would delay placing orders until the end of the day, Pacific Time, requiring TI to staff groups in Houston and Dallas, who stayed late in the Central Time Zone, to book and ship these orders within hours in case pricing fell before morning in the Pacific Time zone.

46

DIGITAL SIGNAL PROCESSING

DSP Solutions become TI's primary focus.

"TI wasn't just a participant in real-time processing; we really started the DSP market. We were the experts in signal processing, and we had all the pieces to put together signal processing solutions," said TI Chairman Tom Engibous as he reflected in February 2005 on the company's business refocus. It didn't happen fast, and it wasn't always easy. Moving into the 21st century, TI redefined and built the company around its expertise in digital signal processing (DSP) solutions.

Texas Instruments' legacy in analog signal processing in oil exploration, then its experience in digitizing analog data and building computers for seismic processing, coupled with its skills in semiconductor integration and software development, all contributed to a revolutionary concept—the single-chip DSP. In 1979, at TI's strategic planning conference in Dallas, Harvey Cragon, TI senior fellow, explained how a dedicated signal processing microcomputer chip could become a leadership product. "All tradeoffs," he said, "were to favor digital signal processing." Cragon was asked to put together a study group to outline an architectural concept and design philosophy for the technology.

The first programmable DSP chip, as superimposed on Harvey Cragon's pencil sketch of the Signal Processing Computer chip. This architecture, with modifications by the Houston team, led to TI's introduction of the single-chip DSP in 1982.

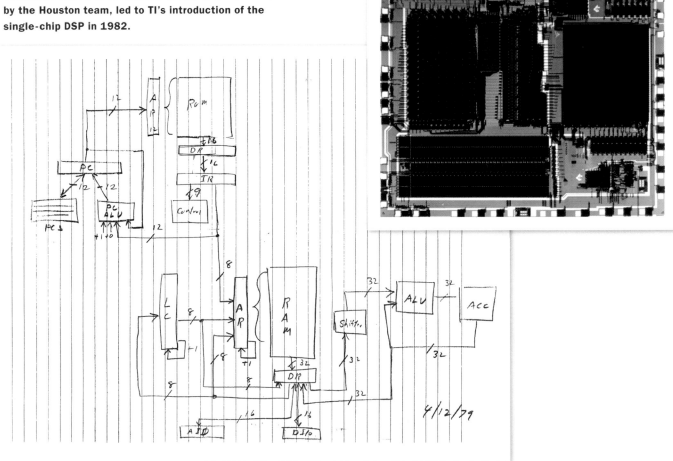

TI President and CEO Rich Templeton, looking back on this period in February 2005, said it was a difficult time for the company. "We were losing our competitiveness. We were mostly a commodity logic company and a commodity memory business." TI wanted a winner in the microprocessor market after seeing competitors achieve major success, and the company planned to hang its hat on its real-time DSPs, hoping they would be the company's specialized processor to perform mathematical computations instantaneously with a high level of precision.

Using his years of experience designing TI computers to perform signal processing, Cragon played a pivotal role in convincing the company that the project should be funded. The company then gave its microprocessor team in Houston the task of investigating DSP development, using $150,000 to fund the study. The Programmable Products Division was tagged to design and produce the new chip as TI's specialized microprocessor. The team took shape in the late 1970s under the direction of Tony Leigh from TI's United Kingdom design center. John Hughes provided marketing support; Ed Hassler provided the simulation and Computer Aided Design (CAD) support. Based on his microprocessor experience, Ed Caudel designed the machine architecture, Wanda Gass worked on the analog interface, and Surendar Magar provided the design experience to determine whether the architecture could be produced using available processes. This team drove a major design decision to use a fast multiplier feature in the architecture, differentiating TI's processor from other approaches.

The programmable product design team faced the task of designing a processor for a market that did not yet exist. Later, Mike Hames, now a TI senior vice president and manager of Application Specific Products, pointed out, "In Houston at the time, we didn't have a lot of successful products, and we were hungry for business. We had a lot of ideas; we had a lot of brilliant people, but we really had not turned a product into a big business. Our attitude was that DSP was

TI's DSP business was built around support, documentation, and design assistance. This display from an early ad shows the range of support, from software development tools to training manuals—everything customers needed to get their products to market.

so new and changing the way people do things. We felt like we were on a mission."

In early 1982, the team delivered the first single-chip DSP. Marketing literature touted the new TMS320™ signal processing chip as *"an important new microcomputer for a dedicated function...capable of processing digitized signals in real time. The processor section is a 32-bit arithmetic logic unit, which achieves an operating speed of 5 million instructions per second (MIPS), comparable to the speed of many mainframe computers."* Once the concept had been proven and demonstrated to customers, the team turned its attention to releasing the product and building a market infrastructure.

"I think the power of what we had was that we had a passionate team of 20-30 people down in Houston who thought they could change the world," said Templeton. "It took 15 years before the rest of the world could even spell DSP, let alone announce that they wanted to try to compete with it, at which point we had established a very strong business in that space."

Hames credits the team's staying power with the support of people like K. Bala, Rich Templeton, John Scarisbrick, and Wally Rhines. "They trusted us. They empowered us. They

With the new millennium came new generations of DSPs. TI's TMS320C64x and TMS320C55x DSPs drove much higher performance and lower power consumption than previously available, helping to create today's portable internet and multimedia communications markets such as digital cell phones and consumer electronics.

sheltered us," he said. "They allowed us to continue. But some days, the bigger battle was just believing in it yourself. When you're starting a new business, you've got to have energy and enthusiasm because the people around you will sense that. And if they think you're excited and that you believe, then they want to believe, too."

Even as the market for TI's DSPs moved slower than the company hoped, Rhines led a team that conceived an architectural concept called function-to-function architecture (FFA) to guide their future product roadmaps. The FFA provided a framework for defining semiconductor products that could fulfill major functions within new systems being developed by TI's customers. This concept laid the groundwork for TI's next-generation families of fixed- and floating-point DSPs.

After the development of DSP technology, TI faced an even greater challenge—market perception. As *The Wall Street Journal* reported, *"In the past, TI had a reputation for developing a product and then telling customers why they needed it. But before launching its first DSP in 1982, TI began rounding up backers through seminars and electronic bulletin boards. It created 'tools' software for writing programs the chip could execute."* Building an infrastructure became a key

element of its DSP marketing efforts.

When Bill Sick became head of the semiconductor business in 1982, he studied the program with Rhines and recalls, "Although the size of the potential market for the DSP was still not very clear at the time, it appeared that DSP was the major proprietary product that TI needed to shift its product mix from largely commodity products to more profitable proprietary products."

The biggest challenge was convincing designers that DSPs were the future of electronics. TI knew it had a winning processor, but customers were skeptical about moving to a new technology when they had little or no knowledge of it. The team realized they would need to evangelize the merits of using DSPs in systems.

Since most digital signal processing work was being done at the university graduate level, TI began to reach out to university engineering departments, paying for textbooks and giving away computers and programming tools. Sick, a member of the advisory committee of Rice University's engineering school, worked closely with Professor Sidney Burrus, head of the school's electrical engineering department and an early digital signal processing pioneer. They agreed that TI and Rice would develop joint DSP technology programs, which in turn inspired Professors Burrus, Tom Parks, and John Treichler to write textbooks containing application information and code for designing with TI's DSPs. As a result, a whole generation of engineers was trained in the use of TI's technology. Students became comfortable using TI's DSP in new designs; TI was educating its future customers while they were still in college. Throughout the country and then the world, TI's DSP university programs supported the study of digital signal processing across the curriculums from undergraduates through the Ph.D. level, allowing the company to proliferate the technology across a wide, diverse, global potential customer base.

The TI third-party program was another key element of early marketing efforts. To proliferate TI DSP technology within its customer base and to make it easier for customers in the design phase, TI began to bring in other companies familiar with TI's technology to provide hardware, software, and design assistance to customers. The third-party program was born. This program combined with the university program built an infrastructure that supported further development of the technology. TI began hosting conferences to bring these communities together with customers to talk about and evangelize their work.

DSP marketing manager Jim Huffhines and his team knew they had to get the semiconductor sales force on board if they wanted to reach new DSP customers. It was a challenging transition, as the sales force was comfortable with easy-selling memory chips. The DSP team resorted to game-show tactics, handing out $20, $10, and $1 bills to sales reps who correctly answered questions about their presentations. Managers and chip designers responded immediately when a potential customer called with an idea—even if it meant meeting an entrepreneur in his living room.

"Our feeling was DSP was going to go the same way the microprocessor had ten years earlier, so we went around the world trying to preach the gospel of DSP. It was a missionary role because when we started, the market for programmable DSP was nothing," recalls Hames. It became a multi-billion-dollar market.

During the early years, TI's top ten DSP customer list changed dramatically from year to year. Some early customers used a DSP as a prototyping device, which they then shifted to an application specific integrated circuit in production. In 1985, when the company brought out the first DSP using its complementary metal oxide semiconductor technology, the DSP performance level greatly improved while reducing power consumption.

When TI announced the first DSP in 1982, the company had fully expected the U.S. market to grow from $25 million to $175 million between 1983 and 1985. By 1986, however, TI's DSP sales were a disappointing $6 million.

The first quarter stockholders' report in 1986 stated, *"In signal processing, we have initially captured more than half of a market that is expected to grow to more than $600 million by 1990."* By 1988, the company reported that "the cost and performance of these processors have permitted their use in a much broader range of applications." As customers found new uses for TI's DSPs, the market expanded, and TI optimized its product line to meet the requirements of different applications.

"Things began to occur that changed our path," said Gene Frantz, TI principal fellow. "We got blindsided by our customers. We did these early devices thinking about speech synthesis and speech translation coding with an eye

EDN NAMES TI AS TOP INNOVATOR IN TWO AWARDS
★ ★ ★

At its annual award event held on March 7, 2005, EDN magazine named TI's TMS320C55x™ DSPs the "Greatest Innovation in the Past 15 Years" and the TMS320C5000™ Low-Power Design Tool Suite as the winner in the "Software" category for Innovation of the Year for 2004. First introduced in 2000, TI's low-power C55x DSPs are the integral processors that helped propel the rapid adoption of wireless digital cell phones and other communications and consumer product innovations. They beat out Intel's Pentium Processor and products from HP, ADI and others for the honor.

Recently, TI announced that it has shipped more than 1 billion TMS320C5000 DSPs to Nokia, the world's largest cell phone maker. In addition to digital cell phones, TI's C55x DSPs are used in digital still cameras, Internet audio players, digital radios, and portable instrumentation.

TI's C5000 Low-Power Design Tool Suite is the first comprehensive tool suite to eliminate the guesswork in determining actual DSP power consumption during product design. It includes software to implement the power-saving features of the C55x DSPs in real-world applications.

A panel of *EDN* technical editors chose the finalists in each category, and then *EDN* readers crowned TI DSP products winners in an online ballot. The winners were announced during a special ceremony at the Embedded Systems Conference in San Francisco.

on the telecom industry. Then all of a sudden, we started seeing people like the hard disk guys and modem companies recognizing the advantage of using DSP." Customers realized that the technology offered lower cost, ease of manufacturing, and higher performance.

As Hames pointed out, "If you keep your ears up and listen to the pulse of the marketplace, you start figuring out what the key enablers are, and then you turn that into a strategy. A lot of our best ideas came from spending time with customers in the marketplace, learning about the obstacles and problems they faced, then deciding how our products could solve them." The evangelism paid off; DSPs had a market, and it would become big.

TI's development tools, including those offered by third parties, and sales strategies focused on supporting designers' needs to integrate DSPs into their system designs. So, TI moved to a systems-related approach, as opposed to a product-oriented one. Engibous set up separate business units to address various application areas, such as wireless, broadband, and emerging end equipments.

According to industry statistics, the DSP market, including single-chips, programmable DSPs, and general-purpose and custom ASICs, became nearly an $8 billion market by the end of 2004. TI's market share was about half of it.

Years of perseverance and dedication paid off.

As Engibous pointed out, "Digital signal processing is the engine that enabled the real-time digital revolution. In DSP, we are determined to have two to three times the market share of any competitor. We are playing to win."

FINDING THE "LUNATIC FRINGE"

Through the University Program, TI introduced DSP at the undergraduate level. In the mid 1980s, many engineering Ph.D.s were leaving college and forming their own companies to use DSP products. They came up with wild ideas such as digital cell phones, digital cameras, digital audio, digital television, and cable modems.

"They are what I like to call the lunatic fringe," said Gene Frantz, TI Principal Fellow. "They have what appear to be crazy, far-out ideas, but 20 years later they're considered just genius." TI cultivated these geniuses, working closely with them by providing support, encouragement, and the technologies needed.

"They may have begun as the lunatic fringe, but they were considered mainstream as soon as their products became successful in the marketplace," said Frantz.

Frantz, a proud member of the lunatic fringe himself, believes the first wave of the DSP revolution was telecom, changing the way we do land-line, modem, and wireless communications.

A mature market today, it still has room to grow.

"The second wave is entertainment. We've seen audio and TV go digital; radio and images go digital. We're seeing the first and second wave combine to what we're calling 'streaming media,'" said Frantz.

In 2005, Frantz said he plans to work with the new lunatic fringe to find the third wave of the digital revolution as it affects transportation, medicine, security, and education.

"There may be a way to use DSPs so automobiles can sense what's around them," he said. "We need medicines that can improve the quality of our lives. We want our safety and privacy protected with better security. And it has always troubled me to see teachers writing on a chalkboard, using century-old methods to teach new technologies."

He believes DSP is becoming multi-dimensional with video and imaging processes. "That takes a lot more performance," Frantz said. "But the strength of TI has always been creating capabilities to provide more performance."

47

DSP GOES TO SCHOOL

TI's DSP University Program invests in the education of future generations of engineers.

As soon as TI began to understand the potential of digital signal processors (DSPs), the company realized it faced a formidable challenge in the expanding world market. Few customers could comprehend the technology and the difference it was destined to make in the changing business environment. TI made a strategic decision to invest in the education of engineering students in far-reaching DSP applications and leading edge semiconductor technology. Led by Mike Hames, now senior vice president and manager of the Applications Specific Products division, the

TI University Program was established in 1982 to facilitate the inclusion of digital signal processing in engineering classrooms, research labs, textbooks, and course curricula.

Early in 2005, Rich Templeton, TI's President and CEO, reflecting on the decision to invest in university engineering education, said, "We spent 10 years evangelizing about programmable DSPs and how you could uniquely solve problems in a different way. The work that was done with universities and third parties was to create new ways to apply programmable DSPs to old problems that had previously been done with open-loop control, bit-sliced, or analog solutions."

By 2005, more than a thousand universities around the globe were members of the program, establishing TI's TMS320™ DSP family as the digital signal processing standard. In the European Union alone, more than half the universities have a TI DSP lab putting TI software and hardware development tools into the hands of students. Each year, universities in India are graduating 20,000 engineering students who have TI DSP lab training. Professor H.S. Jamadagni of the Indian Institute of Science in Bangalore said, "The TI education program was the best I had seen from the industry. The program supports course and lab development projects, research and mentoring

A team of students from Technion, the Israel Institute of Technology, wins the $100,000 prize in TI's DSP and Analog Challenge in 2001 for its project "Real-Time Digital Watermarking System for Audio Signals Using Perceptual Masking." Left to right: Gene Frantz, (TI); Nimrod Peleg, Advising Professor, Technion; Shay Mizrahi, Team Leader, Technion; Jack Kilby, Nobel Laureate, inventor of the Integrated Circuit; Yuval Cassuto, Team Member, Technion; Michael Lustig, Team Member, Technion.

In 1999, TI boosted its university network and established the DSP Leadership University Program. Its goal was to speed-up DSP education, applications, and algorithm development. Inaugural members of the pilot program were Rice University, Georgia Tech, and Massachusetts Institute of Technology (MIT). Leading faculty members are pictured here (left to right) with Gene Frantz, TI Principal Fellow: Jim McClellan, Georgia Institute of Technology; Sidney Burrus, Rice University; and Alan Oppenheim, Massachusetts Institute of Technology.

of students, which was as important as the material support. Response of TI to our needs was always excellent and at lightning speed." For TI, improving the quality of engineering education with an emphasis on DSP was essential to building the strong foundation for technology that had given birth to the company's new direction.

Teaming with the Institute of Electrical and Electronic Engineers, TI was an early supporter of the International Conference on Acoustics, Speech, and Signal Processing, which focused on theoretical work. TI began exhibiting digital signal processing applications at the conference and facilitated a closer coupling of theoretical and application spaces. Other programs like TI's DSP Solutions Challenge and Elite Lab projects gave students hands-on experience, challenged them to work on cutting-edge projects, and taught skills that made them valuable candidates in the high-tech job market. TI has facilitated the education of a DSP-literate engineering workforce worldwide through its many programs. Many of those students would ultimately work for TI's current customers or become new customers themselves at other companies. They would bring with them a predisposition to TI's technology. As the number of DSP-savvy students grew, so did TI's base of new markets in regions where the university programs were located—the Americas, Asia, Europe, Israel, Japan, and India.

———

By building relationships with educators, TI bridged another gap—between businesses and the academic world. TI's strategy was to provide educators with tools to help them teach real world, real-time signal processing, making it more exciting, relevant, and affordable for students to begin developing ideas for future products. Working with top academicians, TI was able to have DSP platforms incorporated into more than 30 textbooks as well as into teaching kits the company provided. By partnering with universities and their brightest engineering students, TI extended its research capabilities. The company provided university researchers with tools, making it possible for them to use DSP while solving next-generation problems and developing innovative roadmaps for markets, technologies, and solutions.

Al Oppenheim, a professor at MIT, explained, "TI recognized the need for research in universities to be very uninhibited and in a style that is highly creative and speculative. Another part of the magic has been a tight linking of theory, hardware, and applications through ongoing exposure of the universities to interesting industrial problems and exposure of industry to exciting emerging theory and ideas. This linking, when effective, keeps theory from going off in esoteric directions that may be mathematically interesting but of less practical significance and allows for exciting technology transfer. That's why the opportunity to work together with industry is so critical to universities."

In 1997, TI established a DSP University Research Fund to extend the company's lead in DSP solutions. TI's focus was on such areas as wireless communications, high-speed networks, and smart motor control while, at the same time, educating the next-generation of electronic designers on TI DSPs.

University-based research plays a key role in technologies that drive the DSP world and makes significant advancements in communications, entertainment, and information. In 1999, TI boosted its university network by establishing the DSP Leadership University Program, whose goal was to accelerate DSP education, applications, and algorithm development. Inaugural members of the program were Rice University, Georgia Tech, and MIT.

———

Craig H. Richardson, vice president and general manager of Polycom Installed Voice Business, became acquainted with digital signal processing through TI's affiliation with Georgia Tech. As Richardson explains, "Learning DSP through a textbook makes it seem very theoretical and abstract, while real-time examples help the student understand, at the next level, what is happening. Not having the hands-on aspect of a real-time signal processing environment would be like studying transistors without ever building a circuit. Working with real-time hardware and software reinforced the basic principles and made them come alive. By having exposure to real-time hardware, you are more confident and have more tangible experience. In fact, I hire an overwhelming majority of my engineers from schools that provide TI's real-time DSP experience, and there are at least 50 engineers in our company who deal with the aspects of signal processing every day."

Building a future workforce through higher education primarily emphasizing engineering, math, and science—TI advanced its commitment further. The company developed partnerships and programs, offered expertise, donated equipment, and contributed grants totaling more than $75 million. Mike Hames explained, "We made a strategic decision early in the program not to expect a grade on our investment; it was truly a leap of faith. We believed if you educate people and do the right things, it will result in revenue and profitability. And now 23 years later, that leap has paid off.

"The University Program remains a talent pipeline for recruiting the brightest engineers for us and our customers, which provides a true competitive advantage. In addition, some of the most important advances in algorithmic and application breakthroughs are seeded in our universities. This is where the next-generation wireless systems, futuristic electric cars, and keys that unlock medical mysteries are being hatched."

RESEARCH IN ACTION

★ ★ ★

In 1995, TI's DSP Solutions Challenge offered a $100,000 grand prize in a worldwide contest that encouraged college students to use DSPs in new applications.

First-place money was shared by Dilip Krishnan and Showbhik Kalra from the Nanyang Technological University in Singapore. The second-year computer engineering students together devised a way to restore damaged motion picture frames quickly and effectively.

Their restoration process erased damaged areas of the film and filled in the resulting empty space with information captured automatically from elsewhere in the film.

Lead judge Gene Frantz, TI Principal Fellow, said, "It caught the imagination of the judges. We all know that old films, which we like to watch, are pitted and scratched. This fixed that problem. It's something we experience in everyday life."

Today, Krishnan works for a company in Singapore doing digital restoration projects. Before leaving to pursue his MBA at Harvard Business School in Boston, Massachusetts, in 2004, Kalra had worked in the digital cinema industry.

Dr. Man-Nang Chong, who was advising professor of Krishnan and Kalra, now CEO of GDC Technology Limited, a pioneer in digital postproduction and exhibition technologies, said, "By participating in TI's DSP Solutions Challenge competition, our passionate R&D work was made known to the world, including Hollywood studios. The exposure and experience we gained enabled us to pursue our successful careers in the digital film entertainment industry."

The contest brought in entries from 230 teams consisting of 700 students from 26 countries. Other winners included three students from the University of Maryland, who used DSPs to develop a compression system for real-time video communications over existing telephone lines, and a team from Ecole d'Ingénieurs des technologies des l'Information et du Management (EFREI) outside Paris, France, who developed a processor for an advanced Doppler radar tracking system for smaller airports.

TI's DSP Solutions Challenge design contests have awarded more than $360,000 in cash prizes since the program began. The winning entries have ranged from applications in video processing to direct broadcast television to audio processing. Winning design teams have hailed from around the world from such places as Singapore, Italy, and Israel.

In 1996, Dr. Man-Nang Chong led a team of graduate students from Nanyang Technological University, Singapore, to win TI's DSP Solutions Challenge contest. Now, imaging expert Chong, founder and CEO of GDC Technology, has introduced the first Digital Cinema in China using Christie's DLP™ Cinema projector.

The first consumer application of the integrated circuit was in Zenith's miniature hearing aid, as shown in this early advertisement.

48

THE MAGNITUDE OF ANALOG TECHNOLOGY

TI moves into world leadership in analog integrated circuits, one of the most stable and profitable semiconductor markets.

Before digital technology became prevalent, TI operated efficiently in a world of analog data in oil exploration, in military equipment, and in its first computers. Even after technology shifted to digital techniques, analog integrated circuits maintained a steady and profitable position within TI's business strategy. When communications and entertainment applications surpassed personal computers as the technology drivers, TI emerged as the global market leader for analog semiconductors. The company combined its digital and analog capabilities into real-time signal processing solutions for customers in communications, computing, consumer electronics, industrial, audio, video, and automotive markets.

During the 1950s, the company's linear transistors amplified signals in hearing aids and later went into radios, television sets, stereos, home music systems, and a wide range of consumer products. In 1962, the Minuteman Missile carried TI's customer linear and digital integrated circuits, and four years later, IBM emerged as one of the company's largest customers for analog devices.

In early 1972, TI reported that production quantities of linear integrated circuits, were being delivered to major television set manufacturers in the U.S., Europe, and Japan. In the U.S., TI estimated that most color TV sets would have TI's linear integrated circuits performing automatic fine-tuning for picture

quality, sound information processing, and color processing for color quality. Even though its linear business was steadily growing, TI's analog technologies rarely received the same attention as the company's memory and microprocessor thrusts, but TI's analog business delivered profits.

When Del Whitaker joined TI in 1971, he was told analog was a dead end. He didn't listen. He was there during the mid-1970s when Ed O'Neill talked management into pursuing an analog business that could compete with the industry leaders. O'Neill put together a special team consisting of Don Brooks, manager; Tim Smith, engineering manager; and Whitaker, marketing manager.

Whitaker recalled, "Ed took us into a room and said that he wanted TI to be a leader in manufacturing op amps." Competitors had produced a bipolar field effect transistor (BiFET) that sold for $5 each.

Whitaker contended TI should make BiFETs to sell for less than a $1 each or, better yet, make four BiFETs to sell in a package for $2.50. When he was told it was impossible, he insisted that TI could do it.

Smith, working alone, designed the process, and it worked. The price point came in exactly where Whitaker thought it should. Whitaker recalled, "TI was the only company in the world that had the technology. It was three years before competitors were able to second source it." By then, TI's parts were already designed into many customers' applications, and today, TI's BiFETs are one of the highest -volume analog circuits on the market.

TI attributed many of its business successes to its results with dynamic random access memory (DRAM) and microprocessors.

Both were marketed to large customers who ruled the computer world. As Whitaker said, "TI's DRAMs and microprocessors sold for a lot of money, but there were only a few customers for them. Our BiFETs, on the other hand, sold for only a few dollars each, but we had a lot of customers. You could find customers all over the country who didn't buy DRAMs or microprocessors. But you couldn't find any customer who didn't buy analog products. Even on a memory board, you had to have analog voltage regulators to supply the energy."

In those early days, Tom Engibous, who joined TI in 1976 as a linear design engineer, recalled the linear circuit business had its own culture. Designers were independent, he said, "and didn't follow the recipe." They were more gregarious, and eager to break the rules. "Usually," Engibous said, "you would see them wearing shorts and sandals or sitting barefoot at their desks." They were a different breed who helped build a valuable business.

For both designers and engineers, Engibous pointed out, it wasn't unusual to work all night. "They wanted to see how their

new circuit came out and didn't dare go home before finding out if it would work. On more than one occasion, we had our supervisor come in the morning and explain it was a TI policy to come to work clean-shaven. He had no idea we had been working all night and hadn't had time to sleep, much less shave."

The analog market had no limits. From the beginning, the analog business unit had been virtually self-funded; it never received much funding from corporate, and the team knew it had to generate enough cash from its last project to invest in its next venture. A major change came in the 1980s when TI began developing its mixed-signal process technology capabilities, placing high-voltage standard logic, and high-current drivers on a single chip. It was a technology most competitors did not yet have, and it allowed TI to capture a higher volume commodity business.

Whitaker remembered, "There had been a lot of papers written on the fact that a double-diffused metal-oxide semiconductor (DMOS) transistor couldn't be integrated onto an integrated circuit. But we had a very talented engineer who hadn't read any of those papers. He didn't know it couldn't be done, so he did it. And that technology allowed TI to develop products that moved us into the automobile industry."

In 1982, TI reported the company added 62 new linear products.

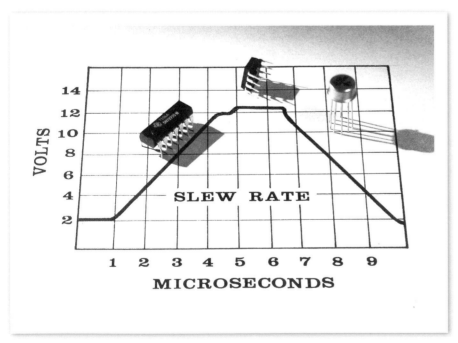

This drawing appeared in a TI press release featuring a new operational amplifier semiconductor. The plot of voltage versus time shows the linear relationship giving rise to the generic name of the product family, which was later changed to analog.

At about the same time, the company recognized the need to begin applying its advanced technology in areas outside memory. In February 1983, TI introduced the industry's first complementary metal oxide semiconductor (CMOS) operational amplifier. The device operated from a single power supply, and provided higher speed with greater operational stability and lower power dissipation. In the early 1980s, with only about 2 percent of the linear market using CMOS, TI applied its CMOS expertise to broaden and improve its analog product line. Between 1983 and 1985, the number of analog products grew from 273 to 600. As Whitaker explained, "Our goal was to be known as the 'new product' company. With CMOS and mixed technology capabilities, we had the ability to spin at least 10 new products off one single-chip design. And by leveraging other TI technologies, such as standard logic and packaging, we had the ability to build products at a much lower cost than our competitors."

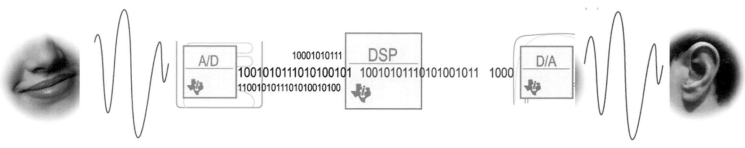

In digital end equipment using DSPs, such as the cell phone application shown above or a digital still camera, analog chips act as translators to change sound or light—real world signals—into the 1s and 0s of the digital world. The DSPs then compress and process these digital signals instantaneously, altering and improving the signal. Analog chips on the other end translate the digital signal back into the "real world" so that people can understand the information.

By 1987, TI began to sense the impact DSP could have on its analog business. In April, the company reported: *"Recently, we added a new thrust—advanced linear—to take advantage of the growing trend toward merging analog and digital functions. TI's traditional strength in both*

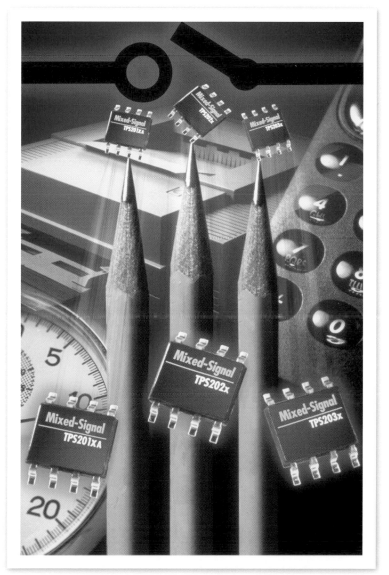

By the 1990s, TI was expanding its offerings of mixed-signal chips, which combined analog functions with a digital signal processor on the same chip.

analog and digital circuits puts us in an excellent position to serve the market." And that was only the beginning.

Tom Engibous remembered, "As DSP took off, so did integrated DSP solutions, and it began pulling through a lot more analog business. DSP had a positive impact. It opened the door for us to build more complex analog circuits than we had probably intended to do. TI's analog growth was a conscious effort because the company understood just how valuable a business analog was and could become."

During the early 1990s, TI targeted the fastest-growing communications markets and began devoting more design resources to analog products. The company's emphasis may have appeared to be on digital systems, but analog functions were keeping up a swift pace. Two decades earlier, TI languished far below the top 10 analog semiconductor suppliers. By 1992, however, the company had climbed its way to number six in the U.S. analog market. The analog team developed a roadmap for growth, looking at areas such as mass storage, digital cellular, printers/paper media, modems, and interfaces. As the decade closed, TI held the number one position in the U.S. analog market.

In the early 1970s, TI's analog revenues were in the tens of millions of dollars a year. They grew to roughly $400 million a year by the end of the 1980s and reached $4 billion a year at the turn of the century.

A complete digital audio solution includes digital interface, digital audio processing, and digital amplification systems. All the components work together to recreate sound infinitely closer to the source.

Today, TI's analog products are rolled into two groups: High Volume Analog (HVA), and High-Performance Analog (HPA).

The HVAL division, (which includes logic) under the direction of senior vice president C.S. Lee, addresses large-volume vertical businesses, such as hard disk drives, printers, displays, and automotive. The company offers analog products along with whatever else is necessary, including software.

Under the direction of senior vice president Gregg Lowe, the HPA division provides TI with a high-margin business, a large customer base, a broad product portfolio, products with long life cycles, and lower production costs by utilizing depreciated, older wafer fabs, which are no longer used for manufacturing advanced logic products.

Acquistions played an important part in moving the company into the high-margin HPA market. By acquiring Unitrode Corporation in 1999, TI had access to a major designer and supplier of power management components, the fastest-growing segment of the market for analog semiconductors. The acquisition strengthened TI's analog catalog portfolio of standard products targeted at a breadth of customers and applications for the mass market. That same year, TI acquired Power Trends, a leading supplier in the emerging and fast-growing market for point-of-use power solutions.

In 2000, TI acquired Toccata Technology ApS, based in Copenhagen, Denmark. The company was one of the world's leading developers of digital-audio amplifier technology and board solutions. The move enabled TI's digital-speaker technology to bring high-end audio system quality to all types of audio equipment, including personal computer speakers, audio-video receivers, car stereos, and home theater systems.

Three months later, TI acquired Burr-Brown, strengthening TI's position with digital-to-analog (D/A) and analog-to-digital (A/D) data converters, at the highest end of the precision and speed range, and amplifiers for emerging applications for third generation (3G) wireless phones, Digital Subscriber Line (DSL) modems, Internet audio players, and digital consumer audio systems.

In 2001, TI added a new category to its HPA and mixed signal portfolio with the purchase of Graychip, a technology leader in reconfigurable D/A and A/D data converters for high-speed communications.

"With the acquisition of these highly respected companies, TI is now in a clear position to provide customers with a leadership portfolio of high-performance analog products," said Lowe. "Over the past several years TI has introduced a plethora of outstanding products based on the synergies of those acquisitions and our customers are more excited than ever about TI and our analog portfolio."

In 2003, TI was recognized as the global leader in the $26.8 billion analog chip market. Engibous explained, "DSP is critical, but at least 50 percent of the solution is analog components, ranging from power-supply management to data conversion. We've taken the opportunity to optimize our analog products to work together with signal processors."

The analog market grew to $31.4 billion in 2004, and TI gained market share as its analog revenues increased 26 percent to $4.35 billion.

As Rich Templeton, current TI president and CEO, said, "We now have the ability to deliver better performance, lower power, more integration, and better cost, but deliver it in trusted, high-volume ways that our customers can count on."

With continued investment to build a portfolio of differentiated catalog products and highly integrated custom solutions, TI is committed to extending its analog leadership position. Templeton said, "Analog will be the largest semiconductor market for a very long time. TI is the world leader, and analog can continue to be the great core financial engine for the company. The company has, I believe, a wonderful paradox. The more the world goes digital, the more analog components are required. And we intend to be in a position to really serve that segment well."

ANALOG AND ACADEMIA
★ ★ ★

TI realized it faced one serious problem that might prevent the company from growing its analog business at a rapid pace. Universities simply weren't graduating engineers with a background in analog technology. They all wanted to be part of the digital world.

Only three U.S. universities, Georgia Tech, Iowa State, and Texas A&M, had a substantial analog focus. TI began investing in academic chairs and grants for graduate students in those universities and hiring professors for summer jobs to educate them about the expanding analog market needs.

Del Whitaker remembered, "One year, Texas A&M graduated 20 students with a master's degree or Ph.D. in analog. TI hired 17 of them."

In 2005, Greg Lowe reported that the university programs were essential and producing good results. During a summer job at TI, Professor Rogelio Palomero from the University of Puerto Rico contributed to TI's product strategies and was later able to use the experience to improve his course curriculum. Palomero recommended Omar Torres, an electrical engineering graduate student, for TI's co-op program, a 3-to-6-month work experience, to "test his wings." Torres "integrated easily into the product development engineering team" and was hired after he graduated.

Lowe said, "I think it's the relationship that develops between technical mentors and students during their co-op programs and beyond that motivates and inspires them to exceed expectations."

49

IMPACT OF SOFTWARE

TI turns its DSP software strategy into a competitive advantage.

As TI's success in digital signal processors grew, the company recognized the need to provide software tools to help customers program the devices. Later, the company expanded its capabilities to include "application" software to support customer needs as well. "What we are doing will revolutionize the digital signal processing industry and pave the way for faster growth with new DSP applications," said Tom Engibous, TI then-president and CEO. "Technology gets you to the table. Software wins the game."

When it was launched in 1999, eXpressDSP™ Real-Time Software Technology garnered attention at trade shows and conferences with media and customers by its ability to reduce development time by up to 50 percent. TIer Geof Cohler (left) demonstrates the technology at a conference in San Jose in September 1999.

Early on, TI recognized the need for a good development tool strategy to program DSPs. "We invested in compilers and debuggers to enable DSP programmability," said TI Fellow Reid Tatge. "At the time, however, we were not involved in providing the application software that actually ran on our DSPs. Writing code was left entirely to customers and third-party companies."

A key ingredient for customers is the compiler, a translator that turns program statements into a collection of ones and zeros the computer can understand and act on. To support this need, TI formed the DSP compiler team in 1983 and delivered the industry's first DSP compiler two years later. By the late 1980s, TI had excellent compilers for traditional DSPs, and was introducing new DSP designs every year.

By 1990, the company was designing more sophisticated multi-processing chips, using Very Large Instruction Word (VLIW) architectural concepts. At that time, TI's existing compiler was not designed to generate code for VLIW processors. The compiler team had begun developing a new "rapidly retargetable" compiler infrastructure to address the increasing varieties of TI's DSPs. With the emergence of these new DSPs, the compiler strategy was expanded, and the first VLIW DSP compiler was introduced in 1992. The initial product generated effective VLIW code, but it had limited optimization capability. Customers' results were disappointing. It was clear that good VLIW compilers with optimization capabilities were needed and that they would provide a competitive advantage.

TI first considered a "quick fix" by purchasing or licensing compiler optimization technology, but the compiler team wasn't sure

TI's eXpressDSP™ software and development tool suite enables customers to speed new products to market and turn ideas into reality.

the technology would work with its DSP architecture. The compiler team had been successful with its new compiler infrastructure, and TI needed to build on that capability. "We knew we had the technology, the knowledge, and the people to build very high-performance state-of-the-art VLIW compilers," recalled Tatge. "We also recognized that we had rushed the initial compiler to market before all the optimization technology had been finished. Finally, we were also very aware of the difficulties of integrating different technologies, a problem which is widely prevalent even today." Tatge argued the compiler team was the company's best option. After several rounds of discussion, management agreed and announced it would invest in the innovations of its own people rather than buy technology outside the company. To augment TI's existing team, the company acquired Tartan Labs, a leading DSP compiler developer in Pittsburgh, in 1996.

Between 1993 and 1996, TI invested heavily in optimization technology for VLIW instruction sets. The company realized that to grow the market, it would need to increase the number of DSP developers. During this period, DSP developers often wrote all their own software, consuming precious development time writing code. Two issues surfaced as a result: the need to make easy-to-use DSP software to attract novice developers, and the need to create an easier "plug-and-play" environment to provide developers with the flexibility to buy and use code modules.

DSP strategic marketing director Leon Adams and a team of TI software developers recommended TI create a foundation for an easy-to-use integrated development environment and an open-standard software framework that supported multi-vendor software "plug-and-play" interoperability and reuse. Thus, eXpressDSP™ Real-Time Software Technology was born. It includes four key elements: an open, graphical user interface for code development and debugging; a Real Time Operating System (RTOS) as a fundamental real-time code base; broad third-party support; and the TMS320™ DSP Interoperability Standard, guidelines that third parties can use to develop algorithms for TI

TI's Code Composer Studio™ Integrated Development Environment graphically enables designers to slash overall DSP coding time and eliminate in minutes many real-time problems that would normally take weeks.

DSPs. "We needed to make all of the development tools work and play well together, just as your email, word processor, and other applications on your computer do now," said Mike Hames, now TI senior vice president and manager over application-specific products.

The team's research identified several strategies for obtaining the necessary technologies. In 1997, TI acquired Go-DSP in Toronto, which added its graphical Code Composer™ Integrated Development Environment (IDE) and DSP debugger, and shortly thereafter acquired Spectron Microsystems, which gave TI expertise in real-time operating systems—the birth of DSP/BIOS. TI's investment strategy signaled the DSP industry that TI was serious about building world-class software development tools to support its DSP products.

TI then focused on how to reduce its time to market and to provide reusable software. A network of external vendors already existed, though it focused mainly on creating algorithms designed for the expert user. TI encouraged current network members and recruited new ones to use its eXpressDSP Interoperability Standard when developing new algorithms, which ultimately led to the creation of thousands of software products designed for easy use with TI DSPs.

Bob Frankel, TI Fellow and co-founder of Spectron Microsystems, said, "We must focus on producing interoperable software modules and creating a plethora of third parties, hundreds and hundreds of third parties, providing a tremendous value web around our products—something that is unmatched in the DSP industry." The third-party developers' network grew to more than 700 companies writing application-specific software for TI DSPs. David McKeehan, chairman of TI's Software Opportunities, said, "We want to go from thousands of people writing software for our DSPs to hundreds of thousands. So if I'm a customer, I can say, 'Look at all these tools and software libraries available to me that make it easier to get my product to market if I buy a DSP from TI.'"

Instead of expecting the customers to write 100 percent of the code required to use DSPs in their new applications, TI recognized the company needed to do much of the "solutions" programming up-front and provide much of the end equipment application-targeted software along with the silicon. Instead of requiring the customer to build a bridge to the DSP, TI needed to build a bridge to the customer.

During the next five years, TI invested aggressively—acquiring

TI'S SOFTWARE CULTURE
★ ★ ★

From the early days of the computerization of seismic processing in GSI, TI has been writing "software" programs. First, these programs were called "seismic analysis programs," which included their own operating systems. TI was talking about computers and "programs" in the 1950s when computers were being developed. The term "software" was not commonly used until the computer field expanded in the 1960s. Then, software functions were separated into "operating systems" and "application" software. A common operating system for each computer processor type performs housekeeping functions, eliminating the need to re-create a new system when developing applications software.

By the time TI finished the Advanced Scientific Computer (ASC) in 1972, the company had operating systems, compilers, Computer Aided Design (CAD) software and infrastructure for complex computers. Ed Hassler, one of the creators of Design Automation Technology, later a manager of several computer-related organizations, said, "The consensus of the ASC designers was that the parallel programming FORTRAN (Formula Translation) compiler and the computer aided design CAD tools were world-class. This software and the embedded algorithms were the key to the success of the ASC. Designers could design logic, and the system designed the interconnect system with the embedded algorithms. Seismic software writers wrote logically correct programs, and the compiler used the embedded code to utilize the parallel vector processors. Algorithms express the interface between the natural world we live in and digital representation of processing for that world."

The ASC's complexity is now surpassed by today's DSPs. Computing power that once filled large rooms and consumed hundreds of kilowatts of electrical power is now available on a chip the size of a silver dollar and consumes just a few watts of power and operates at room temperature.

companies with critical DSP software expertise. These companies—including Telogy Networks, Amati Communications Corporation, and Alantro Communications—were industry leaders in their application domains. Acquiring them enabled TI to quickly ramp products to market, leveraging DSPs. All these companies owned intellectual property critical to the telecommunication markets, such as DSL modems and cable modems.

In 1998, TI established a $100 million venture capital fund to seed start-up companies that write software for TI DSP architectures, capturing the industry's attention by extending incentives to companies that developed around TI architecture. Early in 2005, Engibous, reflecting on TI's decision to build its software capabilities, said he "never envisioned that we'd have more people writing software than we have designing integrated circuits. The net results are that this has greatly altered TI's competitiveness in the semiconductor industry, because those vertical businesses created by software solutions have turned out to be a very large part of the semiconductor market. The product-line-dedicated companies aren't competitive in participating in those vertical businesses, so we've become larger."

People depend on TI "application" software every time they talk on a cell phone, download music, send an e-mail message, or access television programs with a set-top box. Strolling through an electronics superstore, a consumer could easily fill a shopping cart with products containing TI DSPs: digital still cameras, Internet wireless music players, digital video satellite TV receivers, state-of-the-art pagers, X2 modems, digital cellular telephones, disk drives, and 3-D video games. And TI software, more than ever before, is used in products consumers never see on store shelves, such as automotive and aircraft navigation systems, recording studio controllers, and cellular base stations.

TI's programmable DSP strategy changed the course of the company. Software—development tools and application software—became an important factor in every silicon sale. As the DSP business grew, TI became a "solutions" company—providing both the hardware and the software to customers. Moving forward, customers can expect that trend to continue.

TI software and systems specialists at the company's software design center in Bangalore, India, around 1988. The satellite dish was purchased and installed by TI and, by contract, given to the Indian National Telecommunications Company in return for the use of one channel for five years. All the companies in Bangalore, including IBM and Hewlett Packard, were ported through this antenna until fiber optic underwater circuits became available several years later.

50

WORKING WITHOUT WIRES

TI defies the odds to build its wireless technology into a multi-billion-dollar business.

In 1989, TI made its first precipitous inroad into a competitive new market that would radically change the way people lived, worked, and played. A small TI team headed by Gilles Delfassy decided to make a bold bet on digital wireless communications as a way of building the company's European business. Fifteen years later, wireless would become a $3 billion business for TI, comprising over one-fourth of TI revenues. The tale of that journey is a story of innovation and persistence, risk and reward—and even a burning coat.

In 1994, Gilles Delfassy was based in TI's operation near Nice, France, when he was assigned the task of building a billion-dollar semiconductor business for digital cell phones.

It began in Villeneuve-Loubet, France, with Gilles Delfassy and his TI team working to create a strategy for digital signal processing in Europe. All obvious applications seemed to point toward the computer, but Delfassy knew Europe had not developed a thriving computer industry, and he didn't have access to products that might fit any other possible targets. For three days, his team explored ideas and opportunities at an off-site meeting near Nice, France. The days were becoming long and depressing. The pressure they all felt was virtually unbearable.

TI made an earlier attempt to work its way into the wireless communications business, but the electronic giants of Europe—Nokia, Siemens, and Ericsson—had all selected other suppliers, which was even more frustrating for Delfassy's team. The communications market was owned by corporations already entrenched in a competitive overseas environment. As Delfassy remembered, "The odds were all against us. So the only thing we could do was bet it all on digital wireless."

There was one large potential problem. Digital wireless communications was only in the early stages of development. No one had any idea that wireless would one day become a multi-billion- dollar business for TI, spurred on by this entrepreneurial group of TIers who would not give up or take rejection as a final answer. Delfassy referred to his team as "streetfighters," and perhaps they were.

When Delfassy joined the start-up team in 1989, it had only one customer—Matra—a small European manufacturer that produced an inexpensive cell phone. Soon, the imaginative team saw the potential for a breakthrough by developing Time Divide Multiple Access base stations for Ericsson. The project, however, required TMS320C5x™ technology, and the C5x was still being designed not close to production. Most even considered it impossible to build because the die size was so large. Delfassy wasn't fazed. He made commitments that stretched the boundaries of what was possible, but he also realized his group would probably not survive without the Ericsson business. "Ericsson wanted a RAM-based version for the base station, 10K of RAM, which at the time was huge," he said. "So we agreed to build it in volume, and that was unheard of, since it was only considered to be a prototyping tool." The ramp-up of the C5x was difficult and expensive, producing very low yields in a wafer fabrication facility where capacity was severely limited. The first few

The Nokia cell phone became the market leader, powered by TI's advanced DSPs and analog technology.

thousand devices were sold at $42 apiece. But the cost to manufacture each device soared to $900—a considerable loss. Delfassy remembered the finance controller calling to ask, "What is this program where you are sacrificing precious manufacturing capacity and losing money?"

Delfassy, determined to defend the fledgling C5x program, said, "Trust me, and one day wireless will be big and profitable. Don't kill this." It worked. TI gambled on the technology and on Delfassy's team, allowing the program to continue.

In 1993, TI won a pivotal contract with giant mobile phone maker Nokia. The contract was for a new DSP optimized for digital cellular baseband applications, codenamed "LEAD." Shortly thereafter, TI won a second pivotal contract with Nokia for a single-chip baseband processor for cell phones, codenamed "MAD." It ended up significantly reducing the cost, size, and power consumption of mobile phones and became an industry milestone. The project also marked the beginning of a long, respected relationship between the two companies. At the time, TI feared it would have to choose between Ericsson and Nokia, the two leaders in the market. They were fierce competitors, and it seemed improbable that TI would be permitted to work for both. But the improbable happened: not only did TI keep both customers, but in time it was producing power management and DSP devices for the third powerhouse, Motorola, as well.

———————

By 1994, TI, recognizing the vast potential in the market, formed a wireless business unit led by Delfassy. Tom Engibous, then head of the TI semiconductor business, had one directive for him: "I want you to achieve very aggressive revenue and profit goals. Your mission is to get $1 billion worth of business by the year 2000."

Delfassy didn't entertain the thought that the gauntlet Engibous tossed him might be beyond his reach. Still, he and his team found the road to a billion-dollar goal had more rough spots than they

had anticipated. Their first hurdle was a potential loss of business from Ericsson. The Swedish company was ready to select a supplier for Second Generation (2G) phones; it was concerned because TI did not want to integrate DSP cores with standard cells. Ericsson's engineers wanted to drop TI, and it appeared there was no room for discussion.

Back in Dallas, Rich Templeton—then newly promoted Worldwide Applications Specific Products manager—took a different view. He supported Delfassy's idea for a standard cell strategy. The Application Specific Integrated Circuit (ASIC) business didn't want to support standard cells, but wireless believed there was a definite use for them. Delfassy committed to inventing a standard cell strategy if it had a chance of salvaging his Ericsson business. He remembered, "My phantom standard cell strategy was a foil set, which I came up with in three days and had no buy-in from the company."

Templeton met Delfassy, and the two men walked into Ericsson with the intention of selling them on a strategy no one else at TI knew about. "Rich started the meeting and tried various ice breakers to create a warm atmosphere. There was silence in the room. No word from Ericsson. It was very cold. You could have cut the tension with a knife," Delfassy said.

It was chilly outside as well. Someone from TI-Stockholm had hung a coat on a halogen lamp, and while Templeton was trying to ease the unhealthy and growing tension, a voice shouted, "Fire! Fire!"

The lamp was hot. The coat was smoking. It soon became difficult to breathe. Then, everyone stumbled outside into the cold morning

Someone joked about the coat. There was a chuckle, then laughter. By the time the smoke cleared, TI and Ericsson were talking again. Delfassy explained TI had decided to produce a standard cell library, which was a huge revelation for TI and Ericsson both. Delfassy finished his presentation, and, shortly after the meeting, Templeton instructed TI ASIC management to implement the new standard cell strategy. Ericsson would not be leaving after all.

———————

In 1996, TI introduced its first internally-designed chipset, which was quickly adopted by several leading handset manufacturers. The transition from analog-to-digital technology had begun, and the wireless industry was running wide open on a fast track. The wireless market would allow TI to match the success of its DSP and analog capabilities.

During 1996, it was estimated that TI's wireless-optimized DSP Solutions had been incorporated into approximately 22 million digital cellular phones worldwide—more than half the digital cellular phones manufactured that year.

The secret of TI's success in the burgeoning wireless market was described this way by Steve Pardee, controller for TI's wireless operations, "From the leadership team on down, there was the spirit of always trying to find a solution, trying to find a way to satisfy the customer even if it meant multiple passes. First pass fail, then regroup. Find a way to succeed and never give up until a solution was found."

By 1998, two years ahead of the deadline imposed by Engibous, TI's wireless organization achieved $1.3 billion in revenue.

During the next two years, TI expanded its wireless expertise with the acquisitions of Butterfly, ATL, Dot Wireless, and Condat. The company's wireless business unit had the foresight to understand that the industry would transition from voice-centric to an applications-intensive environment. Determined to achieve market leadership and remain there, the unit initiated significant and deliberate technology development that would shape its future—the definition of its OMAP™ (Open Multimedia Applications Platform) application processor architecture. The vision of the wireless business unit was cemented as TI moved rapidly into new technologies,

manufacturing disciplines, and logistics models. "The evolution of wireless was nothing short of supersonic," said David Solomon of wireless operations, "Things changed so fast it was like getting up every day and getting on the biggest, fastest roller coaster there was and riding it. It scared you a lot, but at the end of the day you went home exhausted but thrilled at the same time."

———————

Delfassy believed TI's culture fostered the drive to be continuously inventing things. "Innovation," he said, "was synonymous with TI, and our intellectual property was a tremendous source of competitive advantage. We took on a pioneer spirit because the unit was clearly breaking ground for the company. Our goal was a worldwide organization without boundaries, with all the team members focused on delivering a winning solution for the customer.

"We achieved several major OMAP design wins from Japanese customers that were the result of combined efforts by marketing and applications people in TI-Japan, systems and design people in TI-France, and design people in Dallas," he said.

TI's skills at building customer relationships also helped. To quote Nokia: *"We do not have a comparable partner to TI. TI is on a level of its own. The breadth of cooperation, starting with top management down to*

The use of TI DSPs in digital cell phones in the mid-1990s accelerated the growth of the DSP business.

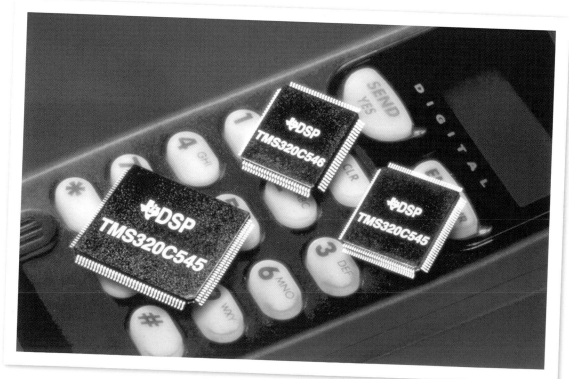

the engineer, is a benchmark for us internally. The key parameter, however, is the trust we've always been able to build together at all management and working levels. It's built on common interest, openness, and a real desire to work together to be the best. This may be the best partnership that exists in the industry, a real success story."

The growth in cellular phone sales increased the demand for powerful, inexpensive, battery-saving integrated circuits that formed the guts of digital cellular systems. During 2004, the wireless business unit topped the $3 billion mark. Close collaboration with customers, systems integration expertise, and a broad network of multimedia application developers contributed to TI's position as a driving force in next-generation wireless phones. Live digital television, custom ring tones, music, 3D games, and multi-megapixel cameras were among the innovative applications fueling the growth of cellular technology.

The technology was able to miniaturize the living room entertainment experience without sacrificing performance. Meeting consumers' expectations for a secure mobile entertainment experience was a strong step toward making trendy mobile features "must-have" revenue-generating services for TI and the industry as a whole. No longer just devices to make and receive calls, cellular phones with Third-Generation (3G)

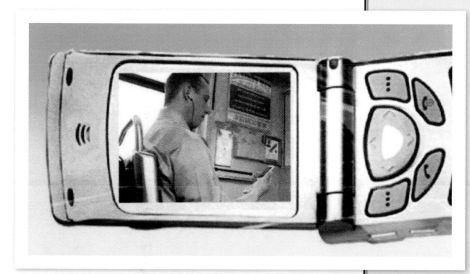

In October 2004, TI announced the development of the "Hollywood" chip, designed to receive live digital TV broadcasts using new television infrastructure that is being developed for cell phones.

technology are now a universal communications and entertainment system.

By 2005, mobile phones represented four to five times the unit volume of personal computers, with sales of more than 700 million units. The cellular phone, in fact has been recognized as the single most important electronic platform in the technology industry. In February 2005, Templeton reflected on the future of wireless, "Even as large a business as wireless is today, we are going to be shocked at what a cell phone is going to be five years from now. With our continued innovations and investments in the technology, we'll be able to drive some of the growth. Our product organization is connected with customers and in the long term that's the healthiest way to make sure you have good returns and innovative areas in which to invest."

TV ON THE GO
★ ★ ★

In October 2004, TI announced the company was working on the first digital TV chip for cell phones. Through it, users will enter a new era of watching television broadcasts.

Code-named "Hollywood," the chip will have the capability of doing for cell phones what High Definition Television (HDTV) did for home television sets. According to Gilles Delfassy, general manager for TI's Wireless operations, "The Hollywood digital TV chip combines in a single handset two of the biggest consumer electronics inventions of our time—the television and the cell phone. With this new chip in cell phones, users will be able to enjoy digital, high-quality TV in real time no matter where they are."

Samples of the Hollywood chip are planned in 2006. Field trials are being conducted in the U.S., Europe, and Japan, and it is expected that manufacturers will be able to launch products that include this technology in 2007.

51

THE BROADBAND STRATEGY

A series of strategic acquisitions boosted TI into the rapidly expanding broadband business.

The information superhighway had extensions in several directions, and TI wanted to travel as many of them as it could. According to Rich Templeton, senior vice president of the semiconductor business in 1994, "Our experience tells us very clearly that the information superhighway, whatever it turns out to be, represents explosive growth opportunities for the semiconductor industry, especially in the area of digital signal processors (DSPs)."

Texas Instruments understood early the need to communicate globally on a real-time basis. The company pioneered communication systems to address this need. In 1965, TI, as did many other companies, communicated via AT&T's Telex and Teletype devices over networks of copper wire. The next year, TI needed a better technology for transmitting seismic data and began using international cable. Two years later, it switched to low-level satellite links allowing TI in Dallas to communicate at the computer-to-computer level with its seismic data center in Croyden, England.

A major communication breakthrough for the company came in 1973, with the creation of the TI electronic message system, known as the MSG system, providing private message communication via terminals within the company. With the advent of the Internet, this system was replaced with the email system in use today. As early as 1978, TI began wiring company sites and intersite communications with Local Area Network (LAN) technology. In 1982, TI used fiber optics in the towing cable for the seismic sensors to communicate with the equipment onboard GSI ships.

By 1988, TI emerged as a leader in geosynchronous satellite communication, deploying satellite links connecting sites in the U.S., Europe, and India. A satellite base station on top of an office building in Bangalore, India, provided the single source for satellite data communications for companies with facilities in that city for several years.

The advent of LANs provided a major semiconductor product opportunity for TI. Ethernet and Token-Ring were two competing LAN standards. Starting in late 1981, TI entered into a joint development program with IBM to develop the Token-Ring standard and a chipset that implemented the standard. Announced in late 1985, this resulted in one of TI's most innovative products. As Ethernet became the most prominent LAN standard in the early 90s, TI worked with Compaq to develop a chipset that implemented both Token-Ring and Ethernet. Called ThunderLAN™, it was followed in 1996 by ThunderSWITCH™, a single-chip Ethernet switch.

As an outgrowth of TI's early networking expertise, along with its development of DSPs, the company began moving into broadband communications in 1997. In time, TI's Broadband Communications Group would include such technologies as cable, Digital Subscriber Line (DSL), Voice over Internet Protocol (VoIP), and Wireless Local Area networking (WLAN). TI realized early it would have to invest substantially in strategic acquisitions to obtain the range of technologies necessary to make broadband a viable part of TI march into the 21st century.

The company created a new product organization, the Access Products Group, to help implement its strategy for providing end-to-end interoperable solutions for networking original equipment manufacturers (OEMs). By taking advantage of TI's technological leadership in DSPs, mixed-signal components, and networking hardware and software integration, the Access Products group focused on developing system-level solutions for access equipment.

As Greg Waters, the group's director at the time, pointed out, TI has the technologies that OEMs need to develop products offering faster, denser, interoperable access for the Internet, high-speed digital data links, videoconferencing, digital TV, and a variety of other end-user applications. Now TI is well positioned to assist OEMs in the creation of new, highly differentiated products that will reach the market quickly."

Meanwhile, the company's DSP research and development team and strategic marketing organization were separately exploring the potential of broadband. One of TI's top DSP customers urged the company to add DSL to its technologies.

Residential Gateway

- Multiplayer gaming
- Video on demand
- Home security
- Digital audio

DSL Internet Access

TOTAL 5,530 pts.

Front door

Wired PC

- Streaming video
- Print/file sharing

Wireless Laptop

- Distance learning
- Video calls
- MP3 downloads

IP Phone

PDA

Recipe

Printer

- Internet access
- Multiple voice lines
- Wireless printing
- Wireless IP phone

Home Networking

At the heart of the digital home sits the residential gateway distributing a host of enhanced content and services without the need for wires.

The PC-driven technology market has given way to a new era driven by communications and entertainment. TI is well positioned to help customers succeed in this era through a comprehensive portfolio of broadband and consumer electronics solutions. With TI technology, consumers can enjoy digital content anywhere, anytime, from any location without the hassle of wires.

Earlier in 1997, TI began working with U.S. Robotics to deliver a family of hybrid modems supporting both dial-up access and Asymmetric Digital Subscriber Lines (ADSL).

The opportunities were intriguing, and the company debated over whether DSL should be developed internally or acquired. As the discussions dragged on, TI consolidated the Broadband Access Group under George Barber, merging the networking business in Houston, the Asynchronous Transfer Mode (ATM) business in Sherman, and the Access Products Group in Dallas. But by the time TI solidified its strategy to pursue the broadband market, the company was already behind the market in the race to develop DSL technology.

There was one way to catch up—acquiring Amati Communications Corporation, a world leader in DSL technology that had long been using TI's TMS320C6x™ DSP family and mixed-signal components to build a DSL chipset. It would cost some money, but would expand TI's influence as a DSP innovator in broadband more quickly. Another company

was attempting to purchase Amati as well, but TI's offer won out. The acquisition strengthened TI's leadership role in providing critical DSP solutions for high-speed Internet connectivity. Amati's xDSL software allowed ordinary phone lines to transmit data as much as 200 times faster than typical analog voiceband modems.

During the summer of 1999, TI made two more strategic acquisitions: Telogy Networks and Libit Signal Processing. Telogy Networks was a VoIP software and systems company and a TI DSP third party that had been wrapping networking technology around TI's TMS320C55x™ DSPs. It had also become the leading provider of TI DSP-based Voice over Packet (VoP) embedded software. The purchase of Telogy Networks helped propel TI to become the VoIP market leader and drove internal software methodology across many other

173

DSP-based businesses. TI was able to penetrate the emerging, fast-growing market for Internet telephony. Two major players in programmable DSPs had come together. TI was now well positioned to become the engine of the communications market as it transitioned from circuit-switched to packet-switched networks. This shift was potentially even larger in scale than the migration from analog to digital in wireless telephony. In late 1999, Mike Hames, then vice president and manager of TI's worldwide DSP business, explained, "Over the next decade, close to 700 million phone lines will transition to digital voice. This acquisition will potentially put TI in every phone, every interface to the telecommunications infrastructure, and every Internet appliance in the digital communications network."

Acquiring Libit Signal Processing was important to TI because the Telecom Act of 1996, requiring telecom companies share their twisted pair access lines with marketing companies, had impeded DSL deployment by telecom companies. Cable companies, on the other hand, were not subject to this regulation. As a result, cable modem deployment was much faster than DSL. With this in mind, TI decided to participate in the cable modem market as well. The Israeli company Libit had already designed, developed, and manufactured highly integrated silicon solutions for cable broadband access. Hames pointed out, "With Libit and Telogy, TI now has all the pieces to play in the large broadband communications market."

With these acquisitions, TI was positioned to become a major competitor in DSL, VoIP, and cable—the critical broadband technologies available in the market during the late 1990s. The company had the capability of enabling service providers to deliver data, voice, and video simultaneously over a single installed line or via cable modems or DSL modems.

In late 1999, four out of five Voice over Digital Subscriber Line original equipment manufacturers had chosen TI DSPs for their systems. Dano Ybara, vice president of Flowpoint, reported, "TI's programmable DSP technology provides the high performance and flexibility needed to execute sophisticated algorithms for required voice processing algorithms, while achieving optimal system costs and ultra-low-power consumption." Kiran Munj, vice president for Accelerated Networks, echoed his words: "DSL is an ideal transmission technology for delivering a bundle of services to subscribers. TI's DSP technology helps us ensure toll-quality

voice delivery while maximizing the bandwidth offered by DSL for delivery of both voice and data over the same line." The VoIP technology split voice and data into packages sent over packet networks, such as the Internet. The packages were then reassembled at their destination.

———————————

John Hughes, director of new business for TI's Broadband Access Group, had been saying that TI needed more than DSL and cable modem access technology if the company hoped to climb to the top of the competitive business. Hughes believed that bringing broadband into the home would

TI introduced the industry's first fully integrated Asymmetric Digital Subscriber Line (ADSL) modem-on-chip, which *EDN* named "Innovation of the Year" in 2003. TI has extended the AR7 family by integrating wireless and voice functionality for complete residential gateways. The chipset's popularity with customers made TI the top DSL supplier in 2004.

become a key factor in the growth of the market. In addition, a longtime customer had been asking TI to get involved in a wireless home networking technology called the IEEE 802.11 standard. TI responded to both in June 2000 by acquiring Alantro Communications, a leader in the development of technology that had set the standard for supporting the emerging market for WLAN. Alantro brought TI world-class signal processing expertise, in-depth application knowledge, and design implementation proficiency. TI's George Barber explained the acquisition was "one more step by TI to bring broadband into and throughout the home or office. DSL and cable modem chipsets from TI will deliver billions of bits of bandwidth to the home. Alantro's technology will distribute that bandwidth throughout the home or office without the need for wires. Untethered access to intelligent networks means you can be connected wherever you are whenever you want, all at the speed that broadband offers."

In 2002, TI acquired Ditech's Telinnovation echo-cancellation software unit, recognized as the industry benchmark for DSP-based voice enhancement and echo cancellation. It was a specified component for equipment purchased by major telecommunications carriers when they transitioned to wireless and packet-switched networks. By combining TI's silicon and software platforms with Ditech's echo-cancellation software and expertise, TI could provide customers with complete, high-performance carrier-class VOIP solutions.

A year later, TI acquired Radia Communications, a fabless semiconductor company specializing in the development of radio frequency (RF) semiconductor, subsystem, signal processing, and networking technologies for 802.11 WLAN radios. TI's customers now had a single source for all the components required to build WLAN products.

Through acquisitions, TI expanded its broadband business globally with design and marketing functions in Texas, California, Maryland, Germany, Israel, India, Taiwan, Japaan, and China.

By 2003, TI's WLAN and DSL businesses gained momentum. The company shipped 14 million 802.11 WLAN ports and 24 million DSL ports. The DSL growth was triggered in part by TI's development of the AR7, the first single-chip modem designed to help ADSL modem manufacturers deliver enhanced home networking for consumers worldwide. The

momentum continued to build dramatically when voice and WLAN capabilities were added to the AR7. In 2004, TI achieved an 80 percent share in Internet Protocol phone and VoIP gateway markets. By November of that year, the company had shipped 2 million lines of voice-over cable, which established TI as the undisputed market leader.

In 2003, TI shipped 32 percent of the total broadband ports worldwide. By the end of 2004, more than 140 million subscribers had broadband connectivity around the globe. The extraordinary growth was driven by the demand for high-speed Internet access, with new applications integrating voice, video, and capabilities introduced to provide new revenue opportunities for service providers.

Texas Instruments' broadband solutions enabled the low power consumption, smaller footprint, and higher system-level integration required to deliver differentiated, cost-effective products, while dramatically decreasing a manufacturer's time to market. Manufacturers could deliver products with unprecedented flexibility, using TI's common customer premises equipment platform, integrated software/hardware architecture, and application programming interfaces.

As Mike Hames reported in a 2004 satellite broadcast, "With the startup of the Broadband Communications Group, our number-one priority was to gain scale by focusing on revenue and market-share growth. After just a few years, this business has grown to become a near half-a-billion dollar business. Thanks to the efforts of its employees, TI is already widely recognized as a leader in this highly competitive market. These years of experience have helped us understand the challenges and what it takes to excel in this market.

"High-speed bandwidth is becoming ubiquitous on a global basis. The enormous worldwide growth in DSL, cable modems, wireless LAN and voice over IP is just the beginning because the world truly is moving to an environment where broadband is everywhere. And our Broadband Communications Group will be there as well."

Rich Templeton captured the essence of the future of broadband and other emerging technologies when he noted, "None of us can guess what wonders human genius will conceive any more than our grandfathers could have guessed at the marvels the computer has brought into life today. We can only be sure that the pace of innovation will quicken as the technological limits to creativity fall away."

52

A SEA OF IDEAS

Digital Consumer electronics reinvents the way the world works, plays, and dreams of the future.

The foundation for an emerging new business is developed by listening to customers' needs, understanding the nature of the products those customers want to create, and bringing those ideas back to the engineering minds within the company. It is all about finding ideas with promise and figuring out how to make them realities.

During the mid-1990s, Rich Templeton, then vice president and manager of Application Specific Products, and Tom Engibous, then TI president and CEO, mapped out a strategy to place the responsibility for developing ideas for new business on teams working directly with customers around the world. They called in Doug Rasor, vice president and strategic marketing manager, and asked him to develop "a sea of ideas." None were too small, too large, or too outrageous to consider. TI viewed customer demands as seeds of opportunity. And in a world of exploding semiconductor technologies, no one could predict exactly what the next big thing might be. As Engibous told Rasor, "We can't afford to miss it."

Rasor later commented, "TI

began creating external venture capital programs to tap into the entrepreneurial community outside of the company to find the 'fish in the sea.' " It was his job to use his experience to recognize a good business plan when one suddenly came his way, then work with those involved to transform the concept into an end-equipment market. It was obvious to him that a marketable idea needed to have the technology, a value proposition, and an internal entrepreneur to drive the business.

"After trying a couple of approaches, we decided to focus on technologies where we were differentiated. We came up with business doctrines to determine what attractive markets looked like, and then we tried to apply them to the 'sea of ideas.' Emerging markets, unfortunately, didn't have much, if any, market projections, so a lot of our decisions were based on judgment and little else."

Templeton asked Rasor to select his six top emerging end equipment areas. Each business would be launched with a team of 10, would be treated as a start-up company, and have the corporate protection necessary to operate independently. After study and deliberation, Rasor chose digital still camera, Internet audio, Universal Serial Bus audio for personal computer speakers, digital motor control, high-level operating systems for cell phones, and raster image processing.

During 1997, TI intensively studied the needs of one of the identified top emerging end equipments—the digital camera. Hewlett-Packard approached the company for a custom camera chip, even though TI's marketing strategy had not been announced.

So Rasor met with Dr. Raj Talluri in digital video research and development to suggest that he begin working on a prototype. Talluri proposed creating the

Doug Rasor, vice president and strategic marketing manager, led the "sea of ideas" process to explore markets well-suited to TI's digital signal processing solutions.

The HP R707 digital camera, featuring Hewlett-Packard's proprietary Real Life Technologies and HP Image Engine, utilizes TI's digital media technology to ensure a perfect picture every time.

THE ROLE OF THE DSP IN CONSUMER ELECTRONICS
★ ★ ★

The convergence of the wireless and digital consumer electronics markets was driving the multimedia experience all around the world, and TI recognized that the intersection of those two hot markets presented major opportunities for everyone participating in the value chain. In the quest to establish their place in the chain, TI invested capital in releasing a new family of high speed digital signal processors with the capability of processing an amazing 5 million instructions per second (MIPS). And in 1983, they were successful. Now, TI produces DSPs that can process 8 billion operations per second...a 1600-fold increase. This has enabled an entire new generation of consumer electronics such as cell phones, audio players, home audio/video receivers, digital cameras, digital video cameras, digital radio, and video phones with the ability to process voice, images, and data in real-time.

versatile disc (DVD), and car entertainment applications were located in either TI's Tsukuba or Atsugi technology centers.

Whether it is in Japan or anywhere else in the world, consumer electronics is an incredibly fast-paced market. In order to be a solid contributor, the technology must keep up with latest application ideas. Rasor explained, "For TI, it already means taking our strong position in wireless and consumer electronics, channeling that into delivering the most advanced Third Generation (3G) wireless

Intempo's PG-01 digital radio, based on TI's digital audio broadcast (DAB) baseband, is a kitchen radio design popular in the U.K.

image pipeline in software rather than using a custom chip. He developed a prototype about the size of two sheets of copy paper placed next to each other. It was the first software-based camera ever developed, capable of producing video graphics array (VGA) quality. Rasor said, "If a picture is worth a thousand words, a demo is worth a thousand pictures."

As TI embraced the possibilities of innovation within the digital camera market and the other identified emerging end equipments, the company in 2002 established the Digital Consumer Electronics Solutions (DCES) division based in Tokyo, Japan. A staff of several hundred enabled the division to work more closely with and provide total solutions to Japanese companies recognized as world leaders in consumer electronics. Application-specific departments for video and imaging, digital audio, camera and TV cell phone, digital solutions and the most compelling multimedia applications. As such advances in applications appear, the potential 3G barriers consumers once faced, including high-priced, bulky handsets with short battery life, will continue to dissipate and focus the buying decisions more on the compelling services and content that 3G delivers." According to Rasor, reliable communications, when combined with such "cool applications" as live digital television, custom ring tones, mobile music, 3D games, and multi-megapixel cameras, are turning the traditional cell phone into a universal remote control, "allowing our on-the-go society access to entertainment and productivity with just a click."

Through TI ingenuity, these ideas were transformed into digital consumer products that completely revolutionized every day life and continue to do so.

With the handheld RCA LYRA A/V Jukebox, a Thomson product, users can take movies, photos, and music with them anywhere.

HIGH-TECH SPORTS
★ ★ ★

Sonic Instruments, a TI customer based in Germany, recently announced the industry's first watch-sized, radar-enabled measurement system that enables skiers, joggers, and cyclists to more accurately measure speed and distance. Sonic's radar technology is unique in sports measurement and is three times more accurate than that of competing body movement-based measurement products.

The new lightweight Radar Speed System (RSS) watch, speedometer, and optional heart-rate monitor use a full range of TI technology. At the heart of the watch is the industry's lowest-power, 16-bit microcontroller unit (MCU) that calculates distance, speed, and average speed, and then displays the information through a Liquid Crystal Display. Power management features, based on TI's analog and 16-bit MCU devices, enable the RSS watch to operate for two years before it requires new batteries according to the manufacturer. The MCU calculates a user's heart rate from heart rate information transmitted from an optional pulse measurement unit worn separately. The pulse measurement unit uses the same platform (the 16-bit MCU) to collect the user's vital statistics and transmits this information to the watch via a wireless transmitter-receiver.

Within the belt-worn speedometer is a TI low-power DSP for processing the radar calculations that continuously measure the wearer's progress relative to stationary objects. With its real-time performance, the DSP calculates the shifts in frequency between the transmission and reception of low-power radio pulses, and then passes this data on to the MCU for speed and distance calculations.

THE NEW SENSORS

New technologies in sensing and radio frequency identification create market opportunities for TI's Sensors & Controls business.

When it was introduced in 1988, no one would have predicted the huge success of TI's first foray into automotive pressure sensing—the Automotive Pressure Transducer (APT)—despite the fact that it was touted as the automotive "product of the future." And no one would have predicted that TI's radio frequency identification (RFID) technology developed that same year would one day change the face of security, logistics, and retail payment methods around the world.

In 1988, after a long history of developing electromechanical controls, switches, circuit breakers, and thermostats for the appliance, automotive, and industrial markets, TI's Materials & Controls (M&C) business delivered a solid-state pressure sensor to the automotive industry. Capitalizing on M&C's experience in the automotive market, especially with pressure switches, and TI's applied integrated circuit technology, TI engineers developed a small, competitive sensor for use in automotive air conditioning systems. General Motors' Oldsmobile division was the first customer to sign on, incorporating the device in its 1989 automobiles. The APT family of products grew rapidly, expanding to include antilock braking, air conditioning, engine controls, transmission, suspension, and power steering applications.

In the late 1990s, mounting competition led to the design of the next-generation APT sensor, known as APsquared™ was launched in oil pressure sensing applications at General Motors in 2002. The next-generation product followed in 2005. M&C, now reorganized as Sensors & Controls (S&C), was producing some 40 million APT sensors a year and shipping them to leading automotive customers in Europe and Asia, as well as North and South America.

TI's move into pressure sensing led to the division's first acquisition in 1999. Acquiring Integrated Sensor Solutions, Inc.—a company that specialized in pressure sensors for advanced vehicle stability systems and low-emission engines such as common rail diesel fuel injection—gave TI an entry into new applications important to European automakers. This European focus led to the development and launch of another type of sensor, TI's Microfused Strain Gauge (MSG) pressure sensor. The MSG sensor, with its redundant temperature/pressure signal conditioning, quickly found its way into leading-edge braking and vehicle stability control systems, and MSG derivatives began multiplying. By 2000, thanks to the success of these portfolio developments, its acquisition strategy, and global market focus, TI achieved the number one position in automotive pressure sensing. By 2004, the MSG technology was being deployed in occupant weight sensors for use in next-generation smart air bag systems. S&C's sensor products portfolio had also grown to include position and inertial sensors. In 2005, Martha Sullivan, TI vice president and manager of TI's Sensor Products business, estimated the worldwide automotive sensors market to be about $9 billion. Based on a combination of market foresight, business acumen, and technological know-how, the S&C business had intercepted the opportunity and achieved worldwide leadership. The result was 10 consecutive years of revenue growth for its Sensor Products business.

Persistent in its pursuit of business applications for its new technologies, TI began exploring applications and potential markets for RFID devices. During the Vision 2000 sessions in 1989, (organized by Jerry Junkins, TI president and CEO), the RFID team identified RFID as an opportunity—based on the tracking project for the Dutch pig industry. After those sessions, the project was renamed TI Registration and Information Systems (TIRIS).

An RFID tag consists of a thin antenna looped around a dime-sized computer chip. It automatically broadcasts its stored data without batteries. The signal from an electronic reader provides enough electricity to turn on the tag so it can transmit a signal each time a reader scans it. The brief burst of data can contain anything from serial numbers to encrypted medical information or credit card numbers.

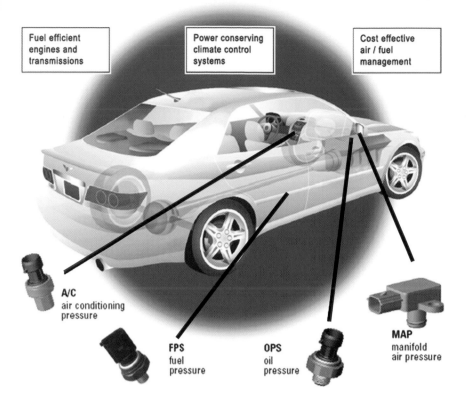

Fuel efficient
engines and
transmissions

Power conserving
climate control
systems

Cost effective
air / fuel
management

A/C
air conditioning
pressure

FPS
fuel
pressure

OPS
oil
pressure

MAP
manifold
air pressure

TI's pressure sensing devices are used in many
automotive systems, including engine and transmission
controls, climate control, and fuel management.

In 1998, TI introduced a breakthrough with Tag-it™ smart label transponder inlays, which enabled the first commercially viable disposable RFID label. Zebra Technologies and Symbol Technologies, leading providers of automatic identification solutions, formed a strategic alliance with TI to develop and market Tag-it tags for product authentication, baggage, and parcel tracking applications. Other applications followed. London's Heathrow Airport installed the world's first experimental RFID baggage delivery system, and the Vatican Library in Rome adopted Tag-it tags to identify and manage its collection of 20 million books and documents. Before the introduction of Tag-it tags, administrators had been forced to close the library for months to verify its contents. Books and documents that had been misplaced or misfiled with the Vatican Library's manual system—essentially "lost" for extended periods—now could be accurately located and accounted for with a quick scan of the shelves, using a handheld reader.

The company debuted its TIRIS technology at agricultural shows throughout Europe in 1990, and the response was "heartening." A year later, TI announced its formal entry into the RFID systems markets with worldwide introduction of the technology. In 1993, Ford company (in Europe) became the first company to use RFID technology to reduce car theft when it implemented a TIRIS device in its U.K. and German versions of the Escort. By 1995, TI had developed a new ultrahigh-frequency TIRIS product platform as the core of California's electronic toll and traffic management system. These TIRIS applications led to the expansion of its uses across a wide array of applications in access control, factory automation, waste management, livestock management, vehicle identification, and security.

In the 1990s, TIRIS devices were used to time runners in the Boston Marathon and provide security for athletes at Atlanta's Summer Olympics. Mobil startled the gasoline service industry by implementing Speedpass, a new pay-at the pump program using RFID from TI. And, in September 1997, a European Union mandate required all vehicles sold in member countries to be equipped with immobilizers to prevent theft, a move that boosted TI's RFID-based immobilizer business.

The Port of Singapore used TI's RFID system to track thousands of multi-ton cargo containers while managing the arrivals and departures of as many as 50 ships a day. Scanpro, a Dallas medical technology firm, began using TI's technology to create RFID bracelets and military "dog tags" containing the medical data of wounded soldiers, civilians, and enemy combatants in Iraq.

In 2003, Wal-Mart mandated the use of RFID tags on pallets and cartons shipped to the store starting in January 2005. In 2004, the Food and Drug Administration (FDA) issued directives which required the implementation of RFID to track pharmaceutical products.

Each plastic tag, the size of
a postage stamp, contains
a computer chip that can
store data, and a minuscule
antenna that lets the chip
communicate with a reader
attached to a network.

TRACKING PIGS

★ ★ ★

The technology was sophisticated enough, but the application didn't quite measure up to traditional TI standards. By happenstance, Gerry Bekkers, manager of TI-Holland, met a businessman from The Hague, who told him about a problem the Dutch Meat Board had keeping track of some 20 million pigs. All pigs were "earmarked" with a numbered plastic flap that allowed authorities to trace any diseased animal to its home farm. Unfortunately, the plastic flaps often fell off, and many pigs could not be identified.

The board looked into implementing an advanced registration system that used radio frequency transponders. Such a system would make it possible for the government to act immediately if a problem was detected, and it gave farmers a management system for automatic feeding, as well as automatic counting, when the pigs were transported.

Bekkers contacted TI's semiconductor facility in Freising, Germany, and Joe

Schuerman immersed himself in the project, aptly named "Porky." Bekkers recalled, "The essential task was to demonstrate we could read the transponder at a distance of 80 centimeters. Until this point, the industry only had transponders with a 5-centimeter readout, which was good for pets, but not for pigs. We got ready for our first demonstration to the Meat Board in Almelo with Juergen Frieling, Joe Schuerman, and the Freising team. The meeting had been scheduled, but we needed more time. Yet, postponing it would create doubt about TI's capabilities. The last rehearsal test failed, but, fortunately, at the crucial moment, the actual demonstration was a big success."

Unfortunately, the Dutch government decided to phase down pork production and project "Porky" was no longer needed. But TIRIS technology survived and thrived in many other applications.

By 2005, with the RFID market poised to grow, TI closed in on production milestone of 500 million RFID tags and was gearing up to produce billions of chips, straps, inlays, and reader modules for retail supply chain "contactless" commerce and pharmaceutical applications. Addressing thousands of attendees at RFID World 2005, Julie England, vice president of TI and general manager of the TI-RFID Systems business, predicted a critical mass of the technology would spur innovation and new applications across the enterprise value chain.

"Wireless RFID data acquisition for value-chain applications will create new business models, much like the cell phone has shifted the market from voice-only to a range of messaging, data, and transaction services," England said. "At the edge of wireless and sensor networks, RFID is converging with Electronic Product Code and sensor technology to unlock new applications that go beyond identification to include everything from authentication to temperature, time expiration, pressure, and condition monitoring.

"TI's objective," she said, "is to empower a host of new RFID applications and innovations that drive core business process transformation."

54

MIRRORED IMAGES

With its DLP™ technology, TI delivers images with incredible resolution, brightness, contrast, and color.

There was no magic in the creation of a new technology that, as Dr. Larry Hornbeck said, would be the world's first truly digital imaging capability to beckon at the end of the information highway. The innovative pursuit of Digital Light Processing™, or DLP, technology was a journey littered with mistakes, failures, and shattered concepts, all fueled by dogged perseverance and sheer determination that refused to quit on an idea destined to revolutionize the television and film industry. As Hornbeck, a noted physicist, would remember, "If you're afraid you may fail, then your actions may not be as bold, aggressive, or creative as you need them to be in order to accomplish your goal. You may play it so conservative you never get there." Hornbeck was determined to get there.

Dr. Larry Hornbeck received an Emmy Award in 1998 for "outstanding achievement in engineering development for DMD technology" from the Academy of Television Arts & Sciences.

Reflecting on this pursuit, Rich Templeton, TI president and CEO, explained it this way, "Persistence may be the greatest attribute for the success of DLP, that or stubbornness, depending on how you want to describe it."

Today, nearly 30 years after Hornbeck began his work, DLP technology has changed the face of the display industry, bringing clear, sharp pictures to large-screen TVs, and projectors for business, home, and digital cinema.

"It has been a long road to success," said John Van Scoter, TI Senior Vice President and General Manager, DLP Products. "It took a lot of hard work from a lot of very determined and visionary engineers to bring DLP technology to where it is today."

At TI's Central Research Laboratories in 1977, Dr. Hornbeck and his team began work to develop one of the world's most prolific display technologies even though no one had yet conceived of a practical consumer application for a process that was ultimately able to place as many as 2 million movable micromirrors on the face of a silicon chip not much larger than a postage stamp.

The search for applications well-suited to the technology would continue for more than 15 years. The starts and stops, however, were not lost, because Hornbeck and his team improved the technology with each engagement.

In the early 1970s, TI worked with the Defense Advanced Research Projects Agency to investigate the possibility of using charge-coupled device (CCD) imaging chips as a moving-target indicator for military applications. Although this project did not result in a product, it led to a subsequent project in 1977 with another Department of Defense agency to use CCDs in conjunction with deformable surfaces using metallized membranes for optical target recognition. By 1981, Hornbeck shifted to all-metal, electrostatic reflective mirrors driven by analog signals, which were easier to build in a standard semiconductor fab. He also began to look for commercial rather than military applications, where the payoff to the company would be much greater.

At the same, time Dr. Ed Nelson, an expert in optical imaging, joined Hornbeck and expressed his conviction that the technology was well suited for printer applications. In late 1983, Hornbeck filed the initial patents for his deformable micromirror device (DMD). Several engagements with printing manufacturers followed.

The analog concept, no matter how grand it appeared in theory, had not lived up to its expectations. So, Hornbeck began using the micromirrors as simple on-off switches and implementing pulsewidth modulation techniques to generate a digital image. Thus, the basis for what would become today's DMD was underway.

In 1987, a 512 x 1 "digital" DMD was built and tested. Although the technology had much to offer, it was a radical departure from the technology and product roadmaps of printer manufacturers. By late 1990, TI delivered an 840 x 1 DMD, its first commercial DMD application for printers, driven by the technology. The customer was TI's own printer division.

But, the road remained rocky for the DMD. Some managers couldn't see a future for the technology and getting space in the semiconductor development wafer fab to build the devices was a continuing struggle. One ally, TI Chief Technical Officer George Heilmeier, provided a little funding to keep the team going and, perhaps more importantly, he provided encouragement to Hornbeck.

In 1988, Jeff Sampsell, manager of research for the optical processing branch, learned of an upcoming defense research program to explore the concept of High Definition Television (HDTV). Sampsell was convinced that DMD was the answer,

NAMING THE BABY

★ ★ ★

Early in the development of the DMD technology, the company faced a major marketing challenge: how should the company position the DMD technology in the video display market?

Cathode Ray Tube (CRT) technology was the technology of choice for most video images and Liquid Crystal Display (LCD) technology was the default winner in the burgeoning projection display business. TI knew it had a technology that would resonate beyond its competitors. In fact, TI wanted to drive the advantages associated with the technology to the consumers as a technology brand.

A distinctive brand identity would bring increased value to TI's customers who chose to use DLP technology in their products. With this in mind, Digital Light Processing, or DLP, technology was born.

Today, manufacturers display the DLP logo on

The logo for TI's DLP business was a key element in the branding strategy for the technology.

their projectors and TV products, digital movies show a DLP Cinema™ trailer to audiences, and an extensive www.dlp.com website is continually updated to educate the public on the technology and on the manufacturers that use it. In addition, TI's marketing campaigns have driven education and recognition to consumers. In fact, many people began asking for "DLP TVs" at retail.

In January 2004, *Reuters* noted, *"Perhaps the real magic behind DLP is that Texas Instruments has succeeded in turning the technology into a veritable brand name."* In late 2004, TI took a huge marketing leap and launched an eight-market U.S. advertising campaign for DLP TVs, featuring TV, radio, and web advertisements, which will likely be the first of many.

even if the application would need an array of 2 million micromirrors. To Hornbeck, the project seemed like a huge leap. It would require going from 840 to 2 million mirrors. Nevertheless, he and his team moved forward.

A packaged DLP chip contains up to 2 million tiny, moveable micromirrors, individually controlled to produce a high-quality image.

Sampsell and his team were dismayed when their proposal did not make the cut, primarily because it used 2 million micromirrors as digital switches for the display, which was not an easy technology to either envision or understand. Sampsell did not accept defeat. He argued that the technology had not received a fair hearing, and a special DoD team came to Dallas to review the DMD technology. Although difficult to comprehend, the DMD theory made sense, and, in February 1989, TI was awarded a $12 million television HDTV development contract.

By year-end, Rank Corporation, a major player in the motion picture and entertainment industry, added to the development coffers by investing $5 million for TI to develop a concept using beam-splitting prisms and three DMD devices to create high brightness, large-screen projectors.

The combined investments probably made the difference between success and failure for DMD technology. They allowed Hornbeck and his team to keep working. When they began to

This photomicrograph shows the tiny micromirrors compared to an ant's leg. These micromirrors switch 5,000 times per second to reflect light and create an image.

TI's DLP technology is now designed into more than 75 DLP TVs from more than 20 manufacturers. The Samsung 56" Widescreen Pedestal DLP TV, pictured here, is one such example.

concentrate on the digital signal processing aspects of the DMD projector concept, they realized that the strength of digital light processing was its ability to trick the eye into thinking it was actually seeing a continuous moving image in real time, even when it wasn't.

TI CEO Jerry Junkins and a few of his managers were convinced that DMD technology could become the foundation of a major business. In 1991, a corporate-level venture project was formed, a dedicated wafer fab was built, and TI decided to focus on two key business applications—digital network printing and digital video display. It was time to develop manufacturing processes, design device structures capable of withstanding the heat levels of arc lamps, and address the technology's unique packaging concepts.

———————

By 1996, the team saw a natural fit for its DMD technology—the digital projection market for conference room use. Current projectors weighed 25-35 pounds each and cost $12,000-$18,000 each.

TI knew that DMD technology would not immediately bring lighter projectors at lower costs, but it did know that DLP technology would enable superior images and bring the weight and cost advantages eventually. Competition was still tough with manufacturers of projectors that were first to market; they were improving their products, and building awareness with advertising.

As for printer applications, there were no paying customers on the horizon. Printer companies that showed interest initially had made significant improvements in print quality and lowering costs. It wasn't feasible for them to switch technology development paths at the time. Although the future looked brighter for TI's DMD technology, it was hard to remain convinced without paying customers.

In mid-1996, Tom Engibous, TI's new CEO, decided to augment the project with senior managers from various parts of the company to help work through the problems. TI needed to develop a process to build the DMD device at competitive costs. Otherwise, two decades of hard work would be for nothing. The initial strategy was simple enough. Create projectors that were "down in size and weight and up in brightness and resolution."

It was also clear that TI, being a semiconductor company, should focus on a chipset product offering rather than integrated projector subsystems. Furthermore, managers agreed that TI would focus on video displays and terminate any pursuit of printer applications.

From Hornbeck's DMD, a digital light switch on a silicon chip became TI's DLP technology. It integrated the DMD with TI digital signal processors and memory, adding software, optical, and electrical components while utilizing an illumination source to create a digital light imaging system. DLP technology allowed traditional analog and digital images to be digitally captured, manipulated, and optically reflected from the mirrored aluminum surface of a DMD display.

Hornbeck pointed out, "Sir Isaac Newton said, 'If I have seen farther, it is by standing on the shoulders of giants.' His quotation directly related to DMD. We're standing on the shoulders of a semiconductor giant."

Looking back at how everything finally came together, Sampsell said, "To see a static image on the screen coming off an integrated circuit for the first time was truly an experience. It was exciting because it worked. Everything we said would work did work, and all the math made sense. Things switched on and off, and we could really see a picture. We determined the sky was the limit. Nothing could hold us back now. We had already been through all of the challenges, all of the problems, all of the issues."

TI wondered, "What will the world ask of this revolution?" The company knew it was imperative to forecast those opportunities successfully and move immediately far out in front of the competition, using TI's entrepreneurial skills and quick response mechanisms to take advantage of a waiting marketplace.

By the end of 1996, TI was working with InFocus Systems, the world's number one projector company, to develop a projector that was twice as bright and weighed less than seven pounds—less than half the weight of projectors in the market. When the product was introduced a year later, it revolutionized the conference room projection market. DLP technology quickly captured a 20 percent share of the market, and pressure mounted for DMD array sizes to be increased from 500,000 to more than 1 million micromirrors. The semiconductor fab team was undaunted. In time, DLP projectors would weigh less than two pounds and cost less than $1,000. Today, there are more than 275 DLP projectors available from the world's top manufacturers for both business and home entertainment use.

TI's semiconductor manufacturing expertise played a significant role in the commercialization of DLP products. Major achievements were made in DMD process development, yield, assembly/test, volume ramp, and vendor/subcontractor fan-out from 1996 through 2003. Although DMD fabrication uses standard TI material, equipment, and processes, it proved to be a significant challenge when considering not only electrical, but also optical, and mechanical performance. These challenges were met, resulting in growth from a small laboratory environment producing thousands of units per quarter to a worldwide mass production environment of multiple factories producing more than 1 million units per quarter.

Once TI DLP technology achieved success in the front-projection space, TI set its sights on the rear-projection TV market. TI's Bob England recalled demonstrating to board members a unit of a large Japanese TV manufacturer, and one of them remarked, "This is one of the best plasma TVs I have ever seen." England knew immediately TI had achieved the image quality it needed to break into the

DLP technology received a second Emmy Award® (Copyright ATAS/NATAS) in 2003 for "pioneering development of mass-produced digital reflective imaging technology for consumer rear-projection television." (Photo courtesy of the Academy of Television Arts & Sciences.)

AT THE MOVIES

★ ★ ★

During the early 1990s, TI sought to create large screen image quality that would rival and ultimately replace film in the motion picture industry.

The benefits of digital media were simple to understand. There would be the easy, non-physical distribution of the video content and non-degradable image quality without scars or scratches. It would mean no more reels to change or complicated machinery to operate. Mainstream digital projectors would be as simple to operate as pushing a button or pointing and clicking on a computer screen.

The industry, however, wasn't convinced.

Movie studios feared that pirating could represent a serious loss of revenue. Unlike a videocassette, the digital medium did not degrade when multiple copies were made of a motion picture. And, theater owners did not relish the thought of increased financial investment in new projectors.

To address the industry's concerns, in 1997, TI's Digital Cinema team began meeting with the Hollywood creative community—producers, directors, and cinematographers, along with those individuals responsible for editing and duplicating movies. They took notes from distributors, movie theater owners, agents, actors, audiences, and even ushers about what made a great picture. And the team began incorporating the ideas they heard into a new prototype for the projector. These improvements were incorporated into the other DLP products as well.

George Lucas opened the door for TI in 1998 when he announced he would shoot his new *Star Wars: Episode I, The Phantom Menace* in digital format and exhibit it with digital projection. The results were spectacular, when shown using two DLP Cinema projectors in New York and Los Angeles.

As *Menace* producer Rick McCallum said, "For filmmakers, this brings the in-theater experience a lot closer to what could be seen on the set during shooting, which is what the director wants the audiences to see. This is a turning point in film exhibition."

At last, the industry was ready for the benefits of DLP Cinema technology.

---

large-screen TV marketplace.

In 1998, with the promise of HDTV on the horizon and the increased consumer preference for large screen sizes, several Japanese customers decided to develop DLP televisions. The new sets received critical acclaim at home and abroad. Unfortunately, the retail prices that ranged from $10,000 to $15,000 were more than the market would bear. Samsung led the charge with the second generation of DLPs in 2002, which featured smaller, sleeker cabinets, and price points in the $5,000 range. Today, DLP TVs are available from more than 20 companies, including seven of the top nine TV manufacturers. Prices have gone as low as $2,500, with the expectancy that the prices will continue to drop. The hope of General Manager John Van Scoter is that in time, "there will be a DLP TV in every home."

The success of DLP technology and the increased recognition of the DLP brand have driven TI back in front of the consumer. The *Wall Street Journal* reported, *"Some analysts think DLP ultimately could be as ubiquitous as Dolby sound in stereos."*

By the end of 2004, more than 5 million DLP products for projectors and TVs have been shipped. Consumers can select DLP TVs from more than 75 different models at 11,000 retail outlets worldwide. *Red Herring*, a respected technology publication, referred to TI as one of the *"brightest stars in the digital universe."* The DLP technology would ultimately bring clear, sharp, vibrant images to business, home entertainment, and professional venue projectors, as well as large-screen HDTVs and digital cinema. Mitsubishi, Toshiba, Sharp, and Skyworth had joined InFocus, LG Electronics, Panasonic, and Samsung to add DLP TVs to their product lines.

THE PEOPLE OF TI

Cecil Green underscored TI's philosophy when he said, "Getting ahead depends not on working people but on working with people." Their ideas, innovations, inventions and commitment shaped the company, and the company worked diligently to establish programs to benefit its employees. TI embraced all races, ages, genders, religions, thoughts and ideas, pointing out, "Our diverse workforce makes us better," especially when networking in a global society. Profit sharing, communications, training and continuing education programs all encourage TIers to reach their potential at the office, while Texins Activity Center provides a way for TIers to reach personal goals.

TI was built on ingenuity of people, and continues to reward employees for all the things that help propel the company toward the future.

The many recreational and hobby interests of TIers were featured in a cover story in *Life* magazine (September 3, 1971). Clubs of the Texins Association ranged from archery and aircraft, to fishing and dancing, to other types of indoor and outdoor sports.

55

SHARING THE WEALTH

GSI pioneered a profit sharing plan and shared the wealth with employees.

Former president Erik Jonsson was a visionary, so few were surprised when he introduced a profit sharing program for GSI employees in 1942. Yet his idea was met with some skepticism. Jonsson, however, realized good people are a company's greatest asset. His plan would reward those who helped build the foundation for GSI as its new ventures brought in substantial revenues. He saw profit sharing as a way for long-term employees to build sizable financial accounts.

By building on Jonsson's plan, remaining flexible, and making positive changes in the benefits programs, TI could attract and retain some of the best and brightest minds in a complex industry.

During the instability of World War II, GSI management worked to instill confidence about the company's future in their employees. In a bid to retain GSI personnel in 1942, Jonsson developed an innovative profit sharing trust, designed to give employees ownership and emphasize the point that costly errors—as well as any wrecked, junked, or abandoned field equipment—could jeopardize profit at the end of the year. Employees realized good production schedules and accurate survey results would ensure higher profits as well as customer satisfaction. Through combined efforts, revenue in 1942 reached $1.2 million, with profits of $128,000 to share among the partners and GSI's 370 employees. As founder Cecil Green said, "Getting ahead depends not on working people but on working with people."

In a 1982 interview, Jonsson remembered, "During World War II, wages were frozen and prices were locked, as were commodities and materials. If we didn't have flexibility, we

TURNING TEXINS INTO TEXANS

★ ★ ★

In 1953, 11 TIers pooled $5 each and petitioned the Texas Banking Commission to create an organization to promote thrift and provide low-cost loans to TI employees. On October 8, 1953, the Texas Banking Commissioner signed certification that created the Texins Credit Union, a state-chartered credit union. For nearly 40 years, membership in Texins was limited to TI employees and their family members, but in 1991, membership was opened to employee groups outside TI. In 1998, membership expanded again when a smaller credit union merged its operations into Texins. This merger resulted in the addition of several communities to membership, as well as more employee groups. To better reflect the diversity of the credit union, the name was changed from Texins to Texans in 1998.

One of 25 branches of the Texans Credit Union, serving more than 130,000 customers in North Texas, Austin, and Houston.

Carl Skooglund, former TI vice president said, "A few years ago when we were ready to reach $1 billion in assets, we invited John McCormick, one of the original founders of the credit union, to deposit another $5 to put us over the top. It was, of course, a symbolic event, but a very significant one." Today, Texans Credit Union serves more than 130,000 members in various companies, professional groups, and communities.

couldn't survive. There was only one thing we could do, and it was rather new in American business, too. We established a profit sharing plan that was different from most. Profit sharing plans in general were constructed to take care of top-level management, and sometimes, there was more consideration of middle management. But there was little attention paid to the rest of the people. We never felt that way. We included the janitors pushing brooms just the same as we did executives."

According to an April 1955 issue of *texins*, the company newsletter, the trustees of the profit sharing fund followed a conservative policy for its investments. (A year earlier, net assets of the trust had reached more than $2.2 million.) TI continued to modify the trust as new operations were acquired, allowing new employees a chance to participate. In 1955, the U.S. Treasury Department approved an amendment making it possible for five-year participants to authorize trustees to buy TI stock for their individual accounts. By 1959, employees with three or more years' service could authorize trustees to invest either 10, 25, or 40 percent of their vested interest in TI stock.

During the late 1950s, day-shift employees would file into Moody Coliseum at Southern Methodist University, the only place in Dallas large enough to accommodate them all. Assisted by four large projection screens, President Pat Haggerty presented the previous year's results and corresponding profit sharing awards. The final numbers were always closely guarded, which filled the annual meeting with anxiety and anticipation. For Haggerty, it was an opportunity to inspire and motivate employees as they faced a new and often unpredictable year.

Tommy Chaddick, a machinist, recalled, "The enthusiasm of the people who came out of there was just unbelievable. We

A LOT OF DOUGH

★ ★ ★

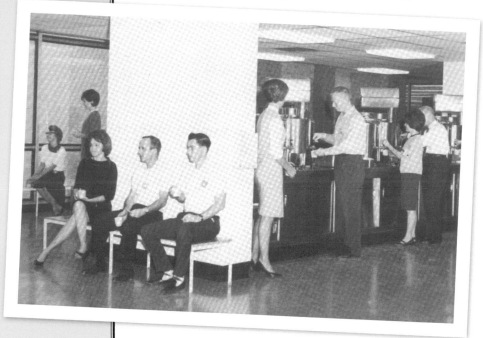

TI's unwritten policy of offering free coffee and donuts to employees each day began at the Lemmon Avenue Plant. Thelma Peacock, who started at TI in 1953, remembered when employees had two coffee breaks each day. Trays piled high with freshly baked, glazed donuts would be rolled from the cafeteria into the hallways at 9:50 a.m. and 2:50 p.m. Employees filed out of their offices and workplaces, and donuts were gone before the final cup of coffee was finished.

The tradition spread to the new semiconductor plant when it opened in 1958 and made its way to other buildings as they were added to the Expressway site. Depending on local customs, TI operations around the world followed a similar trend.

At first, donuts were purchased from local bakeries, but as quantities grew, TI made its own. However, during the 1960s, baking donuts for 20,000 people and getting them ready to serve became a daunting and costly task. Cafeteria employees came to work long before daylight to make the batter and wait for the yeast to work its magic. The recipe was secret, and it never varied.

During the business crunch of 1968, TI made the difficult decision to discontinue free coffee and donuts. Vending machines took their place, with a percentage of the profits designated for employee recreation.

Some of those last donuts have survived the test of time. One donut was bronzed and another encapsulated in plastic as mementos of the sweet days gone by.

would come out of there thinking, 'Boy, what in the hell can we do next?' At that time, we had divisions, but it wasn't each division working for itself. It was every division working for the whole team. That was the good of TI."

Haggerty's schedule didn't let up after the Dallas meeting. The profit sharing meeting was repeated for night-shift employees in the cafeteria at the semiconductor plant, and then again with TI personnel in the Houston plant the next day. Eventually, the Houston group grew so large it had to be moved to Rice University Stadium.

As TI expanded around the world, with more people becoming eligible for profit sharing, the group meetings were replaced by video teleconferences.

In the 1990s, the profit sharing plan was again revised. Employees were given more flexibility and the power to diversify their TI stock holdings. They were also able to access their accounts on the Internet and obtain up-to-date information about investment opportunities. Later in the decade, employees were given cash payouts.

The largest profit sharing payouts in TI history were awarded in 2000 and 2004.

In addition to profit sharing and the 401(k) plan, TI introduced and modified several other incentives including stock option purchase plans, merit bonuses, and custom reward plans. Each was tied to financial performance, and each kept the company competitive in benefits.

56

PEOPLE: THE SPIRIT OF TI

TI is known worldwide for its innovative technologies, but from the beginning it has been a people company.

TI is known for revolutionary technologies, but it is the people who are the foundation of the company. The fabric of TI is woven from the commitment, the dedication, and the inspiration of thousands of people whose day-to-day efforts help the company re-engineer the world. They all have stories of importance, humor, and inspiration, and what follows are a few of them.

Although many TI secretaries had responsibilities similar to each other, a few found themselves navigating the unfamiliar waters of "black" programs, those top secret Department of Defense operations that were an integral part of supporting TI's defense group.

This photo shows TIers in the early 1950s in a typical office with tile-covered floors and gray Steelcase desks at the Lemmon Avenue plant in Dallas.

On one project during the early 1980s, the government demanded a turnaround time of six weeks. The urgent deadline not only put the engineers under stress, it became a nightmare for secretaries who had to produce the details of the proposal in final form.

Four women worked an average of 18 hours a day, seven days a week, using Mac 2s (small-screen Macintosh computers) that, for security reasons, had never been networked.

Some brought sleeping bags to work, slept in the offices, and showered each morning at the Texins Activity Center.

By the time the proposal was completed, it consisted of 20 volumes bound in one-inch binders. A secretary delivered the 50-pound box on deadline—personally carrying the proposal to Washington, D.C., despite an accident at the airport when the oversized box slipped off the baggage carrier, leaving her to wrestle with the top secret documents in the middle of the crowded terminal. Undeterred, she completed the mission.

In 1967, K. Bala came to the U.S. to obtain his master's degree in Electrical Engineering from the University of Rhode Island. When he was about to finish his studies in 1969, one of his friends invited him to visit Southern Methodist University, so K. Bala applied for a job with TI, figuring he could get a free plane ride to see his buddy in Dallas.

He got the free plane ride, but he also got a job offer as MOS Design Engineer in Houston. He accepted. K. Bala still takes many flights for TI, now as Chairman of TI-Japan.

One day in 1973, there was a massive power outage at the TI plant in Kuala Lumpur, Malaysia. Zaiton Ahmad, a quality inspector then, was working in the factory when everything went dark and all the equipment shut down. Zaiton recalls, "It was thought that the power outage would last for a week, so we were all sent home." The power, however, returned after three days. Since telephones were not available in most homes and cell phones were not yet invented, TI had to come up with an alternate plan to call the employees back to work. Ultimately, it was decided to use national television and radio. The plan worked; most employees, including Zaiton, returned the next day.

Larry Brantingham was working as a design engineer in the late 1970s when his module in the TI-Lubbock plant was rearranged to house both the design group and assembly/test group. Management had decided it would be good to emphasize the importance of the production side to the product development side.

Brantingham remembers, "Maybe my concentration was lacking, but I just couldn't hold a complex design in my head while listening to a battery of air-powered screwdrivers. I did some work at home, but we were living in an efficiency with our new baby while our house was being built, so the only real work that I accomplished was in the very early hours of the morning."

Then one cold morning on his way to work, Brantingham

saw a Laundromat and pulled into the parking lot on an impulse. It was the perfect solution to his problem: it was warm inside; there was lots of white noise, and it was mostly empty. Since logic design was done at that time with a pencil, template, and vellum, it wasn't any harder to work on the clothes folding table than at his office. Brantingham's ability to "think outside the box" enabled him to design synthesizers, but his ingenuity allowed him to work outside the box as well.

Mary Ellen Weber joined TI's Semiconductor Process & Design Center in 1988. She was later selected by NASA to become an astronaut, flying on both the *Discovery* and the *Atlantis* space shuttles. TI's Phil Bogan, on the other hand, became a reluctant astronaut.

One of Bogan's assignments during the 1970s was to produce TI floats for the New Year's Day Cotton Bowl Parade in Dallas. One year, in celebration of TI's involvement with NASA's *Voyager* mission, TI decided to replicate the *Voyager* as it orbited around the planet Saturn.

Bogan received special permission from NASA to borrow

During the 1970s, TI entered floats in the Cotton Bowl Parade which wound through downtown Dallas each year on New Year's Day. The theme of this TI float was space exploration, graphically demonstrating TI's role in getting man into space.

two authentic spacesuits for a couple of models to wear during the parade. The suits were shipped to Bogan's home, and, after a quick inspection, his two sons tried them on for size. They convinced their father one of the suits might fit him.

He tried one on.

Bogan remembered, "The suit went on just fine. But then I couldn't seem to bend my head enough to get it back through the metal neck ring. I guess astronauts were a little shorter than I was. I spent most of one whole day trying to get out of that suit. Just as I was prepared to have my wife saw through the neck ring, she and my sons gave it one more huge try and, at last, I was released from the suit.

"My biggest fear, as I lounged around wearing the spacesuit that day, was having to explain to NASA why one of their expensive suits had been returned with a slight alteration."

———————

Just after 4 p.m. on July 16, 1990, a rumbling sound thundered from the ground in Baguio City, Philippines. Seconds later, the earth shook violently. Everything swayed sideways, then shook up and down. Roads cracked and buildings collapsed. When the 7.7 magnitude earthquake was over, employees at TI-Philippines (TIPI) huddled in parking areas in a state of shock. It was a miracle that none of the 800 plus personnel in the factory were injured.

After the company ensured that each employee had the basic commodities and assistance for any family member who suffered injuries, their focus turned to operations at the plant. Producing units was possible, but shipping them was a huge challenge. Only one main thoroughfare, Naguilian Road, remained partially passable. Trucks couldn't cross the bridge, so boxes of semiconductors had to be painstakingly hand-carried from the truck coming from Baguio to the other end of the bridge, where the other truck bound for the international airport in Manila waited.

TIPI started shipping products in 12 days, a record time, since the original assessment had been 90 days.

———————

In 1991, Ed Pouliot was a new business planner in Dallas for Application-Specific Integrated Circuits. He had only been with the group a few months when he received a call from TI-Austin—they didn't have enough of the devices that he was responsible for. They had pre-assembled as many

boards as they could without this device, and if he did not get these parts to them now, the customer would be in a serious situation. Pouliot had just received a small quantity of devices from the local assembly subcontractor, so he worked on the test floor all day carefully watching the devices as they went through the final stages of processing and packing. Finally, at 2 a.m. on the last day of the quarter, the parts were ready to go. There was no way to have a courier pick up the material, so as a last resort, he decided to take the parts to Austin himself. He had driven his motorcycle to work, but the boxes were just small enough to fit in his saddlebags.

Pouliot loaded everything, and without sleep, headed to Austin. He was about 50 miles outside of the city when he realized he had no idea where the Austin plant was located. A former member of the National Guard, Pouliot went to the only point of reference that he had for the area—Camp Mabry. Once there, he started making outward circles, and as luck would have it, he stumbled onto the TI plant just seven miles away.

It was 7 a.m. when he arrived—exhausted and wind-burned, but just in time to hand off the parts to the assembly manager. In the end, the parts were added to the preassembled boards, the customer received the devices as scheduled, and TI received $4 million in revenue for the quarter.

———————

Amy Treece was communications manager of TI's military division when a personal invitation arrived from the Commander of the Naval Air Systems Command. He wanted TI to send a representative to the 2004 Navy Science and Technology Engineering Workshop in San Diego. She recalled, "Al Steel, who was the government liaison for our division and a former Navy F-14 pilot, was the natural choice."

As soon as Steel arrived at the conference in California, the Commander cornered him and said, "Al, you've got to help me. The Admiral is trying to fill some slots for a 'Distinguished Visitors' trip to a carrier in Norfolk, Virginia, on Sunday morning. It would be great if you could get me a TI senior-level vice president to go."

Steel called his boss, John Goff, in Texas, and they made a list of potential candidates. Unfortunately, all had prior commitments. Finally, it was decided Steel would go, but there was a problem. He was in California, and it was Friday. He needed to arrive at the Norfolk, Virginia, Naval Base on the

East Coast by midnight Saturday. Steel's race against the clock was on.

Time wasn't on his side, and neither were circumstances. On Saturday, airport security noted his driver's license had expired before he caught his flight to Chicago, and he had to convince them to allow him to continue his trip. Then, a major storm system threatened the Midwest and delayed his flight for two hours, and finally, above Chicago, the plane encountered a low-level wind shear, missed the approach, and had to try again before landing. The next flight to Norfolk was canceled and so was the next, but close to midnight, Steel finally made it onto a plane headed for Baltimore.

Baltimore was closer to the goal, but it was still 250 miles from Norfolk. The rental car counters were closed, and no limo driver would go that far. After a series of negotiations, one taxi driver finally agreed to take Steel to Norfolk, but insisted, in a thick foreign accent, that the fare would be $400 cash. Steel was out of options. He climbed into the cab and together, they headed for a gas station with an automatic teller machine.

At 5 a.m. Sunday, the two arrived at Norfolk Naval Base where Steel's credentials and letter of introduction from the Naval Commander got them past security. After they entered the gate, the driver smiled, pointed to himself, and said, "Twenty years, Russian Navy."

"What irony," Steel thought. "Twenty years earlier, our countries were at odds, and now, the two of us were together at the largest Naval Base in the world in a post 9/11 environment."

By 7:30 a.m., Steel and the other distinguished visitors boarded a helicopter for a bumpy, 90-minute flight to the *USS Enterprise*, CVN-65. Steel hadn't slept for more than 24 hours.

Steel said later, "For me, it was a pleasant homecoming. The sights, sounds, and smells were just as they had been during my Navy tenure 23 years earlier. As I stood there, I realized this trip had been well worth the trouble."

A FAMILY AFFAIR

★ ★ ★

For the Stringfellows and Jakubiks, TI is a family business. Tom Stringfellow and his wife, Marianne, started working for TI in 1965. Over the next 30 years, Tom supported a variety of business groups, became site manager of the TI-Temple plant in 1986, and retired in 1995.

Susanna Jakubik, the Stringfellows' daughter, hired on at TI in the summer program as an assembly line worker following her graduation from high school. The next summer, she took an internship in the marketing department, and the position sparked her imagination. She is currently the manager of DSP Media Relations.

When Mac Stringfellow, one of Tom and Marianne's sons, graduated from college in the early 1990s, he followed in the family footsteps and went to work for TI. He remained at the Austin plant for a few years before joining the Marine Corps.

In 2000, John Jakubik, Susanna's husband, applied for a position in business planning. He currently supports the Advanced Embedded Controls group.

The Stringfellow-Jakubik family have a combined 47 years of experience with TI.

Stringfellow-Jakubik family (left to right): John Jakubik, Tom Stringfellow, Susanna Stringfellow Jakubik, Marianne Stringfellow, and Mac Stringfellow.

57

TEAMWORK

TI's teamwork-centric environment is a legacy.

Teamwork at Texas Instruments is nothing new. From the earliest days, when geophysical exploration crews worked together in remote locations, often in difficult terrain, success or failure depended on how well the team functioned. Later on, it sometimes was the brilliant insight of a single inventor, but more often, it was the team—where the different skills and approaches of the individuals came together to accomplish something that no one thought could be done.

Texas Instrument's history is a story of teamwork. TI's first transistor was the result of a small team, as was the development of the first transistor pocket radio, the first handheld calculator, the Speak & Spell™ learning aid, and the digital signal processor.

The company invested in the creation of programs to foster collaboration. In 1999, TI began a program called Innovators in Action in which teams from around the world are nominated for their ingenuity in creating devices, refining processes, and meeting the needs of the market. Winning groups, such as the ADS5500 High-Speed Data Converter Development Team and the Digital Light Processing™ (DLP) Fast Track Pixel Team, are selected by a panel of senior managers and featured on TI's *Worldwide Quarterly Perspective* satellite broadcasts.

ADS5500 High-Speed Data Converter Development Team

When it was announced on December 1, 2003, the ADS5500 analog-to-digital converter was a major technological breakthrough. The ADS5500 began in December 2002 when Bobby Mitra, Managing Director of TI-India, set out to develop a device that allowed increased system capabilities in advanced communications, industrial, test and measurement, medical, video and imaging applications. The TI-India team's steady focus and willingness to try unconventional design architecture, soon paid off.

At the same time, Mike Koen, senior design manager at TI-Tucson, and his team organized a symposium for TI designers to share ideas and best practices in the design of high-speed analog-to-digital converters. Members of the TI-India team attended the symposium, presented a paper, and then stayed for extended talks. Ultimately, the product development took off as a joint effort spread across three sites: India, Tucson, and Dallas.

In the end, the ADS5500 was a winning product that opened new doors and an outstanding example of true innovation and collaboration across the company.

DLP Fast Track Pixel Team

The Digital Micromirror Device (DMD) is an optical semiconductor containing a rectangular array of up to 1.3 million hinge-mounted microscopic mirrors. Each of these micromirrors measures less than one-fifth the width of a human hair. When a DMD chip is coordinated with a digital video or graphic signal, a light source, and a projection lens, its mirrors can reflect an all-digital image onto a screen or other surface. Challenged to meet increased demand and reliability of these DLP™ products, TI created the Fast Track Pixel Team, whose mission was to create a revolutionary new pixel design.

"Three ingredients made the new DLP pixel design a success," noted Rabah Mezenner, DLP program manager, "sound judgments on the part of management; technical sacrifices made by team members from several groups who were often behind the scenes, yet responsible for building the project's foundation; and the support and encouragement of management each step of the way."

Collaboration with the other groups was important throughout the project. "Having Make [manufacturing] involved from the beginning ensured the manufacturability of the new concept," said Jerrell Carroll, DMOS5 DMD Module manager, "and to have the first device qualify in just six months is remarkable."

Communication and feedback helped optimize the design processes. "A methodical approach involving feedback from each area involved helped to optimize the designs for the given process," said Mark Strumpell, DMD Modeling and Tool Development manager and the other team leader. The new design dramatically reduced the number of steps in the manufacturing process. It also increased simplicity and stability, while improving yield, quality, and performance.

TEAMWORK ON A GLOBAL SCALE

★ ★ ★

Knowing the Market

"I look for broad market trends, identify requirements not yet satisfied, and translate these into high-level product and solution requirements compatible with TI's technologies, both existing and planned."

– Sujatha Garimella
   Strategic Marketing

Identifying the Potential

"Knowing what questions to ask about potential product requirements is essential to identifying those that will satisfy the customer's requirements."

– Kazuo Muramatsu
   Business Development

Seeing from Another Perspective

"By looking at our portfolio from the perspective of our customers, we can ensure that we produce the right products for their applications."

– Markus Staeblein
   Worldwide Account Manager

Making It User-Friendly

"We develop and market a set of software tools that makes it possible to create complex information systems from reusable software components that can be rapidly assembled and customized. It's a novel approach—one that promises to help customers make good decisions, and make them quickly, by putting the data they need right at their fingertips."

– Philippe Lafon
   Software Design Engineer

Optimizing Production

"As semiconductors make their way into more products, it's becoming a challenge for manufacturers to meet demand. TI has developed a management system we call the 'virtual fab.' It links our worldwide manufacturing sites into a close-knit network. Rather than operating as autonomous units, all the fabs now work together to produce the maximum output for our customers."

– Adrian Salinas
   Process Engineer

Delivering on Time

"Getting products delivered on time means tracking multiple projects across multiple continents on a real-time basis."

– Donna Knottek
   Planner

TEAMWORK ON A GLOBAL SCALE

★ ★ ★

Exploring the Possibilities

"The breakthrough manufacturing processes we develop will serve as the technology base for TI's leading-edge solutions."

– Juanita DeLoach
  Research & Design

Putting the Idea to Paper

"Designing circuits can be challenging, especially when all the performance parameters must fit 'inside the box.' The specifications sometimes conflict with each other; improving one parameter causes degradation in another. The trick is to get the right balance among all the specifications."

– LaRita Buchanan
  Design Engineer

Meeting Expectations

"Attention to detail is critical. Ensuring that products meet specifications saves money for us and our customers."

– Kevin Treece
  Product Engineer

Certifying Quality

"Quality assurance is an ongoing process that not only includes checking standards, but also providing the tools, processes, and products that allow both us and our customers to stay on the competitive edge."

– Richard Biddle
  Quality & Reliability Assurance

Supporting Beyond the Sale

"It's often said that two heads are better than one. We've long used this approach to build new business for digital signal processing solutions. In most cases, we don't invent the end-use applications. Instead, we co-invent them with thousands of customers around the globe—a strategy that's helped our components become the invisible enablers behind many of today's hottest technologies."

– Kyle Castille
  Applications Engineer

(Illustration courtesy of David Lesh.)

58

A TRADITION OF CORPORATE GOVERNANCE

TI was one of the first technology companies to incorporate non-employee and independent directors.

During its earliest years, the TI Board was composed of the founders, officers, and a handful of directors affiliated with TI through acquisitions. In 1967, TI added its first independent director, former Texas Governor John Connally. As the company grew, Pat Haggerty decided to consider a broader independent representation on the Board. It was a well-conceived strategy that would put TI among the early innovators in corporate governance.

In 1966, as Chairman of the Board, Haggerty wrote a memo to TI's directors, noting that the company was nearing $1 billion in sales and pointing out that it was becoming increasingly difficult for TI's senior operating officers to *"spend the time necessary to study, to think quietly about, and to comprehend the importance of this rapidly changing internal and external environment."* He believed *"some real pioneering in the structuring of a Board of Directors"* was required to govern an institution as large and complex as TI. Haggerty felt that long-term strategic planning should be the function of the Board, and a year later, he went public with his views at TI's annual stockholders' meeting.

Haggerty realized TI would have to address the need for succession throughout many facets of the organization since members of the company's management team were nearing age 55. Haggerty needed a tactic to enable a new generation of leaders to emerge and take charge.

Haggerty felt executives should move toward "second" careers in which they could contribute in new ways different from their first careers. He understood the need for a system that allowed new people to become top managers as a way for the corporation to remain strong and healthy.

Haggerty also understood the importance of addressing a corporate reform movement. He explained, *"Governments everywhere are participating increasingly in our corporate actions—often as a customer, but just as frequently as regulator, policeman, judge, and jury."* Rather than having the company report to a federally constituted regulatory watchdog, Haggerty wanted TI to develop a strong, independent Board whose duty was to protect shareholders' interests. Under his leadership, TI became one of the first technology companies to incorporate non-employee and independent directors.

Haggerty proposed two categories of director—retired employees no longer involved in the day-to-day operations of the company and outside directors who had no affiliation with TI. Eventually, TI stopped appointing retired employees as directors and focused on the appointment of independent Board members.

Managers accepted the Board's involvement on crucial decisions, which created a certain measure of self regulation. They were not inclined to push questionable tactical risks or make unethical decisions because they knew the Board would be reviewing those actions.

As the years passed, the composition of the Board changed, becoming more diverse with the addition of women and an African American director. Outside directors brought unique perspectives to the company. The commitment of the Board's independent directors and active CEOs amounted to roughly nine full days a year. The number of committees has varied over the years, but there are now three—Audit, Compensation, and Governance & Stockholder Relations. The Board's main function now is oversight, albeit a powerful oversight.

The Board receives its information in a variety of ways. Insightful materials are always available at regular meetings. TI conducts an annual strategic planning conference with the Board. Committee chairs are routinely briefed by TIers who are experts in certain fields, and senior TI managers keep Board members up-to-date on the direction of the company's expanding technologies and markets.

One of the Board's greatest jobs is to choose a CEO and ensure a steady succession plan for the company. To make the right decision, it is vital that directors have a working understanding of the TI strategy as well as insight into the

The TI Stockholders Meeting in 1980 was held in the North Building Cafeteria on the Dallas Expressway Site with Chairman Mark Shepherd presiding. More than 1,500 attended the meeting, most of whom were TI employee stockholders.

background and contributions senior managers have made to the company. Board members need to know the candidates on a personal level in order to form opinions on an individual's integrity, commitment, vision, and communication skills.

———

Under the leadership of Jerry Junkins, the Board frequently discussed the direction of TI and its next generation of leaders. The Board had to deal with the issue of succession much sooner than anyone anticipated when Junkins unexpectedly died in 1996 on a business trip overseas. James R. (Jim) Adams, retired Group President of SBC Communications and independent TI director, was named Chairman of the Board, and became a TI employee. After accepting the role, he said, "The biggest surprise was that there weren't any secrets between Jerry, the other leaders, and the Board. They had been very candid with us over the years. I found everything just as it had been presented. I think that's probably unusual when you walk into a company, and you haven't previously been there day-to-day."

The TI Board requires its directors to be outstanding achievers in their careers and possess a breadth of experience, sound judgment, analytical skills, the ability to contribute to a diversity of views on the Board, and have the time to devote to Board activities.

Through the years, TI's Board of Directors has provided the leadership, the strategies, the perspectives, and the influence the company needed to build TI into a multi-billion-dollar, global company. By 2005, TI's tradition of a strong, independent Board had spanned four decades.

59

WORKING HARD– PLAYING HARD

An association for employees grew out of a passion for bowling and expanded to three locations, 20 clubs, and 3,500 members.

In 1952, TI formed the Texins Association to provide a venue for employees to become involved in clubs, recreational programs, and community service. From its inception, Texins has been one of TI's most valuable perks, allowing TIers, their families, and others to participate in a broad range of interests.

During GSI's early years, employees from the Lemmon Avenue plant formed bowling teams, eventually growing to 48 teams in a league (believed to be one of the largest leagues west of the Mississippi), along with softball and baseball leagues.

By June 1952, the TI newsletter reported that 27 TIers had formed a group of stargazers, the Texas Instruments Astronomical Society. One of the group's first projects was the development of large telescopes that permitted members to survey and study the heavens. About the same time, other TIers formed an Amateur Radio Operator's Club and a Camera Club.

When the Texins Association was officially chartered in 1953, Al Morel (who had been the first employee hired by the company in 1930) was named chairman, and, under his leadership, the organization began growing in numbers and scope. There was no fee for participation, although some clubs charged dues to cover expenses.

During the mid-1950s, TI formed a 12-member basketball team, coached by Tom Fritz, that competed in the Longhorn Commercial League against such teams as General Electric, Hormel Packing, and Continental Gin. The teams squared off every Wednesday night in the automobile building at Fair Park.

Prior to 1958, the company had a tradition of sponsoring Christmas parties, which progressed from small gatherings to company-wide get-togethers. The TI Christmas party of 1957 was said to be the largest holiday party in Dallas, and some employees began to wonder if there might be a better way to spend the funds. A survey of TIers recommended that the Christmas party money be used to create a more varied recreational program. The next year, Pat Haggerty, president of TI, presented a check for $32,000 to Morel, who later established a facility for TI extracurricular activities.

By 1959, membership in Texins reached more than 2,100. TIers and family members participated in 17 clubs and athletic activities, ranging from archery to tennis. A year later, T. E. "Smitty" Smith, who had worked in the company's defense business, became the association's first full-time director.

In 1960, Texins secured a 20-year renewable lease for 20 acres on the shores of Lake Texoma—a woodland recreation site for boating, camping, and fishing. Over time, cabins were built and leased to TI employees and retirees for a modest fee. By 2005, the property featured a full-time, on-site manager and was available for year-round use by the Texoma Club. Members had leased and made improvements on more than 200 lots.

In 1961, Texins was given the use of an existing farmhouse on land bought for TI's Expressway Site. The building hosted general group meetings and was used by the radio, bridge, dance, astronomy, rock, camera, and model train clubs. During that year, members voted to invest a half million dollars from the Facilities Fund to build the Texins Activity Center. The 26,000-square-foot facility opened in Dallas in January 1964 with a gym, exercise and steam room, club and activity areas, a snack bar, softball fields, and tennis courts. During the early 1960s, the association acquired 52 acres in Allen, Texas, for a Rod and Gun Club. This club was closed years later when the surrounding area became a residential development and the lakes became a feature of Bethany Park.

The 1970s saw a sudden national passion for health and fitness. This zeal was mirrored in the September 3, 1971, issue of *Life* magazine, devoted to America's recreational boom. It featured a story on Texins that described its array of activities, pointing to TI's Texins as the nation's premier example of what a recreation association in industry should be.

Texins hired a full-time fitness director in 1979 and began

one of the industry's most comprehensive health and wellness programs. Free health screening procedures, such as mammograms, were instituted in 1987, and *Better Health and Living* named TI one of the 25 healthiest companies in the U.S. TI established a Texins Health Fitness Council, which became a driving force in the company's Clean Air Program. Smoking was eliminated from all TI offices and facilities many years before this became standard corporate practice. TI has remained on the leading edge of health concerns. The programs Texins instituted have had a positive impact on the health and medical costs of TI employees and their families.

In 1986, musically talented TIers formed an award-winning 20-piece big band—the Texas Instruments Jazz Band, which has performed hundreds of concerts throughout Texas, Oklahoma, Louisiana, and even Switzerland. An offshoot of the Jazz Club, a quintet known as the Jazz Engineers, plays music for corporate dinners, award banquets, wedding receptions, and private parties.

Other clubs Texins sponsors include Amateur Radio, Archery, Art, Badminton, Bass Fishing, Bowling, Aquatics, Flying, Genealogy, Golf, Sailing, Running, and the TI Alumni Association.

Nate and Faye Rainey, TI employees, are pictured with their children at Texins Kids' Room, a child-care service provided to members while they use one of TI's fitness and activity centers.

TIers in 2004 take advantage of the Texins Activity Center to shape their future. (Photo courtesy of the *Dallas Business Journal*'s "Best Places to Work" issue.)

In 1991, Texins won the two top honors from the National Employee Services and Recreation

Association—the first time any company had won both in the same year. President and CEO Jerry Junkins was named employer of the year for TI's strong support of employee services and recreational activities, and the organization was recognized for having the nation's best overall program for providing employees opportunities to develop physically, mentally, and socially.

A new $8.2 million facility for Texins was opened on the Expressway Site in 1995. By this time, more than 40 percent of the Dallas-area TIers were participating in one or more of the activities the association provided. Those using the jogging trail could thank, in part, Joe Zimmerman, a TI vice president, who became a moving force behind leadership with regard to employee health.

Two years later, TI retained Health Fitness Corporation (HFC) to take over operation of all the Texins facilities. A renovation of the facilities in 2000 incorporated 117 new pieces of strength training and cardiovascular equipment, a new high-tech entertainment system, a massage therapy area, a power cycling room, a juice bar overlooking the pool, a new pro shop, and additional programs for children. Personal trainers with specialized skills were available to work with heart and arthritis patients, as well as provide lifestyle and weight management consulting.

When HFC assumed its management role, TI-owned assets in the centers were sold, and the proceeds of more than $1 million were given to the clubs to provide them with long-term financial assistance. At the same time, the organization was divided into the Texins Activity Centers and the Texins Association Clubs. By 2005, TI had 110,000 square feet of facilities in three locations, more than 20 clubs, and a membership of more than 3,500.

60

AN INVENTIVE EDGE

TI's inventions generate patents that protect existing technologies and help fund new technologies.

For more than seven decades, innovation and invention have been the genius behind TI's competitive advantage and continued leadership within an ever-changing, ever-expanding marketplace. TI has designed many important inventions, including the first commercial silicon transistor, first integrated circuit, first single-chip microcomputer, and first electronic handheld calculator. The contributions of TI's engineers, scientists, and technicians helped shape the present and will shape the future of society.

In its first 15 years, the company applied for more than 10 U.S. patents for seismic equipment used in the search for potential oil-bearing strata. In early 1952, TI established a patent department, with Samuel M. "Mack" Mims as its first patent attorney. The stage was set for the company to enter the semiconductor business with a transistor license secured from Western Electric. A second license followed six years later, and TI agreed to pay royalties from the sales of transistor devices. TI paid a premium for the licenses because the company, at the time, did not hold a patent position in the semiconductor business.

With creation of its Central Research Laboratories in 1953, however, the number of TI patent applications increased, primarily because of key inventions by Willis Adcock, Boyd Cornelison, Mort Jones, and Gordon Perry. By 1958, TI held some 60 patents, many of which would play an important role in the emerging semiconductor industry.

One of the company's most significant patents was awarded to Jack Kilby in 1964 for his invention of the integrated circuit, which had occurred six years earlier. TI had recognized the importance and immediate value of Kilby's invention and filed applications in the U.S., as well as in Europe and Japan. TI

experienced patent conflicts, confronting U.S. and Japanese companies in court battles to maintain the integrity of Kilby's invention and establish TI's sole ownership position. In Japan, it took almost three decades to resolve the issue, when all the major Japanese semiconductor companies signed licensing agreements for the Kilby patent, except Fujitsu, which contested the patent in court.

Mack Mims, TI's first patent attorney, and his administrative assistant, Audrey Worthington, handled applications for patents from all TI divisions and subsidiaries.

Robert Noyce, a co-founder of Intel, while working at Fairchild Semiconductor, made a significant contribution to development of the integrated circuit. T.R. Reid described in his book, *The Chip* (published in 1985 by Random House), how Noyce came to the idea of a monolithic integrated circuit in early 1959, which was several months after Jack Kilby. Reid commented that Noyce *"began at a different starting point than Jack Kilby's, but reached the same destination."* Reid also detailed the patent litigation that ensued between TI and Intel, and the decision made by the companies in 1966 to cross-license each other, after a lengthy court battle. Kilby later commented, "Bob Noyce of Fairchild developed a similar idea, along with a practical means of manufacturing it." Kilby and Noyce are both recognized in the industry as giants for their contributions.

In the 1980s, led by Chairman Mark Shepherd, TI embarked on a more aggressive patent strategy than it ever had before. It was based on the concept that competitors using TI's patented technology should pay a fair royalty. It would prove to be a turning point in the way the industry viewed intellectual property.

Dick Agnich, TI's general counsel, led a team that filed a patent lawsuit in 1985 against several Japanese and Korean semiconductor companies. After a series of negotiations and court actions, TI emerged from the lawsuit victorious, and, gradually, the revenue TI gained from its technology,

protected by patents, helped offset skyrocketing research and development costs. During the second half of the 1980s, TI's patent royalties enabled the company to invest more than $2 billion in research and development.

As TI recognized the importance of inventors to its long-range strategy, the company established the Technical Ladder in 1968 to provide them with a unique track for career growth and personal recognition. All exempt employees working in technical job classifications are eligible for Technical Ladder nomination as they meet job-grade requirements and contribute to shareholder value through exceptional technical innovations. The value is measured in three categories: direct contributions to revenue and profit, the development of top technical talent, and the ability to influence external decisions favorable to TI. Election to the six-rung ladder, still in effect more than 35 years later, is made by technical peers and approved by management.

In the early years, TI inventors received a token $1 for their contribution. Then in 1979, TI created the Patent Incentive Award program to recognize employee contributions to the company's patent portfolio. TI inventors were compensated at the time of filing a U.S. patent and again when the patent was issued. Inventors often received additional grants in selected subsequent years based on TI's use of the invention, the importance of the patent to TI's product portfolio, and the use of the patented invention by other companies.

Photocopy of the U.S. patent issued for the invention of the Miniature Electronic Calculator (handheld calculator), dated June 28, 1974.

Entering the 1990s, TI already had a strong foundation of key patents in semiconductor manufacturing technology, packaging, circuit design and structure, system-level solutions, software, and business methods. But soon, significant research and development investments would be made in applications, including reference designs that demonstrated ways in which TI innovations

In TI-Houston, one section of the "Wall of Patents" displays DSP patents awarded to TIers.

could be used to produce end products.

TI's patent program had three objectives: to ensure the operational freedom of the company's businesses, to ensure fair compensation from competitors using TI technology, and to provide incentives, as well as rewards, to inventors for their innovations. The aggressive efforts of TI's inventors and patent attorneys resulted in about 1,000 patent applications being filed annually. The company maintained and protected a strong patent portfolio and often licensed patents to other companies or signed cross-licenses to give TI access to technology generated by competitors. On rare occasions, TI chose not to license its technology and instead retained exclusive rights, as it did with its Digital Light Processing™ patents, because they offered a revolutionary business opportunity. By the end of 2004, TI had been issued more than 15,000 patents.

Its employees have always been TI's most valuable asset. Their inventions have proven to be the company's most valuable resources. TI built its foundation on inventions, innovations, and technology. TI's intellectual property protected by patents has enabled the company to re-invest in the future.

WHERE'S MY DOLLAR?

★ ★ ★

Over the years, a strong collaboration evolved between TI's inventors and patent attorneys, but for Ed Millis in his early years at TI, something was missing.

"My first try at inventing something was a failure. I was disappointed, but soon after, a second idea burst forth," recalled Millis. His invention used a TI phototransistor, modified to make a mechanical motion transducer. He wrote the patent disclosure and optimistically submitted it to Mack Mims, TI's only patent attorney at the time.

In December of 1955 Mims called Millis to his office. "We're going to file your invention of the transistor transducer with the patent office,' he told Millis, 'and I need you to sign the assignment form. This turns over the rights of your invention to Texas Instruments. Sign here, please."

Millis was excited. "This was how Edison started," he remembers thinking. Millis read the brief form and found more good news—in addition to receiving a patent, TI would pay him a dollar.

"So," Millis asked Mims, "where's my dollar?"

"Mims puffed on his pipe, then smiled and replied, 'We don't actually give you a dollar,' he said. 'That's just legal stuff.'"

Millis recalled, "For some reason, it upset me. This great big company can't even supply me a token dollar on this great day? I wanted something to frame."

Millis declined to sign the form and left Mims' office. Days later, still miffed, Millis shared his story with colleague T. E. Smith, "a man older and wiser than I, who agreed it was a bum rap." Smith said he'd take Millis' case to the TI Supreme Court, namely President J. Erik Jonsson.

The following week, Mims again summoned Millis to his office, but this time to ask him to fill out a check request for a dollar.

"T. E. won the battle for me, kind of, and broke down the mythical dollar barrier. Soon the patent department, namely Mack, had a bundle of nice crisp dollar bills for TI inventors. So, finally, I not only got my first patent, I got the first TI dollar. Thanks, Mack."

61

A PLEDGE OF DIVERSITY

TI understands the competitive advantages that come from a diverse workforce.

"Diversity is all the ways in which we differ. This includes the obvious differences such as race, gender, age, disability, and more subtle differences such as education, sexual orientation, religious affiliation, work styles, and thoughts or ideas. Diversity is part of building a future for individuals, the company, and our communities. We believe our diverse workforce makes us stronger." —TI Diversity website

Texas Instruments began focusing formally on diversity in 1989 during the tenure of CEO Jerry Junkins. He believed the company could always replace things and buildings, but TI's success would be predicated on the brains, creativity, vision, and dedication of its employees. Junkins formed the TI People Initiatives with groups focused on women and minorities in the workforce, procurement from women- and minority-owned businesses, the workforce of the future, and employee skills.

Junkins said, "People are the source of our competitive advantage. Everything we do at TI can be copied, bought, or licensed, except our people. Our people and their creativity are what make TI unique. That creativity is crucial to our success, and it only comes through diversity—that is, through the interaction of different ideas and different kinds of people. In order to win in the marketplace, we've got to continue building a working environment in which every TIer feels comfortable, trusted, and respected."

Employees took up the diversity banner, and during the 1990s, a series of grassroots initiatives were formed to gather people with similar interests. One of the first was the Women's Initiative in Corporate Services, which helped TI's

management understand the growing role of women in the workplace. In time, TI sponsored more than 30 diversity initiatives dealing with the concerns of various ethnic groups and people with disabilities. In 1993, these initiatives came together to form the TI Diversity Network and name the first network co-chairs, Bill Brown and Shaunna Sowell.

In 1989, the company made a commitment to use minority- and women-owned suppliers. TI's defense business led the way, but the concept soon spread throughout the company. TI was planting the seeds for prosperity in the community, as well as opening doors for smaller suppliers and helping them navigate through a large company. TI not only awarded contracts, but company leaders also worked to mentor and assist minority- and women-owned companies to help them become more effective and competitive. By 1996, TI had reached its goal of 5 percent minority procurement, representing a value of $189 million from more than 650 minority-owned firms, and in November 2004, TI received the Pacesetter Award from the Dallas Together Forum in recognition of the company's procurement from minority-owned businesses and hiring and promotion of minorities.

The Dallas community was facing similar calls for diversity in the workplace, so The Private Sector Covenant for Workplace Diversity and Economic Opportunity (a private sector coalition of

TI won the Catalyst Award and achieved national recognition for its efforts to advance women in the workplace. CEO Jerry Junkins accepted the award for TI in New York in 1996.

individuals, organizations, and companies who work together to improve race relations in the city) was formed. More than 180 companies joined the minority covenant and the Dallas Women's Covenant to work toward improving race relations and broadening opportunities for minority- and women-owned suppliers.

The company realized its initiatives weren't enough—especially in education, since there were not enough women and minorities entering the engineering field. The company partnered with such organizations as the Dallas Women's Foundation to create educational venues.

TI also realized that work and life balance issues were of concern to many employees. In 1992, the Semiconductor Women's Initiative Network formed a small team to look at work and family/personal life issues. The team convinced the Human Resources department to do a full needs assessment which resulted in the creation of TI's work/life strategy. As a result, TI has been on the *Working Mother* magazine's list of 100 Best Companies for nine consecutive years.

TI is proud of its legacy in diversity. Its first woman supervisor was Ethel Brooks, who joined GSI in 1948. Dorothy Kubicek was TI's first woman field sales engineer in the Semiconductor Division in 1974. Mary Ann Potter was the first woman fab manager. Morris Chang became TI's first Asian officer in 1967. Duy-Loan Le and Wanda Gass were the first women fellows. Duy-Loan is also the first woman and first Asian to be named a Senior Fellow. Phil Gomez was TI's first Hispanic officer. In 1992, TI named its first woman, Gloria Shatto, president of Berry College, to the Board of Directors. James Mitchell and Bart Thomas became the first African Americans named vice presidents of TI. Terri West is TI's first woman Senior Vice President on the leadership team for the company, and Melendy Lovett, as the Senior Vice President of Educational &

Productivity Solutions, is the first woman to oversee a major business segment.

In 1995, the company introduced a worldwide diversity statement underscoring diversity as a core TI value. It mandates that every TIer must work to create an environment that promotes diversity, and that each TI business must develop and maintain diversity strategies and measurements. Teams of diverse employees work together to handle business challenges and opportunities because TI believes participation in teams, in a diverse workplace, enables employees to appreciate cultural differences, increase innovation, and achieve better business results.

———

According to Dave Martin, who formerly managed some of TI's international operations, "There are many issues companies face when they're dealing with customers. They include different cultures, different languages, how to work in a multicultural team, and how to negotiate inside a company to resolve an issue or negotiate outside the company with customers and suppliers. We have to get beyond the belief that English is the language of business around the world. The language of business is the language of the customer."

Over the past few years, through 16 robust business and site diversity teams, organizations have taken ownership

Dancers help ring in the 2005 Chinese New Year at a lunch celebration.

209

Diwali Nite, a gala event presented by the TI Indian Initiative, features excellent Indian music, dancing, and food.

for diagnosing and removing barriers to diversity at the local level and have developed custom solutions to address them. Although specialized external diversity training is still offered, many organizations have developed and deployed training in partnership with the TI Diversity Office.

This approach has kept contemporary diversity issues in front of the company. Presentations on different cultures, global participation in diversity conferences, active grassroots employee diversity initiatives, and opportunities for continuous learning have all contributed to TI's diversity effort.

The TI Diversity Network of employee initiatives has aligned its annual priorities with those of TI businesses and has contributed to business projects. New diversity and worklife "tips," along with a monthly diversity column, posted on TI's diversity website, have been effective in providing diversity and work/life information and tools.

Terry Howard, TI Diversity Director is pleased with TI's success. "When it comes to a culture that encourages inclusiveness and allows pushing the envelope, TI excels."

STRIDES IN DIVERSITY

★ ★ ★

TI has seen tangible results in its hiring, retention, and promotion practices. The number of women and people of color in management positions is close to five times what it was when the company began its diversity efforts. Currently, 26 percent of TI officers in the U.S. are women or people of color.

TI has won 35 prestigious awards for its role in promoting the benefits of diversity, and for seven years, TI has been listed on *Fortune* magazine's list of The 100 Best Companies to Work For.

62

GETTING THE WORD OUT

TI communicates with employees around the world.

TI's strategy was that connectivity was the precursor to productivity. Communication in all its forms— talking face-to-face, printing information in a company publication, or trading ideas electronically—was crucial to the company's ability to climb from exploratory seismic surveys in the oil patch to the pinnacle of a complex world ruled by digital and analog technologies.

During 1944, GSI established the company's first employee newsletter, the *GSI Grapevine*, which evolved from a typewritten sheet to a small-format magazine that doodlebuggers in remote reaches of the oilfield could fit into their pockets. Dot Adler, an editor of the *Grapevine*, recalled the newsletter was published for 44 years, ending only when a majority interest in GSI was sold to Halliburton in 1988.

Derrick Painter, a former GSI doodlebugger, remembered, "We would be on the boat a year to eighteen months, and the *Grapevine* reduced our feeling of isolation. One would eagerly scan for the mention of one's own ship or, the ultimate, one's own name. The *Grapevine* did a lot to make the remote crews feel part of a family."

Norm Harding, a GSI gravity manager, called the publication "a morale builder." He said, "The folks who wrote the articles and took the pictures were able to show administrators in Dallas how well our good, tough, hard-working people were able to cope with work-related problems involving everything from 115 degree desert

temperatures, 40-below Arctic blizzards, floods, mud, or tough living conditions. It helped give these guys credit for jobs well done."

In 1953, the *texins* magazine was launched to provide information on the expanded TI business operations. Issues featured stories about the company's rapid growth, organizational charts, educational pieces showcasing new technologies, working procedures, an in-depth update on company investments, and personal news about TIers and their families.

The *texins* magazine was replaced in 1967 by *TI World*, a less-expensive, tabloid-format newspaper that provided more space for more corporate and personal news. As the number of manufacturing operations outside of Dallas expanded, TI eased out *TI World* and introduced *The Dallasite*, created to cover the company's multiple facilities in the Dallas area. Much of the publication's popularity was based on its candid letters to the editor, several pages of service anniversary photographs, and the Trading Post, a classified ads page for employees who wanted to buy or sell anything from cars and

The first *GSI Grapevine*, the company newsletter, was a single-sheet multilith copy. It began in November 1944, as the first editor, Bill Edwards, noted, "To be published from time-to-time as we have the time."

boats to tools and homes.

In the 1970s, TI launched a "site" newspaper network, developing individual publications to focus on TI operations in Houston or Sherman, Texas; Versailles, Kentucky; and

Dot Adler, editor of the *GSI Grapevine* in 1964, works with the *Grapevine's* first editor, Bill Edwards, on the 20th anniversary issue of the newsletter.

(MSGIDs), later known as e-mail addresses, TIers in 1971 began communicating person-to-person electronically, making the company one of the earliest pioneers in conducting business via e-mail. The system streamlined global communications by eliminating dependence on telephone calls and their inherent timing and translation issues. TI's Ed Hassler remembered, "We quickly developed an early dependency on e-mail. If you didn't e-mail, you didn't communicate."

The capabilities of the TI On-Line Reporting system, developed to share production data among manufacturing sites, were co-opted by savvy TI communicators to launch *T News*, one of the first electronic newspapers in the world. John W. Wilson was its first editor, and he made sure the online newsletter provided daily updates on TI business news, stock prices, even world news and sports. The publication was quickly recognized as the de facto "hot news" source within TI facilities around the world.

Attleboro, Massachusetts. Later, international sites such as Japan also began dedicated publications, and by 1990, the network was producing publications for 16 plant sites within the U.S. and 19 locations abroad.

By 1984, the defense and semiconductor businesses were publishing their own technical journals as a means to share technological expertise among the organizations. A dozen years later, the journals went online, with Portable Document Format (PDF) files of each issue posted on the TI Intranet. The printed publications ultimately became online editions.

In 1985, TIers began formally using the Internet by exchanging e-mails with the U.S. research community via the Computer Science Network system. At first, TI could only exchange e-mail from the Computer Science Center, but the links soon reached other business units within the company. By 1992, TIers could communicate with the outside computing world, but first they had to stop at the "lobby" fire-

As early as the 1970s, TI linked a global computing network into its information management system. The network eventually became home to the manufacturing, financial, and communications systems throughout the company. A decade before the Internet was introduced, TIers in Dallas already had the capability of viewing the same information on a computer screen that other employees were seeing on the far side of the globe. In functionality, they were using a concept that would one day be termed "Intranet." By 1985, about 33,000 terminals had been connected to TI's information management system, giving TI one of the world's largest single-image, interconnected, worldwide communications/data processing networks.

Using four-character electronic message IDs

One way that TI currently communicates with employees is *INFOLINK*, an online newsletter that is updated daily.

wall and verify their credentials to access the network. Two years later, a special TI Internet Team redesigned the firewall system so TIers could have direct access to the World Wide Web.

TI's home page was launched on the World Wide Web in April 1995, and Ralph Oliva, director of corporate marketing communications, pointed out, "Our presence on the Internet opened up a whole new channel of communication for the era ahead. Our customers had direct, online access to information about our products, our services, and our company."

During the mid-1990s, TI invested in a network upgrade that opened the door for more advanced office software, graphic-heavy e-mail and Internet sites, as well as online communications and meeting tools. Many of the technologies were experimental at the time, but TI's commitment never wavered. PowerPath allowed the company to reach offices or manufacturing operations in 30 countries with 36 major sites or buildings, communicating with 59,000 computer workstations in all TI business operations.

Communications capabilities were exploding at the turn of the 21st century. TI established a video teleconferencing system to broadcast its quarterly CEO updates worldwide, and transitioned the printed Dallas newsletter into an electronic magazine known as *TI-Dallas Connected*. This, in turn, became *INFOLINK*, a continually updated online publication reporting on TI's businesses and employees.

Communications keep TIers linked even after retirement.

Communications at TI currently feature interactive global satellite broadcasts where questions can be asked by TIers via the computer, phone, or fax. Tom Engibous and Rich Templeton headline the broadcast.

Members of the Texas Instruments Alumni Association receive a customized newsletter and can access the association website (www.tialumni.org), maintained by retiree John Byers.

When it comes to getting the job done, effective communications systems made, and continue to make, the difference.

A RAPID RECOVERY

On January 16, 1995, at exactly 2:51 p.m., TIers in Plano knew something was dreadfully wrong in Japan. Working in the TI Worldwide Command Center for information technology, they suddenly lost all contact with TI's joint venture wafer fab in Kobe, Japan.

An earthquake had struck, registering 7.2 on the Richter scale.

Fortunately, no TIers were killed or injured, but one of the company's major regional computing centers was knocked offline, shutting down manufacturing information systems required for chip production.

TIers from Dallas, Plano, Osaka, Miho, and Kobe immediately rallied to implement the company's disaster recovery process. In five days, all critical computer systems and the stored data were restored at a remote computer center more than 300 miles from Kobe. Within eight days, the plant manager declared the plant fully operational.

63

DOING THINGS THE RIGHT WAY

A high standard of ethics has always been part of the company's culture worldwide.

Even during its early days in the remote oil fields, when business was risky and competition often combative, TI understood the value of ethics. In a business where deals were made on the basis of a handshake, a man's word was his bond. This was the company founders' gift to the generations who followed them from the oil fields to the high-tech, complex world of electronics.

When the company was small, TI's employee population worked closely with each other and with management. But as the company expanded around the world, that day-to-day interaction between the founders and employees became less frequent. Top management felt the company had an obligation to communicate the ethical principles guiding TI, and, in 1961, a booklet, *Ethics in the Business of TI*, was printed and distributed to employees.

In its fifth printing in 1990, Jerry Junkins, chairman, president, and CEO, wrote in the preface: *"We will not let the pursuit of sales, billings or profits distort our ethical principles. We will always place integrity before shipping, before billings, before profits, before anything. If it comes down to a choice between making a desired profit and doing it right, we don't have a choice. We'll do it right. We must do it right, in every detail. Expedient compromises or short-cuts for near-term gains are not acceptable."*

TI had operated in a variety of industries, from geophysical exploration and defense systems to semiconductors,

The ***Ethics in the Business of TI*** booklet was translated into various foreign languages. The flags of the nations of TI's major locations are shown in the background.

calculators, materials and controls, and a constantly growing array of digital consumer products. Each of the industries had its unique challenge, and TI became recognized globally for high ethical standards. During the 1980s, many defense contractors were alleged to have fraudulently billed the government millions of dollars. TI took its responsibility seriously and joined a group of 24 leading defense contractors to establish the Defense Industry Initiative, to emphasize the need for ethics-based corporate self-governance. TI has continued to take leadership roles in worldwide industry associations in which ethics were central to the organization's charter. The Defense Industry Initiative, the Conference Board Council on Global Business Conduct, and the Ethics Officer Association all recognized TI for its contributions.

In 1987, the TI Board of Directors established the TI Ethics Office, appointing Carl Skooglund as its first Ethics Director. The office had three major functions: it ensured that TI's business policies and procedures were aligned with the company's strong ethical principles; it communicated those principles while educating employees, customers, and suppliers in ethical business practices and expectations, and it provided multiple channels for feedback so employees, customers, and suppliers could ask questions and raise issues in a non-confrontational atmosphere.

As Skooglund pointed out, "Ethics is nothing new for TI. We've always held to the strong, fundamental principle that we will conduct our business in accordance with the highest ethical and legal standards." He believed, "The old maxim 'let your conscience be your guide' sounds good, but it just won't work in our complex business environments. Although our commitment to 'doing the right thing' has not changed over the last 55 years, many situations arise today in which 'right' and 'wrong' are not always obvious."

TI Standard Policies and Procedures, the *Control and Treasury Handbook*, and other documents were combined to integrate ethical business practices into the company's manufacturing processes. During the 1990s, TI expanded its ethics program literature with seven pamphlets called *Cornerstones*, which addressed such topics as "Ethics and the TI Procurement Process," "Gifts, Travel, Entertainment ... and TI Ethics," "TI, Ethics, and the U.S. Defense Business," and "Employee and Employer Rights." Each of the brochures targeted specific TI employee populations requiring more information in a particular area presenting potential ethical risks.

TI's commitment to "doing it right" made an impact on its

TI ETHICS TEST

One of the most frequently referenced elements in the TI ethics program is a quick inventory that provides a simple, yet valuable, tool for employees:

- Is the action legal?

- Does it comply with our values?

- If you do it, will you feel bad?

- How will it look in the newspaper?

- If you know it's wrong, don't do it.

- If you're not sure, ask.

- Keep asking until you get an answer.

employees. Ron Shelly remembered, "TI had two primary characteristics. It was hardworking, and it was highly ethical. I don't think that any company could stand any taller than TI when it came to ethics. Doing the right thing was the only way—no matter how difficult it was."

In 1997, TI published a simple philosophy outlined in the booklet *The Values and Ethics of TI*. TI's three basic values were integrity, innovation, and commitment, and each could be described by three guiding principles.

Integrity: Respect and value people. Be honest.
Innovation: Learn and create. Act boldly.
Commitment: Take responsibility. Commit to win.

The company considered it impractical, if not impossible, to provide a policy manual addressing every day-to-day business decisions. As Tom Engibous, then president and CEO,

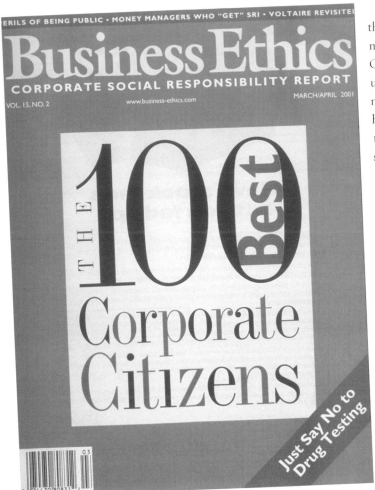

the years. Isolated incidents like these have only served to make TI try harder to meet the highest standards. In 1976, Chairman Mark Shepherd said, "The Corporation will ultimately be judged by society on the basis of its ability to meet the world's material needs. We must do so with the highest standard of ethics, with a deep sense of obligation to the societies in which we operate, and with a willingness to stand before the public and defend our commitments as well as our capacity to carry them through."

TI's commitment to business ethics is ingrained in employees proud to be working for a company that stands behind its beliefs. As Engibous said, "Policies and rule books will not act alone to maintain a company's ethical standards. In fact, policies and rule books do not act at all. People, specifically employees, either behave in an ethical manner, or they do not." He was proud of the efforts that TIers made each day to maintain the company's high ethical standards.

Rich Templeton, TI's current president and CEO, continues to propel the importance of ethics at the company. At the 2005 Annual Shareholders Meeting, he said, "Over the past 75 years, we have changed in many ways. But we have had one thing that has been very stable and unchanging throughout that time. And that is our foundation, our commitment to our values."

TI was recognized as one of the "100 Best Corporate Citizens" by *Business Ethics* magazine in its March/April 2001 issue.

pointed out, "For TIers to be successful in this highly competitive global marketplace, we must be creative, fast to act, and we must work together effectively. We must make our choices in an informed manner—in the field and on the factory and office floor. We cannot do this by referring every decision to a book of rules or policies, but rather from adopting, understanding, and following the company's values and principles."

TI continued to reinforce those values and principles in its people. In 2003, under the direction of Ethics Director David Reid, the company rolled out a web-based training course titled "What Would You Do?" Lessons provided real-life situations and problems offering TIers the knowledge and skills to make good decisions during difficult and, at times, unclear circumstances.

In a company with 35,000 employees around the world, poor judgment calls and bad decisions have occurred over

LEAVE THE ROOM

★ ★ ★

Few TIers will ever forget Mark Shepherd's leadership in ethics. Almost every TI planning conference, sales meeting, or quarterly financial review started with a reminder from him about TI's values and ethics. He had a simple and forceful message. TIers were not to engage in any price discussion with competitors. If a TIer ever found him or herself in a room where the subject of price came up, the TIer was to "get up and leave the room." Then Shepherd paused, looked everyone square in the eye, and repeated it.

64

TI'S TRAINING GROUND

Through the years, training has evolved to meet the needs of changing technologies.

Early on, TI management realized it would be necessary for a company committed to developing its own innovative and revolutionary technologies to provide training to keep its employees up-to-date and ahead of the learning curve. New directions required new knowledge, and TI was always headed in bold new directions. TI wanted its employees to develop their full potential and was willing to invest in educational assistance and training programs that would give them that opportunity.

During the 1930s, GSI crews were scattered in isolated locations around the world, and on-the-job seismic survey training was conducted in the field. By the 1940s, however, some employees were being trained in Dallas to develop special skills.

Cecil Green, responsible for field operations, dedicated himself to raising the standard of professionalism in geophysics. He worked with Robert Shrock, professor of geology at the Massachusetts Institute of Technology, to develop the MIT-GSI Cooperative Plan. The program was launched during the summer of 1951 with 14 college students, all interested in tracking faraway hinterlands in search of oil. During the next 14 years, more than 300 students from 78 colleges and universities spent 10 summer weeks attending seminars and working with GSI crews in the field.

The MIT-GSI Cooperative Plan would ultimately inspire the creation of engineering co-op programs and summer development programs in TI's defense and semiconductor businesses. Students were exposed to leading-edge technology while gaining valuable experience in an industry that would re-engineer the world. It was not uncommon for these students to return to TI and join the company as soon as they graduated.

In 1953, Cecil Dotson began teaching classes in Work Simplification, one of TI's first formal training efforts. Various departments throughout the company, aware of Dotson's success, began holding classes that related to technologies important to their particular areas. When Jim Nygaard and his team developed the first front-end system (the front end of the integrated circuit manufacturing process) classes were soon taught on the process. In the 1970s, three separate training organizations emerged. The semiconductor business expanded the front-end classes into a

J. C. Dearden receives his graduation certificate from Cecil Dotson, who directed the first work simplification program at TI in 1953.

training organization led by John Baum. TI's defense business established a training organization under the direction of Erskine Hightower. And Corporate Marketing established the TI Learning Center, which commercially provided training and books, mostly written by TIer Jerry Luecke and area university professors. The books covered a wide variety of subjects, from microprocessors to optoelectronics.

Ralph Dosher developed a series of orientation seminars for new employee training in 1977, and he discovered that

TI employees from the Wireless Technologies Business Unit participate in a Leadership Learning training activity designed to help them work as a cohesive unit.

many attending the classes were expressing an interest in learning more about TI technologies. In addition, many TIers were taking engineering courses through an interactive television network called TAGER (The Association for Graduate Education and Research) to qualify for degree credit. Based on the input he received from employees, Dosher pushed the programs forward by asking the TI Management Committee to establish a corporate-level training and education organization to provide advanced technical training and the centralized management of TAGER courses. His proposal was accepted, and Dosher, in 1979, officially put the innovative new training program in place.

At about the same time, training activities were being expanded to all TI organizations worldwide. To assure uniform policies and procedures across the company, Dosher established a Training and Education Council, composed of training managers from various TI organizations. The council reviewed programs already in place and determined the need for new courses. A catalog of courses was developed in all divisions around the world on the Texas Instruments On-Line Reporting system, and employees had the opportunity to enroll online even before the advent of the Internet.

In addition to TI's own courses, Dallas-area universities offered graduate-level courses through the company's new corporate-level education organization. Initially, three subject areas were taught on site at TI by professors from the universities: Artificial Intelligence, Computer Science, and Microelectronics. By the mid-1980s, TI had more graduate-level engineering students than any of the area universities.

As CEO Jerry Junkins would tell employees in 1985, "In the markets TI serves, our products must reflect some of the most advanced technology available. To do so, TI engineers and scientists must be technically competent. One of the best ways is to participate in TI's continuing technical education program. Because new technologies are continually emerging, education is an ongoing process. I encourage all TIers in our technical community to take advantage of this important program. TI's future depends on your technical currency."

During the 1990s, TI committed to make training a top priority, measuring every employee's training hours. Individuals established their own personal development plans, and the company made the investment necessary for each employee to have 40 hours of training annually. The organization's name was changed to Training and Organization Effectiveness (T&OE), and it was focused heavily on the semiconductor business.

TI established a partnership with The University of Texas at Dallas in 1994 to provide a program that could lead to a Master's Degree in Change Management. The majority of the company's training professionals in T&OE earned the degree between 1995 and 1997.

Gloria Olson took the leadership reins of T&OE in 1996. During the next two years, several training entities in TI were combined under the T&OE umbrella. Between 1996 and 2001, the training organization provided performance consulting and organization development. The T&OE organization also recognized the advantage of establishing partnerships with external training firms, and used a wide catalog of training companies to supply the content for the company's major training programs. T&OE also began e-learning as a strategy to reach the far-flung sales force, as well as capture and deploy essential information gleaned from vital learning events.

TI forged a partnership with The University of Texas in Austin in 1999 to increase the company's management bench strength by establishing a company-sponsored executive Master's Degree in Business Administration program.

Since 2001, Kathryn Collins has provided the leadership of T&OE. The strategy of utilizing outside partners was expanded to include using General Physics to administer and deliver all standard business and professional training. Leadership Learning teams and Symposia became the focus of internal training professionals, while most classes were delivered by external partners. T&OE expanded offerings globally. E-learning and the use of technology in training enabled TI's training efforts to reach employees wherever they happened to be.

A group of TIers takes time from cooking at the Hotel Martinez in Cannes, France, to pose for a picture. This February 2003 activity taught leadership lessons in a fun, hands-on way.

SHE NEVER STOPPED LEARNING

★ ★ ★

Ann Minnis, a young Hispanic woman, joined TI in 1963. Recently married, and badly in need of a job, she took the only job available—an operator on the third shift in germanium transistor manufacturing in the Semiconductor building on the Expressway site in Dallas. She adjusted to sleeping in the day as her husband Bill went to his day job. In the next 25 years, Minnis progressed from production operator to office worker to administrative assistant for senior managers and then moved into management. She took advantage of TI's educational assistance program to complete an Associate's Degree from Richland College.

In 1988, Jerry Junkins asked her to work with the TI Foundation in the area of preschool education, which launched a second career for Minnis. Encouraged by Mike Rice and Win Skiles, she completed a Bachelor of Science Degree in Rehabilitation Science from The University of

Texas Southwestern Medical Center's Allied Health Sciences School in Dallas, while continuing to work. She managed the TI Foundation's office as Director and Grants Administrator and was the first woman to become a member of its board. When she retired in 2003, Tom Engibous recognized Minnis, a co-founder of TI's Hispanic Employees Initiative Forum, for her diversity leadership in mentoring Hispanic men and women. Minnis continues to have a passion for education. She consults with school districts as well as educational institutions and is sought after as a speaker and advisor. Minnis commented that she "considers herself a product of TI's educational assistance program." Like Minnis, thousands of other TIers have benefited from the company's educational assistance program.

TI AND THE COMMUNITY

From the beginning, the founders of Texas Instruments understood the value and importance of instituting a spirit of giving, caring, and providing for TI communities around the world through education and philanthropy. They provided endowments and scholarships. They were instrumental in establishing The University of Texas at Dallas. Their concern and commitment became deeply ingrained in TI's culture, flourishing as brightly in 2005 as it did during the early days of GSI. The legacy of Eugene McDermott, Erik Jonsson, Cecil Green, and Pat Haggerty continued to be sustained by the ongoing contributions of the TI Foundation, as well as the company's determination to keep education as one of TI's top priorities. TI's time-honored dedication to community service was underscored by employees and retirees who banded together to augment corporate-sponsored programs with their own grass-roots efforts. TI was determined to make a difference, and it did.

TI employees, clad in red T-shirts, gathered on October 2, 2004, to support the Juvenile Diabetes Research Foundation by participating in the Dallas Walk to Cure Diabetes. Almost $150,000 was raised through the effort.

65

A PHILANTHROPIC LEGACY

TI's Founders worked almost as hard to give their money away as they did to earn it.

TI's Founders and their wives—Eugene and Margaret McDermott, Erik and Margaret Jonsson, Cecil and Ida Green, and Pat and Beatrice Haggerty—were bound not only by their deep connections to Texas Instruments but by a common interest in improving the lives of people around them. As they witnessed extraordinary technological advances, they came to understand technology's role in shaping the future and preparing new generations to pursue a potential that was limited only by their own genius.

The Founders and their wives applied the same analytical skills that paid off in business to their interest in philanthropy. They held their beneficiaries to business plans and goals and became involved with the organizations they supported. They worked hard to find new ways to make the most of their charitable investments.

Eugene McDermott was born in Brooklyn, New York, on February 12, 1899. He earned a master's degree in Mechanical Engineering in 1919 from the Stevens Institute of Technology in Hoboken, New Jersey, and another master's degree in physics from Columbia University in New York in 1925. He was granted two honorary degrees, a Doctor of Science from Stevens Institute of Technology and a Doctor of Humane Letters from The University of Dallas. McDermott is credited with some 10 inventions, including geochemical and anti-submarine warfare applications; he held five U.S. patents. He married Margaret Milam in 1954. They had one daughter, Mary

**Eugene McDermott
(1899–1973)**

McDermott Cook, who serves as president of the McDermott Foundation.

McDermott believed that science neglected individual and economic growth. As a result, he served on a national committee to teach businessmen of their responsibilities. He envisioned education as the foundation for individual success and believed that "learning begins when a child starts looking at the world." He and Margaret promoted quality education to maximize "everyone's capacities for thinking and doing." In 1954, the couple gave stock valued at $1.25 million to help fund the building of the Stevens Institute of Technology Center in Hoboken, New Jersey, and, in 1960, began funding scholarships at MIT. Other schools receiving the McDermotts' support included The Lamplighter School in Dallas, the Dallas Junior College System (Dallas County Community College System), Southern Methodist University, the University of Dallas, The Hockaday School in Dallas, and The University of Texas system. The McDermotts helped found St. Mark's School of Texas and helped establish what is now The University of Texas at Dallas.

McDermott was involved in medical projects at various universities, including Columbia and the University of California. At The University of Texas Southwestern Medical Center at Dallas, he supported a visiting professorship in anesthesiology and research laboratory. In 1973, he established the Eugene McDermott Center for the Study of Human

Growth and Development, and, in his honor, the Center established two professorships: the Eugene McDermott Distinguished Chair for the Study of Human Growth and Development and the Eugene McDermott Distinguished Chair in Molecular Genetics.

McDermott began his career in exploration geophysics, but his scientific interests became increasingly coupled with a concern for others. His interest in helping young people discover their natural aptitudes led McDermott to focus on a broad spectrum of education and research pursuits at Columbia, Case Western Reserve, The University of Texas, and the University of Oregon.

McDermott shared his wife's interest in the Dallas Public Library, the Dallas Museum of Art, and the Dallas Symphony Orchestra. The McDermotts helped establish the Margo Jones Memorial Theater at SMU, and they served as directors of the SMU Fine Arts Association. The McDermotts established a trust fund for the Dallas Art Association. Their foundation gave one of the world's largest collections of Navajo blankets to the Dallas Public Library, and in 2003, they contributed $10 million to the Dallas Center for Performing Arts. McDermott served as director of the Dallas Theater Center. MIT's Council for the Arts established the Eugene McDermott Award in 1974 to honor his support of the institution. In a speech to the Society of Exploration Geophysicists, which McDermott led as president in 1933, Cecil Green said, "Eugene McDermott can be variously referred to as a pioneer, geophysicist, scientist, engineer, businessman, and philanthropist. But best of all, we are proud to know him as a wonderful human being."

In 2004, Margaret McDermott received The University of Texas System's highest award, the Santa Rita Medallion, for her donations to The University of Texas at Dallas. She gave the school $32 million, the largest endowment in the history of the school, to establish the Eugene McDermott Scholars Program, which covers four years of tuition and expenses for 20 qualified students each year. The Santa Rita is awarded to individuals who show commitment to higher education and serve as an example of selfless and spirited public service. Cecil Green, Erik Jonsson, and Margaret's husband had been prior recipients of the award. In 2005, the Trinity Commons Foundation, responsible for raising private funds to construct three bridges spanning the Trinity River in Dallas, announced that one of the bridges would bear Margaret McDermott's name in recognition of her support of architect Santiago Calatrava's designs for the bridges.

John Erik Jonsson was born in Brooklyn, New York, on September 6 in 1901. He married Margaret Fonde on February 8, 1923, and the couple had three children, Margaret, Philip, and Kenneth. Jonsson earned a Bachelor's Degree in Mechanical Engineering from Rensselaer Polytechnic Institute in Troy, New York, in 1922. He ultimately held 10 honorary degrees, including a Doctor of Laws from SMU in Dallas and Carnegie Mellon University in Pittsburgh, and a Doctor of Civil Laws from the University of Dallas. He served on the board of trustees for 11 educational groups and institutions, including Tulane University, the University of Dallas, and the Texas Governor's Committee on Education Beyond the High School. Jonsson wrote two books: *Of Times and the Cities*,

**J. Erik Jonsson
(1901–1995)**

published in 1968 by Mechanical Engineering, and *Avalanche: the Cities and the Seventies*, published in 1969 by the Gantt Medal Board of Award. He received more than 30 awards from professional, civic, and business organizations, including the Horatio Alger Award, UCLA School of Medicine Lifetime Achievement Award, Dallas Man of the Year, and the 1980 American Society of Swedish Engineers John Ericsson Medal, of which he said, "It's almost as lofty a distinction in this discipline as the Nobel Prize is in others." Jonsson was one of the first four living Americans elected to the Hall of Fame for Business Leadership.

After their daughter attended Skidmore College in upstate New York, the Jonssons donated 1,000 acres in Saratoga Springs for the construction of a new campus. They gave money for a hospital at Baylor University Medical Center in Dallas, a cancer research center at the University of California at Los Angeles, an engineering center at Rensselaer Polytechnic Institute, and a theater at the University of Dallas.

The Jonssons supported Bishop College in Dallas, the Dallas Symphony Orchestra, the Salvation Army, MIT, Tulane University, Carnegie Mellon University, and virtually every non-profit hospital in the Dallas area. Jonsson's children have continued the family legacy of giving through their own philanthropic foundations.

On November 22, 1963, as president of the Dallas Citizens Council, Jonsson was to serve as host for a luncheon speech by President John F. Kennedy. When word reached the Trade Mart crowd that the president had been shot, it was Jonsson who had the grim responsibility of stepping up to the podium and making the announcement. Jonsson was appointed mayor of Dallas on February 3, 1964, to complete the unexpired term of Earle Cabell, who resigned to run for Congress. As former Mayor Steve Bartlett remembered, Jonsson took "the city from the lowest point in our history to one of the highest."

Goals for Dallas, a program that involved the citizenry in defining long-range objectives for the city, was Jonsson's brainchild. He applied some of the same planning and goal-setting techniques used at TI. "It turned out that goal setting intrigued Dallas people in general," Jonsson recalled. "They needed something to do, to talk about, and to work with that was as far apart from the assassination and its grieving as it could possibly be. I think that we were fortunate to hit on this, and we took full advantage of it."

Among the major public works completed, expanded, or conceived during Jonsson's tenure were the new City Hall, the Convention Center, the Martin Luther King Jr. Recreation Center, nearly a dozen branch libraries, and major portions of the city's roadway system. In 1967, at his urging, city voters approved a $175 million bond issue—three times larger than any previous such proposal—to finance an array of overdue improvements, from road and sewer extensions to renovations at Fair Park.

Jonsson, who stepped down as mayor in 1971, was the driving

**Cecil H. Green
(1900–2003)**

force behind a partnership between Dallas and Fort Worth to fund and build a centrally located airport. He served as chairman of the Dallas/Fort Worth International (D/FW) Airport Board of Directors and helped the two fractious sides reach a compromise construction site. D/FW, at the time the world's largest airport in size, opened in 1974 on a 17,800-acre site between the two cities. As Tom Sullivan, D/FW Airport's first executive director, said of Jonsson, "He didn't let anything get in the way of finishing that airport."

During his retirement years, Jonsson said, "My job today is to find ways to reduce the cost of education of appropriate quality and give people a chance to be what they can be. That was part of the name of the game at TI and still is."

Cecil H. Green was born on August 6, 1900, in Manchester, England. He married Ida Mabelle Flansburgh in 1926 in Schenectady, New York. Green began his undergraduate work at the University of British Columbia and finished his B.A. and M.A. electrical engineering degrees at the Massachusetts Institute of Technology. Sponsored by Erik Jonsson and Roland Beers, Green became a naturalized U.S. citizen in the Dallas Federal Courthouse in 1936. He would ultimately hold 13 honorary degrees, including a Doctor of Science from SMU, Oxford University, and The University of Sydney in Australia. Green received 24 awards and honors from educational and medical institutions, as well as from professional and humanitarian organizations.

Green was introduced to the power of geophysics when he witnessed the great San Francisco earthquake in 1906. In a 1982 interview, he recalled living in a tent at Golden Gate Park: "We watched the whole city burn. I can still remember a soldier breaking a store window to get me a pair of shoes."

Early on, Cecil and Ida Green crisscrossed the country, establishing temporary residences in auto camps and tent hamlets as Green searched for a challenging career. He said, "It took me six years to figure out what I wanted to do. The geophysical exploration business offered a happy combination of technology and people." In their early years with GSI, constantly moving from one oil field to another, the Greens noticed the poorest among them lacked even the simplest amenities, including access to education. He and Ida vowed someday to do something about it.

In 1982, Green said, "Intelligent giving is not easy. In fact, Ida and I have discovered that lots of time, effort, and thought are necessary to make sure that our giving would have a multiplying effect by triggering new and healthy growth in relation to the finally selected project."

The Greens spent time and effort investigating a potential project before pledging a donation. If they liked what they saw, the Greens frequently expanded their pledge and became personally involved, serving on boards or committees and planning new developments.

Internationally recognized as an engineer, geophysicist, philanthropist, photographer, and bibliophile, Green devoted his energies to cultivating the human mind. The couple's generosity was evident throughout Dallas and around the world; their names grace buildings, facilities, programs, and professorships. Green's giving was broad, and he supported education from kindergarten to post-doctoral studies. Although the Greens stretched their philanthropy from Australia to England, much of their giving was focused on such Texas institutions as The University of Texas at Dallas, SMU, The University of Texas Southwestern Medical School, Children's Medical Center of Dallas, St. Mark's School of Texas, Texas Christian University, and Austin College.

In addition, the Greens supported many of the world's most prestigious universities, including the University of British Columbia, MIT, Stanford University, Colorado School of Mines, the University of California at San Diego, and The University of Sydney in Australia. For his generosity, Green was recognized as Philanthropist of the Year in Dallas and San Diego.

Perhaps Cecil Green's most unique honor was being appointed Honorary Knight of the Most Excellent Order of the British Empire in 1991. Queen Elizabeth II honored him for his 1979 donation toward the establishment of Green College at Oxford University. Green College was the 39th college at Oxford, the first to be built in 200 years.

Ida Green's bequests totaled more than $41 million; the couple's combined giving exceeded $150 million. The Greens made contributions to 50 academic, medical, and civic buildings. They supported 20 special instructional and research facilities, funded 28 endowed chairs at 15 institutions, and donated land to educational and civic organizations.

In 2004, the Cecil and Ida Green Foundation made the final distribution of its assets in a $12.8 million gift to the University of Texas Southwestern Medical Center. The money was used to establish a center that would enable scientists to use information technology to link research on molecules and cells with analysis of the functions of biological systems. Since they had no children, the Greens decided early on to distribute all of their wealth to philanthropic causes.

Green once quipped, "I want to have all the fun of giving my money away in this life. When I die, all I want left is a nickel."

Pat Haggerty was born on St. Patrick's Day, March 17, 1914, in Harvey, North Dakota, the son of a railroad telegrapher. As a child, he built a prize-winning radio and became one of the state's first ham-radio operators, which perhaps fueled his idea for TI's first "pocket" radio called Regency. Haggerty entered Marquette University in 1931 with a scholarship and graduated summa cum laude in 1936, earning a bachelor's degree in electrical engineering. Two years later, he married Beatrice E. Menne, and the couple had five children, Sheila, Kathleen, Teresa, Patrick, and Michael.

At Erik Jonsson's urging, Haggerty joined GSI in 1945, and early the next year became general manager of the Laboratory and Manufacturing division. Years later, Jonsson called his hiring of Haggerty his "best contribution to TI." Though not one of the original owners of GSI, Haggerty was later considered a TI founder for his legendary contributions to the company.

Haggerty became concerned with what he called America's "productivity malaise," and in front of international audiences he advocated improvements in productivity that permitted steady price reductions in the face of increasing inflation. His

Patrick E. Haggerty
(1914–1980)

leadership inspired many contributions to the electronics revolution, and *Fortune* magazine called him "*a star example of the engineering-executive breed.*"

Haggerty dedicated much of his life to science, technology, management, and art, and he worked tirelessly at the national level to improve educational opportunities for engineers. He supported many professional organizations, including the Institute of Electrical and Electronics Engineers, Texas Academy of Science, and the National Security Industrial Association. Haggerty believed the disciplines he championed would receive greater benefit if he backed national organizations rather than focus on individual groups. He served

as co-chairman of a committee that recommended the merger of the Institute of Radio Engineers and the American Institute of Electrical Engineers into IEEE, which became one of the discipline's most prominent professional organizations. In 1968, Haggerty received the IEEE's Founders Medal.

Under the leadership of Haggerty's daughter, Teresa Parravano, the Patrick and Beatrice Haggerty Foundation continued the family's philanthropic legacy. Established in 1968, the Foundation in 2002 gave $100,000 to the creation of the Old Red Museum in Dallas and in 2003, donated to the Children's Medical Center's "We Promise" campaign to fund facility improvements and hire additional physicians. Before the end of 2003, Beatrice Haggerty, in conjunction with her 90th birthday celebration, made a $1.4 million pledge to fund expansion at Children's Medical Center in Dallas. The announcement came in the Center's chapel, which, in appreciation of her gift, was renamed the Beatrice Menne Haggerty Chapel.

Over the years, financial support from the Haggertys created the Patrick and Beatrice Haggerty Library at Mount Mary College in Milwaukee, Beatrice's alma mater, and the Patrick and Beatrice Haggerty Museum of Art in Milwaukee. The couple also gave generously to Marquette University, helping fund an art museum on campus, as well as the Haggerty Engineering Building. Marquette established the Bea Haggerty Outstanding Student Service Award, given to College of Engineering students who exhibited organizational leadership, promoted diversity, and completed community service. The couple also made generous contributions to the University of Dallas.

In remembering her mother after her death in 2003, Sheila Haggerty Turner said, "Our mother was born wanting to make a difference. She died with that wish totally fulfilled."

The same could be said of all four of TI's Founders. They made a difference in their company and in the world around them. In addition, TI is indebted to other founders who contributed to its history: H. Bates Peacock, one of four GSI managers who purchased the business in 1941; John Clarence Karcher, a co-founder of GSI who pioneered reflection seismography; and Everette L. DeGolyer, who financed the startup of GSI in 1930.

66

TI FOUNDATION

TI's Founders sought to improve the quality of community life by establishing a way to ensure perpetual corporate giving.

TI Founders Cecil Green, Erik Jonsson, Eugene McDermott, and Pat Haggerty created a legacy of personal philanthropy through the family foundations they established to ensure perpetual giving to the Dallas community. In turn, their philosophy was embraced by the company when it created what is now known as the TI foundation.

In 1952, TI's Board of Directors approved the creation of the TI-GSI Foundation and designated its funds for "charitable, scientific, literary, or educational purposes or for the prevention of cruelty to children or animals within the U.S. or any of its possessions." The Foundation's first trustees were Jonsson, Green, and W. C. (Bill) Edwards. During the first three years, funds were given to 47 organizations, including Dallas Pilot Institute for the Deaf, the Dallas School for Blind Children, Southern Methodist University, the University of Illinois, and Texas A&M University.

Education was set as an early priority for the Foundation and, by 1959, TI reported that a substantial part of the Foundation's funds were being allocated to educational institutions to improve the quality of education and provide opportunities for individual development. Around that same time, the Foundation pledged $250,000—its largest commitment at the time—to help start the Graduate Research Center of the Southwest, which later became The University of Texas at Dallas.

In 1964, the TI Foundation was incorporated as a non-profit corporation to support service organizations in cities where the company operated plants. With $290,466 in assets held primarily in government bonds, the Foundation allocated the largest share of its grants for educational programs, but also gave to health and human services, arts, and cultural organizations.

Mike Rice, a TI senior vice president, was appointed president of the Foundation in 1984, and Ann Minnis was named its director in 1988. Together, they began working with the Foundation's beneficiaries to adopt business plans and

Ann Minnis (foreground) and Mike Rice (background) of the TI Foundation lead the Head Start class to its graduation ceremony in 1992. The Margaret Cone Head Start Center in South Dallas is funded in part by the TI Foundation.

measurable goals, ensuring that the Foundation's investments were spent wisely.

But it was the foresight of TI CEO Jerry Junkins that truly set the ball in motion with early childhood development, one of the TI Foundation's biggest success stories. Initially, the Foundation provided funding to the Margaret H. Cone Center, serving a predominantly African-American population in South Dallas, for supplemental health and salary increases for teachers, as well as nutritional, social services, and extended-day programs for children. The results were encouraging, and students made significant gains in social skills. However, they lagged behind their peer groups in language and cognitive abilities. So, the Foundation, in conjunction with SMU, created LEAP (Language Enrichment Activities Program), a pre-reading curriculum that began showing impressive results in just a year.

Encouraged by the outstanding results, the Foundation's leadership worked to perpetuate the model through Texas' Ready to Read program. Texas First Lady Laura Bush used the program as the basis for her education policy initiatives in Texas, and later, she embraced early childhood education and the Ready to Read program in her national platform.

Martin's son, also David, and is located in a neighborhood near Fair Park.

Besides early childhood, the Foundation has focused on activities in education that strengthened the company's ability to grow a future work force. The Foundation made a particular focus on programs to attract more minority students to engineering with major grants to Prairie View A&M, The University of Texas at El Paso, and Paul Quinn College. At other points in the education continuum, TI's Foundation funded grants aimed at improving girls' math skills and bringing an engineering curriculum to high school students. The Foundation supported the Advanced Placement (AP) program, where students who enrolled in AP classes received financial assistance and cash awards. Teachers also received stipends proportional to student performance. It was yet another Foundation program that showed measurable results and could be easily replicated by others.

Although education remains the highest priority, the Foundation continues to make major grants that impact

The Foundation was instrumental in the creation of other Head Start centers as well. To honor Jerry Junkins, the TI Foundation, the Patrick and Beatrice Haggerty Foundation, and the Eugene McDermott Foundation endowed funds for the construction of the Jerry R. Junkins Child Development Center, which opened in April 1997 in the predominantly Hispanic West Oak Cliff community in Dallas. The third Head Start Center called Davids' Place was supported by Nancy Shelby and retired TI executive Dave Martin. The center was named after Shelby's son, David, and

The TI Founders IMAX Theater opened in 1996 at the Science Place in Fair Park, Dallas.

the quality of life in Dallas. In June 1996, with the addition of a $3 million contribution from the TI Foundation, the TI Founders IMAX Theater at the Science Place Museum in Fair Park opened. The Foundation made the gift in honor of Junkins and the

Front view of the Jerry R. Junkins Electrical Engineering Building on the SMU campus in Dallas, as shown during construction in July 2002. (Photo courtesy of *Dallas Morning News*.)

company's Founders. In 1996, Win Skiles, senior vice president, Public Affairs, said, "Jerry and the TI Founders committed themselves to education and technological innovation. In one tribute, both of those legacies will be commemorated."

In 1999, the TI Foundation and the Junkins family gave SMU two gifts totaling $5 million for the construction of a new electrical engineering building named in honor of the company's former CEO. The Jerry R. Junkins Electrical Engineering Building houses classrooms, faculty and graduate student offices, and instructional and research laboratories.

Supporting efforts during catastrophic events has also been high on the list for the Foundation. Recent examples include the 9-11 disaster and the devastating Southeast Asian tsunami in 2004.

The Foundation also continues to be committed to the United Way and makes an annual contribution upwards of $1 million. In arts and culture, the Foundation's intent is to fund organizations that can attain "world class status." For example, in 2004, the Foundation announced a major gift of $500,000 to the Dallas Black Dance Theater during its capital campaign. The grant allowed the dance troupe to establish a permanent home.

The TI Foundation's Matching Gifts Program enables employees who are on the TI U.S. payroll or a TI subsidiary, along with retirees, directors, and retired directors, to determine how to use a portion of the company's philanthropic resources. The Foundation matches employees' tax-deductible contributions dollar-for-dollar up to $10,000, but not less than $50 per year. The donations go to colleges, universities, and arts and cultural organizations. In 2004, 274 educational institutions received more than $1.2 million, and 138 cultural and arts organizations received more than $450,000. More than 40 percent of those matching gift donations were contributed by retirees.

Jack Swindle, a retired senior vice president, became president of the Foundation, and Ann Pomykal was named

Director of Corporate and Foundation Giving when Mike Rice and Ann Minnis retired in 2003. However, the philanthropic goals remained as solid as they were in the vision of TI's Founders.

Since 1964, the Foundation has given more than $64 million. Today, the TI Foundation continues to ensure that its money is invested where it can do measurable good for future generations.

READING BY THE THIRD GRADE

★ ★ ★

With math and science as their focus, company leaders understood the importance of igniting the curiosity of students and instituting programs that could develop a core of engineers. But students needed the necessary reading skills to develop math and science aptitude. In 1992, CEO Jerry Junkins asked retirees Ralph Dosher and Jim Fischer, who both were working with the Dallas Independent School District (DISD), "What will it take to get all DISD third-grade students reading at grade level?" Dosher and Fischer developed a plan and implemented it in the lowest performing school in the DISD. By 2002, with leadership from the principal, teachers and numerous TI volunteers, the Julia Frazier Elementary School achieved the goal and became one of the highest performing schools in Texas.

67

BIRTH OF A UNIVERSITY

TI was instrumental in creating The University of Texas at Dallas to improve regional opportunities for advanced education.

While pursuing ambitious growth plans during the 1950s, the company scrambled to attract and retain skilled engineers and scientists. Yet the company often found itself battling other technology companies throughout the country for graduates with high-tech degrees and facing the additional challenge of attracting this talent to Texas. Their solution was to create a top-flight institution in the North Texas region to educate and train engineers. That idea led to what is now The University of Texas at Dallas (UTD), which is becoming one of the nation's leading engineering universities.

On an airplane flight in 1958, Erik Jonsson and Lloyd Berkner, head of Associated Universities Inc., discussed ways to develop much needed expertise for TI. Berkner had recently joined TI's board of directors, and Jonsson appointed him to study the problem and find a workable solution. Berkner discovered that, in 1959 alone, Columbia University conferred 560 doctoral degrees—more than all the universities in the southwest combined. Berkner recommended the establishment of a laboratory and research center for Dallas, staffed with a top-tier faculty, that would attract the best and the brightest students throughout the country and keep those from Texas at home.

Cecil Green, Erik Jonsson, and Eugene McDermott did not hesitate to act on Berkner's proposal. They began working with Dallas-area business and education leaders to make the concept come to life.

On February 14, 1961, the State of Texas granted the Graduate Research Center of the Southwest its charter as a non-profit educational institution. Although the new institution did not grant degrees, students could earn their diplomas through programs in established colleges and universities in the region.

Students walk to class outside the Erik Jonsson School of Engineering and Computer Science building. Built in 1986, the school has the largest undergraduate enrollment at UTD. Students study in state-of-the-art classrooms, featuring servers and workstations connected via fiber-optic networks. (Photo courtesy of UTD.)

The TI-GSI Foundation donated $250,000 to turn the idea into reality, and TI Founders, along with their families, agreed to match the donation. They later purchased a 1,200-acre site for the campus in Richardson, Texas, just 16 miles north of downtown Dallas and six miles from TI's Expressway campus. Berkner headed up the center and spearheaded a fund-raising campaign. By 1963, there were some 100 faculty and staff members, and on October 29, 1964, the school dedicated its first building, the Laboratory of Earth and Planetary Sciences, later renamed the Founders Building.

In 1965, the school's name changed to the Southwestern Center for Advanced Studies (SCAS). By this time, TI's Founders realized their original plan was not working. They envisioned that universities in the region would send their best graduate students to SCAS to complete their doctoral work and continue post-doctoral research. However, few did.

So the Founders turned to The University of Texas System, which agreed to accept the school's assets and provide funding for development of a full-fledged university. Since some of

The UTD Mall serves as the university's main esplanade and provides access to most of the buildings on campus. (Photo courtesy of UTD.)

the best scientific talent in the world was now on campus, the Texas legislature in 1967 concurred with the vision of TI's Founders and agreed that Dallas needed a proper academic forum for science, research, and technology education. McDermott, Green, and Jonsson donated the campus and its land to The University of Texas System, and on June 13, 1969, Governor Preston Smith signed the bill creating The University of Texas at Dallas.

Enrollment began with 408 students at the upperclass and graduate levels, and it grew to 3,500 during the next six years. By 1977, enrollment exceeded 5,300, and the university began to admit freshmen in 1990.

In 1986, the university established the J. Erik Jonsson School of Engineering and Computer Science in honor of Jonsson's contributions. Many of the 500 high-tech companies within a five-mile radius of campus allowed UTD students the opportunity to work part time, complete summer internships, or alternate semesters between the workplace and classroom. As many as 70 percent of the school's students held co-op positions or internships with North Texas businesses prior

to graduation. Two-thirds of the university's freshmen came from the top 25 percent of their graduating high school classes.

The families of the Founders consistently provided strong financial support for UTD and its vision. For example, Cecil and Ida Green donated $2.4 million to the university in 1991 to establish the Cecil and Ida Green Center for the Study of Science and Society. The center promotes the effective use of science and technology to better understand and deal with issues threatening our global future. In addition, experts routinely appear on campus to engage in focused, cross-disciplinary research and analysis. The center presents an annual distinguished lecturer series and houses Cecil Green's documents, photographs, and memorabilia.

In 2000, Margaret McDermott honored her late husband by giving a $32 million grant to establish the

Eugene McDermott Scholars Program for 20 of the nation's brightest students each year. The program covers all educational expenses for four years, including travel, participation in special programs at home and abroad, room, board, and supplies. McDermott Scholars are expected to have a strong influence on their university and their society, possess a record of academic excellence and active engagement with their school, and exemplify leadership, scholarship, and citizenship.

In November 2002, The University of Texas at Dallas initiated three new Ph.D. programs: Telecommunications Engineering, the first doctoral degree of its kind in North America; Software Engineering, the first doctoral degree of its kind in Texas; and Computer Engineering.

Texas Instruments announced in June 2003, the company's plans to build a new 300-millimeter wafer fab on a 92-acre site near the UTD campus. Chairman Tom Engibous said, "An important factor in our site selection was finding a climate that encouraged advanced research and extreme innovation. In considering Richardson, TI asked the state to make a significant commitment to the engineering school at UTD, and they are devoting $300 million in public and private funds, over five years, for the Erik Jonsson School of Engineering and Computer Science."

During groundbreaking ceremonies, University President Dr. Franklyn Jenifer thanked TI for its long-standing support of the school: "If it weren't for Mr. Green, Mr. Jonsson, and Mr. McDermott, and if it weren't for their company, Texas Instruments, UT Dallas wouldn't be here."

With an enrollment exceeding 14,000 in 2005, the campus has become home for thousands of engineers, scientists, and managers from high-tech companies in the Dallas community, as well as for students from around the world. UTD offers more than 115 academic programs within its seven schools. More than 45,000 students have graduated from the school since its founding, and approximately 23,000 of those graduates are still living and working in North Texas.

In 2004, UTD awarded more computer science degrees, combining bachelor's, master's, and doctoral, than any other university in the United States. The university also ranks 15th in the nation in awarding engineering degrees to women. Over the years, UTD has attracted three Nobel laureates, and two remain on the faculty today, exemplifying the university's growing stature nationwide.

FROM THE WORKPLACE

In 1965, Cecil Green sought a way to provide employees in the workplace the same instruction that college and university students were receiving in the classroom. He pledged funds, then collaborated with Dallas area universities to establish TAGER, The Association for Graduate Education and Research, one of the world's first one-way video and two-way audio interactive television networks.

TAGER opened at the Graduate Research Center of the Southwest, and, in 1967, a 250-foot television tower on campus began broadcasting instruction to remote classrooms across North Texas. The closed-circuit television system offered a talk-back feature, permitting students to interact directly with instructors in distant classrooms.

Bob Olson, a key figure in TI's entry into the semiconductor market, served as the first president of TAGER. As services expanded, the name was changed in 1982 to The Association for Higher Education of North Texas. A decade later, the program was renamed Alliance for Higher Education.

During ceremonies at Southern Methodist University in 1981 honoring Green as the architect and father of TAGER, Dr. Donald Shields, SMU's president, paid tribute to Green "for his pioneering spirit, visionary leadership, and commitment to community." Dr. Shields pointed out that Green's idea and his determination to make it a reality "enabled thousands of individuals, who could not otherwise have done so, to earn advanced degrees by television." At the time, an estimated 18,000 students had benefited from the distance-learning network.

68

IMPROVING A COMMUNITY'S LIFE

Backed by the generosity of its employees, TI became one of the largest corporate contributors to the United Way of Metropolitan Dallas.

TI Sr. Vice President Cecil Dotson (right) presents an enlarged TI pledge card to L.S. Turner, Jr., President, Dallas Power & Light, who headed the Dallas United Fund (United Way) campaign in 1970. This represented a commitment by TIers of more than $740,000.

It may have had a variety of names during its history, such as the Community Chest, the Red Feather Campaign, and the United Fund, but its mission remained the same as did the commitment of TI employees to be one of the biggest supporters. The United Way of Metropolitan Dallas, as it is known today, embraces the mission of improving the quality of life in the community by responding to priority health and human service needs.

Dating back to TI's earliest days in Dallas, TI employees have always been active in community support. During the early 1950s, GSI employees led drives to support local charities, including the Dallas County Community Chest, which supported 36 area agencies. TIers formed teams from every department within the company, encouraging them to support the Community Chest by contributing one day's pay. It was a great success and set in motion a commitment that is still around today.

In 1961, the name became the United Way, and its first board president was Erik Jonsson, one of TI's Founders, who had been recognized as one of the true pioneers of modern Dallas. The *Dallas Times Herald* would write of Jonsson: *"A man previously known for his business acumen and corporate leadership proved to be a public leader who was wise, sensitive, determined, and talented."* Spurred by his civic involvement and leadership within the United Way, TI became a major corporate

contributor to the Dallas-area organization's annual fund-raising campaign.

During the next decade, employees donated $258,000 to the United Way. With TI's support and Jonsson's leadership, the United Way expanded its coverage to 61 agencies. And with 80 percent of the company participating in the annual pledge drive, TI became the largest corporate giver in the Dallas area. In 1976, the company achieved a milestone by pledging $1 million dollars to the organization.

To underscore the importance of giving, TI provided buses during the United Way campaign season to take employees to agencies supported by the United Way. During department meetings, managers showed videos starring employees from plant sites in Dallas, Houston, Sherman, and Lubbock who had benefitted from services United Way agencies offered. Tom Engibous, who chaired the company's United Way campaign from 1997 until 2003, said, "Corporate citizenship is a legacy that began with the Founders of our company, and I can assure you that it will continue in the future." CEO Rich Templeton chaired TI's 2004 and 2005 United Way campaigns.

TIer Gina Copeland understood. The day her son walked into his first-grade classroom for the first time, she began college. But she needed a day-care program for her youngest child. She found it at a United Way supported agency. As she

From left to right: Kyle Flessner, Steve McQuay, Lou Hutter, Todd Marvin, Chris Love, and David Lassiter. The South Building (SB) Managers' Pie Challenge, featuring six managers, was held in the SB Cafeteria to benefit United Way. The winner, Lassiter, employed a "face-first, no-questions-asked" strategy, and for his heroic effort was awarded movie passes.

pointed out, "I think that some people take United Way for granted until it impacts their lives in some way." Her degree earned her a job at TI, and she remembered, "It was a dream come true. I'm a product of the American system. A lot of single mothers in this country might be able to lift themselves out of poverty if they could only take advantage of the programs available to them."

In 1988, employees set a TI pledge record of $4.8 million with 91 percent of the company participating. The drive was spearheaded by the Pacesetters, some 64 percent of employees who had volunteered to donate 3 percent of their salary.

Tom Shaw, the expansion project coordinator in Dallas Logic, was a TI Pacesetter. He later commented, "Times have changed a great deal during the past 50 years. Everyone used to look out after their neighbors. The Dallas community is just too big and the problems too great. Being a United Way Pacesetter is an important part of my working for TI. More than a responsibility, it is an important part of my obligation to live in this community."

A s the company divested itself of numerous businesses in the late 1990s, pledges declined. In 1998, TI introduced online pledges, allowing employees to make contributions via the company's Intranet. By 2004, employee contributions and TI Foundation support had rebounded to more than $3.2 million a year.

Over the years, employees contributed more than money to the United Way. Many volunteered to find ways to show other Dallas-area companies how TI's annual pledge drive worked.

TI loaned employees to the campaign, each responsible for contacting a minimum of 32 businesses. When Jerry Junkins was CEO and Chairman, he served as the Dallas agency's 1989-90 general campaign chairman. TI won four James F. Chambers Awards for Outstanding Campaign Communications.

TIers have built a tradition of devising creative ways to raise funds. The first United Way Slam Dunk Celebration, held at the Dallas Texins Activity Center in 1997, included a basketball shooting contest between two business units, pie-throwing venues, and dunking booths where water-logged managers kept taking a dive for donations. TIers held car washes, carnivals, ice cream socials, hallway golf-putting competitions, bake sales, and tugs of war, where the vice presidents on losing teams found themselves pulled unceremoniously into pits of spaghetti.

The events were fun, and the reason for hosting them was serious. And TI matched all proceeds from each social, celebration, or event.

Gary Godsey, the President and CEO of the United Way of Metropolitan Dallas, thanked TI for its participation saying, "Texas Instruments is a model corporate partner. Because of the unwavering support of TIers, the United Way continues to build a stronger organization, better equipped to meet the changing needs of our community. Congratulations on 75 years of service."

Rich Templeton (left), Terri West (center), Phil Ritter and Mary Templeton (far right), sit with yellow-shirted members of the Boys & Girls Clubs of Plano, a branch of the Boys & Girls Clubs of Collin County, Texas. This CEO United Way tour took place on July 16, 2004, prior to the 2004 United Way campaign.

69

MAKING A DIFFERENCE

TI and employees reached out with corporate and grassroots volunteerism to improve their communities.

TI's Founders and leaders always believed they had an obligation to become a positive force in the communities they called home, and they set a high, enviable standard with their personal involvement and generous philanthropy. They left a legacy of concern and compassion that would guide and inspire generations of TIers to become more active and more involved in improving the world around them.

Early in its history when GSI established roots in Dallas, many employees followed the lead of the company's managers and took active roles in chambers of commerce and industry associations. During World War II, the company began a strong tradition of supporting War Bond campaigns and blood drives. In 1945, as the war edged toward a climactic end, GSI held a drive to collect clothing that could be shipped to citizens of liberated countries.

For TI, education had always been a top priority. TI volunteers, both active and retired, rode buses or drove their own cars during the school year to tutor and mentor students

The Tech Smart-Big Heart logo was developed by Public Affairs in 1999 to help build community awareness among TIers.

in programs designed to improve performance standards in the classroom. As Annette Campbell, an executive assistant at TI pointed out, "I love reading. I love words. I work in a technical environment, and it's important to me for these kids to be able to survive in today's world. I'm trying to show these kids how to reach for a goal and make something of themselves. I'm hoping I'm making a small difference. If there's something I can say to make them pass, it'll be worthwhile."

TI also supported learning opportunities outside the classroom by working with Junior Achievement, a national organization that gives high school students real-world business experience. The company began sponsoring Junior Achievement companies in 1956 with four supervisors, and, by 1980, the company had 32 advisors attached to 19 businesses.

TI volunteers like Phyllis Jefferson were helping students pick up some of life's basics that weren't being taught elsewhere, making sure they understood the importance of staying in school. "We can't wait for the government to do what needs to be done," she said. "We all need to lend a hand where we can. Working with these great kids recharges my batteries. It's also my small way of giving something back to the community. TI can help these kids succeed in life."

Texas Instruments and its employees applied the same vigor to helping their communities as they did to enriching education. In 1959, the General Products Department of the Semiconductor Division began working with the Lighthouse for the Blind in Dallas to create employment opportunities for the blind, developing a process that allowed unsighted workers to salvage diodes and leads for reuse. Other TI programs included on-the-job training for deaf students, a first in the United States, and computer training for the disabled. And TI remained actively involved with Special Olympics as more than 200 employees assisted with the Sports Carnival in Dallas in 1993. Cathy Garcia, a software technician, understood more than anyone about the value of the games. She had a son who competed, and pointed out, "Special Olympics gives these young people a chance to compete and show what they can do. I know it doesn't matter to Santiago if he comes in first, second, third, or just gets a ribbon. He gets tremendous enjoyment out of it."

One of the company's most avid and visible cheerleaders in North Texas was Jerry Junkins, chairman, president and CEO

Children of employees view one of the award-winning Christmas trees decorated by TIers in Corporate Legal in the 1980 contest. After the judging, the trees were donated to local charities.

from 1988 until his death in 1996. His leadership was evident outside of TI in education, trade, race relations, and many other issues that made Dallas and the nation better places. Junkin's fingerprints left an indelible mark and proved that one person could be a catalyst for change.

Almost from the company's beginning, TI employees took the initiative to launch their own community support projects. In 1966, rather than exchange holiday gifts among themselves, 40 Materials & Controls employees in Attleboro, Massachusetts, handed out presents at a Veterans Administration Hospital. In 1990, TI employees in Austin launched a multi-year program to set up computer labs at high schools and middle schools.

It was never unusual for the company to loan executives to area organizations, continuing to pay their salaries while they applied their expertise and management skills to address specific issues facing communities.

For example, TI's Gerald Borders with Facilities and Joe Zimmerman, TI senior vice president, worked several years as advisors for campus development at the predominantly

African-American Paul Quinn College. They realized a growing need to renovate and restore several buildings. A special TI team showed up to help wire, heat, and repair the structures so students could concentrate on their coursework.

Borders said, "The students and faculty looked at us as miracle workers because of the conditions they were used to. But we saw them striving and wanting to do more, and TI had the talent to help them. It was pleasing to be able to breathe new life into the campus." By the time the TI team left, the cafeteria had earned its health permit on the first inspection. The basketball team was pounding the boards on its home court, and students were able to stay warm when the winter temperature turned cold.

TIer Jimmy Hosch plants one of 12,000 trees to beautify North Texas lakes in 1992.

Through the years, TI managed to maintain an active role in supporting selected arts and cultural programs. In 1953, 50 employees formed a TI-GSI Choral Group that held benefit performances for charities. In 2000, TI had become a title sponsor of the Dallas Symphony Orchestra Classical Series, with 2,000 TIers attending the first "TI Night" at the symphony. TI donated $500,000 to bring the Women's Museum to Fair Park in Dallas to showcase significant contributions made by women in the disciplines of science, math, engineering, and technology. The company is recognized as a strong contributor to the Dallas Arboretum, the Dallas Opera, and the Dallas Museum of Art.

Compassion ran deep throughout TI during times of emergencies and crisis. Employees contributed funds and bottled water to aid tornado victims in Jasper, Texas. They pledged money and provided labor to help rebuild a school damaged by a typhoon that tore through India. They joined together to raise more than $300,000 to assist survivors after a 1995 earthquake killed almost 5,000 in Kobe, Japan. They donated more than $100,000 to benefit families suffering losses in a powerful earthquake near the company's site in Taiwan in 1995. In 1997, TI-India began hosting blood donation camps on the country's Independence Day, August 15, and Republic Day, January 26. In 2002, TI began working with voluntary blood banks to organize donation camps only as needed. That year, TI-India held two camps and 135 employees donated blood.

TI and its employees donated more than $1 million to the Red Cross and Salvation Army disaster-relief efforts through the TI CARES: Project 9-11 Campaign after the Twin Towers fell in New York.

Then, when disaster struck again in late 2004 as a tsunami swept ashore in Southern Asia, killing more than 200,000, the company and employees from around the world joined to contribute almost $1.5 million to support those whose lives had been devastated.

Many TI employees took their passion for community involvement into their retirement years. In 1974, the company began hosting monthly and annual retiree functions. In lieu of paying membership dues, retirees pledged to complete 10 hours of volunteer work each year. In 1999, TI helped officially form the TI Alumni Association, keeping retirees and former employees aware of community service opportunities through a website and newsletter. Among other things, the retirees have raised more than $100,000 for The Senior Source, a United Way agency, through annual golf tournaments.

In 1990, Erik Jonsson said his life had been enriched by donating time and money to community projects. He spoke for thousands of TIers who together had built a rich heritage of community involvement. They cared about those around them. They had compassion. But, more importantly, they didn't just talk about making the world a better place. They made something happen.

With supplies borrowed from DMOS6 in Dallas and the "Making of a Microchip" video, TIers at the Longmont, Colorado, site gave youngsters a chance to dress up in cleanroom suits and learn how TI turns silicon wafers into microchips for the annual "Take Your Daughters and Sons to Work Day."

70

EXCELLENCE IN EDUCATION

TI's efforts to improve math and science add up.

Viewing education through a competitive lens, TI sees the need to broaden the pool of engineering and technical talent in communities where it operates. The company understands the need to support educational programs that help students prepare for life in a technology-based economy.

Ralph Dosher, Jr. of TI sits in on a Project SEED class taught by Hap Vaughan of TI in November 1982. Dosher coordinated TI's involvement with the program.

Texas Instruments was built on the innovation and ingenuity of highly skilled and educated employees. As the company grew, it competed from coast to coast, and globally, for the best and brightest minds. Ultimately, TI decided the most effective way to find future engineers and scientists was to increase the talent pool.

As TI Chairman Tom Engibous pointed out, "With the advent of the Information Age, the need for technologically skilled people was escalating. Meanwhile, the number of skilled American high-technology workers had actually declined. We are faced with a reality, not a theory. That's why TI vigorously supports a wide range of initiatives designed to promote effective education. We began putting more emphasis than ever on our core areas, such as mathematics and science education. We are also doing more to expand our focus on educational opportunities for women and minorities in order to significantly increase their representation in technical fields."

With its sights set on increasing the number of technically skilled graduates, TI initiated programs that changed the way mathematics and science are taught. In 1997, the company teamed with the Dallas Public School's Science & Engineering Magnet (SEM) High School and donated half the price of a transmission electron microscope

for its science classes. TI's Wireless Communications business unit later offered paid summer internships to SEM graduates. And, in 1999, the company helped design the nation's first high school course that incorporated the fundamentals of digital signal processing.

In middle and high schools, TI's innovative programs made it possible for students to connect math and science to real-world situations. In 1993, two TI engineers, Ted Mahler and Steve Marum, served as guides for a group of high school students during Engineering Day at the company's site in Sherman, Texas. They noticed students' interest rise as they viewed a video of college freshmen building a robot at MIT. The two knew TI had the technology and expertise to support a similar, but more comprehensive program. So, with help from Texas A&M University, they created the North Texas BEST (Boosting Engineering, Science, and Technology) competition. More than 2,000 students representing 250 teams from five states now gather annually before a sporting-venue audience to build remote-controlled robots with the capability of solving a defined challenge during an allotted time. With TI and Texas A&M continuing to support the competition, the robot-building extravaganza was moved in 2004 to Southern Methodist University.

TI's "World in Motion" program supports science education. TI volunteers taught elementary students in Attleboro, Massachusetts, the art of designing and racing small sailboats by applying the concepts of friction, aerodynamics, measurement, and force.

Through its calculator business, TI created T³ (Teachers Teaching with Technology) in 1986 to help teachers from kindergarten through high school learn the latest math and science teaching methods. The program appealed to students' different learning styles by using TI graphing calculators and data-collection devices to help them visualize math and science concepts. By 2005, T³ workshops had trained more than 100,000 teachers worldwide.

In 2001, TI's Educational & Productivity Solutions (E&PS) business introduced the TI-Navigator system, incorporating handheld graphing technology—the TI-83

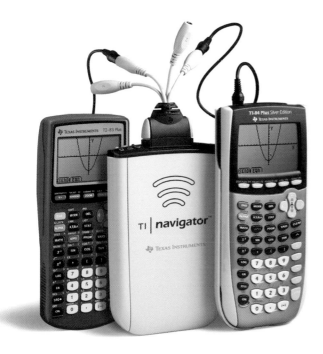

TI graphing calculators, shown with the TI-Navigator, make it possible for teachers to track students' progress in the classroom in real time. By 2003, TI had shipped more than 25 million of the calculators.

Plus—with a set of wireless hubs to create a wireless networked classroom. Teachers could access lesson plans and materials, view students' work with a handheld unit, and send questions to individuals or the entire class. Educators could also monitor students' progress in real time, allowing them to immediately address questions or issues.

In conjunction with the Semiconductor Industry Association, TI supported a variety of technology-based instruction, including the Southeastern Consortium for Minorities in Engineering, known as SECME. The partnership with universities increased the number of minority students who were prepared to complete science, math, and technology studies. Created and developed in 1975 by the deans of seven southeastern universities, SECME involved 38 colleges and reached more than 56,000 minority students in more than 770 schools—kindergarten through grade 12—by the end of 2004.

As a world leader in digital signal processors (DSP) and analog chips, TI had a keen interest in supporting university research projects. Over two decades, TI invested more than $50 million in DSP education and research to help university students explore applications for wireless communications, high-speed networks, and smart motor control. TI's DSP University Challenge offered a $100,000 grand prize to the winning team of college students that could develop the best new applications for digital signal processing.

At Rice, Georgia Tech, Stanford, and Texas A&M—universities engaged in analog, DSP, and electrical engineering research—TI provided a series of grants worth almost $30 million to endow professorships, graduate fellowships, and general research in signal processing. A $5.1 million gift to Texas A&M led to the creation of one of the nation's premier university analog programs. The company's $2.2 million grant to Georgia Tech funded the TI Graduate Scholars Program in Analog Integrated Circuit Design, recognizing the university's outstanding history of awarding engineering degrees to minority and women students. Rice University received a $7 million donation for facilities and long-term cooperative research in engineering.

Most of TI's university programs were conceived and developed to make sure the latest semiconductor technology and programming tools were available in engineering, education, and research programs. For more than 1,300 institutions participating in the DSP University Program worldwide, TI provided affordable access to technology, discounts on development hardware and software, lab equipment, and technical assistance.

Education had always been a key business priority for TI. Gene Helms, former manager of corporate strategic planning, said in 1990, "You can talk about capital investment, marketing skills, management, capabilities, and all the rest.

TI has endorsed and supported a statewide effort to introduce Advanced Placement (AP) coursework in schools across Texas through the Texas Science and Technology Council and the North Texas Science and Technology Coalition. TI underwrites AP test fees for students enrolled in Dallas magnet schools and provides graphing calculators as learning tools.

But when it comes right down to the basics, competitive advantage is based on knowledge. In the long run, TI is going to be at a competitive advantage, or disadvantage, based on how our people's knowledge stacks up with the rest of the world."

TO INFINITY AND BEYOND

★ ★ ★

In 1999, TIer Torrence Robinson, responsible for the company's university relations programs, and Dr. Geoffrey Orsak, a professor who became dean of the SMU School of Engineering, cast aside traditional approaches and turned cell phones, digital cameras, and MP3 players into teaching tools. They called it the Infinity Project.

The Infinity Project is an unusual curriculum for high school students, emphasizing the application of math and science fundamentals to the creation and design of technology that is useful and relevant to young students. Its approach was the first to incorporate state-of-the-art engineering and advanced technology curriculum in classroom instruction.

The program was originally intended to help meet TI's growing demand for engineers. As the

program expanded, however, it began tackling a larger issue—the widening gap between the annual number of U.S. engineering graduates and the high-tech industry's need for highly skilled engineers.

At the time, Europe and Asia both were graduating three to five times more engineering students annually than universities in the United States. The Infinity Project has been integrated into 120 high schools in 22 states, as well as the District of Columbia, and 17 educational institutions of higher learning throughout Texas.

Students can view engineering design and technology as the gateway to a future without limits. For them, the world of math is no longer just a maze of fractions, formulas, and equations. It makes real-world sense.

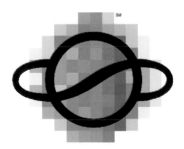

THE INFINITY PROJECT

THE COMMITMENT TO ZERO

TI implemented strong measures and policies to ensure the safety and health of its employees.

TI's commitment to ethics, integrity, and fairness long solidified the foundation of the company's Environmental, Safety and Health (ESH) stewardship program. It has always been management's belief that employees represent TI's most valuable asset, and the company creates policies and procedures to guarantee that TI employees work every day in a safe environment. TI also ensures that company operations have minimal negative effects on surrounding neighborhoods and the natural environment.

Zero became the heart of TI's ambitious ESH goals. Zero wasted resources. Zero injuries. And zero illnesses. Employees at TI's Oyama operations in Japan, for example, did not miss a day because of a work-related injury in 10 years as they worked toward national recognition, reaching 10.5 million work hours without an accident or on-the-job injury.

In 1949, TI developed one of the high-tech industry's earliest safety standard policies and procedures. The guideline required employees to receive safety training, demanded that knowledgeable safety professionals work with all TI operations, and required that safety goals were set and tracked across the company. Environmental science continued to evolve and, for more than 20 years, the majority of TI's sites have had ESH committees led by site-level senior management. The committees, intimately involved in the investigation of all incidents, ensured that employees had a safe and healthy workplace and set the ESH stewardship culture, celebrating the accomplishment of goals and taking

corrective action as needed.

In 1973, TI established a formal policy and company-wide program promoting energy conservation. By 2005, TI employees had created plans to reduce energy consumption at more than 40 different business locations around the world. The company implemented thousands of individual projects that included such simple programs as turning off lights and unused equipment to purchasing more efficient equipment. The projects usually paid for themselves in less than two years and significantly reduced nitrogen oxides and carbon dioxide emissions.

When TI launched its worldwide ESH audit program in 1984, corporate and on-site ESH professionals identified and shared best practices among manufacturing facilities, reporting to management on TI's compliance with its standards.

Five years later, TI introduced one of the world's first lead-free semiconductor component finishes. Although the amount of lead the semiconductor industry used was relatively small, TI took a major step by developing and introducing a nickel-palladium finish for leadframe packages in the late '80s and

Logo for TI's eco-friendly programs.

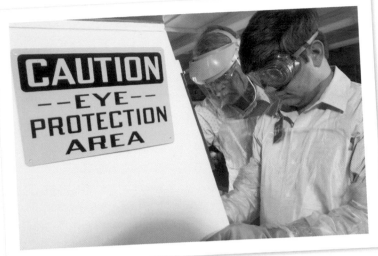

TIers are trained to wear safety glasses
in eye protection areas marked by
familiar yellow and black signs.

early '90s, and converting to nickel-palladium-gold in 2000.
For ball array packages, TI developed lead-free options using
industry-standard tin-silver-copper balls.

During 1994, TI broadened its ESH approach to set new
standards of excellence in the industry. Shaunna Sowell, serving
as vice president of ESH Services, worked with TI's Leadership
Team to create one of the industry's most rigid ESH goals of
zero illnesses, injuries, and wasted resources. The corporate
goals became the predecessor of incremental annual goals for
sites and business groups, calling for the reduction of energy
and water use, hazardous waste generation, and recordable
work injuries. The program also increased non-hazardous
solid-waste recycling. In a universal move to effectively
accomplish the goals, TI sites around the world incorporated
a new level of innovation into their safety and environmental
programs.

For example, during the 1970s, TI was building a fab
atop a mountain in Hiji, Japan, when residents expressed
concern about the effects of waste water in nearby Beppu
Bay, home to Shiroshita Karei, a unique fish considered
a delicacy in the country. The company allayed fears by
designing a system that discharged no waste water into the
bay or the environment. TI recycled water used by the fab
and trucked the particulates captured by a waste treatment
system to a disposal facility.

Beginning in 1990, TI operated a non-hazardous, solid
waste reduction program. By 2005, TI was recycling
approximately five out of every six pounds of all non-hazardous
solid waste generated by its operations. Employees recycled
such materials as office paper, corrugated fiberboard, aluminum scrap, electronics, a variety of wood products, and
plastics. By the end of 2004, the recycling program had returned over 722 million pounds of non-hazardous materials
to the global materials market.

TI works closely with its employees and communities
where the company operates to understand surrounding
environmental, safety, and health issues. In Campinas,
Brazil, a local institution collected recyclable materials
and used the proceeds to fund social services. In Hiji, Japan,
disposable packing materials were sent to another company
for use as fuel, and money earned in a community recycling
bazaar benefited a charity. Cafeteria waste in Taipei, Taiwan,
became feedstock for a pig farming operation. And, in Kuala
Lumpur, Malaysia, more than 300 tons of plastic mold runners
were recycled each year, and then used as a component for new
cement.

In 1992, TI in North Texas received the Environmental
Excellence Award in Solid Waste Management from the U.S.
Environmental Protection Agency for its recycling efforts
the previous year. Employees recycled 4.5 tons of materials,
reducing the need for waste transportation and disposal. In
addition, many materials were reused either through the sale
of the materials TI no longer needed or by the reuse of such
materials as paper.

A TI booth at an Earth Day fair highlights
the company's broad array of environmental,
safety, and health programs.

Texas Instruments uses large amounts of water in its manufacturing operations around the world. Using state-of-the-art management systems in rinse efficiency, re-

TI employees work with the Neighborhood Service Council to clean up Cottonwood Creek in Richardson, Texas.

cycling, reclamation, and conservation, some TI fabs in 2004 had significantly recycled more than 50 percent of their rinse water. TI had become an industry leader in water-use optimization, recycling, and reusing more than 1 billion gallons of water annually at facilities around the globe.

In Stafford, Texas, TI tapped water from its own on-site wells to reduce its public water consumption. In Miho, Japan, town officials and local fishermen were pleased with the analysis of discharged water samples at TI's facilities. In the Philippines, the company installed new water treatment and conservation technology to reduce the use of regeneration chemicals and waste-water treatment. The new system integrated ultra filtration, saving 60 gallons of water per minute, about 28,800 gallons over eight hours, compared to the previous system.

Despite state-of-the-art technology, many employees helped invigorate the environment the old-fashioned way. Employees and contractors planted 500 saplings in the Philippines to restore a watershed as part of the Worldwide Reforestation Movement. In Sherman, Texas, employees

planted trees donated by TI at schools and other locations throughout the community. In Oyama, Japan, employees sowed flower seeds and planted bulbs during the town's annual beautification contest.

In 2003, TI was recognized by the Semiconductor Industry Association as the safest semiconductor company among its members. TI's safety success was based on a strong leadership commitment within the company, as well as an aggressive ergonomics program. As a result, from 1990 to 2004, recordable ergonomics-related injuries decreased by 84 percent.

TI continues to be a friend of the environment and workplace, striving to reach its ambitious goals of zero illnesses, injuries, and wasted resources. For TI's most valuable asset, TIers, zero has become the most important number.

FROM SCRAP TO POWER

★ ★ ★

TI began selling test wafers, which would otherwise be scrapped, for use by a solar cell manufacturer in 2000. The collaboration contributed to the development of alternative energy by recycling silicon, and has saved TI more than $1.8 million. In the same amount of time, more than 998,000 8-inch wafers and 85,000 6-inch wafers have been recycled. The recycled wafers, coupled with solar cell technology, have produced enough power to supply more than 720 average-sized homes with electricity year-round. The emissions avoided through the program are estimated to be almost 131,000 tons of carbon dioxide. That's equivalent to the benefits that nearly 582,000 mature trees can provide for the air.

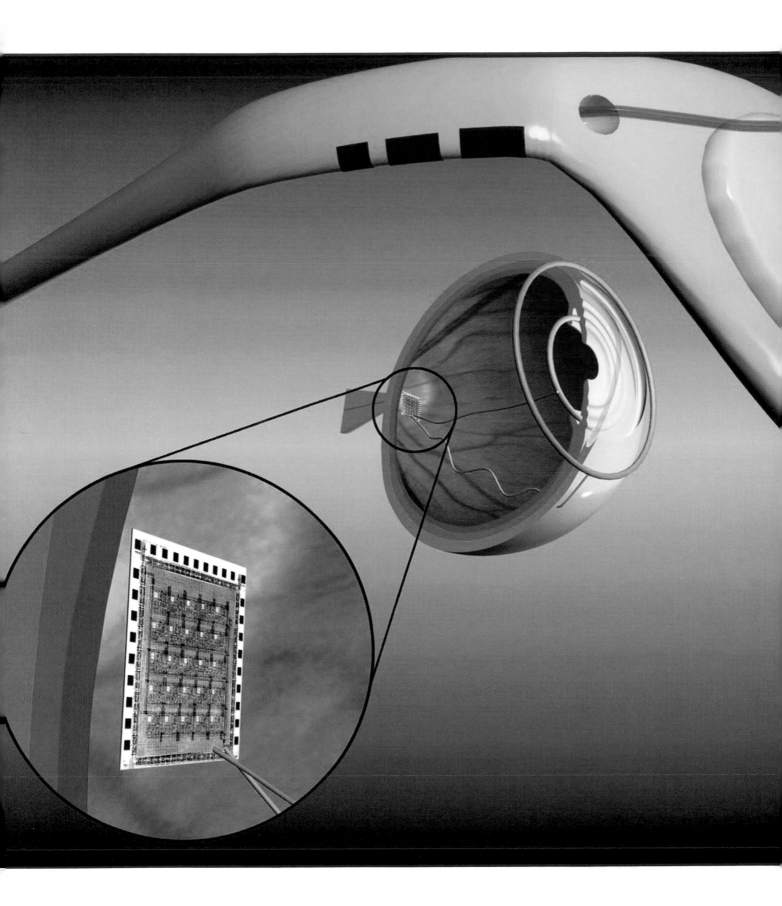

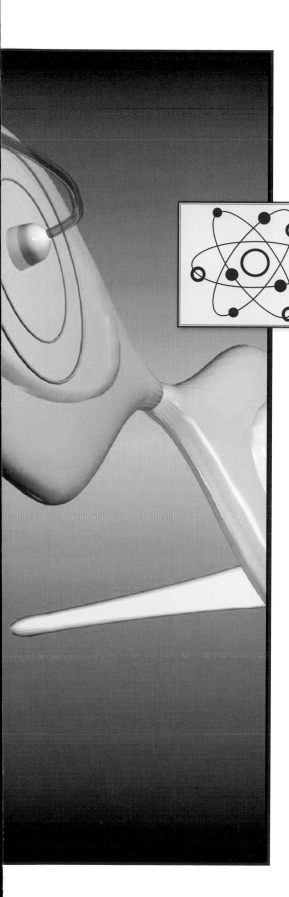

THE FUTURE

In the process of transforming itself and the world during the past 75 years, Texas Instruments chose to lead rather than follow. In doing so, TI pioneered advances in technologies such as digital signal processing and analog—the semiconductor engines of the Internet age. TI's commitment to manufacturing strength through construction of advanced technology fabs enabled the company to remain one of the few semiconductor companies to continue building plants in the U.S. and abroad.

The company may have had humble beginnings in the search for oil, but TI and its people ultimately set the pace in global markets for wireless and broadband access, as well as a variety of emerging markets that showcase digital projection systems, digital audio, and more. As bright as TI's heritage has been, the future appears even brighter in a world where every phone call, every Internet connection, every song, every picture, and every movie will be enriched by advanced technology. The future of TI will be the ongoing story of discovering and applying technology to change people's lives for the better. TI has been inventing the future for 75 years and will continue to turn science fiction into science fact.

The University of Southern California's prototype for an artificial vision system depends on TI's most advanced digital signal processing chip.

72

THE IMPACT OF RESEARCH

Creating an envrionment for innovation in the rapidly-changing world of electronics.

Over the last 30 years, various governmental and commercial groups have formed to assure the continued emphasis on research in technology. They all realized that strategic research and development was essential, not only for industrial profitability, but for the betterment of society. TI has taken leadership roles in these groups because it has embodied the same philosophy since the beginning of GSI. From the earliest innovations which helped geologists see the oil hidden in the depths, to one of the most recent innovations, Digital Light Processing (DLP™) technology, which brings depth, intense color and clarity to movies and television, TI's quest to unlock the future will continue in the research labs, and the impact will be seen around the world.

The Central Research Laboratories (CRL), formed in 1953, under the direction of Dr. Gordon Teal, established the direction for TI's basic research endeavors. The strength of CRL was influenced by the basic research model that Teal had learned at his previous job with AT&T's Bell Labs. Although TI was still a relatively small company, its research efforts were recognized by *Business Week* in a December 22, 1956, article, "Research Packed by Ph.D.s," which noted TI's ability to quickly transfer innovations by central research into product areas to commercialize the ideas. TI recognized the importance of creating an environment for innovation and worked hard to make the company one of the best in the industry.

Over the years, most basic semiconductor research shifted to universities and a few key industry consortiums, such as SEMATECH and IMEC, where companies shared the burden of research in the pre-competitive early development stages. As TI evolved from a diverse corporation to a focused semiconductor company in the 1990s, the R&D function also found itself in the midst of change. TI's Silicon Technology Development (SiTD) team made a concentrated effort to continue advancing Jack Kilby's core ideas.

In 1982, George Heilmeier brought TI's three semiconductor labs—VLSI Lab, Houston Process Development Lab, and Semiconductor Research and Development Lab—under one roof in the Silicon Process and Design Center (SPDC) in Dallas. Under the direction of Dennis Buss, SPDC was able to offset the growing cost of development by consolidating the three almost parallel R&D efforts into a single, more powerful organization.

Heilmeier would later say, "What differentiated basic research from applied research was simply the fact that applied research was conducted with at least one potential application in mind. It certainly might not be the only application or ultimately the most important application, but it was performed with the implications of success in mind. By this definition, research at TI has always been applied research. And while it may have been basic from a fundamental science point of view, it was always relevant to TI's current or future product interests."

When Dr. Yoshio Nishi came to TI from Hewlett-Packard in 1995, he was recognized as "the father of the 1-megabit CMOS Dynamic Random Access Memory (DRAM) chip." Although TI disbanded the memory R&D organization in the economic wake created by plunging DRAM prices, Dr. Nishi did not panic. He believed that advanced R&D would be the foundation for the strong future he envisioned for TI, and he pointed out, "This is just a cycle, not unlike five or six others I have experienced. The wisdom you gain is that a downturn is the best time to invest in R&D. The investment allows you to be well positioned for the upturn." This advice served TI well in the severe downturn of 2001, as the company held its R&D investments relatively steady and benefited in the next upturn with market share gains.

Dr. Nishi became a driving force behind the development of the Kilby Center, which was dedicated on September 9, 1997, with Jack Kilby and Willis Adcock in attendance. When the 584,000-square-foot building on the Dallas Expressway site was conceived, it was intended to be a dedicated 200-mm R&D pilot line. TI management soon realized that devoting a portion of the fab to technology production could help offset the large investment required to build the center. An added benefit was moving the development teams closer to manufacturing and TI's business units.

In 2001, Dr. Nishi returned to Stanford University, and Dr. Hans Stork became TI's Chief Technology Officer. The SiTD team was focused on keeping pace with the competition it faced with the roll-out of new technologies. At the time, TI's 130 nanometer copper process was struggling to reach qualification for production. Dr. Stork moved quickly to implement an organizational change that placed all program deliverables for each process node under one leader.

As Dr. Stork noted, "The expected benefit of scaling CMOS was changing, as far as cost, design, and complexity were concerned. We couldn't just shrink things and expect size, processing performance, and power consumption to all get uniformly better. How we exploited the move to smaller dimensions in terms of cost reduction became critical."

The move to reduce component size was expedited when TI realized that the demand for portable applications was on the rise, and the company's ability to place more functions into fewer packages would enable them to surf the edge of the electronic wave. In parallel, they would need to provide the technology that would enhance the quality and quantity of images/video, voice/audio, and other data, as well as the memory and processing power to manipulate them. Intensive research in these areas culminated in the integration of several TI technologies onto single chips.

The Digital RF Processor (DRP) was a focused effort to bring a stand-alone, specialized analog function (Radio Frequency) on a chip, using low-cost, high-volume, digital CMOS technology. A single-chip Bluetooth product integrating the DRP was introduced in 2002 and a single-chip cell phone was sampled in 2004. Customers could now build more functionality into compact, low-power devices, giving TI the opportunity to steadily increase its share of the total system semiconductor content

Single-chip Asymmetric Digital Subscriber Line (ADSL) and single-chip Voice over Internet Protocol (VoIP) devices were other examples of TI leveraging its analog and digital signal processing capabilities in the development of

highly integrated products. By moving these system-on-chip (SoC) designs onto high-volume, leading-edge manufacturing lines, TI was able to offer a value proposition increasingly difficult for competitors to match.

"There were several applications that needed one of everything," Dr. Stork said. "They needed RF, a power amplifier, and power management, and TI was able to appropriately integrate the analog and digital functions. Integration wasn't something that physics told you to do. It was something that economics told you to do."

In today's economic environment, system integration is critical, especially since it is an important facet of communications. As cell phones advance, integration enables the necessarily robust multimedia applications processing. By delivering multiple key features in one product, TI's OMAP processors have become the world's leading application processors for portable devices. This chip is built in 90-nm technology and integrates a DSP and a microprocessor, a dedicated 2D/3D graphics accelerator, an integrated camera interface and sophisticated Direct Memory Access (DMA)

In September 1997, TI unveiled its new research and development building, named in honor of Jack Kilby, the inventor of the integrated circuit. The Kilby Center, located on TI's north campus in Dallas, is one of the world's most advanced research centers for silicon manufacturing.

important to electronics as Moore's Law which refers to the scaling, or constant shrinking, of CMOS transistors. To continue this trend, TI continues to invest in the research which will bring new generations of CMOS manufacturing processes.

"As CMOS processes become more specialized—and as Moore's Law comes within sight of fundamental limitations—the need to optimize chip design and manufacturing processes will become ever more significant. By the time that Moore's Law eventually ends, TI will be putting about 100 billion transistors on a chip, as opposed to the 400 million transistors it places on a chip today. So, any technology trying to displace CMOS in the mass market must be able to match the performance of 100 billion transistors at the tremendously cost-effective price CMOS can deliver. Alternative nano-electronics will augment CMOS, not replace it—at least not in the next couple of decades."

Nanotechnology, the science of designing, building, or using unique structures smaller than 100 nanometers in size (a nanometer being one billionth of a meter), generates promises ranging from micro-machines that could cure illnesses from within bodies to new materials much stronger and lighter than anything previously available in the marketplace. TI, in the early twenty-first century, had already achieved 90 nanometer process technology and continues to push the technology to even smaller feature sizes.

Dr. Stork, like Templeton, believed nanotechnology would grow over time without ever affecting the overall health of the semiconductor industry. TI visualized that nanotechnology would eventually exert a pervasive impact on business and society far beyond the scope of the semiconductor industry as it exists in 2005, possibly generating the creation of entirely new businesses not yet conceived. In many ways, nanotechnology has the potential to produce technical discontinuities and associated business opportunities similar to those experienced during the early history of semiconductor development.

TI, by virtue of its world-class capability in semiconductor processing, has the potential of taking advantage of its strong core competency in nanotechnology to ultimately create and participate in new semiconductor businesses on the far edge of technologies not yet imagined. One day they could well be part of life itself. And TI will be out front, continuing to work with universities and consortiums to strengthen the environment for innovation and exploring the possibilities long before they can be grasped as reality.

controller, an imaging and video accelerator, internal memory to boost streaming media performance, and full-motion video encode or decode which can output images to an external television.

Rich Templeton, TI's current President and Chief Executive Officer spoke at the IEEE International Conference on Communications in May 2005. He emphasized the importance of TI's focus on system integration for communications. "System integration has become as

TI'S CENTRAL RESEARCH LABORATORIES: A CULTURAL LEGACY

★ ★ ★

The TI legacy and culture of innovation were nowhere stronger than in its Central Research Laboratories (CRL). Gordon Teal set it on this course when he founded CRL. The accomplishments of Teal, Willis Adcock, and others in creating the first silicon transistor set a standard of research achievement that would motivate generations of researchers at TI. The talent that Teal recruited into CRL was astonishing for a small, upstart company like TI. His recruits included the next two directors of CRL, James Ross Macdonald, who arrived in 1953, and Norman Einspruch, who arrived in 1959.

By the 1960s, TI's CRL was recruiting at the Ph.D. level across the nation on par with the biggest and best national research organizations. CRL was regularly recruiting researchers from the top universities like MIT and Stanford, and had arguably become one of a handful of top national research labs in physics and electronics. A culture of academic excellence combined with application-driven research had become deeply rooted in CRL. One aspect of the academic emphasis was the close relationship TI established with universities and the external research community. An outgrowth of this was the annual preparation of a detailed technology forecast intended to apprise TI business units of potential technical shifts or discontinuities impacting their products. An aspect of the application-driven emphasis was the annual evaluation, ranking, and funding of research projects based on their relevance and impact on TI's business.

These elements of culture were preserved and enhanced through successive generations of CRL leadership. When Teal became International Technical Director for TI in 1963, Macdonald became CRL Director. During his tenure, the CRL mission was extended to include support for a number of defense-related technologies, including both infrared and microwave components. In 1972, Einspruch became CRL Director and emphasized an even stronger coupling of research programs to impact business. Robert Stratton succeeded Einspruch in 1975 and achieved the longest tenure of any director in CRL history.

In 1977, George Heilmeier arrived at TI from his post as Director of the Defense Advanced Research Projects Agency and, in 1983, was named Senior Vice President and TI's first Chief Technology Officer. Heilmeier was a great champion and advocate for R&D. He established additional R&D units around CRL, under the umbrella of Corporate Research & Engineering that included the Semiconductor Process and Design Center, the Corporate Engineering Center, and the Computer Science Laboratory. In 2005, Heilmeier was awarded the prestigious Kyoto Prize for his pioneering work in liquid crystal displays at RCA before joining TI.

Eventually, with the growing focus on semiconductors, and the spin-off of unrelated businesses, it made sense to concentrate R&D efforts within the semiconductor business. But the cultural legacy born and nourished in CRL—academic excellence combined with application-targeted projects—remains as strong as ever.

73

THE FABULOUS FAB BUILDERS

TI took a leadership role in building some of the world's most advanced semiconductor manufacturing plants.

The evolution of TI's fabs mirrored the ever-changing growth in size of the wafers and complexity of the products, as well as a corresponding increase in the size, complexity, and quantity of process tools required to produce them. An ultra-clean environment was essential, and it required a greater volume of air being constantly circulated and filtered throughout the cleanrooms. TI quickly realized the evolving semiconductor process needed a new approach to building fabrication facilities, with each possessing reliable support infrastructure.

In rapid succession, wafer sizes in the 1980s kept increasing. It seemed as though they were three inches (75 mm) one day, then four inches (100 mm) the next. The wafers would soon go to five inches (125 mm) and finally to six inches (150 mm). In 1984, DMOS4 in Dallas—a

sister of Miho's MMOS6—opened as TI's newest fab, offering two-level cleanrooms equipped for six-inch processing and boasting some early automation systems. DMOS4 would be the last new fab TI would build in the United States for almost a decade.

The rapidly escalating costs of building fabs forced the company to become an integral part of a number of joint development projects during the late 1980s and mid-1990s as TI struggled to remain competitive in the Dynamic Random Access Memory (DRAM) market. By partnering with other companies—and even with regional governments seeking to establish high-tech industries—TI hoped to share the costs involved with building fab facilities and manufacturing equipment that were becoming increasingly more expensive. The strategy resulted in TI-built fabs rising up in Italy, Taiwan, Singapore, Japan, and Texas, all housing high-volume DRAM manufacturing. Each of the facilities embodied the latest fab designs and traced the evolution of production technology by transitioning from 150-mm to 200-mm wafers. The fabs

A view of the DMOS6 lobby entrance, Dallas, Texas, designed by architect Alfonso Mercurio. Construction began in 1996.

were eventually sold when TI exited the DRAM market, and the agreements with those countries were dissolved. One fortunate outcome of the frantic-paced venture was TI's relationship with architect Alfonso Mercurio of Rome. He had been instrumental in the design of almost all TI wafer fabs in the 1990s, including those in Avezzano, Italy; Hsinchu, Taiwan; Singapore; and the Dallas Kilby and DMOS6 facilities. The other positive outcome was a team of highly experienced TI engineers, who moved site-to-site with their families during the construction and start-up of the fabs around the world. They became know as the "Fabulous Fab Builders."

Most of TI's early fabs had been single-level. But the design evolved over time into a two-level building with massive vane axial fans and large infrastructure spaces, then to a three-level design to accommodate the increasing density of manufacturing support equipment associated with larger, more complex tools. It was vital for the fabs and their support systems to be reliable because TI was counting on $2 billion worth of production equipment running efficiently, without interruption, in the 300-mm fabs. On one occasion, DMOS4 in Dallas transitioned from 150-mm to 200-mm wafers, adding back-end copper interconnect and essentially rebuilding the entire fab infrastructure without ever shutting down production. It was a remarkable achievement.

In 1993, TI announced plans for a new fab, DMOS5, dedicated largely to advanced processors and the integration of multiple functions and technologies onto single chips. The new fab was built in phases and designed to eventually produce semiconductors with measurements as small as 0.12 micron on 200-millimeter (8-inch) silicon wafers.

DMOS6 became TI's first 300-mm fab, but it certainly didn't start out that way. When construction on the building began in 1996, plans called for a 200-mm facility. By the time

DMOS6 is an example of a highly automated wafer fab, with overhead systems moving the products from tool to tool through the entire production sequence.

brick and mortar were in place in early 1997, however, the industry had entered a down cycle, and work on the cleanroom slowed to a halt. The building shell sat empty until April 1999, when work began anew. During those months when the fab remained idle, production equipment suppliers completed development of their first 300-mm tool sets, and TI made a critical decision to implement 300mm processing in DMOS6. The move allowed TI to realize production cost advantages by adding more chips on each wafer. The first 300-mm equipment was installed in September 2000 as TI scrambled to build capacity to support a booming demand.

"The decision to move DMOS6 from 200 mm to 300 mm turned out to be a very fortunate one," remembered Kevin Ritchie, senior vice president of TI's Manufacturing Technology Group. "It turned out to be one of the first few 300-mm factories in the world to qualify, and it put TI in a great position for the next upturn." DMOS6 is a highly automated wafer fab, with overhead systems moving the products from tool to tool through the entire production sequence.

The 300-mm fab era brought about an increase in wafer size and output capability, and it created a new generation of equipment, automated production areas, and larger, even more costly facilities to house them. The issue of escalating fab construction costs became an important point. Leading-edge wafer production had touched all corners of the globe, and research revealed that manufacturers in Asia were able to construct wafer fab facilities for substantially less than in the United States.

———————

The threat of such low-cost competition on foreign shores added to the complexity of a decision on the best location for TI's needed internal capacity. In the end, TI made a difficult decision to build its next fab, called RFAB, in nearby Richardson, Texas. There were clear advantages in keeping a significant portion of its available capacity in-house. The construction team was challenged to reduce the cost of the buildings and infrastructure by some 30 percent. The team rose to the challenge, implementing a remarkable and innovative new design program, relying on the skills of its "Fab Builders." Four basic concepts for reducing costs were identified: function, space efficiency, right sizing, and simple reliability.

TI also targeted "sustainability" as a design objective that could help lower operating costs while, at the same time, positively impacting the environment. Before a design team was even named, a three-day meeting was held with 30 TIers and 12 staff members from the non-profit Rocky

Mountain Institute (RMI). They drafted a list of sustainability improvements that had never been included in a TI fab. The team registered the project under the Leadership in Energy and Environmental Design Program, developed by the U.S. Green Building Council, a voluntary, consensus-based national standard for developing high-performance, sustainable buildings systems.

According to Paul Westbrook, sustainable development manager, "It helped give everyone on the project a common language and a system of measurement for energy savings and environmental issues. Once you established a way to keep score, people became very competitive and tried to score points."

Among the ideas generated from the TI and RMI teams was the decision to use smaller, more energy-efficient pumps and fans, along with implementing larger pipes and ducts that were more directly routed to reduce the number of energy-sapping bends and elbows. The move would create lower operating costs from the energy savings.

Extensive water recycling became part of the design, with two to three uses for each gallon inside the facility. Outside, a 3 million gallon retention pond caught rainwater runoff for irrigation of the site and kept the runoff from entering the streets and drains in the surrounding neighborhood. Native landscaping was chosen for its adaptation to the environment.

A portion of the exterior building shell design included windows and reflectors that brought natural daylight deeper into the building. Artificial lighting was the primary power use in an office, and it was recognized as a generator of unwanted heat. As a result, TI implemented motion and daylight sensors to automatically turn lights on and off. In total, the sustainability improvements reduced projected operating costs by $3 million a year.

Even as TI's latest fab began construction, the ongoing goal of reducing capital investment in manufacturing was being supported by foundries in Taiwan. Research and development investments in the foundries placed them in a position to support TI's most advanced technology nodes. By 2005, TI was sourcing around 50 percent of its most advanced products from foundries, a strategy that freed the company from having to build the large amounts of additional capacity required every two years to support peak demand for each node.

In the end, it wasn't all the motors, fans, pipes, and precision equipment that helped close some of the cost gaps with the Asian fabs. It was those teams of "Fabulous Fab Builders" with years of experience and a dedication to building world-class fabs that could take TI and its customers to higher levels of performance.

HOW TI'S NEWEST SEMICONDUCTOR FABRICATION PLANT WILL IMPACT THE COMMUNITY.

★ ★ ★

In 2005, TI's newest fab—a $3 billion facility—began construction in Richardson, Texas. The plant will employ 1,000 people when fully operational, but those jobs are only the beginning. TI officials worked closely with policymakers who earmarked $300 million in new funding for the Erik Jonsson School of Engineering and Computer Science at The University of Texas at Dallas. That investment in the future will draw more students, and will broaden research and development programs at the school. Economists estimate that the plant and the UTD project could corresponding create more than 74,000 jobs in Dallas-Fort Worth over the next 10 to 15 years, as the TI project attracts suppliers, software companies, engineering firms, and other technology-related businesses.

TI's newest fab, under construction in Richardson, Texas, is located near the campus of The University of Texas at Dallas. (Photo courtesy of *Dallas Morning News*.)

74

TI'S IMPACT

Texas Instruments has built a great legacy of advancing technology and enhancing communities where TI operations reside.

Texas Instruments drove itself to succeed on the strength and technological power of its innovations, and that determination sustained the company through difficult times, consistently elevating TI to new heights of achievement. Along the journey, the company's work, time and again, served as a catalyst for reshaping industries all over the globe.

GSI revolutionized oil and gas exploration three times, first with analog reflection seismology, then with digital seismic techniques, and again with 3D technology. These innovations promoted international production, significantly reduced the cost of finding oil, and allowed the efficient recovery of millions of barrels of oil from proven reserves.

In electronics, TI's silicon transistor breakthrough hastened the industry's shift from vacuum tubes to solid state devices. This innovation effectively created an environment that led to the invention of the integrated circuit at TI, which then set the modern semiconductor industry in motion. The company's early work with integrated circuits and infrared technology was a critical enabler for space exploration and played a major role in restructuring tactical warfare. And TI's relentless pursuit of productivity led to semiconductor cost reductions, a move that helped propel electronics into mass markets—to the benefit of societies worldwide.

Reaching into the consumer market, TI transformed math and science education by inventing the handheld electronic calculator. In 1978, the company gave the world a glance at the future with Speak & Spell™, a personal, portable, and digital device that was the first consumer product to utilize digital signal processing technology.

TI's focus on real-time signal processing led the transition of cell phones from analog-to-digital technology, and, by the end of 2004, more than 1.6 billion people were actively using cell phones. More than half of all cell phones shipped worldwide were engineered with TI technology.

As the company marks its 75th anniversary, TI is spearheading the use of signal processing to make a positive difference in daily life, from portable multimedia devices that let consumers enjoy music and video on the go, to stability control systems that increase the safety of automobiles and even portable magnetic resonance imaging systems that enhance health care. In these and many other ways, TI is enabling higher performance, greater efficiency, lower total costs, and entirely new capabilities.

Jim Plummer, dean of Stanford University's School of Engineering, said, "When Tom Engibous succeeded in shifting TI's full attention to real-time signal processing, I think it probably launched their most significant efforts yet to fulfill the integrated circuit's potential for impacting daily life on this planet."

In international technology standards and professional engineering societies, TI made significant contributions

---

TEXAS INSTRUMENTS NAMED MOST ADMIRED SEMICONDUCTOR COMPANY IN 2004 AND 2005

★ ★ ★

For the fifth straight year in 2005, TI was included on *Fortune* magazine's lists of most admired companies. TI achieved the ranking of the most admired semiconductor company for the past two years, according to *Fortune*'s annual surveys in 2004 and 2005.

THE LEGACY OF JACK ST. CLAIR KILBY
★ ★ ★

There are few men whose insights and professional accomplishments can be said to have changed the world.

Jack Kilby, who passed away on June 20, 2005, was one of these men.

His invention of the monolithic integrated circuit in 1958 laid the foundation for the entire field of modern microelectronics. It was this breakthrough that has made possible the sophisticated high-speed tools of the Internet age.

Kilby was the recipient of two of the nation's most prestigious honors in science and engineering. In 1970, in a White House ceremony, he received the National Medal of Science. In 1982, he was inducted into the National Inventors Hall of Fame, taking his place alongside Henry Ford, Thomas Edison, and the Wright Brothers.

In 2000, Kilby was awarded the Nobel Prize in Physics for his role in the invention of the integrated circuit.

From his first simple circuit has grown a worldwide integrated circuit market with sales in 2004 totaling more than $175 billion. Such is the power of one idea to change the world.

Jack Kilby (circa 1958) about the time of his invention of the first integrated circuit at Texas Instruments.

for decades. The company supported and often led efforts ranging from industry coalitions promoting specific technologies to international bodies such as the Institute of Electrical and Electronics Engineers (IEEE) which actively supports and encourages standards. Technical standards enhanced trade and technology transfer by establishing consistent, interoperable specifications that expanded product offerings, increased competition, and improved the user's experience with new technologies.

Beyond TI's impact on technology, the company had served as a valuable catalyst for positive change in the communities where its operations had been built. From helping build roads in India to working with Dallas-area leaders to create an institution of higher learning that ultimately became The University of Texas at Dallas, TI and its employees proactively identified and addressed community needs.

TI has continued to be a major supporter of education, a tradition established by the company's founders and maintained by the generations of leaders who followed them. As Linda Katehi, dean of Purdue University's School of Engineering, said about Engibous, "Tom's support of engineering education—including his promotion of women and minorities in the engineering disciplines—is bringing the next generation of technological visionaries along."

From the beginning, TI created positive change, whether it was advancing technology or enhancing communities. Such opportunities attracted a special kind of person. But then, TIers always knew they were people on a mission. On his retirement from the company in 1988, TI Chairman Mark Shepherd looked back on his 40 years with the company and commented that one of his personal rewards was helping build an institution, Texas Instruments, that serviced societies throughout the world, made its living with high technology and innovation, created new kinds of jobs, provided TI communities with better educated and more active citizens, created wealth for shareholders, and improved the economy of the countries, states, counties, and cities where TIers lived.

It is quite a legacy.

75

THE FUTURE

TI's history points to its future—the ongoing story of the human drive to discover and apply leading-edge technologies that benefit mankind.

Team Digital Auto Drive is using TI's most advanced digital processors to develop a vehicle—seen here in a U.S. government-sponsored race in 2004 for autonomous vehicles—that drives and navigates itself with no human intervention. (Photo courtesy of Velodyne/Team Digital Auto Drive.)

The history of Texas Instruments is not a story with a beginning, middle, and end. Instead, it is a cycle of beginnings, middles, and new beginnings.

During the early 1990s, a new beginning started to crystallize when company leaders recognized that DSPs and analog semiconductors could become the primary catalysts for achieving the next phase of the digital revolution. In previous stages, mainframe computers were dependent on transistors. TTL/logic products came along to drive minicomputers, and microprocessors powered the personal computer. As the world began to dream and seek to develop technologies that would make the Internet mobile, TI envisioned that digital communications and entertainment would emerge as the dominant drivers in electronics. Applications, however, would require real-time signal processing, and no one could deliver the technology better than TI.

"When Texas Instruments narrowed its focus to DSP and analog, we actually expanded our opportunities," said TI Chairman Tom Engibous. "Real-time signal processing was ideal for applications that couldn't wait, whether it was a voice conversation on cell phones or anti-lock brakes in your car. We knew that TI could accelerate digital technology's penetration into daily life."

Applications enabled by TI's technology included such common activities as more efficient and quiet household appliances or motor scooters that operated without gasoline, a significant development throughout many parts of the world. Other researchers began using TI's most advanced products for applications that bordered on the miraculous: systems that would allow the blind to see, prosthetics that an amputee could control with his or her mind, and vehicles that safely navigated themselves without the need for human intervention.

In the 21st century, TI is focused on creating total system solutions that integrate all the digital and analog functions required by a particular application. The products include packaged components, as well as total solutions on a single chip.

"System integration opens up new horizons for our technology, our customers, and the end user," said TI President and CEO Rich Templeton. "Our new single-chip cell phone solution targeted the pent-up demand for wireless voice communications. It is possible that hundreds of million of people worldwide could experience telecommunications for the first time because of this single-chip breakthrough."

For the high-end cell phone market, TI is integrating multimedia consumer applications into the company's platforms for advanced cell phones. The OMAP™ 2 processors will enable cell phones with DVD-quality video, CD-quality audio, 3D multiplayer gaming, and more. In addition, TI has developed a chip that will permit cell phones to receive and ultimately record broadcast television content.

Real-time signal processing is not the only dynamic technology TI has brought to market. "Some day, TI will be as famous for DLP-based, high-definition televisions as we are for calculators," Templeton predicted. "And if you consider what bar codes did for the retail industry, TI's RFID technology will change things in even more fundamental ways in coming years."

A key factor for the future is that the cost of advanced manufacturing and design is accelerating as components become ever smaller. Innovative developments are more difficult and more expensive to achieve. Many industry experts believe that global semiconductor demand will ultimately be met by a small number of companies with the scale and financial strength to pursue leading-edge developments. TI has all of the ingredients and the commitment necessary to rank as one of those select companies.

As of the company's 75th anniversary in 2005, TI has just begun to mine the full potential of real-time signal processing, focused both on the necessary components as well as software. In fact, development of underlying software is becoming as important to the company as electrical engineering.

"I wouldn't trade our position in signal processing for any other company or technology on earth," Templeton said in 2005. "We're working toward the time when every phone call, every Internet connection, every song you hear, every picture you take, and every movie you watch will be touched by TI technology.

"Even so, our eyes are wide open," he said. "We're always thinking about how the future will unfold. Today, as always, the ability and the willingness to change are two of TI's great strengths. DSP is an essential skill, while high-performance analog is becoming the financial core of this company due to its high profitability and broad demand. This core will help TI's research into new growth areas."

Motorola's Ojo Personal Video Phone used five TI devices. It's shown here with Rich Templeton, TI President and CEO. (Phone photo courtesy of Worldgate, Inc.)

Whatever happens, TI will pursue business success by collaborating with customers to enable people to change their lives for the better. The future of Texas Instruments will be the ongoing story of the human drive to discover, learn, and apply— contained and sustained within one company.

WHAT TI DOES REALLY MATTERS

★ ★ ★

On December 9, 2004, Rich Templeton addressed the company's top managers at the annual TI Leadership Conference. Here is an excerpt:

"When I talk to customers, they look you in the eye and say, 'What TI does really matters,' and what they're really saying is 'You better keep doing it well.' We have a lot of customers that think that, and that is a great opportunity for TI.

"Your work matters because TI is changing lives, and I mean that on an emotional, personal, and human basis. There are 1.6-billion wireless users in the world. More than half of them use a cell phone, compliments of TI solutions. We're changing the way people live. We're impacting medical care, with scanners that are portable,

enabling deaf people to hear, making it possible for blind people someday to see. We're affecting the world around us in profound ways because of the technology we deliver.

"As we look back on all the things that have changed in the past 75 years, a few things stand out that have been consistent through all those generations of managers that have come and gone from rooms like this. TI's attributes of innovation, ethical values, and a global understanding of the world remain as absolute foundations and unique advantages to TI. I think they can go a long way to ensuring that TI continues to make a real difference in the world, and they will help us become the company that we aspire to be."

THE HISTORY OF THE HISTORY
How This Book Finally Came to Be

This isn't the first time TI has tried to write its history. In fact, a book on the company's accomplishments has been attempted at least six times in the past, making the "history of the history" a story unto itself.

From the company's earliest days, the founders sensed the business they started would make a significant impact on the world. There were discussions as early as the 1940s about the need to record the details of the company's great accomplishments, but the people of TI were too busy making history to write it. Fortunately, company newsletters, such as the *GSI Grapevine* and *texins* contained in-depth articles written by employees who were there in the early days.

Erik Jonsson thought for many years about writing his autobiography, and from 1960-1961, Holland McCombs, the Dallas bureau chief for *Time/Life* magazines, spent six months interviewing Jonsson, Eugene McDermott and other TI officers. His work was the basis for a November 1961 cover story on TI in *Fortune* magazine. Ultimately, the McCombs papers were donated to the University of Mississippi and the University of Tennessee at Martin, but no other works were published.

In 1965, TI compiled and published five of Pat Haggerty's presentations in a small hardback book titled,

Management Philosophies and Practices of Texas Instruments Incorporated. Copies were given to managers throughout the company. While not intended as a history of the company, it did contain historical details about certain key innovations and was a valuable reference.

In the early 1970s, Larry Secrest, while a doctoral candidate at The University of Texas at Austin, received a grant from the Moody Foundation to study the 80 most influential people in the building of the state of Texas as it transitioned from agrarian to industrial, and then to post-industrial. He interviewed Jonsson, Cecil Green, and McDermott. The interviews were never published, but the tapes are located in the archives at The University of Texas at Austin.

As Haggerty began to contemplate retirement as chairman of TI in 1976, he thought more about the need to record TI's history. In an interview, he mentioned that he planned to spend 40 days a year working on such a project. Soon after Haggerty's retirement, TI began to collect historical records and interviewed about 50 employees. But Haggerty's untimely death in 1980 brought this attempt to write TI's history to a standstill.

In 1981, TI management took up the project again, hiring History Associates Incorporated to do the honors. Several

---

SPECIAL THANKS

Engineering the World owes its existence to a small group of dedicated retirees and current TIers who spent more than a year researching and editing. All agree that the toughest part of the process was deciding what not to include.

The Retiree Advisory Council consisted of 14 retirees with an average 34 years of TI service. They represented a cross section of experience from all of TI's businesses—current and former. Four of these retirees were already themselves authors or former editors; two were PhDs; 10 were engineers. All were dedicated to documenting TI's achievements and the stories of its people.

Special thanks to these retirees: Jim Adams, Dot Adler, John Byers, Harvey Cragon, Ralph Dosher, Ed Millis, Ed Hassler, Gene Helms, Sherel Horsley, Jon Jackson, Linda Lambert, Jim Peterman, Max Post, and John W. Wilson.

Kathyrn Lang and associates at the Southern Methodist University Press provided valuable editing support and overall guidance to the project.

Finally, a real debt of gratitude is owed to all the TIers in Worldwide Communications, as well as others who helped with the project, including: Janelle Richards, Allen Scott, Cindy Sheets, and Brad Smith.

The TI history book team was honored at a luncheon hosted by Tom Engibous and Terri West on May 16, 2005, celebrating the company's 75th anniversary.

Front Row: Gene Helms, Amy Treece, Cindy Sheets, Sherel Horsley, Max Post, Ralph Dosher, Linda Lambert, Dot Adler, Jon Jackson, Terri West, Tom Engibous. Back Row: Jim Adams, John Byers, Jim Peterman, Ed Millis, Phil Bogan, Harvey Cragon, Ed Hassler, John Wilson. Not pictured: Janelle Richards and Brad Smith

people were involved in the work, including writer Ken Martin. History Associates spent 33 months on the project, starting with interviews in 1982. Although a book was never published, the interviews proved to be a valuable resource.

The work that began with History Associates eventually led to establishment of a Corporate Archives department, including an artifacts program led by retiree Ed Millis who collected key items such as semiconductors, calculators, defense equipment test equipment, computers, and printers. The archives and artifacts programs were discontinued during financial cutbacks in the late 1990s. However, many of the landmark TI inventions collected and catalogued through this effort were contributed to the Smithsonian Institution and can still be viewed by visiting www.smithsonian.org and searching on Texas Instruments.

In 1996, Mike Lockerd assembled a team, including retired TIers Glenn Bandy and Bernie List, to document TI's key innovations. As a result of their work, a one-hour videotape was prepared for employees, and a summary of their work was used in the History of Innovation section on TI's web site. An outcome of their work also was the popular *TI Innovation Milestones* poster.

Finally, in early 2004, a conversation between former TI president Fred Bucy and then CEO Tom Engibous served as a catalyst to once again resurrect efforts to capture some of TI's great history into book form. At the same time a small group of retirees, some of whom had worked on TI's 50th anniversary celebration, gathered together and generated ideas for the company's impending 75th anniversary. At the intersection of these two discussions was born a collaboration between current TI management and a small band of determined retirees led by Max Post and Phil Bogan. They were later joined by Amy Treece. The effort ultimately culminated in this book of 75 stories.

These 75 stories, collectively titled *Engineering the World*, have been brought together in one place for the people of TI on the special occasion of the company's 75th anniversary. This book is not intended to be a complete or textbook history of the company, but rather a compilation of some of the great achievements of TI people over time. Clearly, it never could have been created without all the earlier efforts to document TI's history.

It is hoped that this book captures both the landmark achievements and the indelible spirit of TI. The intent of this collection of stories is to remind TI people everywhere of the great impact they and their company have had on the world.

INDEX

Semiconductor Manufacturing
International Corporation, 110

Semiconductor Women's Initiative
Network, 209

Sensors, 15, 109, 122, 143, 145, 172,
179, 252

Sensors & Controls, 107, 109, 122,
179

Sevin, L.J., 91, 92

Shanghai, China, v, 109

Sharp Corporation, 141, 187

Shatto, Gloria, 209

Sheets, Cindy, 258, 259

Shelby, Nancy, 228

Shelly, Ron, 215

Shenzhen, China, 109

Shepherd, Mark, 32, 33, 56, 60, 61,
66, 67, 71, 73, 78, 82, 90, 93, 98,
102, 106, 123, 125, 140, 141, 147,
201, 204, 216, 255

Sherman, Texas, 70, 79, 90, 97, 173,
211, 233, 238, 243

Sherill, Jim, 36

Shields, Donald, 232

Shin-Etsu Chemical, 70

Shockley, William, 58

Shrike Missile, 27, 45, 46, 53, 124

Shrock, Robert, 217

Sick, Bill, 103, 112, 152

Sickle, Jack, 50

Siemens, 100, 101, 141, 168

Signal processing, v, 1, 10, 11, 15,
45, 144, 145, 149-151, 153, 156,
157, 159, 175, 239, 254, 256, 257

Signal Processing Computer, 150

Silent700 data terminal, 140

Silicon reactors, 69, 70

Silicon Technology Development,
246, 247

Simcoe, Robert J., 74

Singapore, 106, 107, 149, 158, 250, 251

Single-chip microcontroller, 93, 125,
126, 204

Skidmore College, 224

Skiles, Win, 219, 229

Skooglund, Carl, 190, 215

Skyworth, 187

Slaymaker, Ron, 64

Smith, Billie, 116

Smith, Brad, 258, 259

Smith, Bryan F., 62, 102

Smith, Mark, 15, 16

Smith, Preston, 231

Smith, Sam K., 36

Smith, T. E., 202, 207

Smith, Tim, 89, 90, 93, 159

Smithsonian Institution, 72, 84, 131,
259

Society of Exploration Geophysicists,
223

Solomon, David, 170

Sonic Instruments, 178

Sonotone hearing aids, 75

Sony, 102, 104

South America, 13, 107, 179

South Building, 95, 97, 105, 134, 234

South Campus (Dallas), 95

South Korea, 44

Southeastern Consortium for
Minorities in Engineering, 239

Southern Asia, 237

Southern Methodist University, 32,
191, 193, 222, 227, 232, 238, 258

Southwestern Center for Advanced
Studies, 230

Soviet Union, 35, 38, 57

Sowell, Shaunna, 208, 242

Space Frame, 96, 97

Space Shuttle Discovery, 40

SPARC, 127

Speak & Spell, 131-133, 197, 254

Special Olympics, 235

Spectron Microsystems, 166

Speech recognition, 248

Speech synthesis, 131-133, 153, 248

Speedpass, 180

Spencer, John Albee, 119, 122

Spielberg, Stephen, 133

Sputnik, 38

St. Mark's School (Dallas), 222, 225

Staeblein, Markus, 198

Stafford, Texas, 243

Standard Oil Company of
California, 10

Stanford University, 225, 239, 247,
249, 254

Stanolind Oil & Gas Company, 13,
14, 66, 68

Steel, Al, 195, 196

Steineke, Max, 10, 11

Stevens Institute of Technology, 2, 222

Stoneham, Sam, 11

Stork, Hans, 247, 248

Storm, Al, 9, 11, 30

Strategy Leadership Team (SLT),
143-146

Stratton, Robert, 249

Stringfellow, Mac, 196

Stringfellow, Marianne, 196

Stringfellow, Tom, 140, 196

Stroup, Ralph, 69

Strumpell, Mark, 197

Sullivan, Martha, 179

Sullivan, Tom, 224

Sumatra, 9-11, 30, 62, 64

Sumitomo, 102

Sun Microsystems, 77, 127

SuperSPARC, 127

Suzhou, China, 109

Swank, A.B., 96

Sweden, His Majesty, the King of,
84

Swindle, Jack, 229

System-on-chip (SoC), 247

T News, 212

TAGER, 218, 232

Tag-it™ tags, 180

Taiwan, 44, 105-108, 148, 175, 237,
242, 250-252

Talluri, Dr. Raj, 176

Tantalum capacitor, 118

Tartan Labs, 165

Tatge, Reid, 164, 165

Taylor, Kirby, 42

Teachers Teaching with Technology
(T3), 130, 239

Teal, Gordon, 65- 69, 79, 246, 249

Team Digital Auto Drive, 256

Tech Smart-Big Heart, 235

TI Technical Ladder, 205

Technion, 155

Tecumseh, 102, 120

Telogy Networks, 167, 173

Telstar, 38

Templeton, Mary, 234

Templeton, Rich, v, 77, 127, 146,
151, 155, 163, 169, 171, 172, 175,
176, 182, 213, 216, 233, 234,
248, 256, 257

Terrain-following radar, 35, 36

Texaco, 16-18

Texans Credit Union, 190

Texas A&M University, 84, 227, 238

Texas Academy of Science, 226

Texas Christian University, 225

Texas Science and Technology
Council, 240

Texins Activity Center, 189, 193,
202, 203, 234

Texins Association, 189, 202, 203

Texins Health Fitness Council, 203

Thermal printhead, 128, 140

Third generation (3G), 101, 163,
171, 177, 178

Thomas, Bart, 209

Thompson, Robert P., 9

Thompson, Torger, 57

Thomsen, Carl J., 32, 56, 121

Note: All trademarks mentioned in this book are the property of their respective owners.